PUNJAB UNDER THE GREAT MUGHALS

PUNJAB UNDER THE GREAT MUGHALS

Surjit Singh Gandhi

ATLANTIC
PUBLISHERS & DISTRIBUTORS (P) LTD

Published by

ATLANTIC

PUBLISHERS & DISTRIBUTORS (P) LTD

7/22, Ansari Road, Darya Ganj,
New Delhi-110002
Phones : +91-11-40775252, 23273880, 23275880, 23280451
Fax : +91-11-23285873
Web : www.atlanticbooks.com
E-mail : orders@atlanticbooks.com

Branch Office
5, Nallathambi Street, Wallajah Road,
Chennai-600002
Phones : +91-44-64611085, 32413319
E-mail : chennai@atlanticbooks.com

ISBN 978-81-269-1516-3

Printed in India at Nice Printing Press, A-33/3A, Site-IV, Industrial Area, Sahibabad, Ghaziabad, U.P.

Preface

Punjab has always been crucial in the history of Indian subcontinent. Whether it is ancient India or medieval period or modern era, Punjab's role has always been prominent. This is in part because of its geography, and in part due to its demographic structure. Its locale is such that anyone, whether he or she be a trader or an invader from across the frontier of India or an explorer like Fahien or Hiuen-Tsang, they had to first enter here to reach the mainland of the subcontinent through its passes such as Gomal, Tochi, Khaiber, etc. A large number of invaders and quite a few explorers had come to Punjab over time. Quite a large swath of them chose to settle here. Aryans, Bacterians, Scythians, Kushans, Huns and Turks are such examples. Each wave of settlers brought its own culture and value-system with the result that they had to encounter the original settlers bringing about synthesis or adjustment of values. The process made the people more dynamic and more adaptive. The upshot was that they were always in the front line in any development, may it be political or socio-religious.

The present study focuses on how the Mughal regime functioned and affected the lives of the people, especially of the Lahore Suba of Punjab; what happened to its polity and its constituents such as sovereignty, bureaucracy, governance; how it reacted to different surges at the level of thought as well as at the grass-roots level; and how the Mughal emperors strived to strike an equilibrium between the forces of status quo and those causing turbulence or commotion.

The study also notices the human spirit feeling relatively relieved from oppressions in the past during the reigns from Akbar through Shahjahan and leading to effervescence in art, painting and architecture and remarkable progress in industry, trade and agriculture and then its constriction because of impositions of different kinds such as forcibly establishing Darul Islam, artificially keeping up the tottering Mansabdari system under Aurangzeb and turning politico-socio-religious institutions intractible as a result of opaqueness on the part of the Mughal emperors to the interplay of forces unleashed by renaissance in Europe, discoveries of fresh lands and activated human spirit of a large section of people under the impact of movements such as Bhakti, Sufism and Sikhism.

The study opens with the profiling of the political, social, and economic conditions of Punjab on the threshold of the Mughal rule. Then follows the account of how the Mughal emperors, one after the other, established their hegemony in Punjab. Side by side, the administrative measures which the Mughal rulers put in place have been carefully delineated. The narrative highlights the peculiarities of the concepts and strategies followed by the Mughal emperors and their impact on governance. No wonder that Mughal sovereignty and Mughal governance assumed colors different from the ones identifiable during Sultanate. The Mughal sovereignty was not of Sunni variety. It was Changezian, Timurian, Persianate and Sultanian—all rolled into one. The anchor of governance was not Shariat; it was sovereign-specific. Its scope was not the coverage of the Sunni Muslims alone, but the whole people professing loyalty to the emperor who considered himself as exalted as divine and thus worthy of magnificence deserving to be displayed through progression in architecture, calligraphy, painting and court glamour. This was true, by and large, until Aurangzeb possessed baton and altered the nature of governance to make it Sunni Muslims-specific and anti-non-Muslims, with significant consequences.

The politics which the Mughal emperors initiated from time to time has been amply taken cognizance of in this work. Whereas Punjab developed economically and in terms of stability, certain serious cracks appeared. In the economic sphere, there emerged a need for opening or identifying avenues for industrial surplus to be invested fruitfully. In the social arena, inter-religious and intra-religious tensions needed quick fixes. The bureaucratic apparatus also needed an overhaul because Mansabdari system could neither be expanded nor improved upon because of the shrinkage of crown lands and inability of Mughal rulers to expand horizontally. The situation was essentially crucial and precarious. The prospects looked sombre but could be retrieved only if someone with a vision had emerged on the scene. Aurangzeb, despite his personal qualities of integrity, honesty and perseverance, was too obsessed with Islamic unitarianism to forge a right type of approach to looming problems which continued to cause convulsions in polity and society. His fanaticism led to the downfall of Mughal rule in India.

While preparing the book, an attempt has been made to keep it specifically unique in the sense that it should present Mughal province of Lahore, playing a leading part in framing the policies of the Mughal emperors as also tracing the emergence of socio-religious forces openly challenging the status quo. Such an account needed a lot of mental scratching, vast knowledge of historical circumstances obtaining all around the world, high-profile capability to dive deep into the contemporary and semi-contemporary material in whatever form it was available and a special knack to cull right type of conclusions. I do not claim to have all these qualities. I am a humble explorer, yet I have ventured to take up the job.

Students and academics of History, especially those interested in the history of the Sikhs, the Punjab and the Great Mughals will find the book extremely beneficial in understanding the factors that culminated in the history as we know. Suggestions for further improvement in the subsequent editions of the book will be welcome.

Surjit Singh Gandhi

Acknowledgements

First and always thanks to my wonderful wife, Daljeet Kaur for her love, support and encouragement, putting up with me even when I foisted on her my frustrations which overwhelmed me sometime due either to mental fatigue or the helplessness which I experienced while scratching my head to find adequate answers to the questions which the critic in me posed.

I am indebted to Dr. Kirpal Singh, a doyen of Punjab history, for his proddings to take up the present study and to keep me always on the right track. Many thanks are due to Dr. Jodh Singh, a renowned scholar of Sikh religion and history, at present Professor and Head of the Department of Encyclopedia of Sikhism, Punjabi University, Patiala for enlightening me on various theological issues raking the society in Mughal Punjab. Late Dr. Kharak Singh gave immense help in my portrayal of economic condition of the people of Punjab, and for this I express my sincere thanks.

I am also grateful to Dr. K.R. Gupta, the Honorary Advisor and his brilliant son, Manish, Managing Director and Mr. Harjeet Singh, Publishing Co-ordinator of Atlantic Publishers and Distributors (P) Ltd., New Delhi, who readily agreed to publish the study.

Surjit Singh Gandhi

Contents

Punjab on the Eve of Mughal Rule

1

POLITICAL CONDITION

After the departure of Timur not a vestige of government was in evidence in upper India and the extent to which Punjab suffered during the disorder that followed may be gauged from the fact that when Mubarak Shah, the second Sayyad monarch, entered Lahore in 1421, he found the city in shambles. The Sayyad monarch possessed the needed ability and vigour but the circumstances conspired against him so much so that he failed to stem the tide of disruption. The Mawaties who held the tract between Delhi and Agra, the Hindu Zamindars of Katehar and the Doab and the Turkbachas of Sirhind perniciously kept up the tempo of disturbance. The five adventures of Jasrath Khokhar and the raids of the rulers of Kabul further contributed to this chaotic state of affairs.

With the murder of Mubarak Shah, whatever vigour there was in the Delhi Sultanate, also disappeared and under his successor "the business of the state day by day fell into greater confusion and affairs came to such a pass that there were Amirs at 20 kos from Delhi who shook off allegiance and made pretensions to independence."

In 1451, Bahlol Lodi, the governor of Dipalpur and Lahore, taking advantage of the prevailing anarchy, seized the throne and declared himself Sultan. His shrewdness and tactfulness stood him in good stead and helped to recover a certain control extending from the foot of the mountains to Banaras and in the south as far as the borders of Bundelkhand. Even then with all his ingenuity he failed to control the forces of disintegration. He, however, succeeded in maintaining harmony and amity between the Afghan nobles and Jagirdars in spite of the traditional impatiences of the Afghans with a controlling authority. His pandering to the whims and fancies of the Afghan Sardars, however, undermined a great deal the dignity of the sovereign and reduced him to the position of a peer. It resulted in the rule of innumerable autocrats. It was as dangerous for the common people as for the sovereign. Such a policy might have found favour with the Afghans but it could not inspire any confidence among the non-Afghan residents of India. It was obviously motivated by racial and tribal considerations and was, therefore, narrow and unjust. It carried in its bosom destructive elements which had the potentiality to explode in the shape of tribal jealousies and the dissolution of the artificially bolstered-up Afghan empire.[1] He handed over the reins of the administration of the Punjab to one of the relatives, Tatar Khan Lodi, who aquitted himself well during his life-time.

Sikandar Lodi, the son and successor of Behlol Lodi, had to reap the first fruits of that policy. No sooner did he succeed to the throne than the Afghan tribal leaders insisted on the division of the empire. Had he agreed to the principle of division between his brothers, the logical conclusion would have been the dismemberment of the empire into six principalities. With great reluctance he agreed to share it with Barbik Shah, but soon he changed his mind and reunited the empire. Able, war-like and shrewd as Sikandar was, he realized that father's policy was impractible and decided to enforce discipline and obedience to sovereignty. Washing his hands off the weak-kneed policy, he assumed a high tone in his orders and insisted in the strict observance of court etiquettes. His successes in wars, his personality, liberality and demeanour and above all his popularity among Muslim divines contributed to restore the dignity, authority and power of the crown. But the tribal instincts of the Afghans and their greed for wealth and power were so strong that they looked forward with a suppressed longing to the return of the days of Bahlol. As a counter-measure against the power of tribal leaders as also to enlist the support of the orthodox section of the Muslims by impressing upon them that he was eager to conform to the consent of Islamic state as expounded by their sacred texts he planned to persecute the Hindus. According to Budha Parkash, "The return of stability and consolidation in the early sixteenth century under Sikandar signified the restoration of the old policy of persecution". Mathura, Banaras and other places witnessed a revolting outburst of fanaticism and Nizam-ud-din was constrained to state that Sikandar's bigotry in Islam was so great that in this regard he went beyond the bounds, even of excess. He realised the pilgrimage tax with impunity and forbade pilgrimage to Kurukshetra.[2] Consequently, the opinion of the Muslim population veered round to favour him. Taking advantage of the change in wind, he took stern and quick action against the nobles seething with the spirit of refractoriness. Tatar Khan, who, after the death of Bahlol, had begun to act as if he were an independent ruler, was immediately attached. A fierce battle was fought with Tatar in which he was killed. Punjab then was handed over to Daulat Khan, Tatar's son, for governance.

But even with all these actions, Sikandar failed to achieve any enduring political stability.

The decline of the Sultanate entered its final phase under Ibrahim Lodi who succeeded his father, Sikandar, in 1517. The Hindus remained dissatisfied and the Muslim nobles grew turbulent. Erskine describes the situation under Sultan Ibrahim Lodi in the following words: "These extensive possessions, though under the king, had no very strong principle of cohesion. The monarchy was a congeries of nearly independent principalities, jagirs, and provinces, each ruled by a hereditary chief, or by a zamindar or a delegate from Delhi; and the inhabitants looked more to their immediate governors who had absolute powers in the provinces and in whose hands consequently lay their happiness or misery than to a distant or little-known sovereign. It was the individual not the law that reigned. The Lodi princes, not merely to strengthen their own power but from necessity, had in general committed the government of provinces and the chief offices of trust to their own countrymen, the Afghans so that men of Lodi, Formule and Lohani tribes held all the principal jagirs which from the habitual mode of thinking of their race, they considered as their own right and purchased by their swords rather than as due to any bounty or liberality on the part of the sovereign."[3]

At the time of succession of Ibrahim (A.D. 1517), Punjab was not a single homogenous unit. It was divided into different parts, independent of one another.

Bajaur,[4] the Gate of India, was under Haldar Ali, leader of the Dilazak Afghans. Sawat valley was dominated by Yusafzai Afghans whose Sultan's name was Wais. The Salt Range was being ruled by Jud and Janjua tribes.[5] About A.D. 1480, Ismail Khan and Fateh Khan, the two sons of Malik Sohrab Khan, and Ghazi Khan, son of Haji Khan, founded the three deras which still bear their names (Dera Ghazi Khan, Dera Ismail Khan, Dera Fateh Khan). They overcame the Lodies at Sitapur and established themselves as independents and had no concern with the Lodies. The system of government in these areas was tribal and customary law with an admixture of Islamic law was followed there.

The Lodies ruled only that part of Punjab which included the Sarkars of Dipalpur, Lahore, Sultanpur and Sirhind. Even here the prominent governor, Daulat Khan, paid only lip service to the Sultan. Notwithstanding all this, Sultan Ibrahim started well and embarked upon the policy aiming at the consolidation of the Empire.

He dismissed quite a large number of recalcitrant, disloyal and defiant nobles irrespective of race, rank, status or office and recruited in their places his own loyal persons.

Obviously, an empire threatened on all sides could not afford the dubious luxury of a long drawn-out civil war or allow narrow-minded and mischievous tribalism to stalk freely in the land. True to his policy, the Sultan attended to the affairs of the Punjab. In fact, the Lodies had come to regard the Punjab as if it were their personal Kingdom because it was from here that they had seized the Delhi Throne. Their leader, Daulat Khan, ruled at Lahore as an uncrowned king for twenty years. With him was Alam Khan Lodi, an uncle of Ibrahim Lodi and an old claimant to the throne.

Under the circumstances, Ibrahim was anxious to assure himself of Daulat's loyalty. He called him to the court but Daulat did not go himself and sent his son, Dilawar Khan. The Sultan took Dilawar Khan round and showed him the ghastly exhibition of disobedient commanders and warned if his father harboured any hostile designs, he too would be treated with similar harshness. Dilawar Khan, on his return, conveyed the hint of the Sultan to his father and also informed him of the smouldering discontent among some of the nobles.

Daulat Khan's position was quite precarious. His chief object was to retain the supreme authority in Punjab by hook or by crook. He was fully aware of the designs of Ibrahim as also of the role which his house had played in ousting the Mughals from Western Punjab and naturally feared the movements of Babur on the Western side of the Indus. Under the circumstances, he marked time, probably because he expected that nobles opposing Ibrahim Lodi come to some settlement with him, thereby allowing him respite from that quarter, and with the passage of time, it would dawn on Sultan that in the impending struggle against Babur, he was more important than ever. Similarly, he did not wish to offer any serious resistance to Babur in order to be on his right side. He was not in favour of a settlement between the two because, in that case, his position in Punjab could not remain intact.

The success of Ibrahim on the one hand and that of Babur on the other made Daulat Khan Lodi realise that he would have to decide one way or the other particularly after the conquest of Qandhar by Babur in 1522.

So, he sent his son Dilawar Khan to Babur inviting him to invade Hindustan. Daulat Khan probably thought that like Timur, Babur would shake the very foundation of the Delhi Empire and then he return to Kabul with large booty. About this time, another emissary from India reached Babur's court. He was Alam Khan, the uncle of Ibrahim, who had declared himself Sultan Ala-ud-din without, however, even being able to occupy Delhi. Alam Khan was willing to let Babur had Punjab, if the latter would oust Ibrahim from Delhi and let the former be the King. Apparently, Dilawar Khan's mission clashed with that of Alam Khan. But both most probably compromised, thinking that Babur would not stay in India and might, therefore, leave Delhi to Alam Khan and Punjab to Daulat Khan. Of course, Daulat Khan would have no objection to acknowledging Babur as his overlord and even paying tribute to him. The reasons adduced by both Dilawar Khan and Alam Khan for their invitation were: as firstly, that Ibrahim was an incorrigible tyrant who had decimated a considerable number of nobles and secondly, Alam Khan would be highly deferential and friendly in his attitude towards Babur.

The line of action to be taken was kept vague, perhaps purposely. Babur was asked to depose Ibrahim but there was no mention as to how the nobles of Lahore would help Babur in the task. In fact, the proposal put forward in this connection by Dilawar Khan had enough to lend itself to different interpretations. If Dilawar was cunning enough to keep it vague, Babur was equally clever not to demand any elucidation of the terms.

These overturnes of Daulat Khan to Babur brought Ibrahim's wrath upon him. Ibrahim sent an army against Daulat Khan with instructions to wrest Punjab from him. The Delhi army was not offered much resistance. Towards the end of 1523, Lahore was invaded and occupied. Daulat Khan sought refuge at Multan and waited for Babur's reaction to Ibrahim's occupation of Punjab. Babur, in his turn, felt whipped up to carry out his scheme of establishing his over-lordship over Punjab or the whole country if circumstances permitted. Thus, the occupation of Lahore by Delhi forces brought Babur face to face with the Sultan of Delhi-Agra. Thus, Punjab became a cockpit of struggle among three powers—Mughals, Afghan nobles of Punjab, and Sultan Ibrahim Lodi.

In such an atmosphere of political disturbances and uncertainties many fissures developed in the administration of the Lodi State which had in fact, been going from bad to worse since the decline of the Tughlaq empire.

The Wazarat department which was the king-pin of the Sultanate administration was disorganized and its deterioration was almost complete under the Sayyad rulers. Bahlol Lodi made no effort to improve it, most probably because he did not require any elaborate machinery. Sikandar Lodi showed only lukewarm attitude toward this matter. So did Ibrahim Lodi. The results were obvious. With no strong central agency to keep regular surveillance, the Iqta-holders, Muqaddams, Rais or Chaudaries, started catering to their own ends. The Sultan did exert to make up for the deficiency but without much success. History of the Lodi rule is replete with instances of frauds committed by distortion of figures. Muqaddams, Rais or Chaudaries who were the intermediaries between the State and the people in the case of Shalsa lands, or between Iqta-holders and the peasantry in the case of Iqtas, often indulged in malpractices. The amounts extracted by them from people for exceeded the remittances made by them to the State or Iqta-holders.

Punjab, like the rest of the country area under Lodis was divided into Iqas and Khalsa lands. The Iqa-holders became mini-Sultans in their respective areas. They owed no other allegiance except attending the court, furnishing armies, and remitting the amount of revenue as stipulated between them and the Sultan. Evidently, they enjoyed such a high status that they could attract followers even to be used against the Sultan and assert independence. The fast deteriorating political situation and continued refractoriness became the order of the day. Besides, most of the nobles started indulging in gross misuse of their political power. They exploited the people and robbed them of their hard earned money. No wonder, Guru Nanak was much pained at this gruesome and politically unhealthy situation and uttered in extreme anguish that:

"The Kings have become wolves, and Muqaddams dogs."

ECONOMIC CONDITION

Agriculture

After the fall of the Tughlaqs, an era of anarchy and in disintegration was ushered in Punjab. In these circumstances, it was improbable that any uniform agrarian measures were to be in position. The conditions would make for diversity of practices in assessment and collection, and the probabilities were that each individual dealt with the peasants very much as he chose.[6] Nevertheless, we may guess that group assessment gained ground at the expense of sharing or measurement because it was more suitable to the conditions which prevailed.[7]

In 1451, the Sayyad dynasty gave place to the House of Lodi Afghans. In a general way, the economy of the Lodi dynasty was basically agricultural. Land was divided into Iqtas and the Khalsa. Grandees (Muqtas) of the state were given Iqtas instead of cash salaries by the Sultan for their maintenance. The accounts of the Muqtas were settled at the Wazarat department. During the times of the Lodis, the Muqtas seemed to have been officially called Wajahdars. The terms Muqta, Hakim and Amir were also used for the assignees. Iqtas differed in size. An Iqta might be a pargana, less than a pargana, a sarkar or a whole province.[8]

Khalsa lands were managed by Shiqdars who were the supreme pargana officers. Most of the Shiqdars held the rank of Malik. The subordinate officers posted to the parganas under Shiqdars were Amirs, Amins, and Qazis, the latter being judicial officers. Like the Shiqdars, the Amirs were appointed in the Khalsa parganas by the Sultan. The corroborative evidence contained in the Waqiat-i-Mushtaqi reveals that Sultan Sikandar Lodi never transferred the Amirs whom he once appointed in the parganas.[9] Apart from being revenue collectors, they also took precautionary measures to protect the cultivated land against natural calamities.

As regards the Amin, he seemed to have been appointed in parganas to measure the land under cultivation either for determining the state demand of land revenue or knowing the exact yield (Jama) of a pargana or an Iqta. The Khalsa territories began to shrink during the inefficient rule of the successors of Feroz Tughlaq and these territories nearly eased to exist during the reign of the last Sayyad ruler. Sultan Bahlol drew up a new policy of his own about the Khalsa land after he had occupied Delhi. He did not reserve any extensive territory for the Khalsa, but set aside parganas in every Sarkar. As in other provinces, in the western Sarkars of Punjab, several parganas were reserved. The same policy seemed to have been followed by his successors.[10] The Khalsa parganas during the times of Bahlol, Sikandar and Ibrahim began to be administered through Dewan-i-Ala. Sometimes, the Muqta was required to make arrangements to remit the revenue collected from the Khalsa parganas in his Sarkar to the royal exchequer.

The lowest revenue unit was village, both in Khalsa lands and Iqtas. Its administration was run on traditional lines. The Muqaddams, Zamindars, Chaudhries and Rais—the hereditary chiefs of the villages—were accountable to the pargana officers for the administration of their villages. Being th intermediaries between the State and the peasantry, they rendered important services to both the parties. They were expected to safeguard the interests of the parganas on the one hand and facilitate the work of government revenue officers on the other. They were put under the charge of pargana officers.

There were three systems of revenue assessment—crop sharing, measurement (zabt system) and compounding (indigenous Kankut) prevalent in northern India. Out of the three, the first and the last were common. Sultan Sikandar was very particular about the system of measurement for its merits. To facilitate this system, he introduced his famous *gaz sikandari* (a yard of 32 digits) which was used at the time of every harvest. The patwaris were entrusted with the duty of maintaining the registers of measured land under cultivation, and the work of measurement was done under the supervision of Amin or Amil. This system was in force in the Khalsa territories only, but here too it could not be enforced strictly because of two reason, viz. contumalious behaviour of the Muqtas, particularly in the reign of Sultan Ibrahim and the scattered Khalsa lands in different Sarkars.

So far as the Iqtas were concerned, the Muqtas and Wajahdars were free to adopt any system they deemed more convenient. According to Moreland, "the facts on record justify the statement that the Afghan assignees had something like a free hand in the management of land and the peasants placed under them".[11] In assessment, as distinguished from collection, the assignees appeared to have had at the time a perfectly free hand, at least in practice. Some of the Muqtas were oppressive and even cruel both in assessment and collection.

Notwithstanding the fact that village was the lowest revenue unit, the growing tendency was the group assessment for the purpose of the state. The Qanugo, on the basis of his experience, memory and some record ascertained the future state of a group of villages and assessed the revenue. If the pargana was in the Khalsa, the Muqaddam of the village was required to pay the assessed amount either in cash or in kind. As there was acute shortage of gold or silver during the reign of Sultan Ibrahim, he ordered his officers to collect revenue in kind.

The state share in the agricultural produce was one third and it was collected by the Muqaddams. After deducting his commission, he used to pay it to the state officers.[12]

The agrarian system as explained above suffered from certain defects. The absolute freedom which the Muqtas enjoyed as regards assessment and collection left much scope for them to exploit the peasantry. There are cases on record when the Muqtas collected revenue over and above the stipulated sum for which Iqtas were given to them, and strangely enough if the Iqta yielded larger amount of revenue than it was stipulated by the Diwan, the assignees were allowed to keep it with them.[13] Furthermore, there was no proper system of assessment. Assessment, on the basis of crop-sharing at the time of sowing, was detrimental to the interests of the peasants because none could take into account, even if one desired, the natural factors going to affect the crops. If the process was resorted to at the time of harvest, it was bound to inflict loss on the state treasury on account of the ever-present temptations of the peasants to conceal some of the crop because it was well-nigh impossible for government officials to be present everywhere at the time of harvesting. Similarly, the Kankut system of assessment left scope for the Muqaddams to overcharge the peasants on the one hand and remit less amount to the state. Measurement, no doubt, secured the interests of the state better than any other system, but it was applied only to the Khalsa lands. Besides, it did not ensure justice to the peasants because measurement alone could not determine the quantity and quality of a particular crop.

The condition became all the worse due to certain politic and inappropriate policies of the Lodi Sultans. Behlol Lodi in his efforts to get the throne of Delhi for himself offered assignments on a large scale to those Afghan leaders on whom he depended for military support. The Afghans, accustomed to the tribal ways of life, and firmly attached to the idea of personal independence, regarded the Sultan no more than the first among them, and consequently resented the assertion of sovereign rights on the part of the Sultan. Bahlol tolerated this attitude of theirs to a great extent, but Sultan Sikandar Lodi and Ibrahim Lodi asserted their sovereign rights and powers. They emphatically established the fact that the king was the master of the land and the Iqtas could be assigned or resumed at the royal pleasure.

As a result thereof, Muqtas or Wajahdars began to smart under their rules. The tendency was specially marked during the time of Ibrahim Lodi, because of his sternness in dealing with the disloyal, recalcitrant and defiant nobles, irrespective of any consideration of blood, status or office. Naturally, this alarmed the powerful nobles including Daulat Khan Lodi who ruled at Lahore as an uncrowned king for twenty years.

Since Daulat Khan's chief object in life was to retain the supreme authority he enjoyed in Punjab, he began to prepare for his own safety.[14] In such a situation it was but natural for him to pay less attention to revenue matters and no wonder, the Iqta holders, Muaqddams and other revenue officials including the Shiqdars of the Khalsa lands began indulging in gross irregularities and malpractices thereby causing a good deal of inconvenience to the people and considerable loss to the royal exchequer.

CONDITION OF THE PEASANTRY

The shortcomings of the agrarian structure as mentioned above were sure to spell hardships for the peasantry—the fact which is also borne out by the evidence provided by foreign and Indian writers. Sal Bank while writing about the people between Agra and Lahore, says, "Plebian sort is so poor that part of them go naked." Palssaert, a Dutch visitor, remarked, "The common people live in poverty so great and miserable that the life of the people can be depicted or accurately described only as a home of stark want and a dwelling place of utter woes, their houses are built of mud with thatched roofs. Furniture there is little or none except some earthenware pots to hold water and for cooling." Similarly, Babur witnessed extreme poverty and referred to *Langoti, Kachheri* and poor standard of living of the peasants.

A pertinent question is asked: How is it that the peasants' condition was bad where prices were low and production in agricultural sector had considerably increased? True, both types of crops, cereal and cash, had been produced on a large scale and the prices also had been very low. Yet the plight of the peasants was far from good—rather it was bad. The reasons therefore are not far to seek. The peasants of those days can be classified into three types. The first type comprised those who were holding the ownership rights jointly. In the second type were included all those peasants who held the ownership of their respective pieces of land in their individual capacities. Those peasants who worked on the lands of Jagirdars constituted the third type.

The peasants of the first type were exploited by their own people who were at the helm of affairs. Jagirdars exacted as much as they could from the peasants working under them. These peasants could save themselves only by moving to some other tracts of land or by reclaiming some piece of land for cultivation which they could do, as unclaimed and unowned land was found in abundance, though great physical and mental hardships involved in the process had to be faced. The second type of the peasants also experienced a lot of inconvenience. Whether their land fell in Iqtas or in the Khalsa lands, they had to meet the revenue demand of the State which was often on a very high side, at times approximating to the whole of the surplus produce thus leaving the peasants with only the barest minimum needed for their subsistance. During the periods of political heavels the peasants were forced to part with even more than that because in such times, the Sultans were not feared and the local revenue officers, Shiqdars, Iqtadars, and Jagirdars were free to exploit the peasantry without any fear from any quarter.

Another factor that told upon the economic health of the peasants was the emphasis laid on the realization of the state revenue only in cash. Jagirdars too preferred to take their share in cash.

To meet the demand of the State as also of the Jagirdars the peasants had to arrange for the cash, which many of them did either by selling their crops to the advantage of traders or by getting loans from money-lenders. Both these processes entailed hardships on the peasants. According to K.M. Ashraf, "the peasant experienced severe hardship during the later half of the fifteenth century and the first half of the sixteenth century."

TRADE AND COMMERCE

Punjab had a large number of cities, namely Lahore, Multan, Sirhind, Sunam, Dipalpur, Sultanpur, Batala, and Ludhiana, etc. This shows that there was considerable internal trade between cities and cities as also between cities and villages. The specialization of certain cities in manufacturing articles also shows that trade activities were going on a large scale. As a concomitant to these, currency as common medium of exchange began to be used on a large scale. This process received a big fillip from the authorities preferring to receive land revenue in cash. The recognition of a common medium of exchange facilitated the job of traders and new institutions such as brokerage emerged to assist the traders. Understandably, the volume of trade, whether internal or external, increased paving the way for some new factors to emerge on the economic scene. The traders, particularly those engaged in foreign trade, grew rich and accumulated wealth. In Punjab, trade and commerce had come to be monopolised by certain castes among Hindus such as Khatris, Banias, Suds, Mahajans, Bhatias, Bhabras Aroras, and some sects of the Muslims such Bohras and Khojas.

As these people grew rich, they began to exercise their influence on the government and the economy. In many cases they even succeeded in influencing the political affairs by advancing money to the officials or offering their services as assignees. One important economic effect of this was that the tendency began to germinate that the production and commerce should not be subjected to feudal constraints such as various types of exactions by the feudal lords or by the government officials behaving like them.

INDUSTRIES AND INDUSTRIAL LABOUR

Punjab experienced a lot of prosperity in the domain of industry. The major industries of Punjab were textiles, arms, paper, woodwork, durries, carpets. Sultanpur and Multan were famous for their Chintz and Sialkot and Gujarat for their chiffon (Chighov) work. Multan also produced flowered-durris and woollen carpets. Bajwara, near the present-day Hoshiarpur, specialised in fine cloth, gold work, turbans and Kamarbands. Gujarat manufactured swords and Jamdharas. Arrows were tipped in various ways. Sikandar Lodi got his own arrows tipped with gold. Besides, there were many small industries such as cotton, ginning, gold-smithy, metal work, oil pressing, carpentry, leather work, masonry, etc.

With the increase in trade activities, the industry also progressed. But the artisans had to work under many constraints. They were not given dignified status by the Hindu society as also by Muslims who attached more importance to their nobility and Ulemas. They were also asked to pay a monthly market tax. Besides, another tax which was levied on shops and workshops was realised from the traders.

Rahdari, control duty and duty on each item which an artisan or a trader brought to the market for sale were other taxes to be paid by the artisans and traders. Examples are available in the contemporary historical literature to show that the oil-pressers (Telis), soap-makers (sabungaran), the makers of neel (Nealgaran) and many other craftsmen were subjected to heavy taxation. According to Ibn Batuta, whatever the earnings of the traders, one-fourth of that was taken by the State.

In addition to the artisans and craftsmen who worked independently, there were artisans who were not free and worked in the factories of Sultans and Nobles. In Alauddin's factories seventeen such types of artisans worked while in Muhammad Tughluq's factories which manufactured cloth to cater to the needs of the royal harem and royal court, four thousand workers worked. But this type of craftsmen was on the wane.

During the period of our study, a class of craftsmen working on wages also came into being. In the words of K.M. Ashraf, "In the sixteenth century, the wage earners strength sufficiently swelled and the questions relating to the extent of wages were often discussed".[15]

The artisans, craftsmen and workers as a class were not accorded a respectable status in the society. However, new consciousness dawned upon them and they developed over the years a sense of abhorrence for the various taxes imposed on them by the ruling classes. Abul Fazal's book *Ain-a-Akbari* also records the new trend. In this book, the celebrated author counts four planks on which the prosperity of a kingdom rests. Among these planks were included army, artisans and traders, Ulemas and farmers, and government servants. It is significant that in the order of precedence traders and artisans were ranked second.

RELIGIO-SOCIAL CONDITION

Islam

The majority of the Muslims in Punjab were Sunnis, who were patronised by the State. The Qizis, Muftis and Ulemas were invariably taken from among the Sunnis. The ultimate authority in their religious life was the Qu'ran. Besides, the Hadis, sayings of the prophet, also served as a principal source of authority. The books embodying interpretation of the Qu'ran (Tafsir) were also regarded by the Sunnis with great esteem. Collections of Hadis, prepared by al-Bukhari, and Zama Khshari's celebrated commentary on the Qu'ran, called the Kashshaf, were very popular in Punjab as also in India. Al-Ashri's (A.D. 873-93) book *Maqalat* was considered to be a good guide as far as Sunnis ideas and institutions were concerned.

As a rule, Sunnis believed only in one God, who is all-powerful, just, majestic, inscrutable, righteous and merciful. They had no regard for idol worship, observed five daily prayers (Salat), kept daily fast during the month of Ramdan, went on pilgrimage to Mecca (Hajj) and give charity (Zakat) to their Muslim brethren. They also believed in the unity of the Muslims, the collectivity of the faithful—which in its turn is derived from the conformity of members to the religio-ethical codes and principles enunciated in Qu'ran and the Hadis.

Next to the Sunnis, the most important sect of the Muslims in Punjab, as elsewhere in the Muslim world, was that of the Shias. The distinction between the Shias and the Sunnis had its roots in the dispute between the Alids and the Umayyads in the year following Khalifa Uthman's assassination (35 A.H.). In its origin, this distinction had nothing to do with Islam as such but was wholly concerned with the question of succession to the leadership of the Muslim community.[16] The Alids (the followers of Ali) on their side claimed that they were the legitimate Khalifas because they descended from the Prophet's daughter Fatima and his cousin and intimate companion, Ali. The Ummayyads, on the other hand, claimed that they held their position by the choice of the Muslims themselves. Besides, among the Sunnis, the Khalifa was regarded as a political ruler essentially, while the Alids regarded the Prophets' successor as a religious guide and, therefore, preferred to designate him as the Imam of the Muslim community. It was assumed that his physical descent from the Prophet secured to him not merely the divine right but also the divine endowment of grace and wisdom. They recognised twelve Imams in line from Fatima and Ali. The last Imam Mohammad Ali Mehdi was believed to have disappeared from the world in C.E. 880 and it was expected that he would reappear to restore justice and righteousness. The Shias recognized the authority of the Qu'ran and the prophet-hood of Muhammad but had no faith in the first three Khalifas.

Ismailis and Qarmathians were the other Muslims sects in Punjab. The Ismailis reposed faith in seven prophets ending with Jafar-us-Sadiq and Ismail. They claimed to derive their teachings from a hidden source which must receive absolute obedience.[17] The laws of the *shariat*, according to Ismaili belief, were not meant for those who possessed esoteric knowledge.[18] The Qu'ran itself, they said, had inner meanings.

Qarmathians[19] believed in Muhammud Ibn Ismail as the last Imam who was expected to reappear on the last day. They denied all divine attributes holding that the divine essence has given forth light by which various forms of intelligence and matter have been created, beings having no real individuality. The divine essence which was alone in the beginning, will be alone in the end. The initiates were taught to use speculative philosophical reasoning, as a result of which doubts were raised about the systems of religions including Islam.

Shias, Ismailis and Qarmathians were generally disliked and occasionally persecuted by the Sunis.

However, the most important form of the religious life next to that of the Sunnis was reflected in the beliefs and practices of the Sufis, the mystics of Islam. The fact that in the work of Minhaj-us-Suraj, Ziauddin Barni and Shams-i-Siraj and Afif, there are references to Mashaikh, clearly indicate the increasing importance of the Sufis and also the change in the religious life of the Indo-Muslims. Already before the mid-sixteenth century, the influence of the Sufis had penetrated nearly all the layers of Muslim society. The low-caste Hindus, the craftsmen and others who had embraced Islam at the instance of the Sufis naturally looked upon them as their *Pirs* (religious leaders).[20] The Sultan and the nobles, in the late fifteenth and early sixteenth centuries, were anxious to associate themselves with the Sufis. Sikandar's visits to Sheikh Samauddin, Sheikh Neamatullah, Sheikh Hussain, Sheikh Jamaili are eloquent testimony to his general regard for the Mashaikhs. No wonder, the Sufi influence in Punjab during the late fifteenth and early sixteenth centuries was considerable. There were many important centres of Sufi learning. Baha-ud-din Zakariya of the Suhrawarthy Silsila was the first to establish his centre. Sheikh Yusaf in the beginning of Lodi period and his grandson Sheikh Baha-ud-din Qureshi at the end were at the helm of affairs of the centre.[21] Of the other Sufi centres in Punjab, the most important was the *Sajjadah of Ajodhan* (Pak Pattan), the seat of Sheikh Farid-ud-din Ganj-i-Shakkar who was by far the most popular Sheikh of Punjab. In the early sixteenth century, Sheikh Ibrahim was on the Sajjadah of Farid.[22] He was very popular among people and out of veneration was called Farid-i-Sani, the second Farid. In Lodi period, Musa Ahangar was a popular Sheikh at Lahore while Abu Ishaq Qaderi and Ishaq were on their way to rise into prominence at the same place.[23] In fact, all the towns of the area had a Sheikh of minor or major importance.

Thanesar, Hansi, Narnaul and Panipat were other important centres of Sufi activities, particular of the Chisti order. Panipat, apart from serving as the venue of activities for the Chisti order, was also a centre of Qalander Sufis. Sharafuddin Bin Ali Qalander maintained his Khanqah at this place.

The Sufis derived their inspiration from different sources. Their first source was the Qu'ran. The Sufis adopting the Shia principles of allegorical interpretation (ta-wil) were able to prove to their own satisfaction that every verse and word of the sacred text hides treasures of meaning which God reveals to the elect. So much being granted, one can imagine that it was easy to show Quranic authority for any mystical doctrine whatsoever and to maintain that Sufism was really the esoteric teaching of the Prophet communicated by him to his son-in-law. No wonder various quotations from the Qu'ran served as the basis of mysticism of the Sufis.

The next important, or perhaps even more important, source was the mystical experience itself. It is also possible that non-Islamic ideas might have influenced them. Apart from the influence of Christianity, Neo-Platonism, and Buddhism, atleast in the initial stages,[24] the contemporary jogis and siddhs also affected the course of Sufism. References to contact or contest with the jogis in particular confirm this impression.[25] According to Sheikh Muhammad Gauri, the jogis related the truth of *gnosis* only in different language from that of the Sufis.[26] Similarly, Muhammad Ghauri sees many parallels between yoga and sufi theosophy.[27]

Admittedly, there were many contacts with beliefs in other religions and some exponents even seem to have over-stepped the Islamic limits, e.g. Abu Yazid of Bistam[28] and Hallaj. Yet Sufism was essentially related to the Qu'ran and Muhammad.[29]

The developed Sufi doctrine distinguishes between what is called station (maqam) and state (hal), the former representing the Sufis's efforts on the path or stages on the spiritual journey, the latter being divine gift of grace pertaining to each such stage. The chief stations have been identified as repentance, trust in God. The states have been called meditation, nearness to God, love, fear, hope, longing, intimacy, tranquility, contemplation and certainty, A Sheikh (Murshid) who must be obeyed is necessary for one starting on the path. The sufi seeks union with God and this is attained in ecstasy. The words 'Fana' (passing away) and 'Baqa' (remaining) indicate the necessary preparation and goal. By 'Fana' one transcends passions and desires and finally reaches cessation of conscious though; 'Baqa' means that one has arrived at the stage of unity where one is conscious of continuous survival in unity with God.[30] There had been pantheistic tendencies within Sufism, but the normal Sufi was faithful to his Islamic theology, howsoever difficult it might be to reconcile the idea of union with Islamic doctrine of God who is altogether different from his creation.

Muslim Social Groups

Although the conception of equality and brotherhood (Millat) remained as a ideal for the Muslim society, there were already four major social grades within it during the period of our study.

The upper class consisted of nobles, the exact number of whom it is difficult to mention. In point of composition, they were a heterogeneous body composed of all sorts of foreigners and Indians. In the beginning of the Muslim rule, almost all the nobles were of Turkish extraction. The Afghans came to be incorporated at a later date. Feroze Tughlaq was the first monarch who extended his favours to the Afghans, though the latter were accredited on a large scale only during Lodi reign. The Mughal invasions introduced a small element of Mughals who accepted Islam and were given the appellation of 'neo-Muslims' or new converts to Islam. Some Indian converts to Islam also enjoyed the rank of a noble and from the time of the Khaljis they were a force to reckon with.

The nobility as a group had many self-contradictions. Undoubtedly, they were the greatest if not the only prop of the state and their solidarity contributed a lot to the establishment of the Sultanate, yet they developed fissures in their body-social. To begin with, the Turkish nobles consolidated themselves into an exclusive ruling class but with the passage of time, the converted Muslim population also began to demand its share in political, social and economic privileges. The Turkish aristocracy, being jealous guardians of their power and privileges showed reluctance, and as a consequence of it, the Indian Muslims began to struggle for their place in the ruling aristocracy and in the administration of the country. Undoubtedly, the Indian Muslims succeeded in getting their due but not without upbraiding the foreign Muslim aristocracy that always indulged in conspiracies to bring their rivals down with the result that the administrative efficiency suffered considerably.

Besides, the nobility suffered a considerable decline in respect of personal conduct and character. Not a few of them were corrupt, greedy, selfish, self-seeking and un-reliable.

Religious classes formed the second important social group of the Muslims. This group was mainly composed of Sayyads and Ulemas. Of these the most important were the Ulemas. They were collectively known as *Dastar Bandan*—turban-wearers. The Sayyads were recognised by their distinctive head-dress of Kulah and were known as *Kulah Daran* or cap-wearers. Both of them followed the Sunni form of Islam and the Hanafite school of Muslim law. Ulemas were, however, the special favourites and associates of the Sultanate.[31] As a rule, they were well-versed in Muslim law, Logic, Arabic letters and religious literature of Islam in general, namely Tafsir, Hadis, Kalam, etc.[32] and were held in high esteem by the people.

Under the special conditions of development of the Muslim society in Hindustan, it was but natural to expect that the Ulema would acquire an undue prominence.[33] They monopolised practically all judicial, ecclesiastical and educational services. No Sultan, except Ala-ud-Din Khalji in a limited sense and Mohammad Bin Tughlaq in his initial stages, had been able to be independent of them. Sultan Ala-ud-Din Khalji compelled them to confine their activities within the prescribed limits which were to decide on judicial cases and to arbitrate on religious matters.[34] Mohammad Tughlaq went a step further, and in secularizing the state, he put the Ulema on the same footing as other employees of the state and treated them accordingly.[35]

During Feroz Tughlaq, the Ulemas influence again grew and they had recaptured the earlier position and influence when the invasion of Taimur took place. The Afghans, on the assumption of power, treated the Ulemas with marked respect. Certain scholars said that the Afghan rulers[36] did not admit them to any effective voice in administration but the fact that they had much religious influence and the Afghan rulers wanted to make use of it shows that administration could not but take a serious note of their opinions. No doubt, the Ulemas rendered a great help to the Sultans, particularly in the initial phases of the Muslim conquest through interpretation of the Qu'ran and other sayings of the Prophet to justify various acts of the Sultans from the religious angle, yet since their approach, by and large, was primarily narrowly religious, their advice very often was confined to safeguard the interests of the Muslims alone. So far as their personal character and conduct was concerned, it certainly underwent degeneration.

The peasantry, minor officials artisans, shop-keepers, clerks and petty traders constituted the third social group of the Muslims. Though not equal in status with the upper class and the Ulema class, they were not a despised section of the society. Undoubtedly, they were not as rich and opulent and could ill-afford to own a mansion, dancing girls and concubines, and slaves, etc. yet they had a reasonable standard of living. Being the members of the ruling community, they enjoyed a better life than that of their Hindu neighbours.

At the lowest rung of the society were slaves, both males and females. The Muslim society in Punjab, as elsewhere in the world, was marked by the existence of slavery as its integral part. The slaves were employed in household works and various royal karkhanas. Female slaves were of two types: those employed for domestic and menial work and those who were bought for company and pleasure. The former were subjected to all sorts of indignities, while the latter enjoyed an honourable position, sometimes even dominating position in the household. The number of slaves was quite large during the Sultanate period. Ala-ud-Din had fifty thousands of slaves,[37] while Feroze Tughlaq maintained 180000.[38] The slaves kept by nobles were over and above these figures. The institution proved useful for the Sultans in two ways: first, it became instrumental in converting non-Muslims and secondly the slaves constituted a loyal body ever ready to further the cause of the Sultans. Theoretically speaking, since a slave was usually a convert to Islam, he possessed the same rights as any other member of Muslim society; but in actual practice, the position was quite different. "He was usually a prisoner of war, and according to the military usage of the age, his life was at the mercy of his captor who had full power of killing him or otherwise disposing him of".[39] In fact, the salve was considered the property of a conqueror to be given away as gift or to be sold in the market. But no shrewd captor or buyer, however, neglected to take good care of his property, which given proper attention, could be converted into ready money.[40] As a matter of fact, on the whole, a human relationship existed between the slave and the master. This was the reason that slaves sometimes rose to such social eminence as was not ordinarily within the reach of the highest and the noblest in the kingdom. A slave in the service of Sultan was usually manumitted after some time and was provided an honourable position, even with rank and an elevated status.[41]

The institution of slavery after the time of Feroze Tughlaq threw up certain problems which warranted its re-appraisal. The number of the slaves swelled to an alarming extent and the opportunities for their proper employment lagged behind. Further, the social consequences were not very happy. Muslim nobles engrossed themselves in the affairs pertaining to war and pleasure (Bazm) and paid no heed to the domestic work with the result that in due course of time, their code of social behaviour began to view domestic work as unworthy of a gentleman's dignity and honour. Long standing tradition of slavery prevented the development of a sense of human dignity which is one of the essential prerequisites for the growth of healthy morality.

Be that as it may, all this gives to a slave-holding society the stamp of unprogressiveness and a socially unhealthy character.

The social consequences, though not so pronounced, are fairly well-marked in the social development of medieval Indian society.[42]

Not only this, the Muslim society was criss-crossed by many other social groups, ethnic and religious. Among ethnic groups, there were the Gakkhars, the Pathans, the Baluchs, the Junds, Janjhuas and the Jats. So far as their habits and social attitudes were concerned, they were more committed to their own clanish organizations than to the one preached by Islam. Among the religious divisions there were, as we have seen earlier, Sunnis, Shias, Ismailis, Qarmathians and Sufis.

Hinduism

There was a rich variety of religious beliefs and practices prevalent among the Hindus. The authority of the Vedas was recognized by the priests of nearly all the Hindu sects and it was invoked in support of many socio-religious customs. Though the position of the Vedas as 'revealed knowledge' was unique, the Puranas enjoyed greater popularity throughout the medieval period. The six schools of philosophy were also well-known but of them the Vedanta school was gradually coming to the fore.[43]

Shaivism, Vaishavism and Shakatism were the major religious sects of the Hindus. All these sects represented in their origin an urge to break away from or to bring about changes in Hindu religion to conform to the aspirations of the people stirred by new social economic and political forces. But as time passed, these sects directed their energies into sectarian channels. By and large, in the absence of proper direction and goal orientation, the votaries of these sects developed attitudes which were ethically and socially speaking, unsound and unhealthy.

Shaivism

Shaivism was the most popular of the Hindu sect at this time. The main reason for its popularly was its system of monastic orders. According to Sujan Rai, its *sannyasis* were quite numerous, all of them were extremely ascetical in their practices, underwent hard penances and shunned the pleasures of the senses.[44] They could be distinguished by the tilak-mark on their foreheads. Some of the *sannyasis* carried a tiger's or panther's skin on their shoulders. Almost all of them used ashes for the talik-mark which generally consisted of three horizontal lines representing the trident of Shiva. Some used only two horizontal lines with a dot, considered to be a representation of the phallic emblem of Shiva.

Closely connected with the *sannyasis* but distinct from them were the Aghropanthis and Nathpanthis. Nathpanthis were the followers of Gorakh Nath. Only those who went through the last stage of initiation were called Kanpatas. The last stage of initiation consisted in having the ear-lobes pierced with the bhairvi knife for large rings to be worn. These rings were generally called *mudri*.[45]

The movement initiated by Gorakh Nath in Punjab had its origin in the concept of Yoga as the means of attaining liberation. The particular form of Yoga advocated by Gorakh Nath was Hath yoga. The Nathpanthi movement became a movement of considerable importance in the twelfth century but by the fifteenth century it has reached its apex and was on the way to decline.

Vaishnavism

Vaishnavism upto the period of our study had fallen from its heights. In fact, it had degenerated considerably on the eve of the advent of Guru Nanak. The Vaishnavites were satisfied with the worship of Vishnu and his various incarnations, visited punctually and regularly the temples raised to house the icons of the deity and of reading or listening to the Vaishnavite texts. In addition to these they were required to abstain from meat and liquor. The *bairagis* and *sannyasis* who were committed to the spread of Vaishnavism paid scant respect to their duties and freely indulged in malpractices and loose morals. They coloured their clothes as a mark of their order and were a piece of worn-out cloth as a mark of their having joined the *sannyasi* order and taken the pledge to kindle spiritual flame in the people, yet they did nothing of this sort.

Shaktism

Shaktism was another cult which was very popular in Punjab during our period. Various temples raised in honour of the Goddess as also to house her icons bear testimony to it. The Goddess in her various forms and manifestations was a token of primacy given to Shakti, the active principle or the cosmic force which sustains the universe and various forms of gods. People worshipped her and aspired for their identification with her. The votaries of this cult believed in offering animal sacrifices to propitiate her. In all other respects, the general usages of Shaivism were observed.

But as the time rolled by, a new sect emerged in Shaktism. The members of this sect under the influence of Tantrism developed their own philosophy and their own rituals. Their supreme ideal was identification of the individual soul with the supreme soul. Their worship was characterised by 'initiation' irrespective of caste or sex, and by *mantras, yantras* and black rites. It was based on a code of esoteric practices in which sexual representations were much in evidence. In fact, they regarded human body the most reliable and effective instrument of salvation on the assumption that the macrocosm was reflected in the microcosm.

The worship of Vamacharis Tantriks was not a simple affair. It pre-supposed a long and difficult practices. The dharanis and *mantras* were raised to the dignity of a vehicle of salvation and one was supposed to mutter the prescribed *mantras* even while conducting the ordinary daily business. The *mantra* drawn on a piece of cloth was conceived as a miniature temple. The Sriyantra, the finest of them has four openings or flights of steps, and a sanctuary where the chosen divinity dwells. At the same time, the disposition of triangle in the *yantra* represented the male and female sexual organs. The penances and austerities (tapas) and recitation of *mantras* (japas) were to precede the use of the *mandala* as well as the *yantra*. The *mandala* was meant to be an image of the universe and drawn on a cloth, it was believed to support meditation and to serve as a defence against temptations and distractions. The liturgy was expected to discover *mandala* in the human body.

The male partner in the rite of *maithuna* (the bhairo of the vamachairs) was to look upon the nude female partner (the bhairvi) as prakarti incarnate with adoration and detachment.

At a second stage, the Bhairvi was transformed into an incarnation of Shakti and the goddess herself. The supreme goal of the rite of *maithuna* was a complete identification of Shakti and Shiva through the realisation of 'immobility' on all three planes of thought, respiration and seminal emission. *Matsya* (fish), *mansa* (flesh), *maithuna* (coition) and *madya* (wine) were thoughts extremely important by the vamacharis. The ritual indulgence in meat, wine and sexual intercourse was little short of debauchery and the religion could not fulfil any social purpose.

From the above account it is not difficult to surmise that Hindu religion including its important sects had lost much of its vitality and its votaries had confined themselves to performing empty rituals and recitations from sacred scriptures without understanding their meaning and significance. Not only this, some of its votaries as for instance, Tantriks and Vamacharis had been bold enough to incorporate even debauchery in their religious practices. The religious leadership was bereft of any higher motive; they only aimed at their own comfort and had acquired expertise to exploit the innocent people.[46]

Hindu-Muslim Relations

In the initial stages of the Muslim rule in Punjab, the relations between the Hindus and the Muslims were not so good. The Hindus had no love lost for the Muslims. Alberuni writes: "All their fanaticism is directed against those who do not belong to them—against all foreigners. They call them Malechha *i.e.* impure and forbid having any connection with them, be it by inter-marriage or any other kind of relationship or by sitting, eating, and drinking with them because thereby they think they would be polluted. They consider as impure anything which touches the fire and water of a foreigner; and no household can exist without these two things which once has been polluted should be purified and thus recovered, as under ordinary circumstances if anybody or anything has become unclean, he or it would strive to regain the state of purity. They are not allowed to receive anybody, who does not belong to them even if he wished it, or was inclined to their religion." Alberuni gives reasons for this attitude. "The Hindus are haughty, foolishly vain-self-conceited and stolid.[47] They are complacent and believe that there is no other country on earth but theirs, and no created beings besides them have any knowledge or whatsoever.[48] Their language is different from ours.[49] They differ from us in their manners."[50] But there was yet another, rather the most important reason. The Muslim conquerors during the course of their conquests and even after their consolidation meted out to the Hindus the treatment which could never arouse friendly feelings. According to Imam Shiafa and Abu Hanifah, and Imam Ahmed Hanbal, Hindus being no possessors of a revealed book (*Ahl-i-Kitab*) were *Kafirs* and could choose either death or Islam. But as the number of the Muslims was very small and there was danger of the combination of all the Hindus against the Muslim rule, the legal position of the Hindus was changed by the Muslim jurists and they were given the status of Zimmies, meaning thereby that they would pay *Jaziya* as a condition of their existence.

This position of the Hindu was accepted by all the Sultans of Delhi. Once or twice during this period, some religious fanatics demanded a change in the legal status of Hindus, but their approach was neither approved by the rulers nor did it receive the support of the Muslim public. Such demands remained witness of fanaticism and were never seriously considered.

With the passage of time, the rigours of the Muslim rule vis-à-vis the Hindus diminished and cultural relations began to develop. Relations between the Hindu and Muslim traders and the working classes were dictated by trade morality and guild spirit which transcended all other considerations of religion and caste. For instance, the Multani traders were mostly Hindus. They had frequent dealings with the Muslims, including the Turkish nobles.

The fact that a large number of the Hindus were converted to Islam also blunted the sharp edge of the Muslim fanaticism because they had a better understanding of the attitudes of the Hindus and secondly they themselves did observe many a custom of their erstwhile brethren. Moreover, both the Hindus and the Muslims shared the danger of being destroyed at the hands of the Mughals. This common danger further accelerated the pace of synergetic forces. The Sufi saints also played a considerable role in reducing bitterness between these two communities. Their affectionate behaviour towards every human being went a long way to soften the people in their treatment towards one another. According to Nizami, "The earliest references of the contacts between the Hindus and the Muslims that we find in the medieval records are about the Khanqahs of the Muslim saints."[51] The use of a large number of Hindustani words and idioms, and the assumption of some Hindu names by the Muslim nobles (e.g. Malik Chajju) clearly epitomise the improved relations between both these communities.

The state too had to be lenient towards the Hindus as the time passed on. It could not possibly dispense with the services of the Hindu employees in the various branches of the administration particularly at the local level. The ruling Muslims fully realised that it was not possible for them to destroy all the indigenous institutions of administration and hence the services of the indigenous people were imperative. Dr. Tara Chand writes, "When Qutb-ud-din Aibek decided to stay in Hindustan, he had no other choice but to retain the Hindu staff which was familiar with the Hindu administration, for, without it all government including the collections of revenue would have fallen into utter chaos".[52] The Muslims did not bring with them from beyond the Indian frontiers, artisans, accountants and clerks. Their buildings were erected by the Hindus who adapted their ancient rules to newer conditions; their coins were struck by officers. Brahmin legal experts advised the king on administration of Hindu Law and Brahmin astronomers helped in the performance of their general functions.

Still the road was long and much was to be done to reach the destination. The matrimonial relationship was a rarity. Inter-dining among both the communities was almost non-existent. The social intercourse was healthier and on a bigger scale in the villages as compared with the urban areas. Except on certain occasions, when there was a cry of *Jehad*, the stream of life in the rural areas flowed smoothly.

Some Hindu Social Groups

The loss of political power and the subordinate position that the Hindus occupied under the Muslims caused them to cling even more tenaciously to the old values and out-moded pattern of life. They were divided into four traditional castes viz. Brahmins, Kshatryas, Vaishas and Sudras but as a result of Muslim impact, a number of old social and legal functions had passed out side the operation of the caste rules. The position and the legal and formal powers of the Brahmins had undergone a considerable change with the fall of the old Kshatryas or the ruling classes of Hindustan. Some of them qualified as physicians and astrologers; quite a few among them turned to agriculture. Similarly, Kshatryas or Vaishyas adopted professions other than stipulated by the caste instructions. But the caste spirit was as strong as ever, may be even stronger. The Muslim impact did have some effect on the Hindu society and created some new stirrings but it could not knock out the caste spirit, with the result that the Hindu society was a house divided into four water-tight compartments, often looking askance at one another. Moreover, in-caste conflicts were also there. Each caste group was divided into sub-groups; not unoften assuming about itself an air of superiority and taking vicarious pleasure while denigrating or condemning the other groups.

Hundreds of examples can be cited to illustrate this point. Bhardwaj Brahmins disliked Sarawat Brahmins, some Jat groups looked down upon other Jat groups. The same was the case with other caste groups. Beneath the higher Hindu classes came the millions of untouchables. Though the phenomenon of the untouchability was not so acute in the north as it was in the south, yet the feeling of the upper class in north India towards the untouchables was despicable. The Brahmin and other upper classes, though submissive to his Muslim neighbours, were tyrannical in their attitudes towards low-caste co-religionists. The Sudras or untouchables lived a completely isolated life from the rest of the Hindus. The Brahmin priest would not officiate at the house of an untouchable and would not allow him to enter his temple. Likewise, Kshatryas and Vaishyas would not go near them.

In spite of the frantic efforts of the leaders of the Bhakti movement in the country to uplift the downtrodden people of the Hindu society, the status of the Sudras showed no improvement. Even such saints as Kabir and Namdev—could not escape maltreatment at the hands of the higher castes. Namdev, the eminent Bhakta of Maharashtra, was pushed out of the temple on account of his being low-caste tailor. No wonder, many of these suppressed people saw their salvation in giving up Hinduism and embracing Islam. In fact, the majority of the Indian Muslims came to be composed of such Hindu converts.

Apart from the differences born out of caste barriers, there were other differences also which divided the different social groups from one another. Different groups of the people reacted differently to different social customs and institutions. The customary law of the Jats differed from the Hindu Law. Jats, without any reservation or hesitation, practiced *karewas* and entertained no taboos regarding widow-remarriage. Moreover, the Jats, being essentially tribal in their outlook, took more care for their tribal ties than those of castes or creed. They arduously nursed, and faithfully observed ancestor worship called the *Jathera Puja* according to which some important member of the tribe was worshipped by the people of the tribe.

In marked contrast to the tribal *Jathera* concept, the village in south-east Punjab worshipped *Bhumia*. When a new colony or village was founded in the south-east Punjab, the first thing to be done before houses were actually built, was to raise a maund of earth on a spot near the proposed village and plant a *jand* tree on it. The first man who died in the village whether he be a Brahman, a Jat, or a Chamar was burnt or buried on the maund. The fortunate man was deified as the Bhumia or earth god and worshipped by Hindus of all classes in the village as their deity guardian.

In conclusion, it can be said that Hindu society was a house divided against itself. It appeared as if it had resigned to its fate and felt satisfied in clinging to its out-moded beliefs, and out-dated institutions such as untouchability and caste system.

Bhakti Movement

But there were some sensitive minds also in the body-social of the Hindus. They realized the rapidly deteriorating state of the Hindu society and felt the necessity of some early steps to stop this rot. Chaitaya Maha Prabhu in Bengal, Rama Nand, Kabir and Ravidas in Uttar Pradesh, Vallabacharya in Madhya Pradesh, Tuka Ram, Nam Dev and Ek Nath in Maharashtra, Garib Das, Mira Bai and Dadu in Rajputana worked for years for reforming and regenerating the Hindu society. The thought-current of these sants also reached Punjab which went a long way to create new ferment. It will be too much to say that the Bhagats and Sants working in different parts of the country made any radical change in the general character and pattern of the Hindu society. Still their work had a significance of its own. Punjab and Maharashtra, in particular, experienced far-reaching changes as the result of a socio-religious reform movements.

NOTES

1. P. Saran, *Rise and Fall of the Mughal Empire*, p. 22.
2. K.S. Lal, *Twilight of the Sultanate in India*. Also see Ishwari Prasad, Medieval India, and A.B. Pandey, *The First Afghan Empire in India*.
3. *Babur Nama* tr. by A.S. Beveridge, p. 367.
4. *Ibid*.
5. Fourteen miles north of Bhera lies the mountain range written in the *Zafar Nama* and other books as the *Kohl-Jud*. I had not known why it was called this. I know now that on it dwell two tribes, Jund, Janjua. These two, from the old have been the rulers and the lawful commanders of the peoples and hordes of the range and of the country wherein Bhera and Nilab is. *Babur Nama*, p. 379.
6. W.H. Moreland, *Agrarian System of the Sultanats*, Vol. II, p. 67.
7. *Ibid*., p. 97.
8. Iqtidar Hussain Siddiqui, *Some Aspects of Afghan Despotism in India*, Three Men Publication, Aligarh, 1969.
9. *Ibid*., p. 147.
10. *Ibid*., p. 56.
11. W.H. Moreland, *op. cit*., p. 68.
12. *Ibid*., p. 76. "Abhas Khan says that one share of the produce was left to the peasant and half a share was taken by the Muqqadam as state dues during the reign of Sher Shah. As Sher Shah is reported neither to have reduced nor increased the state demand of revenue of the Lodis, we can surmise that it had continued since the Lodi period".
13. Iqtidar Hussian Siddiqui, *op. cit*., p. 149.
14. R.P Tripathi, *Some Aspects of Muslim Administration*.
15. Abul Fazal, *Akbar Nama*, Vol. III, pp. 729, 734.

16. *Ibid.*, p. 117.
17. S.G.F. Braudorn, *Dictionary of Comparative Religion.*
18. J.S. Grawal, *Guru Nanak in History*, p. 68.
19. Qarmthians are considered to be a sect of Ismailis (*Dictionary of Comparative Religion*).
20. J.S. Grewal, *Guru Nanak in History*. Also refer to Ashraf's book, *Life and Condition of the People of Hindustan.*
21. *Tarikh-i-Multan*, pp. 62-67.
22. J.S. Grewal, *op. cit.*, p. 76.
23. *Tarikh-i-Lahore*, pp. 164-66.
24. James Hastings (ed.) *Encyclopeadia of Religion and Ethics*, Vol. 2, p. 11.
25. J.S. Grewal, *op. cit.*, p. 102.
26. *Ibid.*
27. *Siyar-ul-Auliya*, p. 444.
28. Yazid, ejaculated 'glory to me'. How great it of majesty; Hallaj was crucified in A.D. 922 for his statement 'I am the truth.' The Judges took it to be a claim to divinity although he did not mean that. (*Dictionary of Comparative Religion*), p. 593.
29. *Ibid.*
30. *Ibid.*
31. K.M. Ashraf, *Life and Condition of the People of Hindustan*, p. 67.
32. *Ibid.*, p. 68, Although the Quran emphasizes their position in a general way as a separate class of Muslim people, no special provision was made for them in the Holy Book. Spurious traditions soon began to be spread among the people. Holding that the Prophet was repeated to have said: Honour the Ulema, for they are the successors of the prophets: he who honours them, honours the prophet of Islam and Allah thereby.
33. *Ibid.*, p. 70.
34. *Ibid.*, p. 68.
35. *Ibid.* Also consult *Ibn Batuta, Kitab-ur-Rehla*, Vol. 2, p. 54. The Theologians of Sind were charged with misappropriation of state funds and were severely punished.
36. K.M. Ashraf, *op. cit.*, p. 69.
37. R.P. Tripathi, *Some Aspects of Muslim Administration*, p. 220.
38. *Ibid.*
39. K.M. Ashraf, *op. cit.*, p. 76.
40. J.S. Grewal, *op. cit.*, p. 37.
41. Afif, *Tarikh-i-Feroz Shahi*, p. 444. (As Quoted by K.M. Ashraf in the *Life and Condition of the People of Hindustan.*)

42. K.M. Ashraf, *op. cit.*, p. 77.
43. Romula Thapar, *A History of India*, pp. 162-63 as quoted by J.S. Grewal in *Guru Nanak in History*.
44. *Khulasat-ut-Tawarikh*, p. 22.
45. J.S. Grewal, *op. cit.*, p. 110.
46. Edward C. Sachau, *Alberuni's India*, pp. 19-20.
47. *Ibid.*, p. 22.
48. *Ibid.*, p. 23.
49. *Ibid.*, p. 17.
50. *Ibid.*, p. 20.
51. Khaliq Ahmed Nizami, *Some Aspects of Religion and Politics in India during the 13th Century*.
52. Tara Chand, *Influence of Islam on Indian Culture*, p. 137.

Babur, Zahirud Din (1526-30 C.E.)

2

From the account of the political and socio-economic conditions of the people of the Punjab, some un-mistakable conclusions may be drawn. Firstly, there was no cohesion in any section of the Indian society. Civil strife had become a recurring feature. What with palace intrigues and wars of succession, internal factions among feudal elements and deadly animosities between different social and religious groups were sure to bring about disaster. Nor could hope be entertained for Punjab society to throw up good political leadership or set up healthy trends, because society torn as under into different segments on bases of religion, caste considerations and tribal affiliations, etc. each segment steadfastly opposed to the other, was unlikely to do so. There were people working in guilds and in rural areas who had good neighbourly relations and could form the basis of the emergence of a new social structure bringing about harmony among different sections of the people thus releasing a lot of vital force to reshape Punjab but alas, they did not do anything, because, firstly, they were not conscious of the role they could play, and secondly, their number being very small they were not in a position to influence the trends. The liquidation of the existing political machine as also of the unequal value-system in social affairs was inevitable. Progress towards the objective was, however, set in motion by Babar who was the son of Umar Shaikh Mirza and had inherited territory of Farghana after the death of his father in 1494, when he himself was in his twelfth year. Those were the days when Timurides were heading towards their fall. After the death of Funcie (1404), his loosely knit empire was involved in civil war and was exposed to unfriendly powers almost on all sides. Even then, the things were in control upto the time of Abu Said. After his death, with amazing shortsightedness, the successors of Abu Said Mirza divided the empire among themselves and scrambled for supremacy. The division of the vast empire by Changez Khan among his sons was a necessity, and therefore, justified. It was held together by the great Khans for a few generations or at least so long as the inspiration of Changez Khan and the influence of Kuraltai, the grand council of the Mongols survived. But the system did not work with the Timurids. There was hardly any justification for its continuance by Abu Said Mirza, particularly because the empire had shrunk substantially in dimensions and was surrounded by threatening dangers on all sides. But the traditions left by Changez and Timur and fierce rivalries, jealousies and ambitions of princes and clannish leaders would not allow a clear appreciation of political situation and Abu Said divided his empire among his four sons; his eldest son Sultan Ahmed Mirza held Samarkand and Bukhara, Mahkud Mirza was assigned Hissar, Konbuz Badakhshan and Khutan, Alagh Beg held Kabul and Ghazni while Umar Sheikh Mirza possessed Farghana. Of all the Timurides rulers, Umar Shaikh Mirza was the most fiery. He suffered from restless ambition which invited frequent conflicts between himself and his brothers and maternal uncles. Without adequate means—political, material and moral, he wished to repeat the achievements of the great heroes of Firdause's epic and with the help of strong liquor and *majun* (an intoxicating composition) he had worked up his imagination to a dangerous pitch. He was constantly at war with one or the other neighbouring kingdom. Even in 1494 when Umar Shaikh died, he was engaged in the defence of Farghana from a double attack—one by Mughal prince Sultan Mahmud and the other by Sultan Ahmed of Samarkand. After the death of Umar Shaikh, the defence operations were conducted by Babur with such intelligence, boldness and extraordinary intrepidity that Sultan Ahmed thought it prudent to patch up with him. Sultan Mahmud also raised the siege of Akhshi and went back to his country. In way back to Samarkand, Sultan Ahmed Khan passed away. Since the Sultan had no real son to succeed him, the throne of Samarkand excited the cupidity and ambitions of all the rulers of Central Asia and the Mughals.

A perusal of the complicated history of Central Asia shows that there were two dominant impulses which contributed a lot in shaping the historical spirit of the people. One was the grandeur and the concept of Changezi or Temurid empire and the other was the constant quest for riches. These two things inspired so many personalities who did not hesitate even to risk everything to emulate Changez. Except lust for riches and power what other motives inspired the Changezites and Temurides, it is difficult to understand, but there is no denying the fact that very many rulers of Central Asia of the fourteenth and fifteenth centuries burned with the ambitions of playing the part of Timur or Changez. Babur who was brought up in the atmosphere where much was talked about Samarkand (in fact, his father was eneamoured of the city) and Timuride empire could not but resist the temptation of trying for the throne of Samarkand. Politically, the town was the heart of Central Asia. Its climate, fertility, beauty, glory, and historical associations cast a spell on all the Timurides. The circumstances also egged on Babur to try to achieve his long-cherished objective. Just after the death of Sultan Ahmed Khan, the throne of Samarkand was offered to Mahmud Mirza of Hissar. He too died in A.D. 1495 and the throne came to be held by his son Bai Sughar Mirza whose younger brother, Sultan Ali, contended the claim at the instigation of the recalcitrant nobles of the court of Bai Sughar. Such circumstances impelled Babur to march upon Samarkand. Consequently, he laid siege to it (1496). He failed to produce any impression and owing to the advent of cold weather had to retire without achieving anything. In 1497, Babur again tried his luck. This time he was successful in realising his ambition of ruling at Samarkand, though temporarily (November 1497). In A.D. 1500, Babur reconquered Samarkand for the third time, again to lose it to the Uzbeg leader Shaibani Khan in 1501 who gave him a crushing defeat in the battle of Saripul. What to speak of Samarkand, he even lost Farghana. In 1503, Babur actively assisted by his maternal uncle tried to win back Farghana but his defeat at Achian at the hands of Shaibani Khan sealed the fate of the Timurides in Transoxiana and Babur had to seek safety in flight.

While wandering about and marking time, Babur was told at Tirmiz that it was useless for him to loiter about in Central Asia, and that he would do well if he tried his luck in Afghanistan where the government was unpopular and unstable. The affairs at Kabul were favourable for Babur. Ulugh Khan Mirza had died in A.D. 1501, leaving his infant son Abdul Razzaq to succeed him. One Muhammad Muqim Arghun backed up by the Hazaras captured power at Kabul, married a sister of the little king and tried to replace the old nobility by the one of his own creations. This led to disorder in the kingdom. So when Babur descended upon Kabul in October 1504, there was hardly any resistance. Muqim was allowed to go to his father at Garansir near Qandahar. Babur assigned Ghazni and Ningnahar respectively to his brother Jahangir and Nisir Mirza.

Having planted himself successfully in Afghanistan which once formed part of the Timuride Empire, the adventurism in Babur received a pick. Yet he did not allow his actions to overstep the limit of practicability.

From Kabul, he did make a few efforts to conquer Samarkand from Uzbegs and in 1511, he did succeed to capture Samarkand, yet he did not loosen his control over Kabul; and in fact, he had to fall back upon it soon in the wake of his defeat at Kul-i-Malik by Ubaid Khan, the celebrated leader of the Uzbegs after Shaibani Khan.

His repeated failures to get Samarkand were shocking to him, no doubt; yet it tickled his innate resourcefulness and instead of dampening his morale goaded him to think alternatively. He now seriously thought of conquering India. Historians have connected this thought of his with his failure in the conquest of Samarkand. This is correct only in the sense that frustration caused by his failure to occupy Samarkand induced him to think seriously of some alternative. In fact, his failure to get Samarkand had nothing to do with his design to conquer Punjab or India. Just a glance on the series of events which took place before his final failure to get Samarkand would show that since the beginning of his career he had been entertaining the thought of conquering India—particularly a part of it which formed an integral part of his grand design of re-establishing the Timuride Empire.[1] This being so, ever since he came to Kabul, it had been in his mind to move on to Hidustan.[2] However, he led his first expedition in 1505, halted at Jamrud and consulted about crossing the Indus but it was postponed. Then he proceeded to Kohat and after taking it went to the country of Isa Khail and halted in the environs of Tarbala, a village on the Indus in the country of Multan. In May 1505, he returned to Kabul. In September 1507, again he started by way of little Kabul for the conquest of Hindustan but turned back owing to difference of opinion among officers. Then for so many years, he did not attend to the conquest of Punjab as also the rest of India. The reasons were that the political condition did not warrant such a step. In the second decade of the sixteenth century, especially after 1514, the political situation turned in favour of Babur. A balance of power came to be established in Central and Western Asia, between the Ishaelites, the Persians and the Uzbegs. None of the powers, liked to disturb the balance of power because they apprehended war among themselves in case it was disturbed. Taking advantage of this type of situation, Babur turned his attention towards India with seriousness. The unstable political condition of Punjab and the shaky Lodi government at Delhi were also important factors which inveighled Babur to undertake the subjugation of Punjab and then Delhi, but these did not provide the motive which existed independent of them and long before the actual undertaking or the India campaigns.

Babur made his first serious attempt at the conquest of Indian territory in 1519. He stormed Bajaur which fell after a spirited struggle. He looked upon this as the first step on the road to Hindustan. Here he ordered a whole-sale massacre, not because it was to his liking but because he wanted to set an example. The country of Bajaur was entrusted to Khawaja Kalan and he was given a strong contingent to help him in subduing the country around. An expedition was sent against the Yusafzais early in February 1519 and they were made to acknowledge his authority. Babur's Sunni zeal manifested itself in the demolition of the tomb of a heretical faqir, Shah Baz, who had preached among the Yusufzais and Dilzaks. Having reached the borders of Hindustan, Babur crossed the Indus and marched to Bhera[3] which had been present in his mind since the storming of Bajaur. He claimed the countries of Bhera, Khushab, Chinak and Chiniot on the ground that his ancestor Timur had conquered them. At Bhera, Babur acted with restraint and issued orders to his soldiers not to hurt and harm the flocks and herds and fields of the people. Ali Khan, the governor of Bhera, capitulated. Babur compelled the people of Bhera to pay a good ransom. From there he dispatched Mulla Murshid to the court of Ibrahim Lodi whom he considered the lawful ruler of the Lodi Empire, with the proposal of returning to him portions of the Western Punjab, which belonged to his uncle, Ulugh Beg Mirza of Afghanistan. Daulat Khan Lodi refused to see the envoy and prevented him from proceeding beyond Lahore. He probably feared lest Ibrahim should deliver those districts and make friends with Babur, or reject the proposal and thus provoke a war with him in Punjab. Since Babur was not prepared to stay longer in India or embark upon extensive operations, he did not push the matter further. Nevertheless, he was resolved to get them into his hand whether peacefully or by force. After he recrossed the Indus, the Afghans drove out his officers and re-occupied the district.

Next year (A.D. 1520) Babur again conquered Bhera and pushed on as far as Sialkot and Sayyadpur (Eminabad). The inhabitants of Bhera and then those of Sialkot submitted without resistance but not so the people of Sayyadpur. The attempted defence of Sayyadpur proved abortive and a large number of inhabitants were either put to sword or carried into captivity. Guru Nanak and his companion Mardana, in all probability, were near the scene as it is evidenced in one of his verses in *Guru Ghranth Sahib*. Apart from the general massacre, the destruction of horses, mansions, palaces and dishonouring of women gave a strong jerk to Nanak's tender feelings which he expressed in the following lines:

> The wealth and sensual beauty which had intoxicated them became their enemies. To the messengers (of death), the command was given to strip them off their honour and carry them off. If it seems good to Thee, Thou grantest glory and if it pleases Thee Thou grantest punishment. Had they paused to think in time. They would have received no punshmen. But the rulers paid no heed, passing their time, instead in revelry, and now that Babur's authority has been established, even the (Pathan) princes starve. (*Guru Granth Sahib*, p. 417)

The Guru was also pained at the unequal character of the contest. On one side fought the trained organised army while on the other side was the defence force mostly consisting of non-combatants of a peaceful city. Guru Nanak also lamented the neglect which the Lodis had shown towards defence of their subjects. He bemoaned "the dogs of Lodis have spoilt the priceless inheritance, and when they are dead, no one will hold them in regard".

Babur, however, dropped the idea of pushing further because the news of the raid of Shah Beg Arghun of Qandahar compelled him to retrace his steps.

Upto this time, Babur must have found out that the road to Punjab was clear after the Indus was crossed, that the Afghans were either incapable of resistance or for some reason were anxious to avoid a serious clash with him, and that Qandahar must be conquered before any extensive operations in India could be undertaken. The conquest of Qandahar was also necessary for the peace and safety of Afghanistan which, for obvious reasons, was to remain for the time-being the base of his operations anywhere. Moreover, whether for Herat, Kabul or Hindustan, Qandahar was a strategic place.

Babur occupied Qandahar in A.D. 1522 and was now comparatively free to devote his full attention to the conquest of India.

He invaded Punjab for the fourth time in 1524. This time he had been invited by Daulat Khan, the Lodi governor of Punjab, and Alam Khan the uncle of Ibrahim Lodi who thought that

Babur would help them to depose Ibrahim Lodi and enthrone Alam Khan. He had been given full assurance through Dilawar Khan son of Daulat Khan, and Alam Khan who met Babur at Kabul, that they would act under Babur's instructions. The proposal was deliberately left vague as the real aim of the nobles of Lahore was to induce Babur to take steps to depose Ibrahim Lodi without making any positive commitments with him. If Afghan nobles were clever enough to keep the proposal vague, Babur was equally clever in not demanding clear elucidation or precision. Babur, however, was convinced that there was no solidarity among the Afghans and the opportunity was favourable for an adventurous drive. So far, Babur had been thinking only of those districts of the Western Punjab which had once formed part of the kingdom of Timur. Now his vision seems to have included the whole of Punjab, if not the entire Lodi Empire. If the plan worked well, he could rival the achievements of Timur in Hindustan, which would be an adequate compensation for his failures in Central Asia.

Babur set out from Kabul, though the exact date of his departure cannot be ascertained, crossed the Jehlum and Chenab and advanced to, within ten miles of Lahore, the headquarters of Daulat Khan. A little while before the advent of Babur, Ibrahim's forces led by Daulat Khan and Mubarak Khan had overpowered Daulat Khan and had occupied Lahore. Daulat Khan was compelled to seek shelter in colony of Balachis. Babur fought a battle with a Delhi army and defeated it with great slaughter. He made his triumphant entry into the city where the houses were put to flames and the inhabitants were plundered by his soldiers after the fashion common to Babur's tribe.

For four days Babur stayed at Lahore and then marched to Dipalpur. The entire garrison in the fort of Dipalpur was put to sword.

It was there that Daulat Khan along with his three sons joined Babur who then distributed the conquered territories among his Chiefs and allies. Daulat Khan was given Jalandhar and Sultanpur against his long cherished desire of occupying Lahore, Dipalpur and various other territories of the Sultan. Dipalpur was given to Alam Khan. Daulat Khan felt grievously hurt over his share and rose in revolt but having been foiled in it, he took shelter in the hills. Babur, thereupon, handed over Daulat Khan's territory to his son Dilawar Khan. Babur seemed to have realised the importance of Lahore and, therefore, placed it in charge of Abdul Aziz, his master of the horses. Sialkot, likewise, was placed under Kurram Kokltash. Babur had a mind to sack Sirhind but, because of the defection of Daulat Khan, gave up the projected plan and went back to Kabul.

Babur had hardly crossed the Indus on his way back, when Daulat Khan and his son Ghazi Khan revolted. They seized Dilawar Khan and recaptured the Chief of Sultanpur. Alam Khan was also defeated and driven from Dipalpur. Lahore still remained in the hands of Babur's officers who repulsed[4] a force of 5000 men which Daulat Khan had sent against Sialkot. He could not recover his power but succeeded in bringing a portion of Punjab under his control.

Alam Khan fled to Kabul, for, according to *Babur Nama*, he was present there and informed Babur of what had happened in Punjab. He solicited Babur's aid which was promised on the condition that while he would be given the throne of Delhi, Babur should retain Lahore and the whole country west of it in full suzerainty. Babur could not start for Kabul until December 1525 and wrote a letter to his Begs at Lahore ordering them to assist Alam Khan in his plan. He informed them that he would soon come after the trouble in Balkh was over. With Babur's letter Alam Khan went to Lahore and requested help from his officers for a march on Delhi and Agra. This was refused and then, in despair, the Lodi pretender opened negotiations with Daulat Khan and his son Ghazi Khan. The agreement between the two was that Daulat Khan and Ghazi Khan would take all the Begs posted in Hindustan to themselves and seize the country west of Delhi, while Alam Khan was to take Dilawar Khan and Haji Khan and with their help would capture Delhi and Agra.[5] With a force of 30 to 40 thousand men, they advanced upon Delhi and laid siege to it; they were routed by Ibrahim's army. Alam Khan fled the field in darkness and joined Ghazi Khan who had fled into the hills.

When Babur received the news that Daulat Khan and Ghazi Khan had collected an army of 20 to 30 thousand men, had seized Kalanaur and were thinking of advancing upon Lahore, he dispatched a courier forthwith to the Begs at Lahore asking them not to risk an engagement until the arrival of the Padshah.[6]

Babur set out towards Punjab in November 1525 and was joined on the way by Humayun with the troops from Badakhshan. Babur crossed the Indus on December 16, 1525 and began to advance to Sialkot by the hill route. He marched in five stages from the Indus, the sixth bringing him close to the hill of Jud,[7] below the hill of Balnath Yogi, on the banks of the river Harur, at the station of Baikal. After crossing the Jehlum, he was joined by some officers from his Lahore army. He reached the bank of Chenab and rode on to Bahlolpur. Next morning he halted at Pasrur where Muhammad Ali Jang and Khawaja Hussain waited on him.[8]

Leaving Shah Mir Hassan and some officers to guard Lahore, Babur moved ahead with his troops with all possible speed and reached Kalanaur, 17 miles west of Gurdaspur. He was anxious to overtake Daulat Khan Lodi and Ghazi Khan who were now seized with panic and had shut themselves up in the fort of Milwat near Hariana in Hoshiarpur district.

He ordered Muhammad Ahmed and Kutlag Dadaun to pursue them and they were strictly instructed to intercept every move into and out of the fort of Milwat, so that the garrison might not be able to escape.[9]

Babur crossed the river Beas opposite Kahnuwan and encamped at the mouth of the valley of the Shivalik hills in which lies the fort of Milwat. Daulat Khan was completely unnerved and sent word to Babur that since Ghazi Khan had fled into the hills, he would surrender Milwat if his offences were forgiven. Khwaja Mir Miran was deputed to set his mind at ease and to bring him with his two swords, which he had girt to his waist to fight against Babur, hanging down from his neck as a mark of humiliation and surrender. When he was brought before Babur, he was admonished and entrusted to the custody of Khwaja Mir Miran.[10] Daulat Khan and Ghazi Khan who had fled to the hills like a coward leaving his wife and children in Milwat. Ghazi Khan's library was sifted and its contents were given to Humayun and Kamran. Milwat was placed in the charge of Muhammad Ali Jang—who left his elder brother Arghun there with a contingent of 200 or 250 officers to support him. It was about this time that Dilawar Khan also joined Babur, and in consultation with him the blood ransom was settled for prisoners.[11] Daulat Khan's life was spared; he was allowed to go to his village but he died on the way. Babur continued his march and was joined by Alam Khan whom he treated with polite respect.

Babur continued his advance on Delhi via Dun and reached Rupar. It was here that Babur had to descend from the hilly route. His army moved through Kurali to Banur where he was informed that Sultan Ibrahim Lodi was marching towards Panipat. He also learnt here that Hamid Khan, the Shiqdar of Hissar-i-Feroza, had also advanced against Babur at the behest of the Sultan. Babur sent Atka Beg towards Ibrahim's camp to procure intelligence and directed him to find out the movements of Hamid Khan. From Banur, Babur proceeded to Ambala and dispatched Humayun with all the forces under him to reinforce Atka. Hamid Khan was defeated. Humayun's troops entered Hissar-i-Feroza and sacked it. The town was bestowed upon Humayun as a reward for the brilliant success he had achieved in dealing with one section of enemy's army.[12] Babur pushed on and reached Sarswati from where he advanced to Panipat with his army totaled four thousand by two marches on April 12, 1526. It was not a large army, hence he had to take such a defensive position which under favourable situation could be converted to an offensive one. His knowledge and experience of warfare was wide and he had seen tactics employed by the Mongols, the Uzbegs and the Persians. He had, moreover, the advantage of commanding the services of two Turkish officers who knew Qamanalite methods of warfare and the effective employment of fire-arms. For the first time the Afghans were going to face an effective combination of heavy cavalry and fire-arms. Babur made use of the town of Panipat to protect one of his flanks while the other was safeguarded by a ditch and a palisade of felled trees and thorny shrubs. In front, he placed a row of hundreds of wagons tied together by ropes of raw hides. This was, however, not a continuous line. Between a set of wagons there were gaps in which small breast-works were erected to give reasonable protection to musketeers and artillery men, as also to give passage for the deployment of his cavalry at an opportune moment. Behind the line, he arranged his troops in the traditional manner of the east into three sections—the right, centre and left—and posted flanking parties of Mongols on the extreme right and left to effect the charge of the Tulughama—well-known Mongol manoeuvre in order to produce a deadly effect on the enemy. The right was commanded by Prince Humayun, Khawaja Kalan, Sultan Muhammad Duladi Beg, Treasurer Wali, and Pir Quli Sistani, and left by Muhammad Sultan Mirza, Mehdi Khwaja, Adil Sultan, Shah Mir Husain Sultan Janaid Barlus, Qutluq Qadam, Jag Beg, Pay Master Muhammad Shah Hussain Yaragi and Mughal Chanchi. In the right centre were posted Chin Timur, Sultan, Suleman Mirza Beg of Quj Beg, Khalifa, Muhibh-i-ali and Mirza Beg Tarkhan. The advance guard was led by Khusrau Kukulbash and Muhammad Ali Jang and the reserve by Abdul Aziz, the Master of the house.

Ibrahim Lodi came with a large army which has been roughly supposed one lakh but was probably not less than fifty thousand. He had no doubt two thousand elephants which had not been trained to face the new fire-weapons and, therefore, were likely to prove an encumbrance, if not a positive danger. The two armies faced each other for a week. Babur was anxious to force Ibrahim to open an attack. To both, delay was likely to cause demoralization and complications. Tired with provocation caused by the Mughals, Ibrahim held a feast, like those of the Spartans and Rajputs, gave away to officers and men the jewels, pearls and gold which he had brought with him and asked them to prepare for a decisive blow. Next day, a determined attack was opened.

The Afghan army galloped for a vigorous frontal charge, but, finding the front line of the enemy narrow, the flanks hesitated and then converged on it. In doing so, the formation of his army was badly broken and the troops were crowded towards the centre. This was exactly what Babur wished for. He directed his flying flanks to take the enemy on the flanks and the rear and ordered the fire to be opened. These tactics rolled up the Afghan army into a solid mass. It was paralysed and it could not be properly deployed. It was mercilessly exposed to deadly fire.

Ibrahim Lodi was requested by Muhammad Khan to run away for a safety before the enemy closed upto him. The Sultan thought, it would be disgraceful to choose safety in place of martyrdom. He refused to listen and rushed into the thick of the battle with five or six thousand devoted soldiers and was engulfed with them in the Vortex of annihilation. Panic overtook the Afghan army which broke and fled only to be slaughtered (April 21, 1526). The head of the dead Sultan was severed and presented to Babur. Babur's success was, indeed, a success of consummate leadership, superior war strategy and superior weapons. But it was decisive for the Lodi Empire and Punjab. Punjab fell into the hands of Babur not to be challenged by another power of India, immediately at least.

In the very day of the battle, Babur pushed forward two detachments—one to Delhi and the other to Agra—to prevent lawlessness and plunder and to take possession of the public treasuries in those cities. He himself followed and reached Delhi on the third day after the battle. He moved swiftly to Agra after sealing up all treasuries at Delhi.

After the battle of Panipat, Babur could not pay his full attention to the affairs of Punjab, as he was pre-occupied with Rajput and Afghan affairs. He appointed Mir Yunis Ali as the governor of Punjab. He was devoted to Babur and was one of the most trusted, daring and experienced generals who had fought with great intrepidity and wisdom in the battle of Punjab.[13] Even before this when the rebellious Afghans, under the command of Hamid Khan of Hissar Feroza, had clashed with Humayun, Mir Yunis Ali was one of those who had fought bravely and had defeated the Afghans. Being a great general and capable administrator, he succeeded in keeping Punjab under complete control when Babur was heavily engaged in the conquest of the unsubdued provinces of northern India. He was, thus, destined to play a dominant role during the formative period of the Mughal suzerainty.[14] He took steps to put to an end to the depredations wrought by Mohan Mandhar, a Hindu Chief near Kaithal. He issued instructions to Ali Quli Khan Hamdani to take three thousand horsemen and crush the evil doers. Due to the intense cold, the royal archers were unable to pull their bows and thus could not withstand the onslaught of the rural folk of Mohan Mandhar, who had been warming themselves besides the village fire.

Mir Yunis Ali at once despatched Taresam Bahadur and Narang Beg alongwith a contingent to reinforce Ali Quli Khan. They reattacked the Mandhars who now, fortunately for the Mughals, were enjoying festivities. They inflicted a crushing defect on them who were killed in a large number. A tower was erected of the skulls of those who were killed in the encounter. The punishment meted out to the inhabitants of the village struck terror into the minds of the people of the entire area.

Babur, during his short span of rule, did not establish any administrative system better than that of the Lodis. His administration was rough and simple. He accepted the system which he found in vogue in Hindustan. He parcelled his empire into fiefs which he entrusted to Jagirdars dependent upon himself. It is true that they did not enjoy the same degree of independence as they had enjoyed under the Lodis, but the defects of the system stood as they were before the assumption of the reins of government by Babur. He did not organize the administrative machinery to conform to the needs of the times. He did not establish any courts to dispense justice to the people, nor did he evolve any institutions to ensure sound administration and felicity of the people. He did not effect any alternation or improvement in the revenue administration of the province. He accepted the system that was already in vogue. Moreland observes that Babur distributed assignments among his followers soon after the battle of Panipat without any injunctions that they should be considerate while dealing with them as they were much hard pressed, even exploited by the earlier assignees of

Afghan rulers. Babur's casual approach to governance was no credit for him, especially when he had the requisite vision and administrative acumen. He, however, strongly dealt with roving bands of Mandhar of Narnaul in East Punjab who were almost chronic disturber of peace.

Babur Nama is a mirror of his genius, his literary accomplishments, his observant eye, his style of diction, his vast knowledge of flora and fauna, his extraordinary familiarity with the races and people he met wherever he happened to go. According to Alofe Caroe, the celebrated author of *The Pathans*, whatever Babur inscribed in his autobiography about different races/tribes of north western Punjab that was hundred per cent correct. His observations are still valid and ever since he recorded his observations about the races of north western Punjab, very little changes have occurred in their cultural morphology, primarily due to their intransigence and their unreachable habitat. He had a rich legacy of administrative experience as well as of empire building. His ancestry could be traced to Tamerlaine and Changez Khan from father and mother sides respectively. Changez Khan was not only an astute general but also possessed extraordinary administrative capability. He prepared a comprehensive code known as Yasa. Tamerlaine was known not only for his conquests but also for his interest in the welfare of his people as also in architecture and fine arts such as painting. Such precious legacy of his was bound to affect Balbur's demeanor and mind-set. Besides, he was contemporary of Safvi dynasty's rulers ruling over Iran and Ismali Turks exercising their rule over Trukey. He himself had imbibed the fine culture of Samarkand and Herat—both the places abounding in exquisite architectural monuments and excellent paintings by master painters such as Bayazid and his pupils, famous for minature paintings. Babur, as he was acculturated by rich legacy and endowed with wide knowledge of men and matters and profound aesthetic sense, laid out gardens, built aqueducts, bridges and buildings. In Agra 600 persons worked on his palaces and 1491 stone cutters were employed in Agra, Sikri, Bayana, Dholpur, Gwalior, and Koil (modern Aligarh). His son Kamran laid out a garden at Lahore and built a Baradari on the bank of the Ravi. An irony, however, lies in the fact that only two of Babur's buildings survived: One built at Panipat in 1526 and other in Awadh raised in 1530. He brought Yasaf, a pupil of Sinan, a renowned ottoman architect who later on in the time of Akbar raised beautiful edifices.

In one respect Babur's vision of governance was differentially unique. It was all-comprehensive, certainly not particularistic. He was an ideal Muslim himself, but he was not a hater of non-Muslims. In matters of religion, he seldom leaned to one particular section of people. He did not recognize Islamic Shariat as the foundation of his administration.

His personal as well as social stance was that of a latitudinarian or an electic. He had a warm heart for every one, he/she be of any religion or of any social segment. Sikh hagliographical literature such as Janam Sakhi Bhai Bala et al. has recorded that Babur met Guru Nanak, the progenitor of Sikh religion at Sayyadpur (later renamed Eminabad). Guru Nanak denounced the excesses which the Mughal army under his command committed on the people of Sayyadpur. He even versified them both to stir people's conscience and admonish them for their abject cowardice. The remarks of Guru Nanak were duly reported to Babur. He is said to have met Guru Nanak. Instead of venting his spleen against him, he turned an admirer of the Guru and his message. He was not averse to the Hindus or other non-Muslims carrying out their religious and domestic chores in their own ways. "He never indulged in persecution of people on grounds of religious dogma. Deceit and quakry of any kind were hateful to him. He did not issue any edict to conduct wholesale carnage of the lives and property of any segment of people. His concept of sovereignty had a close resemblance to that upheld by Changez or Timur. Both these stalwart Empire builders had accorded status to themselves as that of sovereign which according to them was legitiminised by the light of God that informed them. Babar had inherited this concept and practice although he did not hesitate to temper or modify it as warranted be circumstances including Shariat of his co-religionists. The axis of the structure of his sovereignty was authority which Babar never wanted to share or to get loose".

He did not allow either his bureaucracy or Jagirdars or Mullahs/ulemas to cross boundaries as marked by him. However, he never shrugged from consultation with appropriate persons. He was a man of fine literary tastes and fastidious critical perception. He was an accomplished Persian poet and master of his language Turki. Besides *Babur Nama*, he has left a Dewan, Mubin, a treatise on Muslim law in Turki, a treatise on prosody and metrical translation of Khwajah Walidiyya-Risalah. He introduced a new script called Khatt-I-Baburi. Punjab under him was stirred to think afresh even on unfamiliar Lines.

NOTES

1. "As it was always in my heart to possess Hindustan and as these several countries Bhera, Khushab, Chinab and Chiniot had once been held by the Turks, I pictured them as my own and was resolved to get them into my own hands whether peacefully or by force." A.S. Beveridge, *Babur Nama*, p. 380.
2. From the date 910 II at which the country of Kabul was conquered, down to now (932 II) (my) desire for Hindustan had been constant but owing sometimes to the feeble counsels of Begs, sometimes to the non-accompaniment of elder and younger brethren, a move on Hindustan had not been practicable...." *Babur Nama*, pp. 478-79.
3. Bhera is on the Jehlum; Khushab is 40 miles lower down the same river, Chiniot (Chini-wat) is 50 miles south of Bhera.
4. *Memoirs of Babur*, Vol. II, p. 166.
5. *Babur's Memoirs*, p. 455.
6. *Ibid.*, p. 451.
7. A.S. Beweridge, *op. cit.*, p. 379.
8. *Memoirs of Babur*, Trans. by Beweridge, p. 453.
9. *Memoirs of Babur*, Trans. by Beveridge, Vol. II, p. 169.
10. I called thee Father. I showed thee more honour and respect than those couldest have asked. Thee and thy sons I saved from door-to-door life amongst the Baluchis. They family and thy harem I freed from Ibrahim's prison-house. They crores I have thee on Tatar Khan's lands. What ill sayest Thou I have done thee, that thus thou shouldst hand a sword on thy either-side, lead on army out, fall on lands of ours and stir strife and trouble (A.S. Beveridge, *Memoirs*, p. 459).
11. *Babur's Memoirs*, p. 461.
12. *Tarikh-i-Feriashta*, Vol. II, Trans. by Bridgs, p. 43. *Memoirs of Babur*, Vol. II, pp. 178-79.
13. *Memoirs of Babur*, Vol. II, p. 135.
14. S.K. Bannerjee, *Hamayun Badshah*, pp. 53-56.

Humayun, Nasir-ud-Din Muhammad and Surs (1530-40; 1555-56 C.E.)

3

In 1530, Babur passed away and, after three days of uncertainty, Humayun ascended the throne of Hindustan at the age of twenty-three. The situation at his accession was not, indeed, a very easy one. He was confronted with several hostile forces on all sides, disguised and hence the more dangerous. There was hardly any unity in the royal family. His cousins Muhammad Zaman and Muhammad Sultan were contestants for the throne. Moreover, as the law of primogeniture was not strictly enforced among the Muslims, his three brothers, Kamran, Hindal and Askari also coveted the throne. As Eraskine remarks, "the sword was the grand arbiter of right, and every son was prepared to try his fortunes against his brothers". His court was full of ambitious and jealous nobles who engineered plans to oust Humayun. The army at his disposal was a mixed body, composed of adventurers of diverse nationalities having conflicting interests. Thus, he could not safely count on the support of his relatives, his court or his army. Babur's legacy to Humayun was also of a precarious nature. He did not leave behind him a consolidated and well-organised empire. In fact, he had defeated the armies and broken the power of the reigning dynasties, but the only hold which he or his race yet had upon the people of India was his military force. The Rajputs had been cowed down; they were not subdued. The Afghans were far from being completely crushed. The numerous scattered Afghan nobles, always ready for revolt, required only a strong and able leader to galvanise them, and this they found in Sher Shah. The growing power of Gujarat under Bahadur Shah was also a serious menace to Humayun.

The effect of these hostile forces was heightened by the incapacity of Humayun to make sustained and determined efforts. In the words of Lanepole, "He was incapable of sustained effort and after a moment of triumph would bury himself in his harem and idle away the precious hours in the opium-eater's paradise while his enemies were thundering at the gate."

The adverse factors spelt out above had their full impact in Punjab. Humayun, on coming to the throne, divided the empire among his brothers, probably under the impact of his dying father's will or in harmony with the ancient Turko-Mughal custom, and this process confirmed Kamran in the possession of Qandahar and Kabul which he held even during the regime of Babur. According to Ferishta,[1] he did so because it was in his own interest to win the goodwill of his brothers, and with them to make a united effort to save the empire.

Kamran, very ambitious and never sincere to Humayun, did not feel satisfied with Kabul and Qandahar. He wanted to extend his rule so as to include Punjab. He gathered an army and marched upon Punjab (1531) leaving behind Askari, his favourite brother upon whose support he could generally count, in charge of Kabul and Qandahar. He gave out that he was coming to congratulate his brother and to pay his respects as a loyal servant should. But Humayun knew his brother too well to attach any importance to these loyalist expressions. Being as yet entirely unprepared for any appeal to force, he despatched a messenger to Kamran, informing him that Peshawar and Samaghan had been added to Kabul and Qandahar, and requesting him to retire to his own dominions. Kamran, however, took no notice and pressed on to Lahore.

Mir Yunis Ali, the Mughal governor, who had been appointed by Babur and confirmed by Humayun, organised the defence of the city in such a manner that Kamran's plans to capture the city were foiled. Accordingly, Kamran despairing of being able to take the place by ordinary methods, had recourse to stratagem. Artfully posing to be violently enraged against a confidential officer Qarachah Khan, he inflicted upon him in open Darbar a previously planned slight.[2] The rumours of the breach between the master and the man were carefully fomented and soon it was the gossip of the town that the life of Qurachah Khan was in jeopardy. The Mughal governor was taken in by these rumours and he accorded permission to Qurachah Khan when he, with a small following, craved admittance to the town, crying that he had fled from the wrath of Kamran and now desired only to show his loyalty to Humayun.

Qarachah Khan, by slow degrees and persistent efforts, cultivated intimacy with the governor. At a banquet, Qarachah Khan succeeded in isolating the Mughal governor from the loyal troops and to surround him with the men of Kamran. Suddenly, he threw off the mask and placed Mir Yunis Ali under arrest, threw open a gate whereby Kamran, at the head of a strong force, entered the city, only to occupy it without facing any resistance. Impressed by the valour and loyalty of Mir Yunis Ali, Kamran offered to continue Mir Yunis Ali in the office of the governor; but the loyal servant declined the offer and preferred to join Humayun in Delhi. Kamran accorded the necessary permission and Mir Yunis Ali departed un-hindered. Immediately after this, Kamran over-ran the whole country up to the Sutlej.

With utmost effrontery which was partly the result of his knowledge of his brother's character and partly the product of his victories, Kamran sent an embassy to Humayun, praying to be confirmed in the territories he had seized. Humayun, who was a bit nervous owing to the recrudescence of the Afghans in the east, the seething discontent among the Mirzas and the deep-laid schemes of Bahadur Shah, decided to act cautiously. He confirmed Kamran not only in the governorship of Punjab, but also gave him Hissar-i-Feroza, and the province of Multan. The ostensible reason that Humayun gave for all this was that he wished to fulfil the desires of his father; but in reality, he acquiesced in the fait accompli because he had neither the power nor the inclination to dispute it. Kamran, on his part, expressed gratitude and, in token thereof, composed an ode, certainly a unique mode of covering perfidy.

The importance of the new possessions of Kamran can hardly be over-estimated. He not only got control of the most productive province but also planted himself between his brother Humayun and the regions beyond the Khaibar wherefrom the Mughal Emperor in India could get the fighting material, so essential for the permanence of the Mughal rule in India at this stage. Besides this, Kamran assumed the control of the important road running from Delhi to Qandahar which made it possible for him to stop the stream of adventurers with strong arms and ready swords, thereby cutting the tap-root of Humayun's military power, the strength and efficiency of which were absolutely necessary for the safety of the then infant Mughal dominion in India. "The last acquisition of Hisar Ferozah, which gave him command of the new military road from Delhi to Lahore put the finishing touch to the whole disastrous situation."[3]

Punjab remained under the control of Kamran upto 1540 when he was dislodged by Sher Shah.

Mahammad Zaman Mirza's Abortive Bid to Wrest Punjab

In 1535, Kamran's, authority in Punjab was challenged by Muhammad Zaman Mirza, the rebel Mughal governor of Gujarat, when the former was away to quell the rebellion of Sah Mirza of Iran. Taking advantage of the absence of Mirza Kamran, Muhammad Zaman Mirza marched upon Lahore with a view to occupy it, but instead of resorting to fighting immediately, he opened negotiations with the Faujdar of Lahore for its surrender. In the meantime, Kamran hastened to Lahore. Muhammad Zaman Mirza lost his nerve and abandoned the siege, himself fleeing to Delhi. After this, no disturbance took place in the province.

In A.D. 1530, Kamran made an attempt at seizing Delhi from Humayun at the time when the Emperor (Humayun) was engaged in war with Sher Khan. He was, however, foiled in his attempt by Fakhar-ud-din Ali, the commandant of Delhi, and after a faint attempt to attack Agra retired to Lahore.[4]

Kamran Maintained the Integrity of Punjab

Kamran's greatest contribution to the Mughal empire was that he maintained the integrity of Punjab for a whole decade.

He defeated the Persians twice and did not allow Shah Tehmasap to occupy Qandahar.[5]

In 1540, the political barometer underwent a great change. Babur's victories at Panipat and Gogra had not resulted in the complete annihilation of the Afghan chiefs. They were seething with discontent against the newly-founded rule, and only needed the guidance of one strong personality to coalesce their isolated efforts into an organised resistance against it. This they got in Sher Shah Suri who organised the Afghans and led them against the Mughals. In the process, Sher Khan defeated Humayun first in the battle of Chausa and then in the battle of the Ganges or Bilgram commonly known as the battle of Qanauj (17 May 1540). Thus, the work of Babur in India was undone and the sovereignty of Hindustan passed to the Afghans.

Humayun, after his discomfiture it Bilgram, retreated to Delhi. He could not stay there and had to hasten to Lahore. At Lahore, all the four brothers met. Even in the presence of imminent danger from the Afghans, concord was impossible. With Humayun driven out of Hindustan, Kamran said that he was likely to have to give up his own possession in the Punjab and Afghanistan and the danger of this made him disinclined to join in a hazardours resistance to Sher Khan which might involve the waste of his own resources.

As Sher Shah mounted pressure on Punjab and over-ran its territory, the need for action increased. In view of his slender military resources and the indifference of his brothers, Humayun resorted to negotiations with Sher Shah. He sent Sher Shah a request that Sirhind might be treated as the boundary between the Afghan and Mughal kingdoms. Sher Shah was not prepared to accede to the request of Humayun, because it would have been bad strategy to lose the opportunity of capturing Punjab when it was feasible to do so owing to the acute dissensions in the Mughal camp. He, therefore, offered a straight proposal that he would not use his sword, should the Mughals agree to recognise the Indus as the boundary line between the two kingdoms.

Humayun failed to produce any strategical plan at this juncture. He was pressed by Mirza Haidar to withdrew to Punjab Hills or take shelter in Kashmir. Mirza Haidar asked him that he should be allowed to go to Kashmir which he would conquer in two months and convert it into a safe refuge for their families. It would take at least four months for Sher Shah to reach Kashmir and it would not be possible for him to carry into the hill country the guns or cannons—the mainstay of his army. Hindal and Yadgar Mirza suggested a movement through Sind to reconquer Gujarat wherefrom Hindustan might be again invaded.

Karman was stolidly indifferent to what was passing on. In fact, Kamran feared Humayun much more than Sher Shah, thinking that while the Afghan leader would at least be satisfied with driving him out of Punjab, his brother might wish to resume all the possessions previously bestowed upon him, including Kabul.

With characteristically cold-blooded treachery to his brother, Kamran sent a message to offer his assistance to Sher Khan on the condition that he would be confirmed in Punjab. Although Sher Shah temporized with Kamran's envoys, he was determined to see the ruin of the Mughal imperialists. He forced the passage of the Beas. Mir Zaffar Beg, one of the generals of Humayun, who had been posted to check the advance of Sher Shah, did not succeed and hurried to Lahore to inform what had happened. Sher Shah was soon in the neighbourhood of Lahore. The negotiations into which he had led Kamran prevented army resistance on the part of the only prince who had power to offer it; and Kamran was nearly caught in his own trap. Absolutely unnerved, the brothers abandoned Lahore. Humayun made up his mind to adopt Mirza Haider's scheme for the conquest of Kashmir and moved in that direction. Soon he was informed of the threatening movements by Kamran and his army. Disgusted with the treachory of Kamran his men were now eager to oppose him. But Humayun refused to be hostile to his brother.

Mirza Haidar's plan for the capture of Kashmir was sound. He entered Kashmir via Naushahra, but Humayun, when he reached Bhera in the hope of getting assistance from the local governor, he found that Kamran had already preceded him and forestalled his hopes. Once more, the Emperor was urged upon to take action against Kamran but he refused as he had done at Lahore. Kamran did all this because he suspected that Humayun might dispossess him from Kabul. The road to Naushahra being blocked and it being impossible for Humayun to stay between an envious and unscrupulous brother on one hand and the victorious Sher Khan on the other, he decided to abandon the project of Kashmir and followed Hindal to Sind (end of 1540). A little while before setting out for Sind, there was nearly a clash with Kamran. The forces of Humayun and Kamran met in a defile of the Salt Range near Khushab, at the end of which the roads towards Sind and Kabul diverged, and a dispute arose as to which of them should pass through it first. Kamran's veiled intention of assuming the headship of the family appeared more clearly than ever when he asserted his right of precedence. Humayun's pride was stung and battle seemed inevitable. It was averted only by the remonstrance of a man of saintly repute in the camp of Kamran. Along with his forces which had considerably thinned down owing to desertions, pushed on to Sind, and Kamran then proceeded to his own comfortable domain of Kabul. Sher Shah despatched a force which drove Humayun out of the boundaries of India, followed him to Multan and thence retired. Another force under Sher Shah himself pushed Kamran who was retiring to Kabul, as far as the Indus. In no case was resistance offered and the Mughals were expelled from Punjab as also from India.

After having expelled from India the rivals of his nation, Sher Shah must have heaved a sigh of relief. But there remained hardly the less difficult task of ordering the country. The first thing to be done was to ensure the security of Punjab.

Sher Shah's Frontier Policy in Punjab

Sher Shah marched to Khushab where he halted for about two months to look into the administrative problems and to frame a defence policy for the newly conquered territories. His mind was still full of misgivings about the future. He had to reckon with Humayun in Sindh, Kamran in Kabul and Mirza

Haidar in Kashmir. It was obviously impracticable to pursue a forward policy to crush any of them; so he thought it better to contain each of them where they were, and to isolate them strategically so that they might not combine and make a fresh attempt at recovering Punjab. He could not afford to alarm the Afghan ruler of Sindh by violating his territory in pursuit of Humayun, because he feared that the Afghan ruler might league up with the hostile Rajputana and unreliable Gujarat. Similarly, on the north-west, Kamran and Mirza Haidar might easily combine their forces in the Peshawar Valley, and Qandahar afforded a strategic link between them and the Afghan ruler, should the latter care to make a common cause with them against Sher Shah. So the situation demanded a state of preparedness at three points on this side of the Indus, and the securing of political and military advantages in the tribal territory with the willing allegiance of Baloch and Pathan tribes beyond the Indus. Against a possible descent into the plains of Punjab from Kashmir on the part of Mirza Haidar, it was essential to occupy in strength the country of the semi-independent and war-like Gakhars who lived in the Salt Range and the submontane region adjacent to Kashmir.

In consonance with the demand of the situation, Sher Shah took some necessary steps. The Afghan tribes beyond the Indus were no stranger to him; in fact his own tribe's original habitat was in that area. He was well aware of their mental make-up and their love for liberty. His general attitude instinctively was of deference towards them, being himself a Pathan. They also had soft corner for him. There was another reason for this particular attitude. They had suffered a lot at the hands of Babur and Mirza Kamran. Babur had established a rule of terror in the guise of establishing a regular administration in the country of Roh. The country was divided into Tomain, a heavy revenue of eight lakhs of Shah Rukhis was exacted, and all opposition was crushed with an iron hand. In view of this, the Pathans were not at all favourably inclined towards the Mughals. This being so, the destruction of the Mughal empire by Sher Shah was an event of great Jubilation for them, and Sher Shah's pursuing army was hailed as an army of liberation and avengers of their wrongs against the Mughals.[6]

Sher Shah, therefore, pursued no forward policy in the home country of Pathans. He built no forts, nor did he garrison any strategic place with his own troops. His troops fought an action with Kamran Mirza on the other side of the Indus somewhere near Kohat and Khaibar, in which the latter suffered a defeat.

Side-by-side the caution of keeping the Afghan tribes in good humour, he mobilised the force of Afghan nationalism against the Mughals both at home and abroad. Sher Shah realised that the best safeguard for his Indian empire was the politically conscious Pakhtun nation on the north-west frontier. He made them turn their eyes towards Kabul and Qandahar rather than to Delhi and Lahore. Sher Shah sowed the seeds of Pakhtun nationalism by holding out before them the abject lesson of his own success against the Mughals.

In short, Sher Shah sought no expansion of territory on the west of the Indus but worked for the creation of a strong buffer on the tribal area and left the tribes to themselves. He avoided any demonstration of his authority and power in Roh and treated the tribes as allies against the Mughals. He withdrew his army to the line of the Indus.

Ensuring the Safety of Punjab Frontier from Kashmir Side

Having assured himself of the backing of the Pathan tribes beyond Indus, Sher Shah left Khushab for Bhera at the beginning of the spring season of the year 1541 to deal with the dangers looming large from the Kashmir side.

Mirza Haidar was in Kashmir, making efforts to establish his rule. He was in constant communication with Kamran and had accepted his overlordship. He and Hussain Afghan had read Khutba in the name of Humayun in Sindh and Kashmir respectively.[7] It had been comparatively easy for Sher Shah to seal off Gomal, Bolan and Khaibar Passes against any sudden reappearance of the Mughal from that side on account of his policy of appeasement towards the tribes of Roh; but the same policy was unworkable with two tribes such as the Janjuahas and the Gakhars, Jats, Gujjars, Awans and other tribes who inhabited the slopes of the mountains of Kashmir right upto the interior of the Salt Range.

Sher Shah's policy was two-ranged. He gave extensive help to the Chak tribe who wanted to see their man on the throne of Kashmir. Although, in spite of all this, the Chaks did not get victory during Sher Shah's time, yet his intervention in the affairs was wise and eventually bore fruit. It kept Mirza Haidar too pre-occupied with the Chaks who ultimately defeated and killed him ten years later. Ghazi Khan, the son of Kachi Chak, then, became the ruler of Kashmir in AD 1551. The sagaciousness of the policy of Sher Shah was clearly in evidence when the Chak ruler of Kashmir refused asylum to the rebellious Haibat Khan Niazi and ultimately surrendered the imprisoned Niazi to the Delhi government.

So far as the tribes were concerned, Sher Shah tried through persuation, bribe and love, to enlist their support on his side. The tribes of the Salt Range had been receiving scant attention from the government of Delhi. The Khokhars originally lived beyond Khushab on the Indus. They were the first to feel the heavy hand of Shahabud-Din Ghori who forcibly converted them to Islam, and they had their revenge by murdering the ferocious conqueror at Dhamaik. A branch of the Khokhars known as the Janjuhas had moved eastward and established their hegemony over all the tribes of the Salt Range with the exception of the war-like Gakhars who seemed to have been the original lords of the Salt Range. The Gakhars are thought to be the descendants of the great Yuhohhi Scythians, possibly like some of the Rajput tribes with this difference that having been unreclaimed by Brahmanical culture in their secluded hills, the Gakhars retained much of their untamed savagery and outlandish customs and more of their martial characteristics than other Indian tribes.

The history of this region from the 13th century onward had been a sickening record of wars between the Janjuhas and the Gakhars for political ascendancy, disturbed occasionally by the march of the armies of Delhi Sultanate more for the purpose of military demonstration than for permanent conquest and annexation.

When Babur entered Hindustan, he supported Janjuhas against Gakhars, but later on he changed his policy. Ever since Rai Sarang Gakhar had remained a faithful ally of the Mughals.

Strategically, the region of the Salt Range has always been too important to miss the eye of any master of war since the time of the Greeks, the Yucchis, the Ghaznavides and the Ghoris down to that of Babur and Sher Shah. The reason is that an invader from the north-west can appear suddenly in the very heart of Punjab by stealing a march through this region. So Sher Shah set about consolidating his hold over the Gakhar territory. Sher Shah ravaged the Gakhar country and their Chiefs Rai Sarang and his brother Adam Khan went into hiding. Sher Shah's base of operation against the Gakhars was Hathipur, name after the Hathi Gakhar, and situated between the hills of Rohtas and Rawalpindi.

Sarang Khan was ultimately captured by Sher Shah who flayed him alive and his skull was filled with straw. The daughter of Sarang Khan was seized and bestowed upon his general, Khwas Khan.

Sher Shah did not leave the Gakhars without thrusting a mighty wedge into their hearts which should torment them till the day of resurrection as Makhzan puts it.[8] He chose a commanding height of the Tilla Spur (known also as Jogi Balnath ka Tilla) for the construction of a fort, called the fort of Rohtas. It was magnificently planned on a scale that indicates the grandeur of Sher Shah's conception. Gakhars tried to dissuade labourers to work in the fort but they failed to hinder the proposed construction. The fort commanded the gorge where Kahan river from Kashmir breaks through the Tilla range.

"Its circumference was about 2½ miles, and the walls were about 30 feet thick and 58 feet high. There were 68 towers and 12 gateways, of which the most imposing is the Sohal Gate, a fine specimen of the Pathan style over 70 feet in height with exquisite balconies on the outer walls."

"For a permanent solution of the administrative and military problems of the frontier tract between Dhankot on the Indus and Bhera at the entrance of the Salt Range", he tried to reconcile the interests of hostile elements. The whole of the tract west of Bhera was inhabited not by Afghans but by Jats, Gujjars and Baloches. He found Dodai Balochs at Khushab and Bhera, and they were the ruling race. It was not Sher Shah's policy to disturb the Baloches who were in a position to muster a tribal levy of fifty thousand horses very easily, should they decide to combine against him. The Baloch Chiefs, Fateh Khan Dodai, Ismail Khan and Ghazi Khan who helped Khwas Khan in his pursuit of Humayun, had visited him at Khushab and were confirmed in their possessions in Sindh as well as in this tract. Sher Shah could not have established his authority in the hill country from Bajaur in Bhera without the aid of Ismail Khan Baloch whose army was absorbed and put on the pay-roll like the other regular troops from Hindustan. The Baloch tribes of Dod and Hot from lower Sind had been wandering, northward along the western bank of the Indus during the whole of the fifteenth century, the departure of Timur and were at this time in firm occupation of the whole stretch of the country below the Sulaiman Range from the north of Bolan to that of the Gomal Pass. Under the shadow of the Rajput Langah dynasty of Multan, the Rind Baloch tribe settled in the valleys of the Chanab, Ravi and Sutlej rivers either as mercenaries or as free-booters. The Dods and Hots migrated up the Jehlum and the Indus valleys in search of a new home. Thus, an eventual clash between the Pathan tribes and the Baloches appeared inevitable.

Kamran's fourteen years of rule had aggravated the situation as he followed the policy of playing off the Baloch against the Pathan. When Sher Shah was at Khushab, the dispossessed Pathans of Roh came to him for redress. Sher Shah acted with moderation and caution. He acted in such a way that he did not lose the sympathy of the either group. He prevailed upon the Balochies to give back the lands of Sarvanis in the Indus region, and as a compensation he gave the Baloches the territory of Nandna and Girijhak at the foot of Salt Range. Both these places and the intervening northern fringe of the modern

Jehlum district were of great strategic importance. This was probably given to Ismail Khan Baloch, the founder of Dera Ismail Khan, at the exit of the Gomal Pass and in the neighbourhood of the Pathan country.

Abbas attributes the restitution of the territory of the Sarvanis to Sher Shah's veneration for his remote ancestor. It was, in fact, very much part of Sher Shah's policy, and was a warning to the Balochis that their aggression against the tribes of Roh would not be tolerated. At the same time, he wanted to place between the Indus and the Jehlum, a Baloch block, which in fact already existed, as a safeguard against the trans-Indus tribes, because as an Imperialist his love and trust for his kinsmen were not unmixed with suspicions, and he also had the experience of the Lodi Sultanate before him. "As an empire builder he had after all to take stock of racial antipathies, hereditary feuds, petty ambitions, and clash of economic interests all of which could be exploited for the consolidation of his sovereignty as well as for an extension of his sphere of influence beyond the Indus."

During the short time Sher Shah lived in Punjab, after the erection of the fort, he appointed his general, Khwas Khan, as the governor of this important province. The author of *Makhzan-I-Afghani* states that Sher Shah contemplated the destruction of Lahore, always such a valuable base for the operations of an invader from the north-west, in order to render the return of the Mughals more difficult than ever. As a further safeguard, he intended planting pockets of the Afghans from Roh in the area skirted by the Jehlum and the Ravi so that their swords might serve as a barrier against the return of the enemies of their race. But unfortunately before he could do these things, he was recalled to the east to contend against the menace of the incipient revolt which had broken out in Bengal. But before leaving the province, Sher Shah appointed Haibat Khan Niazi (1540) as the governor of the Afghan forces at Rohtas and issued specific instructions that he would maintain tight control over the Gakhars and also subjugate the country upto the Indus so as to secure for the kingdom a natural frontier. That Haibat

Khan came up to the expectation of Sher Shah, can be seen from the determination and wisdom with which he met the challenges.

In 1543, finding that Sher Shah was pre-occupied with the conquest of Ranthambore, Fateh Khan, the Baloch chief, took possession of Multan, and, to dupe Sher Shah, made it public that he had acknowledged him as his overlord. The Afghan ruler could easily see the foul play. Accordingly, Haibat Khan from Lahore led his army against the Baloch chief who was defeated and captured. He collected together the inhabitants and restored the town to its former prosperity. Sher Shah was highly delighted and bestowed upon Haibat Khan the title of Azam[9] Humayun and Masand Ali. Haibat erected a new quarter as a part of Multan which he named Shergarh in honour of his master.

Similarly, Fateh Khan Jat, the robber chief of Kabula, marched against the Afghan ruler at Pakhattan. He was not alone in his project—rather he was actively assisted by the other robber chiefs, Haidar Khan Baloch and Bakhsha Khan Langah. Haibat Khan with his forces hurried to the spot forthwith and inflicted a crushing defeat on the combined forces of the Jat and Baloch chiefs. So that none might dare to create fresh trouble, a strong fort was established at Shergarh wherein a strong force was stationed to serve as a perennial deterrent to the Baloch and Jat tribes.

Having completed the preliminary settlement of the country, Sher Shah took such administrative measures that made him famous. "The objectives of his activities were five in number—the first was the relief of his subjects from tyranny; the second, the repression of crime and villainy, the third, the maintenance of the property of the realm; the fourth, the safety of the highways; the fifth, the comfort of traders and soldiers."[10]

Under the first and the third of these heads may be considered the revenue system and the military regulations.

So far as the revenue systems were concerned, the whole of the province except Multan and trans-Indus area which was not under Sher Shah was subjected to the measurement system of assessment in suppersession of the previous system, namely

Galla Bakhshi, i.e. sharing. Land was measured at every harvest and assessment of revenue was made according to measurement and in proportion to the produce. According to P. Saran who bases his conclusion on *Ain-i-Akbari* and the tenth farman of the Daulat-i-Sher Shahi, the land was divided into several classes and the rents fixed accordingly. The state share was fixed at 1/3rd[11] of the average produce, payable either in cash or in produce, the former mode being preferred. Over and above this, the peasantry had to contribute probably something towards the fees and maintenance of the surveyors and collectors when they were on active duty.

As regards revenue administration, the lower unit was that of Pargana. The revenue officer of the Pargana was the Amin. He had a treasurer and two or more clerks under him. The peculiarity of Sher Shah's system was that for the convenience of the peasants, he had appointed a duplicate set of clerks for preparing the records in Hindi as well as in Persian. The function of Amin was to assess and then collect the land revenue, as also to keep records thereof. The village headman was a sort of semi-official person to assist the revenue officials in collection and also to serve as a link between them and the peasantry. The case of the peasentry was represented by the Patwari who was a village accountant and kept all the agricultural records of the village. The Qanungo performed the same duties as regards lands of the Pargana.

Above the Amil was the Chief Munsif or Chief Amil in the Sarkar whose duty was to keep vigil on the activities of Amils in the different parganas of the Sarkar. Those Chief Amils were supposed to work in the light of the directions of the Subedars; but that they had direct communications with the central authorities is also amply borne out by the available evidence. The Amils were changed once or twice a year and their work was carefully supervised. They were not allowed to be oppressive towards the peasants for whom Sher Shah entertained the greatest care and concern. The rights of the tenants were duly recognised and the liability of each was clearly defined in the *kabuliat* (deed of agreement) which the state took from him, and the *patta* (title deed) which it gave him in return. Remissions of rents were made, and probably loans were advanced to the tenants in case of damage to crops, caused by the encampment of soldiers or the insufficiency of rain. These revenue reforms increased the resources of the state and at the same time accrued benefits to people. Sher Shah was so much particular about the safety and the protection of the peasant that he punished severely any one suspected of oppressing the cultivators. But in view of the importance Sher Shah attached to the welfare of the peasants, it can safely be presumed that even in the lands which were granted in Jagir to his officers, assessment and realisation of revenue were carried strictly according to the government regulations and under the direct control and supervision of the state.

Underlying the whole of Sher Shah's civil administration was the strong military organisation which he introduced. The exact number of the quota of the provincial governor of Punjab is not known; but undoubtedly Sher Shah's army was reinforced in time of need by the auxiliaries of provincial governors and Ziladars. To achieve the two-pronged purposes, that is to say to guard the kingdom against foreign invasion and internal disorder, Sher Shah created a large number of the forts and posted garrisons in them under capable commanders. The examples of Rohtas and Shergarh are in point. These forts served the purpose well. From Rohtas, a sharp vigil on the activities of the Gakhars was kept and likewise the troops in Shergarh deterred the Baloches inhabiting the surrounding areas from fomenting trouble. The military regulations were carefully devised and set in operation. Assignments were granted to nobles and the system of paying monthly salaries to the soldiers was also in vogue. He told the nobles unequivocally that they should furnish exact contingents which their obligations required. The horses of the troops were branded so as to check any noble or provincial governor to draw grant twice for the same horse.

Under the head of repression of crime and villainy may be considered Sher Shah's police system and his attitude towards religion. He was a firm believer in the principle of local responsibility for local crimes. Thus, the village headmen were made responsible for the detection of criminals, and maintenance of peace in the rural areas. The Muqaddams had to produce thieves and robbers or to make good the loss when a crime occurred within their jurisdictions. Even in case of murder, the Muqaddams were put to death if they failed to trace the murderers. It was the duty of the Amils of the parganas and over them of the authorities who controlled the Sarkar concerned to exact reparation for every offence. That Sher Shah was able to maintain discipline was also largely due to the efficient administration of justice. In the pargana civil suits were disposed of by the Amin and other cases, mostly criminal, by the Qazi and the Mir-i-Adil. Several parganas had over them a Munsafi-Munsufan to try cases. At the capital there was chief Qazi. The highest court concerning judicial as well as criminal matters was that of the Emperor.

Another cause of Sher Shah's success was his attitude towards religious classes of his own community and non-Muslims, especially the Hindus. He treated with special care the pious among the Muslims, and in this way butteressed his rule by the help of the spiritual forces which always exerted a deep influence on political affairs in medieval India. His treatment of the Hindus in general was tolerant and just. Though he did not abolish *jazia*, yet there is nothing on record to indicate that he was contemptuous towards the Hindus. "His attitude towards the Hindus was not of contemptuous sufferance but of respectful deference; it received due recognition in Punjab as also everywhere in the Kingdom". The Sikh Guru Angad Dev conducted his preaching unhampered by external interference and in an atmosphere of tolerance and freedom of expression.

Under the fourth and fifth heads come his system of road building, his patronage of merchants and his care for the well-being of his tribesmen. He constructed main roads, inns and Sarais at a distance of two kos from each other. These were carefully regulated for the comfort both of Hindu and of Muslim travellers and were made of burnt bricks. Each one of them had a well, a mosque, a temple and a watchman to guard the goods of the travellers and provided separate arrangements for the supply of food to the Hindus and the Muslims. In addition to repairing and maintaining the old roads, he built several new ones of considerable strategic importance. The longest of these, the Grand Trunk Road which still survives, extended for 1500 kos from Sonargaon in East Bengal to the Indus. Another road connected Lahore with Multan. Following the traditions of some of the ancient rulers, he got planted shady trees on both sides of the roads.

In the trading community, he evinced special interest. Customs were taken at two places only by royal officials, i.e. on the borders of the Kingdom and at the place of sale, and all other dues were strictly forbidden. The officials were not allowed to buy anything except at the market rates. The result of this was that trade flourished and Punjab became more prosperous than had been the case for the past several years.

Nor did Sher Shah neglect his Afghan brothers. He insisted upon their good treatment at the hands of the employers and gave all sorts of encouragement to the Afghan soldiers.

The over all impact of these policies of Sher Shah was that Punjab became a well-administered province, enjoying peaceful and stable political and social atmosphere, so highly conducive to the well-being of the people. During the short span of Sher Shah's rule, amity between religious communities at regional as well as local levels prevailed. Trade flourished and agriculture prospered.

But Sher Shah's span of life was cut short by his death in 1545. He was succeeded by his son, Jalal Khan who was proclaimed King in preference to his elder brother, Adil Khan in the fortress of Kalinjar on May 25, 1545, three days after the death of his father under the title of Sultan Islam Shah.

Immediately after his accession, he took drastic steps to crush the power of the nobles who had almost over-shadowed the throne and were holding fast to the view that the king was one of them whom they had themselves elected to the premier position. As a corollary to it, the position of the provincial and local administration under such a system was bound to be strong and the control of the central government extremely loose. Sher Shah, undoubtedly, by his extraordinary energy, resourcefulness, tact and personal attention to the smallest details, had cowed the Afghan chiefs into submissiveness who did not dare to defy the authority of his government; but he did not make any change in the theoretical basis of the Afghan monarchy or Afghan polity which was certainly unsuited to the vast kingdom of Sher Shah. Islam Shah took a bold and long stride forward in shattering the pride and power of the greater chiefs and establishing a strict discipline in the working of the government.

Naturally, the nobles clinging to their political prejudices fumed and fretted under Islam Shah. They began to vent their fire of dissatisfaction through many outlets, one of which was their attempt to raise Adil, Islam's brother, to the throne. Kutab Khan, the commander of the Kamaon hills, was one of the vanguards that harboured the aforesaid design, and to assert his contumacy and independence, he plundered the countries in the neighbourhood of the Kamayun hills. Soon after his spirit failed and disconcerted and disappointed, he fled to Punjab to seek refuge or to weave the web of an intrigue with Khwas Khan and Haibat Khan Niazi, and his brother Saeed Khan, trusted noble of Sher Shah who had made good his escape from Agra and was one of the principal intriguers. Other disaffected chiefs also joined Haibat Khan Niazi. At this juncture Islam Shah recalled Haibat Khan to his court. The summon to this effect was interpreted to mean his destruction.[12] This being so, he refused to oblige Islam Shah. He had thirty to fort thousand horsemen in addition to the forces which Khwas Khan commanded. He unfurled the standard of rebellion and had the Khutba read in his name. For a while, it appeared that the history of Ibrahim Lodi was to repeat itself.

Islam Shah could ill-brook this refractoriness and open defiance. He marched to Lahore at the head of his army, and was met at Ambala (1545) by the confederate forces which were more than twice as numerous as his own. The troops were drawn up in order of battle and advanced against the insurgents. Fortunately for the king, a dispute had arisen the previous night among the confederate chiefs as to the choice of a future king. Khwas Khan who still entertained respect for the family of his patron, Sher Shah, was in favour of the election of the Prince,

Adil Khan, while Haibat Khan (Azam Humayun) had views of his own to advance, affirming that the kingdom was no man's inheritance, but belonged to him who wielded the sharpest sword.[13]

Therefore, the following day when the troops on both sides were in motion, Khwas Vais Shervani withdrew with his contingent, thereby weakening the enemy so much that they offered but a feeble resistance. Salim Shah gained a decisive victory and the enemy suffered a heavy loss both in men and material. "Of those who escaped, many were drowned in the swollen stream to the west of Ambala, and many slaughtered. Islam Shah pushed them upto Rohtas. Khwaja Vais Shervani was sent further in pursuit of the fugitives."

After the battle of Ambala the government of Punjab was entrusted to Khawaja Vais Shervani who was appointed its governor in 1548. He had to reckon with a lot of difficulties. Haibat Khan Niazi had still considerable influence within Punjab and also had a large following beyond the river Jehlum. Shervani was no much hard-pressed that he had to give up the post of Rohtas and come back to Lahore. Soon after, on receiving reinforcement from Islam Shah, he inflicted a crushing defeat on the Niazis in the neighbourhood of Dhonkot and forced them to seek the protection of the Gakhars.

Their presence in the midst of Gakhars was extremely intolerable to Islam Shah as also to his governor of Punjab more so because Kamran Mirza having been put to flight by his brother, Humayun, joined the Gakhars in Punjab and Humayun in pursuit of his brother and possibly to regain the lost kingdom in India was advancing towards Punjab.

Islam Shah, just after the news was received, started his march towards Punjab. His alacrity, assiduity and determination were praiseworthy. The bullocks being unavailable at the moment because they were grazing in the country, he procured two thousand men to drag the unwieldy weapons to Lahore. With remarkable speed, Islam Shah and his force reached Lahore. Humayun, however, retreated. But Islam Shah carried fire and sword into the country of Gakhars but failed to subdue the indomitable spirit of the tribe. Niazis were reduced to great straits. Exasperated, they tried to enter Kashmir but Mirza Haider Doghlet foiled their designs. A fierce battle was fought at the village of Sambal, in which Bibi Rabia, the wife of Azam Humayun (Haibat Khan) distinguished herself by heroic fighting. The Niazis were however outnumbered, over-whelmed and defeated. Azam Humayun, his wife and brother were killed and their heads were sent to Islam Shah. Brutish indignities were inflicted on Niazis' women. They were exposed for months in a state of nudity and many were compelled to become harlots.[14]

Islam Shah paid another visit to Lahore, shortly before the celebrated Sheikh Alai was condemned to death on a charge of personating Imam Mehdi and founding a sect called Mehdies. The Sheikh was tried by a body of learned men and, with the king's approval, stripped and whipped to death.

Islam Shah, besides tightening the administration of the province, ordered the construction of five forts—a chain of fortresses on the eastern bank of the Chenab to serve as a check on the Gakhars and the Hill Rajas as also a second line of defence.

Furthermore, Islam Shah, toyed with the idea of destroying Lahore which being a stronghold of the Mughals,[15] the manufacturing centre of war-like material and because of its nearness to the country of Gakhars could serve as a good base for any invader from the north to advance into the interior of the country, thereby constituting a great threat to the integrity of his kingdom. Luckily for Punjab, the scheme could not be put into effect and the Emperor expired in his palace at Gwalior in A.D. 1553.

Sikandar Sur—1553-55

After the death of Islam Shah, the province plunged into disorder on account of the wrangle of different claimants to the throne of Delhi. Immediately after the demise of Islam Shah, his son, prince Feroz, then twenty years of age, was raised to the throne. But he had not yet reigned for three days when Mubariz Khan, the son of Nizam Khan, nephew of the late Sher Shah and brother-in-law of Islam Shah, entered the female apartment and, dragging the young prince from the arms of his mother, Sultana Bibi, his own sister, slew his with his own hand. He then ascended the throne, assuming the title of Muhammad Adil.

But he had no ability to run the affairs of the country. He neglected the affairs of his country, became a profligate, libertine, and under him the court of Delhi was packed with people who had nothing but flattery to recommend. As it always happens with all unintelligent sycophancy-loving persons, Mohammad Adil Shah left everything to the care of Hemu, once a salt vendor in the street of Rewari who, by dint of his hard work and capacity to manoeuvre, had risen to the enviable position of the confident of Islam Shah. With the disappearance of the strong personalities such as Sher Shah and Islam Shah, many factions emerged among the nobles. "Brawls among the rough Pathans became the order of the day and the king proved to be quite incapable of checking these disorders. Mohammad Adil himself was not above jealousy and factionalism. Motivated by these prejudices, he passed secret orders for the arrest of Ibrahim Sur, his own brother-in-law. Ibrahim's wife cautioned him against the intrigue of the kind and he instantly left for Chunar. A strong contingent was sent under Isa Khan to take him to task, but in the engagement Ibrahim came out successful. Thus, elated with success, Ibrahim marched upon Delhi and seized it and proclaimed himself to be the Emperor. Mohammad Adil Shah, finding his position weak, agreed to an arrangement by which he attained the government of the eastern provinces while Ibrahim was allowed to retain the possession of the western provinces. The empire of Hindustan was thus virtually divided between two rival claimants."[16]

Scarcely had Ibrahim Khan Sur assumed the reins of royalty, when another candidate appeared on the scene. This was Ahmed Khan Sur, a nephew of Sher Shah whose sister was married to Muhammad Adil Shah. He assumed the royal title in Punjab where he began to rule under the title of Sikandar Sur. He then marched to Agra at the head of 12000 cavalry with the view of expelling Ibrahim Khan from his western dominion and encamped at Kera, 20 miles distant from that city. Ibrahim marched out with an army of 7000 horses.[17]

A battle ensued between the two armies, in which the imposing hosts of Ibrahim Khan were signally defeated and the king himself retreating to Sambhal, the conqueror took possession of both Agra and Delhi. Three kings now reigned in northern India. The authority of Adil Shah extended over Agra and Malwa and as far east as Jaunpur, that of Sikandar Shah from Delhi to Rohtas in Punjab and that of Ibrahim Shah from the foot of the Himalayas to Gujarat in Punjab.

Reconguest of India by Humayun—1555

These circumstances were obviously tempting to Humayun to put his scheme of recovering the throne of India into effect. On hearing about the confusion that prevailed in the land where three kings claimed supremacy and the dissensions which prevailed among Afghan nobles, he left Kabul and reached Peshawar on December 25, 1554. Bairam Khan and many other officers joined him. Nine days later when he crossed the Indus, Sultan Adam, the Gakhar chief, failed to join him because he feared that Sikandar might not hold his son who was in his court as a hostage.

The advance of the Mughal army struck horror and Tatar Khan Kashi, the Afghan governor of the fort of Rohtas abandoned the fort on receiving the news of the advancement of Humayun's forces, and fled to Delhi. The fort which was built by Sher Shah as a bullwork against the Mughals was captured without striking a single blow. Tatar Khan Kashi seems to have been frightened by a probable combination of the Gakhars and the Mughals.[18]

Similarly, Humayun entered Lahore on February 24, 1555 without facing any opposition. He halted there for some days and made Lahore as his headquarters. From here he sent a detachment under Abdul Mali, a Sayyid of great sanctity, to Dipalpur to quell the Shahbaz Khan and Nasib Khan who had collected a large number of Afghans to put up resistance to Humayun. The Sayyid routed the enemy and returned with enormous booty to Lahore.

On arriving at Kalanaur in Gurdaspur district from Lahore, Humayun despatched a strong body of troops under Bairam Khan and Tardi Beg to bring Nasib Khan, the Afghan general, who lay encamped at Panj Bhain near Hariana in the Hoshiarpur distirict. Bairam Khan, after a long skirmish, compelled the Afghan general to surrender. As a result, a large booty and many families of the Afghans fell into Bairam Khan's hands, but whereas the booty was despatched to Humayun, the prisoners including the families of the Afghan nobles were set at liberty in view of the vow of Humayun that in case of victory, he would allow no man to be made captive.

Besides this, Bairam Khan advanced to Jullundur via Sham Chaurasi where the Afghans had encamped. On the mere sight of the Mughal forces, they fled carrying along with them their total luggage. Several elephants and some of the more valuable properties were despatched to Humayun.[19]

Meanwhile, Sikandar Shah's army of 50,000 horses, under Tatar Khan and Kabul Khan advanced from Delhi against Humayun. Bairam Khan, with prince Akbar, marched to check the army. The weather was cold and the Afghan soldiers had kindled great fires in their camp, on the opposite bank of the Sutlej, to warm themselves at night. Bairam Khan, taking advantage of their situation, crossed the river at night with the whole of his army and fell upon the Afghans and routed them at Machhiwara. The whole of the elephants and the baggage and a number of horses belonging to the Afghans fell into the hands of the Mughal general, while the detachments sent out by him occupied the country almost upto the walls of Delhi. Humayun was so much pleased with the bravery displayed by his general that he bestowed on him the title of Khan-i-Khanan.

Sikandar Shah now advanced to meet the invader at the head of 80,000 horses. Bairam Khan, too weak to hazard an action in the open field, retired into the fort of Naushehra. From this point, he made repeated sallies on the enemy's position and inflicted heavy losses on them. At the same time, he sent urgent messages to Humayun at Lahore begging him to join him which Humayun did without delay.[20] The Mughals cut off the supplies of their adversary and began to harass them by surprise attacks. In one of the raids, Tardi Beg got the better of the Afghans, captured an important supply train and killed the brother of Sikandar Sur. This death naturally infuriated the Afghans who launched a massive attack on the Mughals. A fierce battle took place at Sirhind.

The day of June 22, 1555 is memorable in the annals of India. On that day was decided the fate of the empire in respect of the nation that was to govern it for the next three centuries. The young prince Akbar was in the early morning inspecting pickets of the camp, when the Afghans under Sikandar Shah and Tatar Khan advanced and offered battle at Sirhind. The Mughal army met the advancing columns, and a fierce battle worthy of the great prize for which the two claimants fought, took place. The young Akbar, who was in the thickest of the fight, greatly distinguished himself by his feats of valour. The Afghans were at last defeated with great slaughter and took to flight.

Sikandar Sur narrowly escaped; fled to the Shivalik mountains leaving the whole country in the hands of the invader. Troops were sent in advance to Delhi and Agra which they occupied without opposition. Humayun re-entered Delhi in July 1555, and ascended the throne of his father after an exile of fifteen years. The most notable thing in this battle was that on both sides, humanity and gentleness were practised, so much so that the bodies of those who had sacrificed their lives were reverently made over to their respective friends.[21]

Immediately after this battle steps were taken for the government of the province. Hissar-i-Feroza was assigned to Akbar, the province which Humayun was bestowed upon by his father Babur when he first entered India. Sirhind and some other districts were granted to Bairam Khan in addition to Qandahar which he already held. Before proceeding to Sirhind to reinforce Bairam Khan, Humayun appointed Ghairat Khan as the governor of Punjab and a batch of officers to assist him. Babur Khan was made the military commander Mirza Shah Sultan, the civil administrator, and Mehar Jauhar, the treasurer of Punjab. Shah Abdul Mali was made the governor of Jullundur Doab, presumably to chase Sikandar Sur who had taken shelter in Shivalik hills and biding his time to pounce upon the province. Abdul Mali was ordered to proceed to Jullundur immediately to established his headquarters there to keep a consistent watch on the activities of Sikandar Sur. But, instead of remaining at Jullundur, Shah Mali rushed to Lahore and usurped all the powers from Ghairat Khan and began to act as an absolute sovereign.[22]

The contumacious behaviour of Shah Abdul Mali gave an opportunity to Sikandar to occupy the Jullundur Doab. He came out of the Shivalik Hills and started collecting the revenue. Humayun deputed Akbar, the heir-apparent, to punish him; Bairam Khan was to assist the young prince to put an end to Sikandar's depredations.

But before the governor of Lahore could be taught a lesson, Humayun died of a fall from the staircase where he knelt in response to the prayer-call of the Muazzin. The event took place on 24 January 1556. His death was kept concealed for some time to prevent public excitement which is inevitable on such occasions under personal governments and one Mulla Bakasi who resembled the Emperor in appearance was dressed in the imperial robe and shown every day to the populace. It was after seven days that Tardi Beg caused the Khutba to be read in the name of Jalaluddin Muhammad Akbar.

Humayun, like his father, did not do anything tangible to improve the condition of the Punjab. He divided his provinces among his generals for purposes of administration. But nothing was done to organise the administrative machinery on a sound basis. Even his officers showed the spirit of insubordination and rapacity which he found it difficult to repress. Abdul Mali, the governor of Punjab set up in his province a state within the state and Humayun did not do anything except transferring him to Hissar-i-Feroza and appointed Akbar in his place.

NOTES

1. *Turikh-i-Farishta*, Vol. II, p. 2.
2. Ishwari Prasad, *Life Times of Humayun*, p. 46.
3. *Ibid.*
4. M. Latif, *History of the Punjab*, p. 126.

5. S.K. Banerji, *Humayun Badshah*, pp. 53-58, 237-38.
6. Makhzan.
7. *Akbar Nama* (i), p. 402 for scattered incidental references to relations among these three.
8. *Makhzan*, p. 41.
9. *Tabcat-i-Akbari*, Vol. II, Tr. Elliot and Dawson in their book *History of India* as told by its own historians, p. 109.
10. Ishwari Prasad, *op. cit.*, p. 164.
11. The only exception was the distant country of Multan where the governor was specially ordered to take only a fourth share of the produce as revenue.
12. *Tabcati-i-Akhari*, *op. cit.*, pp. 131-33.
13. *Ibid.*, p. 133.
14. Briggs, tr. by Beveridge, *Akbar Nama*, pp. 188-89.
15. Many Mughal families had settled in the city during the times of Babur and Humayun.
16. M. Latif, *op. cit.*, p. 130.
17. *Ibid.*
18. M. Akbar, *Punjab Under the Geat Mughals*, p. 28.
19. *Akbar Nama*, Vol. II (Beveridge), p. 625.
20. Bayazid Biyat, *Tarikh-i-Humayun wa Akbar*, pp. 190-99.
21. Tr. in English by Beveredge, *Akbar Nama*, Vol. II, p. 623.
22. *Ibid.*

Punjab Under Jalalud-din Muhammad Akbar (1556-1605 C.E.)

4

According to Sheikh Abdul Fazl, when Humayun met with his fatal accident, Akbar, with his tutor, Bairam Khan was in Punjab. Ali Kuli Khan, the express messenger whom the Delhi Umrah sent, communicated the intelligence to Akbar at Kalanaur where he was residing at that time. On hearing the news, Bairam Khan and other officers present at once installed Akbar on an improvised throne on February 14, 1556. Akbar was only thirteen years and nine months old when he commenced his reign. He conferred the high office of the Minister on Bairam Khan, whom he called by the affectional title of Baba, or father. According to Smith, the accession ceremony at Kalanaur was performed just "to register Akbar's claim to sovereignty".

Smith's statement is very near the truth when viewed in the context of the precarious situation which the young Emperor had to face. The party of Muhammad Adil Shah Sur was still in the ascendant in the eastern provinces. Sikandar Shah Sur, though ousted from the throne of Delhi by suffering defeat at Sirhind in June 1556, yet retained some pretensions to be the emperor of India and had, therefore be lodged in the Shivalik Hills to harass the Imperial authorities.

To worsen the situation still further, Adul Mali, the boon companion of Humayun, began to abuse his position by misappropriating royal treasury for his own personal use and coercing his subordinates. In the face of such a grave menace, as a precautionary measure, he was replaced by Akbar with his tutor Bairam Khan in November 1555, but it improved the situation in no way. Mali was feeling sullen at his supersession as also owing to the slight which he had received at the hands of

Akbar who refused to let him sit with him and partake of food on the same royal table, contrary to the habit of Humayun.[1]

Furthermore, Humayun bequeathed to his son a poor legacy. After his restoration he had hardly got any time to consolidate his conquests with the result that the whole of his kingdom, especially Punjab, was in unstable condition. Besides this, the bitter memory of the invasion of Changez and Timur could not be erased from the minds of the people during the short span of time which Humayun could get after his restoration. The masses, although not openly hostile to the Mughal rule, were certainly indifferent to its fate.

But Akbar was lucky that during these difficult times, at last for four years, he was assisted by Bairam Khan who, in administrative ability and unflinching loyalty and generalship, excelled all other nobles at his court. It would not be irrelevant to state that for most of the successes of Akbar during the first four years, the credit goes to Bairam Khan, primarily.

The Arrest of Shah Abdul Mali

On February 17, 1556, a meeting of the nobles was convened to deliberate upon some political matters. Abul Mali was also invited to it but he betrayed hesitation to comply with the royal order. Being pressed, he attended the meeting but only on specific condition about his reception and place of sitting. This sort of behaviour naturally irritated the young Emperor. Consequently, when he was in the act of washing his hands before partaking of the food, he was taken in a tight grip by Tolaq Khan Qurchi who, according to a pre-concerted plan, had slipped behind him quite unnoticed, and was placed in the custody of Pahlwan Gulgar, the Kotwal of Lahore. Bairam Khan wanted to do away with him, but Akbar restrained him from doing so because he did not want to mar his accession with this bloody deed.[2]

Shortly afterwards, Abul Mali found means of escape and his custodian dreading the shame of the charge of treason likely to be brought against him committed suicide and thus atoned for his neglect.

The Campaign against Sikandar Sur

Akbar now directed his attention towards Sikandar Sur. A detachment under Pir Mohammad was sent against him. The Mughal forces reduced the territory around Dhamiri, and pushed forward into the hills. Sikandar, much disconcerted at the news of the enemy's rapid progress, lost heart and took to his heels. The Imperial army, then, laid siege to the fort of Nagarkot. After putting up a little resistance, Raj Dharam Chand gave way and appeared personally at the royal camp accompanied by many other hill chiefs to tender his allegiance. He was accorded a befitting reception and was recognised with the next deserving to get royal favour.

Sikandar Sur, however, successfully eluded the pursuing army which after striving hard for three months, retired to Jalandhar at the commencement of the rainy season.[3]

About this time, Akbar received the news about the fall of Delhi into the hands of Hemu and the flight of Tardi Beg, its Mughal governor. Immediately, Akbar placed the affairs of Punjab under Khizr Khwaja Khan, whom he appointed as the governor of the Punjab and started for Delhi on October 23, 1556.[4]

At Sirhind the fugitive Mughal governors of Agra, Delhi and Sarbhal joined Akbar and counselled him to retreat to Kabul. Bairam Khan, however, decided to risk all in an attempt to recover Delhi and persuaded Akbar to adopt his views. On account of the cowardice shown on the occasion, Tardi Beg was put to death by Bairam Khan. He also imprisoned Khwaja Sultan Ali and Mir Munshi who were suspected to be guilty of treachery and cowardice.[5]

Second Battle of Panipat—A.D. 1556

From Sirhind, Akbar marched towards Delhi. Panipat, which had so often decided the fate of the empire since the old days of Mahabharta, was chosen as the battlefield. Hemu had an huge army and 15000 elephants under his command. The artillery which had been sent in advance was captured by the Mughal vanguard led by Ali Quli Khan. Even after this loss, Hemu possessed superiority in strength.

On 5 November 1556 during the early hours, the contending forces were drawn up in battle-array. Hemu began the action with his elephants in the hope of alarming the enemy's cavalry unaccustomed to those animals; but the Mughals attacked them so furiously with lances, arrows and javelins that they became quite unruly, and disdaining the control of their drivers, turned back and threw the Afghan ranks into confusion. Hemu, mounting on an elephant of prodigious size, still continued the action with great bravery at the head of 4000 horses in the very heart of the Mughal army, but being pierced through the eye by an arrow, he fell into his *howda* unconscious.

His troops believing that he was dead took to flight, but the gallant Hemu, notwithstanding the intense agony of his wounds, raised himself, drew the arrow from the socket of the injured eye, and having bound his head with handkerchief put himself at the head of the fight with the few men who still adhered to him. His elephant was at last surrounded by a body of Mughal horsemen and he was carried prisoner to the Emperor by Ali Quli Khan. Bairam Khan proposed to his majesty to kill the infidel with his own hand and earn the title of 'Ghazi'. Akbar, in order to fulfil the wish of his minister, drew his sword, and touching the head of the captive, became entitled to the appellation of Ghazi, while Bairam Khan, drawing his own saber severed the head of Hemu. His head was sent to Kabul and his body was gibbeted at Delhi as a warning to the persons of the genre of Hemu.[6]

Thus, an end was put to the career of Hemu who, by the force of his genius, had risen from an insignificant position in life to the dignity of the minister of an empire. He was the first Hindu who had risen to the highest destination under the Mohammaden government of India. He proved himself fully worthy of the confidence reposed in him, and, if the Afghans were enabled to contest the Empire of India with the bravest of the Mughal leaders, that was mainly due to the intrepidity and war-like talents displayed by this able general.[7]

From Panipat, Akbar went to Delhi and took possession of it without facing any opposition.

On March 10, 1557, Akbar received intelligence that at the instigation of Mula Abdullah Sultanpuri, Sikandar Sur had descended upon the plains of the Jalandhar Doab and had started collecting land revenue.[8] Khizr Khan, the governor of Lahore, set out to oppose Sikandar near the tow of Chamiari but could not achieve success and had to return to Lahore.

Akbar by this time was free from the harassment caused by Hemu. He acted promptly and despatched quick reinforcement under Sikandar Khan Alam for the help of Khizr. In view of the magnitude of the danger, he himself followed Alam on December 7, 1556. On December 17, 1556 the Imperial forces advanced through Jalandhar to Dasuya and then moved further to Nurpur. The hill Rajas who had sided with Sikandar Sur deserted him and submitted to Akbar.

The turn of the tide disheartened Sikandar who fled without encountering the enemy and shut himself up in the fort of Mankot, a group of four very strong forts constructed on the adjoining hills by Salim Shah Sur (1545-54).

The Imperial forces put the fort under blockade, Adham Khan and Hussain Khan acted most courageously and attempted to take the fort by storm, but all in vain. The garrison under Sikandar Sur held on, encouraged by the hope that an invasion of Delhi by Mubariz Khan Adil would divert the attention of the imperial forces. But to his utter disappointment that attack never materialized.

At long last, Sikandar Sur sent his son, Abdur Rehman, along with Ghazi Khan Sur to the court as a hostage and begged pardon which was granted at the intercession of Ataka Khan and Pir Muhammad Khan.

The fort was surrendered on May 24, 1557 and was put under the charge of Abul Qasim[9] for the time being. Takhat Mal the real master of the fort and a close ally of Sikandar Sur, was arrested and decapitated under the orders of Bairam Khan and Mankot was bestowed upon Bakht Mal, the brother of Takht Mal.[10] Akbar moved from Mankot to Lahore. At Lahore, Adham Khan, the chief of the Gakhars, paid homage to him. Bairam Khan developed some special attachment to him and in the presence of the king reconciled him to his nephew, Kamil Khan.

On December 7, 1557, Akbar left for Delhi leaving the affairs of Punjab to Hussain Khan and reached Delhi on 20 April 1558.

Hussain Khan governed Punjab only for one year after which he died (1557). He is known as the Don Quixote of Akbar's reign. He ordered the Hindus to wear a *patch* (Tukra) near the shoulders and thus got the nick-name of *Tukriya* (Patchar).[11]

Farhat Khan succeeded Hussain Khan in 1558.[12] He administered Punjab with an iron hand.

The most important event of his governorship was the rebellion of Bairam Khan who was constrained to rise in rebellion on account of the following causes.

Firstly, the Turkish nobles in general and foster-parents of Akbar in particular disliked him and constantly induced Akbar to cut Bairam Khan to size. Secondly, Bairam's over-bearing behaviour and his harsh treatment towards the nobles alienated many of them who began to conspire for his downfall. The execution of Tardi Beg had further struck fear into the hearts of these nobles. Thirdly, being a Shia by faith, the Sunnis had no love lost for him and dubbed him as the patron of his own Shia sect. The appointment of Shaikh Gadai and the promotion of his own men to the posts of Panj Hazari to the exclusion of the more deserving candidates made him still more unpopular. Lastly, even Akbar was not prone to pull on with the domineering personality of Bairam Khan who was suspected of harbouring designs of seating Abdul Qasim (the son of Kamran) on the throne. Moreover, Akbar wanted to be a king in reality and hence was not prepared to brook the tutelage of Bairam Khan any longer.

So plans were set afoot to throw him out. In 1560, the Emperor openly expressed to Bairam Khan his determination to take the reins of the government into his own hands. Bairam Khan was asked to proceed to Mecca, which, in a way, implied his dismissal from service.

Bairam Khan, in spite of the advice of his friends to take up arms against Akbar, did not like to stain the glorious record of his life-long service to the Mughal family, and, after some hesitation, complied with the royal command.

When Mir Abdul Latif communicated this message to Khan-i-Khanan (Bairam Khan), he listened attentively and having parted from the Mir, he left Mewat for Nagor. Upon reaching Nagor, he sent his banner, kettle, drum and all other marks of nobility to the Emperor through Hussain Kuli Beg. The surrender of the banner and the insignia of office[13] gratified the Emperor.

"Pir Muhammad Khan Sarwani, whom the Khan-i-Khanan had banished from the country and sent to Mecca was waiting in Gujarat for the proper season (of sails). On hearing of the fate of the Khan-i-Khanan he returned with all possible speed. He met with a very gracious reception and was honoured with title, Nazir-ul-Mulk as well as with a banner and kettle and drum. He was then sent with a force to hasten Khan-i-Khanan's departure."

When Bairam Khan learnt that Pir Muhammad had been sent to pursue him, he was greatly annoyed. He made up his mind to venge this grievous slight and to rid the king of his evil counselors. He marched upon Punjab. He sent Khwaja Musaffar Ali to the governor of Dipalpur to win him over to his own side but he was arrested and sent to the court by the latter.

Akbar, on being apprised of the intention of Bairam Khan, advised him to desist from his evil course, but Bairam Khan remained obdurate and continued his advance. When he reached Tabarinda,[14] he committed his three years old son along with his family and property to the care of Sher Muhammad Diwana, his adopted son. But on reaching Dipalpur,[15] he, to his great distress, learnt that Mohmmad Diwana had turned perfidious and had surrendered Bairam's family to the court. Bairam was perturbed at this news; but being helpless to wreak vengeance upon him, he pushed on to Jalandhar. On the way, Wali Beg tried to invest the fort of Tihara[16] but Mirza

Abdullah's defences of the fort thwarted his ambition with the result that Bairam's advance to Jalandhar was impeded.

At the report of the advance of Bairam, Akbar, as a precautionary measure, put Hussain Quli Khan under custody and issued orders to Shams-ud-din Muhammad Khan Atka, his son Yusaf Mohammad Kokal Tash, Mahdi Qasim Khan, Muhammad Qasim Khan of Nishapur, Ali Quli Khan, Mir Latif Hasan Khan and Ahmed Khan to march towards Punjab. He himself followed them on August 12, 1560.

When the advance guard of the Mughal forces reached Gunachaur, it found itself confronted with the army of Bairam. Both sides began to prepare for action. Bairam Khan divided his forces into two parts. The advance guard was under the command of Wali Beg, Shah Quli Khan Mahram and others. With nearly fifty elephants, he himself took chare of the centre. On the other side were arranged the forces of Alka Khan supported by Shamas-ud-din Muhammad Khan Atka. The right wing was commanded by Qasim while a band of devoted servants formed the vanguard. Yusaf Muhammad Khan Kokal Tash with a modest force took his post between the centre and the vanguard.

The actual encounter took place on August 23, 1560 near the village named Gunachaur. There were brave feats on both the sides. In the first encounter, the advance corps of Bairam Khan displayed such valour and vigour that some of the Mughal ranks gave way and the soldiers took to their heels. At this juncture, an elephant got stuck in the bog. Shams-ud-din Muhammad Khan Atka seized the opportunity and began to shoot arrows upon the elephant. Bairam Khan with a mind to charge the imperial army from the left withdrew a little. This tactical withdrawal was mistaken to be a flight by the soldiers and there was a general confusion. The Imperial forces took full advantage of the pell-mell and sallied forth on the retreating soldiers and wrested victory from them.

The news about the victory was communicated to Akbar at Sirhind, who expressed satisfaction, and leaving his army in the charge of Munim Khan, himself advanced to Lahore.

On September 17, 1560, Shams-ud-din Muhammad Khan Atka gave him a rousing reception and a sumptuous feast. Much pleased as Akbar was with Atka Khan, he bestowed on him and his relatives the best land in Punjab as jagirs.[17]

From Lahore, Akbar returned to Sirhind to arrange manouvres to bring Bairam to his knees who had taken shelter with Raja Ganesh of Talwara.

A detachment advanced into the hills. A great battle was fought between the Imperialists and Bairam's troops at Talwara. Sultan Hussain Talair, one of the most trusted friends of Bairam Khan, died in the battlefield. His head was cut off by his adversaries and sent to Bairam Khan, who seeing it, burst into tears.

Despaired of any success, Bairam Khan deputed Jamal Khan to the Emperor to beg for mercy (October 1560). Akbar's heart was moved and he despatched Maulana Abdulla Sultan to soothe his afflicted mind and bring him to the court. But he declined to appear until Mumin Khan was sent to assure him of his safety. At this, Akbar moved forward, and arriving at Hajipur, he sent Mumin Khan, Khwaja Jahan, Ashraf Khan, Haji Muhammad Khan Sistani to escort Bairam safely to him. Bairam prostrated himself before Akbar in October 1560. Akbar, with tears in his eyes, raised him up and bade him sit on his right hand. Bairam Khan was given a liberal grant and a robe. Soon after, he proceeded to embark for Mecca and in due time reached Patan. There he was stabbed by an Afghan, Mubarak Khan Lohani, whose father had been killed in an action with the Mughals under the command of Bairam Khan. Thus ended the career of this great minister and soldier, and Akbar, now 18 years of age, was left henceforth free to rule.

Akbar now assigned the work of governance of Punjab to Shams-ud-din Muhammad Khan Atka (1560-61) and himself returned to Delhi at the head of the triumphant army on November 24, 1560 where he reached in November 1561. Shams-ud-din Muhammad Khan Atka was the son of Yar Muhammad of Ghazni, who had entered the service of Mirza Kamran as an ordinary solider, and was present at the battle of

Qanauj in 1540. He had distinguished himself in the wars against Sikandar Shah Sur. Akbar honoured him by appointing him as the governor of Punjab and by awarding his a flag and a drum, and the title of Khan-i-Azam in the same year.

Shams-ud-din Muhammad Khan Atka was recalled to serve at the centre while Mir Muhammad Khan Kalan was ordered to take over the charge of Punjab in 1564 C.E.

Mir Muhammad Khan Kalan

Mir Muhammad Kalan's viceroyalty is famous for cutting Raja Ganesh of Nandon[18] to size, reduction of the Gakhars and repelling of the invasion of Mirza Hakim.

Raja Ganesh of Nandon in whose mind the last defeat was rankling marched against Jan Mohammad Bahandi of Birka but was driven back with heavy loss. Mir Muhammad Kalan considered it an unprovoked attack and marched into the hills. Raja Ganesh was so much hard-pressed that he was compelled to sue for terms. At the intercession of Raja Todar Mal, he was pardoned and reinstated in his territory. Now, he had to reckon with the Gakhars, one of the most war-like tribes inhabiting the territory lying between the Indus and the Beas and hemmed in from all sides by the hills. Their relations with Babur and Humayun had been quite cordial; but in the time of Akbar, there was a distinct change. Since 1564, Adham Khan, their chief, had not waited upon Akbar, thereby creating misgivings regarding the loyalty of the Gakhar chief. This being so, Akbar began to wait for his chance.

The chance came in 1562, Kamal Khan, the nephew of the ruling chief who had displayed marked valour and loyalty in the struggle against the son of Adil in Bengal, was offered by the emperor to choose any boon he wanted. Kamal Khan, too shrewd to let this opportunity slip asked for his hereditary territory, unjustly held by his uncle. Akbar, who was already looking forward to some excuse to wage a war upon the Gakhars, issued orders for the division of the territory into two parts; one was to be placed under the Kamal while the other was to be retained by Adham Khan.

Adham Khan refused to comply with the Imperial orders. So the Khan Kalan marched into his territory to put the Imperial orders into effect. The Imperial forces encountered the Gakhar forces near the town of Hilan. The Gakhars were defeated. Adham Khan was arrested. His son Lashkari was also made prisoner to be put to death shortly after.

Having restored the whole of the territory to Kamal Khan, the Khan Kalan marched back to Lahore victoriously.[19]

Besides this, in 1564, Punjab had to face another menace this time from Mirza Hakim, the half-brother of Akbar. In 1564, Suleman of Badakhshan drove Mirza Hakim out of Kabul, who begged for help from Akbar. In response to the Imperial order, Mirza Khan Kalan and other Punjab officers set their forces in motion and crossed the Indus at the ferry of Atakbanaras.

They invested Jalalabad and beheaded Gambar, the governor of the fort. This thing struck terror into the heart of Suleman and he left Kabul.

The Khan Kalan quickened his pace and made a triumphant entry into Kabul.

Shortly after, differences arose between Mirza Hakim and the Khan Kalan because of the former's preference for Khwaja Hasan Naqshbandi whom Khan Kalam did not like. The matter reached such a pass that the Khan Kalan returned to Lahore.

Shortly after, Suleman again marched upon Kabul. The Mirza sent an envoy to Akbar who had already despatched Fardusi to help the Mirza, passed orders for Khush Khabar Khan to speed on to the Indus. The Punjab officers were also directed, if need be, to accompany the Mirza to Kabul.

But fate decreed otherwise. Mirza Hakim, instead of achieving his target, made plans to occupy Lahore. Fardusi, possibly stricken by jealousy for his popular rival Khush Khabar Khan, acted as agent provocateur. Sultan Ali and Husain Khan also added fuel to the fire and whetted his ambition to occupy Punjab.

Accordingly, the Mirza crossed the Indus, pillaged Bhera and advanced upon Lahore. Khan Kalan, Qutab-ud-din Khan and Sharif Khan took concerted measures to defend the fort at all costs. The Mirza tried to get the fort by storm; but he was totally frustrated. In the meantime, Akbar inflamed at the ingratitude of Mirza, hastened to Punjab on November 1566[20] to conduct the operations himself.

The news about the march of Akbar dampened Mirza's spirit. He hurried back to the Indus. Akbar heard this news while encamped on the banks of the Sutlej, but he continued his march. Towards the end of February 1567, Akbar reached Lahore. Qutub-ud-din and Kamal Khan were deputed to see that Mirza was chased out of India. The peasantry that had suffered so much at the hands of the invader heaved a sigh of relief and the Punjab officers were particularly directed to soothe them.[21] The hurried retreat of Mirza was, indeed, an event, highly conducive to the interests of Akbar. For, exactly simultaneously with the rebellion of Mirza Hakim, rebellions broke out in Uttar Pradesh from Sambhal to Jaunpur. The Mirzas of Sambal were in open revolt; the Uzbegs were up in arms and had been joined by Asaf Khan of the Garh Katanga fame. The Uzbegs had already read the Khutba in the name of Mirza Muhammad Hakim. Caught between two fires, Akbar found himself in very great straits. Indeed, since the days of Hemu, Akbar had to face no crisis more serious than this. But the stars were in his favour. The rebel Mirza had no definite plan and could not take any firm and coherent action.

Akbar now with his mind at rest, enjoyed hunting to his heart's content. Preparations for sport were made on a large scale. Within one month nearly 15,000 animals of different species were driven into the area of ten miles to provide ample game to the Emperor.

On March 23, 1567, when the news of the revolt of Ali Quli Khan, Bahadur Khan and Iskandar Khan reached the Emperor, he at once set out from Lahore to quell the revolt.

In August 1568, the Khan Kalan was transferred and the government of Punjab was made over to Hussain Quli Khan.

Hussain Quli Khan—1568-75

Hussain Quli Khan was the son of Bairam's sister. During his governorship, two events of note—the expedition of Kangra and the revolt of Ibrahim Mirza took place. Hussain Quli Khan in both these cases showed his grit and determination and political finesse. In 1570, Akbar once again turned towards Punjab from Ajmer to pay his respects at the shrine of Shaikh Farid at Pak Pattan where he reached on March 13, 1571. On April 16, 1571, he reached Dipalpur where Khan Azim Mirza Koka arranged a sumptuous entertainment in his honour. On May 17, 1571, Akbar reached Lahore and was received by Hussain Quli Khan. At his request, Akbar paid a visit to the newly built quarters in the town. Towards the end of May 1571 the Emperor started for the capital via Ajmer.

Expedition of Kangra—1572

Raja Jai Chand who on some account had incurred the displeasure of Akbar, repaired to the court having committed his son to the care of Raja Govind. According to Muhammad Akbar, Raja Jai Chand was arrested at the court, and Bidhi Chand, presuming that his father was dead, broke out into open rebellion. Hussain Quli Khan, sensing the possible spread of the revolt, acted promptly and moved with his forces to Dhamiri. The Raja Chotu submitted. Then Hussain Quli Khan proceeded to the fort of Kotla which was captured and handed over to the Raja of Guler from whom it had been wrested by Dharam Chand and Jai Chand of Kangra.

Leaving a small force at that place, Hussain Quli Khan wended his way through thick jungles and emerged near Nagarkot. Next day, the temple of Mahamai was invested. All his inmates were done to death and the buildings were dashed to the ground.

After this storming of the main fort began. The gun on an adjacent hillock thundered forth fire, but to no effect. The wall crumbled down and nearly 80 persons including Bhuj Dev, the son of Takhatmal were killed, but Bidhi Chand escaped unscathed and successfully effected a flight into the jungles. Even this failed to dampen the spirit of the defenders.

Three months after the news of the march of Ibrahim Hussain Mirza upon Punjab following his defeat by the Imperial forces in Gujarat forced the Mughal camp to have second thought on the issue of the subjugation of the Kangra ruler. Ali Khan, Yusuf Khan, Karam Khan, and Fattu were in favour of hastening towards Punjab after patching up a hasty treaty with the Rajputs. But Hussain Quli Khan with some others did not favour this proposal because the reduction of the fort was in sight. But in the end, under the weight of the majority opinion, and also in view of the distress of the soldiers in the hilly terrain, he gave way and concluded a treaty with Raja Bidhi Chand. To ward off any risk of personal responsibility in case the Emperor did not approve of it, he was prudent enough to get the statement of each noble duly signed and sealed.

The peace treaty had the following terms:

1. The Raja should send his daughter to the royal harem.
2. The Raja would pay five maunds of gold as tribute according to the standard Akbari weight which was equal to one year's revenue of the temple. Material and precious things of all kinds were usurped by the Imperial army.[22]
3. The coins will be struck in the name of Akbar.[23]
4. Raja Gokal Chand would come personally to pay his respects.
5. Since the province was given to Raja Birbal as his Jagir, a large sum was to be given to him as compensation.
6. The Raja undertook to acknowledge formally the suzerainty of Mehar.[24]

The Rajputs agreed to the terms but demanded that one of the brothers of Yusuf Khan should come to the fort to guarantee the safe return of the Raja. The condition being complied with, the Raja paid his homage. On Friday in the middle of Shawal 830 A.H. (1572 A.D.) a pulpit was erected and Hafiz Muhammad Bagir read the Khutba in the name of the Emperor.

Relieved of the Kangra problem, Hussain Quli Khan attended to the activities of Ibrahim Mirza who having been defeated by Akbar in Gujarat marched to Punjab with 300 men and sacked the town of Panipat, Karnal and was on the way to Lahore. Hussain Quli Khan overtook him near the town of Talamba, as the latter was out for hunting. Without losing any time, the Mughal forces were arranged in battle array. Hussain Quli Khan occupied the centre. The right flank was commanded by Muhib Ali Khan and Yusaf Khan and on the left side were posted Khurram Khan, Dost Khan Sahari, Shah Qazi Khan Tabrezi. Jafar Khan and Dost Khan held the vanguard.

Musud Hussain Mirza, Ibrahim's younger brother, hastily mustering his army marched forward to engage the Imperialists and a terrible battle ensued. A chance fall of the horse of Musud enabled the Mughal soldiers to chain him. At this juncture, Mirza Ibrahim, who was away on hunting arrived instantly and pounced upon the right wing of the Imperialists, but he too was driven back with a heavy loss.

Accordingly, he fled for life to Multan. He was pursued by Hussain Khan Tukariya. At the Giara river formed by the junction of the Beas and the Sutlej, he was suddenly attacked by the Jhuls (Fishermen of Multan) and he had to save his life by seeking shelter with some faqirs. Shaikh Zakariya, after recognising him communicated his presence to Said Khan, the governor of Multan, with the result that he was arrested and intimation to this effect was conveyed to the Emperor who was on his way to Ajmer from Gujarat.

Hussain Quli Khan, in recognition of his services to the Mughal dynasty, was honoured with the title of 'Khan Jahan' and a considerable addition to his Jagir. The Punjab officers under Hussain Quli Khan were issued orders to the effect that they should accompany him to Badakhshan. But Providence willed it otherwise. The death of Munim Khan, the governor of Bengal, necessitated the transfer of Hussain Quli Khan to that province and hence the proposed expedition under the Punjab officers could not be undertaken.

Shah Quli Khan Mehram (1575-78) was appointed in place of Hussain Quli Khan as governor of Punjab in 1575.[25] Formerly, Shah Quli Mehram was in the service of Bairam Khan and he had distinguished himself in the war against Hemu. He had remained loyal to the Khan-i-Khanan during his adversity but was pardoned by the Emperor along with Bairam Khan at Talwar. He rose higher and higher in Akbar's favour. However, he could not properly suppress the turbulent people expecially the Afghans who had settled in Punjab as husbandmen but instead of pursuing their business peacefully they began to commit all sorts of abilities and oppressed the people with impunity. Akbar defeated Raja Todar Mal to crush their wild spirit. His administration began to deteriorate on account of his leniency. Criminals and miscreants went unpunished and thus great disorder prevailed in the province. When Akbar was informed of this state of affairs, he issued orders for his recall in 1578 and Said Khan was sent to take over the charge. Shah Quli Mehram died at Agra in 1601. He erected splendid buildings and had many a large tank dug at Harnaul, where he chiefly lived after his retirement.

Said Khan—1578-85

Said Khan's seven years of governorship are quite significant in the history of Punjab. It was during this period that the orthodox Muslim nobles got tired of Akbar's liberal policy towards the Hindus and other non-Muslims and conspired with Akbar's half-brother Mirza Hakim to overthrow Akbar. It is alleged that the Chief Dewan, Khwaja Shah Mansur, was also a party to that conspiracy. It was a great crisis for Akbar, and he, therefore, moved to Punjab to reinforce Said Khan and also to direct the military operations against the rebels personally. Besides this, Punjab officers were also called upon to attend to the affairs of Kashmir which, being a frontier province, had great importance for the Mughal rule in India. The general administration under Said Khan was quite good. The condition of law and order was also satisfactory. The religious atmosphere too breathed an air of liberalism.

The Sikhs under the able stewardship of Guru Arjan Dev progressed a good deal during this period. The Sikhs increased rapidly in number.

The popularity of the different Sufi orders, particularly of the Chisti and Qadiria orders, also testifies to the liberal atmosphere in the religious sphere. Guru Arjan Dev had a good number of

Muslim and Hindu followers. Hindus held Mian Mir in high esteem. The orthodox Muslims whose centre in Punjab was Sirhind and who had found a leader in Mujadad-Alf-Sani, were not yet in a position to disturb the peaceful atmosphere in the Punjab. It was one of the important reasons that Punjab witnessed much progress in trade, industry and literature.

Kashmir Affair

In 1580, the Punjab administration was asked to tackle the Kashmir affairs also. In 1579, Ali Shah Chak died after a reign of nine years and was succeeded by Yusaf Shah.

Immediately after the death of his father, Yusaf Shah was called upon to fight out his claim for the throne with his uncle Abdul Chak. Abdul Chak was defeated and killed.

Hardly had the state of affairs resumed their normal course, when a faction of nobles led by Sayyid Mubarak sought to set up Yusaf Khan, the son of Hussain Khan, on the throne. On Yusaf's refusal, the nobles turned towards Sayyid Mubarak and proclaimed him the ruler of Kashmir. Yusaf Khan, determined to stem the tide of rebellion, engaged the rebels in the Idgah in Srinagar, but was defeated and had to take refuge in the flight. He approached Man Singh and Mirza Yusaf Khan Rizvi who took him to the court of Akbar where he was received well. Akbar who had since long been looking for an opportunity to have a say in Kashmir affairs turned it to his advantage. He ordered Raja Man Singh and Mirza Yusaf Khan Rizvi to march on Kashmir and restore Yusaf Khan to the throne.

By the month of August 1580, the affairs in Kashmir had taken a new turn. Mubarak Khan was compelled to abdicate in favour of Lahorchak after a month and a half of his mis-rule. Lahorchak was equally determined to oppose Yusaf Khan. At this juncture a change in the mood of the parties took place. At Lahore, Yusaf Khan got disgusted with the attitude of Raja Man Singh because he did not find him ready enough to undertake the campaign of Kashmir.[26] The nobles of Kashmir perceiving the winds of change entreated Yusaf Khan to come unaccompanied by Mughal forces.

Yusaf Shah decided to embark upon the latter course and made for Kashmir without telling anybody. No doubt, he was received by some prominent nobles at Baramula, but Lahorchak despatched Shamschak and Haiderchak to oppose Yusaf's progress. Ultimately, battle between Yusaf Khan and Lahorchak took place at Sonpur. Lahorchak lost the battle and Yusaf mounted the throne.

But the Mughal interest in the affairs of Kashmir did not diminish and Akbar continued to take interest in the affairs of Kashmir as before.

The next event which embroiled Punjab was the invasion of Mirza Hakim. Akbar's liberal policy towards non-Muslims and his determination to be the king of all the people inhabiting his kingdom and his so-called infallibility decree on September 2, 1579 flared up the bigotry of the orthodox section of the Muslims and a fire of discontentment and restlessness began to smoulder nearly all over Mughal empire. The reforms in the administration of Madad-i-Maash executed by Qazi Ali of Baghdad only added fuel to the fire which blazed forth at the Fatwa of Mulla Muhammad Yazdi of Jaunpur and soon enveloped whole of the eastern India. Mohammad Masum Faramkhudi of Ghazipur, Masum Khan Kabuli of Orissa, Mir Muzzul-Mulk, Nayabat Khan and Arab Bahadur took up Cudgels on behalf of the orthodox Muslims and stirred up rebellions in Bengal, Bihar and Orissa.

Mohammad Masud Faramkhudi and Masum Khan sent invitations to Mirza Mohammad Hakim of Kabul to come and save them from Akbar. According to Dr. Smith, they were not troubled at the thought that the man whom they desired to substitute for their gifted monarch was drunken, cowardly and irresolute, incapable of governing the Empire, acquired and consolidated by the genius of Akbar. It sufficed for them to know that Muhammad Hakim was reported to be sound in doctrine. Accordingly, Masum and other rebel leaders in the eastern provinces conspired with several influential personages at the court to invite the Kabul prince to invade India and wrest the throne from its heretic occupant.

The leader of the conspiracy at the court was Shah Mansur, the finance Minister whom Akbar had raised from the humble position of a clerk for his exceptional skill in dealing with accounts and revenue matters.

The rebels of the East were at a great disadvantage: firstly, they were separated from the territories of Muhammad Hakim by hundreds of miles of country strongly held by Akbar and secondly, Mirza Hakim was a contemptible creature, wholly incapable of meeting his brother either in statecraft or in the field.

Their hopes of success rested only on two things: (i) a vigorous offensive from Kabul threatening Delhi and Agra, and (ii) the desertion of high officials capable of paralyzing the administration of the empire of Akbar.

Akbar met the challenge successfully. He sent necessary orders to Punjab governor and himself made preparations on a large scale.

In December 1580, an officer of Muhammad Hakim named Haji Nur-ud-din made a raid into Punjab at the head of a detachment numbering one thousand.

The Haji crossed the river India and began to advance. Mirza Husaf Khan, at the report of his march, acted promptly and sent an army under the command of Hussain Beg to foil him in his design. On his way, he was joined by Said Khan Gakhar. Incidentally, there appeared a herd of deer and Hussain, ever-eager for game, galloped after it. He pierced one of the deer with his arrow and when he, with his few companions, hastened to round up the game, he found himself face to face with Nur-ud-din who had come out of his camp just to enjoy the sport.

There began the duel and the Haji was wounded and he fled, and his followers followed him in confusion. Hussain's valour and Yusaf Khan's promptitude exacted a good deal of appreciation from Akbar but Yusaf Khan, on account of his laxity in the management of the frontier affairs, was replaced by Man Singh who was at that time in Sialkot.

A second en route was made under the command of Shah Daman who crossing the river invested the forest of Nilab, which was defended heroically by Zain-ud-din whom Man Singh had sent in advance from Sialkot. Man Singh also hurried to the spot. A terrible battle took place. Raja Suraj Singh, the brother of Raja Man Singh, wounded and killed Shah Daman in the hand to hand fight. Shah Daman's men took to their heels and dispersed on all sides in confusion. The Mirza lingered on in the vicinity of Lahore for sometime in the fond hope that help from eastern India would arrive. The execution of Shah Mansur has been a subject of controversy among the historians. Father Monserrate and Abul Fazl acclaim it a right decision, while there are some authorities which dub the execution as a 'judicial murder' or a 'foul murder' and attribute it to the machinations of Raja Todar Mal. After a careful study of the various aspects of the incident, we have reached the conclusion that in 1580 some correspondence did pass between the Mirza and the Shah Mansur. Monserrate's detailed account shows that Akbar was unwilling to take strong action on those documents and that it was the third discovery in 1581 which induced him to harden his heart and order the execution. The truth seems to be that his enemies who were determined to compass his destruction forged the last batch of letters in order to force Akbar's hands. This thing does not acquit Shah Mansur of the charge of treason; he had been guilty of sending letters of invitation to Muhammad Hakim in 1581, and that he was actually the head of treasonable conspiracy as stated by Monserrate. The suggestion that Raja Todar Mal was concerned in the alleged forgery does not seem to be supported by any evidence of value. The help never came because the rebels had been scattered by this time. On the other hand, the news about the march of the Emperor reached, striking terror into his heart. Accordingly, he made a hasty retreat crossing the Ravi near Mehdi Qasim Khan's garden, the Chenab near Jalalabad, the Jhelum near Bhera and the Indus near Khip losing nearly 1600 men who were drowned during his hasty retreat. The royal officers desisted from pursuit in compliance with royal orders and allowed him to escape.[29] From the Indus he made for Kabul with his resources crippled on account of this useless struggle.

Akbar, on his part, set out for Lahore on February 8, accompanied by Prince Salim, Prince Murad and father Monserrate. When the camp moved to Sonipat, an incident disturbed Akbar considerably. When Akbar was at Fatehpur, he had received three letters from Man Singh which he had discovered upon the person of Shadman and which were written to Hakim-ul-Mulik, Khwaja Mansur, Qasim Khan, Mir Bahar respectively, purporting to be answered to the letters of invitation and encouragement written to Hakim by those officers. Akbar verified the facts and regarding them as forgeries did show them to Mansur, although he took precaution to take him along with him on his march towards Lahore, lest he might engineer some trouble in his absence. "The arrival of Malik Sani, the ex-Dewan of Mirza Hakim, confirmed his suspicion and he placed Mansur under stricter surveillance".[30] At Shahbad, a few more letters were produced before the Emperor clearly implicating Shah Mansur in the conspiracy of the orthodox to oust Akbar.

Eventually, before a gathering of chief nobles and other officials, Abul Fazal read out the charges against Mansur, who was hanged on the Babel tree on February 27, 1581.

After this execution, Akbar resumed his march to Lahore and, passing through Ambala and Sirhind, arrived at Pail where he received the happy news of Mirza Hakim's flight.

Having determined to humiliate Mirza Hakim completely, he continued his advance. Passing by Machhiwara he encamped on the banks of the Sutlej. Then going upstream, he crossed the river by means of boats and proceeded to Kalanaur.

At this place Mirza Hakim's letter was received soliciting Akbar's pardon. But Akbar paying little heed to the letter passed on. He crossed the Ravi and continued his march. Crossing the river Chenab he reached Qhunia from where he directed his steps towards the Jhelum after crossing which he halted at the foot of the Tilla Balnath. From here, he ordered his forces to reach Rohtas while he himself visited the hut of Balnath. Shortly after, he joined his forces and was entertained by Yusaf Khan, the governor of the fort.

Then via Rewat, Gagar and Hazara, Akbar reached the Indus and encamped there.

A delay of fifty days was caused at the Indus by the mutinous reluctance of the army to advance. Akbar overcame the situation by his airs of unconcern and dignity. Towards the end of June, Prince Murad and Raja Man Singh were sent in advance. One by one, cities fell and on August 3, the Prince and Raja Man Singh made their triumphant entry into Kabul. Mirza Hakim betook himself to the hills of Ghor Band. Akbar reached Kabul on August 9, 1581. At the intercession of Ali Muhammad Mirza, Hakim was forgiven and he was reinstated on the throne. This was the first time that Akbar had made an entry into Kabul. But for several reasons it was not advisable to stay in Kabul. Akbar had been absent from the capital for over six months, and was, therefore, anxious to return as soon as he could.

In the second week of August 1531, Akbar directed his steps homewards. On November 3, the Beas and on November 10, the Sutlej were crossed. At Sirhind, Raja Bhagwan Das, Raja Rai Singh, Sayyid Hamid Bukhari and Jagan Nath, the officers of Punjab, were allowed to depart.[31] Fitch and Leeds paid a visit to Lahore in 1584 but their accounts contain nothing with regard to Punjab.

Lahore as the Imperial Headquarters

In 1585, trouble seemed once again to be brewing beyond the North-Western frontier. At the sudden illness of Mirza Hakim, disruptive tendencies began to raise their heads in and outside Kabul.

From A.D. 1585 to A.D. 1598, Akbar remained at Lahore. The reasons for this are not far to seek. The Uzbegs, who had occupied Badakhshan to the exclusion of Mirza Shah Rakh and Mirza Suleman began to threaten Kabul. The frontier tribes being turbulent and unruly by nature, were also not in a peaceful frame of mind. They constantly hung round the route to Kaul, ready to pillage the travellers and armies alike. Kashmir was also stirring. Swat, Bajaur and Baluchistan were also to be subdued, both for rendering the road to Kabul safe and maintaining peace in the trans-Indus region. The occupation of Sind was also imperative because the economic advantages apart, it commanded an important route to Kabul via Bolan Pass.

Akbar with a view to tackling these various problems stayed at Lahore which was not only near to the trouble spots but also was capable of providing the requisite number of recruits and provisions to the army.

The head of the state being at Lahore, Punjab affairs were directed straightway by him. Punjab problems during this period were viewed from the Imperial perspective and their tackling reflected more of imperial interests and less of local or regional interests.

The first and foremost problem which claimed the immediate attention of Akbar was that of Kabul. After the death of Mirza Hakim certain Kabuli nobles, intended to forment troubles Faridum had the plan to fly along with Kaikubad and Afraisiyab, the sons of Mirza Hakim, to trans-oxiana.

Immediately after, the report of the death of Mirza, Raja Bhagwan Das and Man Singh proceeded towards Kabul without delay. They pacified the nobles who meditated upon returning to Turan.[32] Faridum also submitted and presented Kaikabad and Afrasiyab before Man Singh who took upon himself the responsibility of escorting them safely to the court.

Meanwhile, Akbar being pressed by his courtiers to appropriate Kabul to himself instead of conferring it upon the minors, set out for Punjab on August 22, 1585. On December 7, 1595, he reached Rawalpindi where, on the same day, Man Singh from Kabul reached and presented the persons he had brought with him. Akbar received them kindly and robes, horses and trays of Mohurs, were bestowed upon them. Faridum, however, because of his ingratitude, was placed under the custody of Zain Koka.[33]

The next six months Akbar spent in the devising of plans to curb the refractory Yusafzais, Baluchis and Roshanyas who were creating trouble on the north-west frontier of India.

On April 24, 1586, Akbar received the homage of Shah Rukh's aunts and his son Shah Muhammad. On May 27, he reached Lahore and chose the house of Raja Bhagwan Das for the royal residence.

Next, Akbar attended to the north-west frontier of Punjab which had always been a source of anxiety to the rulers of India on account of the incursions of the predatory Pathan tribes. In Akbar's time, the danger became acute on account of the presence of a formidable rival in the person of Abdullah Uzbeg of Turan and the appearance of one person Pir Bayazid among the frontier tribes. In fact, Akbar was much perturbed by the nightmare of an alliance between Abdullah Uzbeg of Turan and the wild frontier tribes. After the annexation of Kabul, the boundaries of his empire extended as far as the borders of Badakhshan and Persia with the result that Akbar began to view the problem more seriously because the trouble in the north-west of Punjab through which the routes to Kabul lay could have grave repercussion on the security of Kabul.

Accordingly, Akbar, on December 20, 1585, ordered Man Singh, the governor of Kabul, to chastise the Roshanias who under their leader Jalala had taken recourse to rapine and pillage thereby rendering the roads for travellers and traders unsafe. Man Singh after an incessant warfare with them, gave a strong blow to their power, but they were not crushed. Man Singh was transferred to Swat and Bajaur territory to help Raja Todar Mal, and Ismail Quli Khan was despatched to Kabul along with Sayyid Bukhari who was to occupy Peshawar.

In the meanwhile, Mohmand and Ghori tribes joined the camp of Jalala who now at the head of 20000 foot and 50000 horse marched upon Peshawar and inflicted a crushing defeat upon the Mughals. Startled at this, Akbar dispatched posthaste Shah Quli Khan Mahram, Shaikh Farid and Tash Beg Khan under Zain Khan Koka. Another force under Mutlik Khan was sent an April 18, 1581. The Afridis and Aurakzais tendered submission and offered hostages as a guarantee for their future pacific attitude.

In May 1588, Sadiq Khan who was appointed in place of Koka followed the policy of conciliating the tribes. He gave up the plans to march into the heart of the tribal territory, and confined his policy to keep a strict watch on the movements of the tribesmen.

This policy paid rich dividends. Many of the tribes were reconciled to the Mughal authority. Jalal who had planned invasion of Punjab was decapitated by Murad Beg in Hazara on the 26 August 1600. Thus, by A.D. 1600, the menace of the Rashanias was over.

Closely allied with the Roshanias were the Yusafzais who inhabited Swat and Bajaur territory which recognised no law and no authority. On December 20, 1585, Akbar sent Zain Khan Koka along with Hussain Khan, Raja Mukat, Hira Pardhan, Ram Chand, Kabir and Fulad for their suppression. They were reinforced on January 5, and January 13, 1586.

Under the constant pressure of the Mughals, the territory upto the Karakara Pass and the district of Buner was brought under control but the rebels beyond the Karakara Pass were still unsubdued. With the arrival of the contingents under Raja Birbal on January 21, 1586 and Abul Fateh Khan on January 28, 1586, the task of subjugating the tribes was taken in hand. Owing to the dissensions between Birbal and Fateh Khan on one hand and Koka on the other, nothing tangible could be achieved. The Mughals were routed with the loss of 8000 men including Raja Birbal.

Akbar was stunned to hear this debacle. The loss of his favourite minister Birbal saddened him much and he did not swallow even a single morsal for two days. He pounced upon Koka for his alleged perfidious conduct and as an expression of his anger, he excluded him from his presence.

Now Akbar assigned the task of curbing the tribes to Raja Todar Mal and Murad. Todar Mal posted himself near the Lungar Hills while Man Singh who had arrived there after the departure of Murad stationed himself on the banks of the Indus near Chind in the direction of Buner. In this way occupying both the exits Todar Mal carried daily incursions into the tribal territory. Soon they were reduced to extremes and in the words of Abul Fazl, "The country of Swat, Bajaur and Buner was cleansed of evil-doers."[34] Kala, the leader of the tribes, presented himself before Akbar.

The settlement of the north-western region of Punjab made a deep impression upon Abdulla Uzbeg and his ambassador Mir Kuraish (who was at the court of Akbar in March 1586). They were not convinced of the impossibility of marching upon Punjab and conquering India. This feeling turned into fear when an ambassador from Shah Abbas, the ruler of Persia, arrived at Akbar's court in 1591. The Uzbegs now felt as if they were being encircled. Hence, there was no danger to India from Central Asia.

Side-by-side Akbar's attempts at the subjugation of the Pathan tribes on the north-western border of Punjab, the affairs of Kashmir were not ignored. The occupation of Kashmir was also not less important than the problems of the north-western border of Punjab. Akbar wanted to occupy it both for its strategic importance and scenic beauty. But the immediate cause was the estrangement between Yusaf Khan, the ruler of Kashmir and Akbar caused by the suspicion on the part of the former regarding the real intentions of Akbar.

On December 20, 1585, Shah Rukh Bahadur, Raja Bhagwan Das, Shah Quli Mahram, Madhu Singh and Mubarak Khan with 50,000 soldiers and a contingent of Ahadis were ordered to march upon Kashmir. They advanced into Kashmir by the Pakhili route instead of the Bhimbar route. Yusaf checkmated the Mughal forces at Bulyas Pass. Both sides, wearied of warfare, negotiated for peace. But Akbar did not ratify the agreement arrived at and hence the Mughal army pressed on. Yakub Khan, the son of Yusaf Khan who had been conducted to Akbar by Raja Bhagwan Das, was compelled to pay tribute, and to appoint Mughal collectors in his territory. "The proceeds from saffron crop, the Shawl duties and the mint were brought under the direct imperial control. Royal officers were appointed to various departments. The yield of Saffron crop and Silk industry was placed under Qalandhar Beg, the control of the mint was given over to Khwaja Mirkai and Mulla Mazhari was entrusted with the task of looking after the royal game." Akbar accepted the arrangement but did not feel satisfied.

In 1586, a civil war broke out in Kashmir and Yakub was ousted from the throne by Shams Khan, one of the nobles, who proclaimed himself as the ruler.

Akbar despatched Qasim Khan and Fateh Khan to Kashmir. Qasim gave Shams a crushing defeat and entered Srinagar on October 17, 1586. In 1588, Qasim Khan whose energies were taxed to the utmost was recalled and in his place Yusaf Khan was appointed as the governor of Kashmir. In July 1587, Yakub who had been entertaining the hope of gaining the control of Kashmir came out of his hiding place in Kishtwar[35] and submitted, thereby accepting Akbar as the undisputed sovereign of his territory. In the same year, Akbar paid a pleasure visit to Kashmir. Having lived in Kashmir for about a month and a half, Akbar arrived at Kabul on September 20, 1589 and returned to Punjab in the second week of November 1589. On March 7, Eminabad was reached where homage was paid by Quli Khan, the governor of Punjab in his absence. On March 9, 1590, Akbar held a review of the elephants at a distance of 3 kos from Lahore. On March 13, 1590, when Akbar was away in Kashmir or Kabul, important events took place in Punjab. Raja Todar Mal expired in November 1589. Raja Bhagwan Das who was seized with a violent fever on the cremation grounds breathed his last on 14 November 1589. Mirza Suleman of Badakhshan who was conducted to the court by Jagat Singh on February 24, 1587, also died a little before Raja Todar Mal's death on June 23, 1589.[36]

Insurrection in Kashmir—1592

The exactions of Yusaf Khan to whom Kashmir had been farmed at 22 lakh kharwars (one kharwar being reckoned at 16 Dams), told heavily upon the people. The surplus which accrued from the arbitrary rise in the value of kharwar from 16 to 28 dams instead of being remitted to the royal exchequer was embezzled by him and his servants. When intelligence of this fraudulent misappropriation of money reached Akbar, he made a proportionate increase in the revenue in spite of the protests raised by Muhammad Khan. On July 27, 1591, he sent Qazi Nur Ullah and Qazi Ali to hold a thorough investigation into the revenue accounts of Kashmir.

The committee was received with frowns on the part of the people who were involved in corruption and sent Nur Ullah back to the court to intimate Akbar about the danger of rebellion. Measures were taken immediately to thwart the designs of the would-be rebels. Some of the suspects were summoned to the court and various penalties were inflicted upon them. To hold others in check, Hussain Beg was deputed to Kashmir. But these precautionary measures were of little avail in removing the danger. A plot was hatched by Darvesh Ali, Adil Beg Turkoman, Imam Quli, Qiya Beg and other servants of Yusaf. On the refusal of Kamal-ud-din to assume their leadership, they turned towards Yadgar and under his guidance raised the standard of revolt and began to harass the imperial soldiers.

The insurgents gathered more and more power till the revolt assumed quite a formidable aspect and it became impossible for Hussain to live any longer in this atmosphere which might choke him to death at any time. Accordingly, he set out homewards. When he arrived near Hirapur, someone beat the drum with the result that the enemy got alert and smashed down the bridges. For fear of being overtaken by the enemy, he with his men jumped into the water; some were drowned, some were arrested, but Hussain Qazi Ali escaped and pushed on vigorously. However, Gazi Ali lagged behind on account of exhaustion and was attacked and put to death. The fate which befell his companion was not very enviable. When he emerged from the hills, he found himself face to face with the land-owners of that place who robbed him of his luggage and were about to kill him when there arrived on the scene the Chief of Rajauri. His appearance had an instantaneous effect; the band of free-looters being taken by surprise took to their heels. Thus, Hussain was saved from the clutches of death.

The Emperor having received intelligence set his forces in motion on July 22, 1592. He issued orders to Koka to proceed from Swat to Sadiq to move from Begran and to the chiefs of the northern hills from Jammu. The Punjab officers were ordered to enlist more men and to send them off to Kashmir. On August 15, Farid Bakhshi Beg and Prince Murad were ordered to speed on in advance. Yadgar Mirza appeared within sight of the king's troops but he was seized by strategem by Saadat Beg and Ibrahim Khan Koka, officers of the Mughal forces, who put him to death and produced his head before Sheikh Bakshi. The whole province of Kashmir was thus reduced for the second time under the Imperial Government of Akbar. The Emperor himself marched to Kashmir shortly afterwards, and remained there for forty days.[37] The people of the neighbouring villages who had deserted their homes for fear of royal vengeance were persuaded to return, although the active rebels had to face serious reprisals.

On December 29, 1592 Akbar returned to Lahore. In the year 1591-92, Mughal detachments were sent to Sindh from Lahore to reduce the province of Sindh to submission. As a result, the Chief of Sindh submitted and he was given a high rank at the court. During the period between 1590 and 1598 the northern hill states tried to throw off the Mughal yoke three times in 1590, 1594 and 1596. The quick action of the Mughal officers foiled their attempts and brought them under subjugation, although they did not annex them to the Mughal empire.

Famine, Pestilence and State Policy

From 1595 to 1598, a severe famine gripped the whole country. Spread of plague in epidemic form added to the horrors of famine. The deserted towns and cities presented an awful and ghastly picture. There was such a dearth of corn that some people resorted to cannibalism.[38] The streets and roads were blocked with human corpses. Akbar took compassion on the miserable and wretched condition of the subjects and entrusted Sheikh Farid Bukhari[39] with the relief work. Public kitchens were started. Experienced officers were despatched in every direction to distribute food to the starving people. The condition of Kashmir was still worse and the appalling misery of the famine-stricken people shocked the Jesuit missionaries who had accompanied Akbar on his visit to Kashmir.[40]

The Emperor in an attempt to mitigate the difficulties of the people started work on public buildings. The land revenue was remitted and oppressive fief-holders were visited with severe punishments. In the different quarters of the city, free kitchens were opened for feeding the famished people. In Kashmir as many as 55 customs were abolished in order to bring down the price level.

In 1598, Akbar contemplated the project of sending an expedition to Turan. The ruler of Turan died on January 27, 1598 and his country as usual relapsed into a condition of anarchy and chaos. The oppressive rule of his son made the situation still worse. Akbar felt tempted to incorporate the country into his dominion, but at the refusal of Salim to lead the expedition, the enterprise was not launched.

On August 2, 1598, Manuchehar Beg, the Persian ambassador, appeared before the Emperor and presented on behalf of his Master 100 Iraqi horses and mares, 300 pieces of brocade, 50 masterpieces of carpets besides embroidered, mattresses, various shades of 9 goats and 500 Turkoman slaves in rich dresses.[41]

Admittedly, Akbar, during his stay at Lahore, was more interested in the occupation and settlement of the north-western frontier region of Kashmir and Sindh. But his activities were not confined to these problems alone. His innate spiritual curiosity was a constant source of inspiration for him to find out and reveal the principles of genuine religion. Accordingly, Akbar invited some Christian missionaries. Three Christian Missions visited Akbar at Lahore. Rodolfo Aquaviva and Monserrete formed the first mission who accompanied the Emperor's camp to Lahore, and were wonder-struck at the splendour and greatness of the army.[42] The missionaries who formed the second mission in 1591 were Durate Leitao and Christoval De Vega and a lay brother Es-Tevavo Ri-Boriro. The third mission consisted of Jerome Xavier, Emma Nual Pinheriro and Brother

Benedut. This mission arrived at Lahore on May 2, 1595 and was received with utmost hospitality. Xavier was a good Persian scholar. At the request of the Emperor, he wrote a book on the life of Christ in Persian. In this work, Xavier was assisted by Maulana Abus-Sanaran of Lahore.

The Emperor listened to the missionaries with all the seriousness of a genuine seeker of truth, but the missionaries primary aim was to baptize the 'Great Mogor'. According to Akbar, they strove not once but thrice to baptise the Emperor but they met with failure each time, which was but natural, for they had mistaken the emperor's eclecticism for a desire to be baptised. It was this misunderstanding which was responsible for their accusing Akbar of insincerity. Even the modern historian Smith accused Akbar of his crafty tortuous diplomacy, the assessment which was incorrect.

It was during his stay at Lahore that Akbar appears to have introduced those principles of religious toleration which have rendered his name so conspicuous in the annals of Indian potentates. There he seems to have reached the height of his greatness. Religious discussions were held in the Ibadat Khana on Sabbath evenings, at which learned men were invited to attend. The king's court was the resort of learned men of every kind who came from various countries and were admitted to converse with him. Profound points of science, subtleties of revelation, the curiosities of history and the wonders of nature were freely discussed. The Emperor listened with majestic gravity to all that was said, and passed through the most diverse phases of thought adopting all sorts of religious practices and sectarian beliefs. Two buildings were erected outside the city of Lahore for the purpose of carrying on religious discussions. One of these called Khyrapura was intended for the Mohammedans, jews and fire-worshipers, and the other called Dharampura for Hindus.[43] The debates sometimes caused fatal discords. In one of them, a learned Shia, Mullah Ahmed, the author of *Tarikh-i-Alfi*, was assasinated in the streets of Lahore by Mirza Faulad. The assassin was subsequently sentenced to death and executed by tying him alive to the leg of an elephant.

Apart from infusing the spirit of toleration into the body-social and body-politic of the country, Akbar made administrative reforms of immense value. In fact, he was all the time alive to the necessity of making his administrative machinery more efficient and more harmonious.

In 1588, he decreed that the Hindus, henceforward, should be tried by Brahmans instead of Qazis. Another reform was introduced in connection with the currency. The last edict of Azad-ud-Daula that a mohar the deficiency of which did not exceed six grains should be reckoned as of full weight, encouraged counterfeiting and wrought considerable loss on the royal treasury. In 1592, this provision was annulled. The treasurers and revenue collectors were forbidden to demand from the tax payers any particular species of coins. Moreover, they were required to take the deficiency in weight and purity according to the existing rate only. Qulej Khan and then Khwaja Shams-ud-din enforced these decrees with success. The gold or silver were to be sold or bought at the fixed rate including Imperial tariff.

In 1595, the office of Kotwal was assigned additional duties. He was required to keep watch on anyone who entered or left the city. Feasts, marriages, births and deaths were also to be reported by him. He was authorized to employ one obscure person to spy over what transpired in the area under his jurisdiction.

Besides this, an inspector and a registrar were employed to prepare a list of the property of missing persons and childless people with a view to reverting the property to the legitimate heir having deducted what the owner of the property owed to the imperial exchequer. In the case of a banker or mansabdar, the property was escheated to the royal coffers.

Akbar also took a lot of interest to better the social lot of the people and to imbue them with high moral sense. In 1592, he forbade Hindu women to become Sati against their will. In the same year, the slaughter of oxen, buffaloes, cows, sheep, horses and camels was prohibited. In 1597, it was decreed that one should have only one wife unless he was issueless. The rule should be one God and one wife. Hindu widows were permitted to marry.

In 1595, another series of social decrees ere promulgated. A Hindu made Muslman against his will could revert to his old religion. No man was to be interfered with on account of his religion. Everyone was free to adopt any religion he liked. There was to be no restriction if any one chose to build a church or a temple or a Parsi Tower of Silence. Any profligate woman was to go to the quarters of the prostitutes. In case, parents were forced to sell their children, they could get them back later by paying the amount.

How far were these reforms carried out in practice, it is difficult to say with certainty. But a guess can be hazarded that these reforms operated in a limited way. The bulk of the people, being in villages, remained unaffected. Akbar showed sharp sensitivity to the sad plight of the people during the period from 1595 to 1598 when the country was ravaged by a severe famine owing to scarcity of rain and plague. Akbar was much pained over all this. He entrusted Shaikh Farid Bukhari with the relief work. Public kitchens were opened. Experienced officers were despatched in every direction to distribute food to the starving people. The appalling misery of the people of Kashmir received extra attention of the Emperor. Public kitchens apart, work on public buildings was started and considerable number of persons were absorbed. According to M. Akbar, persons received relief and much of the misery was allayed.[44]

Akbar set out from Lahore on 6 November 1598 on an elephant entrusting the affairs of Punjab to Khwaja Shams-ud-din. The Queen mother together with other Begums and prince Khusro were left behind in Lahore. Before crossing the river Beas at Goindwal on 24 November, he went to pay a visit to Guru Arjan Dev. He was much impressed by the hallowed and Charismatic personality of Guru Arjan Dev, and at the Guru's representation, made a considerable decrease in the land revenue of Punjab. He crossed the Sutlej at Ludhiana and reached Sirhind on 2 December 1598 where from he proceeded to Delhi on December 31, 1598.

Khwaja Shams-ud-din, who had been appointed as Subedar of Punjab before Akbar left Lahore worked very efficiently with the help of the capable Kotwal of Lahore, Malik Khairullah. In July 1599, the Kotwal was killed by a few miscreants who surrepticously entered into his private apartment where he was examining a notorious thief and ripped open his belly with their iron claws. Shams-ud-din died in March 1600. He was buried in that quarter of the town which, to this day, known as Khwafipura.

In 1598, Zain Khan Koka was appointed as the governor of Punjab and Kaul in 1600, but was soon recalled to Agra by the Emperor. He died in 1601 on account excessive drinking.

Mirza Qulij Khan[45] was appointed as new governor in 1601. During his governorship the people were not happy, particularly the Hindus. He could not exercise control over the illegitimate exactions on the routes. This fact came to the notice of Akbar and he had to commit the charge of the Lahore route to Farid Bukhari to put an end to the aforesaid undesirable exactions. According to the author of *Akbar Nama*, the cupidity of local chiefs was diminished but could not be finished.

In 1603, Qulij Khan, in pursuance of the order of the Emperor, sent a force to assist Muhammad Quli, the governor of Kashmir who was allotted the task of humbling Ali Rao, the ruler of Tibet. When Ali Rao got wind of the arrival of the forces, his heart failed him and fled without fighting.

In the meanwhile, there arose trouble in the hills of Punjab. In 1602, Raja Basu, who had taken himself to the jungle after his last defeat emerged from his hiding place and started raiding territories of his choice. Some other Hill Rajas also raised the banner of rebellion along with him. The inhabitants of the Pargana of Muzaffarwal were put to great vexation by his guerrilla warfare. At last Hussain Beg and Sardar Umar took up cudgels on behalf of the oppressed peasantry and started from Rohtas to relieve them of their trouble. Hassan Qulij, the son of Qulij Khan, set his forces in motion to assist them[46] in apprehending the Raja. He also sent Sazawals to Hussain Beg and Sardar Umar Taj Khan and, Ahmed Beg and other servants to join Hasan Qulij Khwaja. Khawaja Suleman was made Bakhshi of the forces. In the operation against the Raja of Mau

(Raja Basu), the Mughal forces suffered a lot. Khwaja Suleman was killed by the insurgents. The commotion in the hill states, could, with difficulty, be set at rest; but the Raja of Mau was still at large. In 1603, he came to Prince Alim and requested him to intercede on his behalf before the Emperor but himself remained on the other side of Jammu. Akbar sent Madho Singh privately to arrest him but the Raja came to know of it and fled away.[47]

Hasan Qulij son of Qulij Khan was honoured for his distinguished services to the Empire and in token thereof he was awarded a robe of honour. Qulij Khan was also given a shawl as a mark of recognition of his merit. He remained the Subedar of Lahore till the death of Akbar in 1605.

NOTES

1. *Akbar Nama* (Tr.), Vol. I, pp. 306-07.
2. Abdul Qadir (Tr.), *Badhaoni*, II, p. 3.
3. *Akbar Nama*, Vol. II, p. 35.
4. *Ibid*., p. 36.
5. *Tabqat-i-Akbari*, Vol. II, pp. 15-17. (English Tr. by Elliot and Dawson.)
6. *Ain-i-Akbari*, Vol. I, pp. 338-39. (Tr. by Blochmann)
7. M. Latif, *History of the Punjab*, p. 136.
8. A.S. Beveridge, *op. cit*., pp. 47-49.
9. *Akbar Nama*, Vol. III, p. 91.
10. Hutchinson and J.P. Vogel, *History of the Punjab Hill States*; Elliot and Dowson, *History of India*, Vol. V.
11. *Ain-i-Akbari*, I, pp. 402-03.
12. *Tarikh-i-Ferishta*, Vol. II, pp. 199-302. (Tr. John Briggs)
13. *Akbar Nama*, II, p. 152.
14. It was the fief of Sher Muhammad Dewana, *Ain-i-Akbari*, II, p. 591. (Tr.)
15. Sixteen miles south of Ckara on the old high bank of Beas.
16. Fort of Tihara is situated on the bank of Sutlej to the west of Ludhiana, *Ain-i-Akbari*, I, p. 1140. (Tr. into English by Beveredge).
17. *Tebcat-i-Akbari*, Vol. II, pp. 246, 257. *The Central Structure of the Mughal Empire*, pp. 126-27 by IBN Hasan Munshi Lal Manohar Lal, 1970.
18. Nandon is in the district Jallundur Doab, *Ain-i-Akbari*, II, p. 314.
19. *Akbar Nama*, II, p. 299.
20. *Ibid*., pp. 410-11.
21. *Ibid*., pp. 338-39.
22. *Ain-i-Akbari*, Vol. I, p. 349.

23. *Akbari Nama*, Vol. III, pp. 36-37.
24. *Akbar the Great Mughal*, pp. 116-17, A.L. Srivastav, Shiv Lal Aggarwal and Company, Agra, 1973.
25. *Tabwqat-i-Akbari*, II, pp. 396-97; (Lowe) *Muntakhabat-I-Twarikh*, Vol. II., p. 161.
26. R.K. Parmu, *A History of Muslim Rule in Kashmir*, pp. 1310-20.
27. *Akbar Nama*, III, p. 507.
28. *Ibid.*, p. 511.
29. *Ibid.*, p. 508.
30. M. Akbar, *The Punjab Under the Mughals*, p. 67.
31. *Ibid.*, p. 70.
32. *Ibid.*, p. 73.
33. *Akbar Nama*, III, pp. 713-14.
34. M. Akbar, *op. cit.*, p. 80. Now almost all the historians agree that Zain Khan Koka was in no way responsible for the death of Birbal. Birbal was quite inexperienced in the matters of warfare and had he acted upon the advice of Koka, this disaster would not have happened.
35. *Akbar Name*, III, p. 765.
36. *Ibid.*, p. 836.
37. Mohammad Latif, *History of the Punjab*, p. 141. Before leaving Kashmir, Akbar, at the request of Salim again handed it over to Yusaf Khan.
38. M. Akbar, *The Punjab Under the Mughals*, p. 204; Ida Rahi AD Biyat-i-Delli, Delhi, 1974.
39. Zubatul Twarikh, p. 182.
40. *The Jesvits and the Great Mughal*, p. 53.
41. *Akbar Nama*, III, pp. 11-12.
42. *The Jesvits and the Great Mughal*, p. 53.
43. Mohammad Latif, *op. cit.*, p. 143.
44. M. Akbar, *op. cit.*, p. 107.
45. *Akbar Nama*, II, pp. 1196-1207. *Ain-i-Akbari*, I, pp. 35, 380-82, *Tabcat-i-Akbari* II, p. 638. *Shanawas Khan Maasir-ul-Umera*, Vol. I, p. 435.
46. *Akbar Nama*, III, p. 1207.
47. *Ibid.*, III, pp. 1207, 1254, 1257.

Punjab Under Jahangir, Nurud Din (1605-27 C.E.)

5

During Jahangir's reign, seven persons Said Khan (1605-07), Qulij Khan (1607-10), Murtaza Khan (1610-16), Itimad-ud-Daula (1616-18), Qasim Khan (1618-23), Sadiq Khan (1623-24) and, Asaf Khan (1624-28) held governorship of Punjab one after another. All of them were men of parts and possessed considerable administrative ability. All of them executed the Imperial policies faithfully. Except for the year of succession, Punjab during their terms of viceroyalty, enjoyed a spell of internal peace. The bureaucrats (Mansabdars) in Punjab suffered from little jealousy. They acted in unison with one another as also with the central government. Punjab because of its geopolitical condition continued to be the springboard of politics to be followed in the countries across the Sulaiman Range.

Khusro's Revolt

In the last days of Akbar, the relations between Jahangir and Akbar were marred by bitterness and suspicion. In 1591, Akbar suffered a severe attack of cholic and in a state of unconsciousness accused Salim of poisoning him. The charge was unfounded but it left scars too deep to be healed. In 1599, Akbar had to leave for Asirgarh to conduct operations to subjugate it. Salim was ordered to attack Rana Amar Singh of Mewar. But he did not go beyond Ajmer, and taking advantage of the Emperor's absence, he revolted. In this design, he was egged on by his closest associates such as the grandson of Shaikh Salim Chisti, Sayyid Abdulla and Zamana Beg, later known as Mahabat Khan. To increase his financial sources Jahangir confiscated over a crore worth of cash and property left by Shah Baz Khan Kamboh who had expired recently. Then he moved to attack Agra to catch hold of the treasure of over twenty crore of rupees, but he was foiled by the firm stand of Qulich Khan who was then incharge of the Agra fort.

Thereafter, he went to Allahabad and declared his independence, making Allahabad his capital.

The middle of 1601 saw Akbar back at Agra. Salim came marching thither at the head of over thirty thousand men, robbing and plundering on the way. Akbar had to issue peremptory orders to his son either to dismiss his followers and come to him with a few select attendants or to return immediately to Allahabad.

Jahangir, now awakened to the reality of the situation, returned to Allahabad. Akbar invested him with the governorship of Bengal and Orissa. At Allahabad, he again declared his independence and assumed the title of 'King'. He got murdered Abul Fazal, the most faithful and much loved counsellor of his father in 1602 through the notorious Bir Singh Deo, head of the Bundelas. This thing hurt Akbar greatly, who for twenty-four hours wept and cried like a helpless baby. "If the prince aimed at the kingship", he said, "he should have killed him and spared his friend." Akbar decreed dire vengeance against Bir Singh Bundela but he escaped. He also made up his mind to teach a lesson to his son. However, the intercession of Salima Begum, the step-mother of Jahangir, saved the situation. She went to Allahabad and prevailed upon him to go to Agra to beg pardon from his father. He agreed and was reconciled to Akbar in April 1603. After some time, he was allowed to leave for Allahabad where he assumed independence again.

Akbar was deeply distressed at the deplorable turn which affairs were taking but he was helpless on account of his fast deteriorating health. As his end came in sight, the question of succession began to loom large. Jahangir's dissolute habits and recklessness roused serious misgivings in the minds of all those who were devoted to the cause of the Empire. Akbar had raised the empire to the pinnacle of glory and prosperity. Should it be suffered to be thrown into misery and confusion for the sake of an individual who had no claim to public gratitude? The remnant of the old nobility perceived that the accession of Salim spelt their fall from power. Public spirit and personal interest combined to suggest plans for the supersession of Salim by one who would continue the traditions of the empire and honour of the ancestors of the Imperial service. Daniyal being out of the question, the choice could only fall on Salim's eldest son Khusro, who had reached the seventeenth year of his age and who happened to be connected by the closest ties of blood with the two greatest nobles of the empire. He was the nephew of Raja Man Singh and the son-in-law of Mirza Aziz Koka. He was eminently handsome and possessed agreeable manners and irreproachable character. Akbar himself had directed his training. The political controversies which raged round Khusro awakened his instincts of domination. He readily identified himself with his uncle and his father-in-law, who sought to place him on the throne. Though Akbar's view did not refer to the succession in favour of his grandson, speculation was rife, that he, being tired of Jahangir's contumacy and unbecoming conduct, was not happy with him.

Akbar at long last in August 1604 resolved to reduce the prince by force of arms into a more submissive mood and to keep him at Agra, far from the obnoxious influences of Allahabad. Meanwhile, Jahangir sensing that his absence from the court would enable the supporters of Khusro's succession to advance their designs, thought it prudent to seek reconciliation with his father. He took advantage of the death of his grandmother and gave out his intention of condoling with his father and apologising for his faults in person. Leaving Allahabad in charge of Sharif, he set out with his son Parvez and some of his principal followers, and arrived at Agra on November 9, 1604. He was received in open court with all affection and honour. Akbar took him into his private apartment, reprimanded him, imprisoned him for a while to correct him and to keep him a way from his bad associates. Finally, he was released and raised to highest honours and dignities.

This thing, however, did not completely alleviate the estrangement that had been caused. The rapid decline of the health of Akbar accelerated the activities of the supporters of the rival candidates. The relations between Salim and Khusro were strained to the utmost as became evident from the fight between an elephant of Khusro and that of Jahangir in which both the parties behaved as if they were enemies far from being sports-lovers.

Shortly after the elephant fight, Akbar fell fatally ill. Round his death-bed raged a whirlwind of intrigue and treachery, plotting and counter-plotting, negotiations and strategems. Khan Aziz Koka who then acted as the vicegerent of the Empire, filled all the posts in the fort with his own followers and planned a coup de main. Salim on his visit to his father was to be arrested and placed in confinement. But the plot failed, as it was leaked out by Mir Zia-ul-Malik Qizwani. The proposed coup-de-main having failed, Khan Aziz Koka and Man Singh acted more openly and more audaciously. They called the nobles and officers together and earnestly argued for the supersession of Salim by Khusro. The proposal was strongly opposed by Sayyid Khan Barha, Malik Khair and others with the result that the conference soon broke up after Jahangir was assured of his succession by the dying Akbar himself. He nodded to his attendants to invest the prince with the turban and the robe and to gird him with his own dagger. Immediately after, the Emperor closed his eyes for ever. Aziz Koka transferred his allegiance to Jahangir, Raja Man Singh took a little longer and took Prince Khusro under his charge and prepared to proceed to Bengal. But on receiving an assurance of perfect safety and security for Khusro and for himself, Raja Man Singh presented himself and Khusro to Jahangir.

Jahangir embraced and kissed his son with the warmest affections and dismissed Man Singh in all honour to Bengal. A few days later, Khusro received a lakh of rupees to repair for himself an old mansion in Agra.

But the hearts of father and son had been hopelessly rent asunder. The one could not forgive nor did the other forget the recent past.

Khusro had aspired to the throne and had but narrowly missed the goal. He was hurled down from the dreamland where he was to become the monarch of all he surveyed, he could not reconcile himself to the situation of dependence and humiliation. On the other hand, the part played by Khusro and his supporters rankled in the heart of Jahangir, who, apprehensive of a repetition of the risk he had undergone, placed his son in a sort of semi-confinement within the fort of Agra. The dark prospect of life-long detention alarmed the young prince. Bereft of free intercourse with the outer world and yet allowed the company of a narrow circle, he thought of escaping and making a hazardous enterprise.

On the evening of April 6, 1605, he escaped on pretence of a visit to his grandfather's tomb at Sikandra with about 350 horses, and hurried towards Punjab. At Mathura, he was joined by Husain Beg Badakhshi and his 300 valiant horse then on their way to the court in obedience to an Imperial summons. Soon the numbers swelled to 12000 as numbers of ploughmen and freelancers flocked to his ranks. On the way, the prince intercepted an Imperial convoy of a lakh of rupees which he distributed among his followers.

He flew past Delhi, burnt Sarai Narela and was joined by Abdur Rehman, Diwan of Lahore. Khusro invested him with the title of Anwar Khan and made him a Wazir.[1]

En route to Lahore, Khusro reached Tarn Taran where he sought the blessings of Guru Arjan Dev. He represented himself as a distressed and forlorn individual. From Taran he marched to Lahore, which was fully guarded by Dilawar Khan whom the Prince had failed to persuade to join him at Panipat.

Khusro's raw levies far outnumbered the royal soldiers within the fort. To encourage them Khusro announced that after taking the fort he would allow them to plunder the city for seven days. Khusro burnt one of the gates of the fort; but Dilawar promptly threw up a wall and defeated all his attempts at assault.

The prince had sat there for nine days when he learnt that the Imperial army had arrived within striking distance.[2] Lest he should be caught between two fires, Khusro left a detachment before Lahore and himself came out to offer battle at the head of ten thousand men.[3] Feeling desperate Khusro turned back to prevent the royal army from crossing the river Beas but he was too late. Shaikh Farid Bukhari had already crossed the river with all his army very safely at the ferry of Goindwal.

A battle between the two armies ensued. Jahangir heard about it when he was at Sarai Qazi near Gondwal. He had at that time only 500 horsemen with him.[4] But he showed courage by moving forward rapidly in spite of heavy rains. The rain was more disadvantageous to the prince, as he could not manage his bows and horses.

But he began the fight desperately. The Sayyids of Barha who formed the vanguard were cut to pieces by the Badakhshani horse but the charge of the Imperialist right wing swept all before it. Four hundred Badakhashanis and hundreds of less renowned rebels lay dead on the field. Among the survivors all was confusion and despondency. Several hundreds fell into the hands of the Imperialists.

The prince fled and thought of going to Kabul to prepare and gather an army there and come down again like Humayun to recover his position.[5] In this plan, he was actively supported by Hussain Beg who even offered to place his hoard of four lakh of rupees (in the fort of Rohtas) at the disposal of his confederates if his advice was adopted. But as the prince finally decided to adopt the advice of Hussain Beg, the Indian and Afghan soldiers deserted him and he was left with only a small number of them. The emperor heard the news of his son's defeat at Goindwal from Shansi Jash Allahi, who was given the title of Khush Khabar Khan. The emperor lost no time in taking measures to prevent the prince from escaping. He directed Raja Basu, Mahabat Khan, and Mirza Ali to pursue the prince. Fifteen thousand rupees were given to Mahabat Khan, twenty thousand to the Ahadis and a hundred thousand to be spent on the way.[6] The ferries all over the rivers of Punjab had been forbidden to ply any traffic without proper check long before Khusro's defeat at Bhairowal so as to prevent the escape of the rebels after their defeat. Warning had also been issued to all the jagirdars, chaudhries and superintendants of roads that they should be careful.

Khusro and Hussain Beg tried to cross the river at Shahpur but no boat was available. After that they went to Sadhora but there also they failed. They were soon captured and brought to Lahore.

Khusro was produced before Jahangir with his hands tied and chains on his legs on the left side after the manner and custom of Changez Khan. His companions, Hussain Beg and Abdur Rahim, were made to stand on his right and left respectively. They were ordered to be put in the skins of an ox and an ass. Then they were mounted on asses with their faces to their tails and taken round the city. As the ox-hide dried more quickly than that of the ass, Hussain Beg remained alive only for four watches, and died from suffocation. Abdur Rahim, who was in the ass's skin and to whom they gave some refreshment from outside, took a longer time to die.

Jahangir ordered posts to be set up on both side of the road from the Kamran garden to the city and asked his officers to hang up and impale the seditious Amirs and others who had taken part in the rebellion.

Jahangir also punished with death and penalties, other companions and helpers of Khusro and also those whom he had suspected of having helped the prince. Guru Arjan Dev, the fifth Sikh Guru and the compiler of *Adi Granth Sahib* was also arrested and put to death according to Yasa, a Changezian legal codex. The Emperor notices the event as follows in his autobiography:

> In Goindwal, which is on the river Biyah (Beas), there was a Hindu named Arjun, in the garments of Sainthood and sanctity, so much so that he had captured many of the simple-hearted of the Hindus and even of the ignorant and foolish followers of Islam, by his ways and mean manners, and they had loudly sounded the drum of his holiness. They called him Guru, and from all sides stupid people crowded the worship and manifested complete faith in him. For three or four generations (of spiritual successions) they had kept the shop warm. Many times it occurred to me to put a stop to this vain affair or to bring him into the assembly of the people of

> Islam. At last when Khusro passed along this road, this insignificant follow proposed to wait upon him. He behaved to Khusro in certain special ways, and made on his forehead a finger mark in saffron, which the Indians call Qashqa, and is considered propitious. When this came to my ears, I clearly understood his folly. I ordered them to produce him and handed over his homes, dwelling places, and children to Murtaza Khan, and having confiscated his property commanded that he should be put to death.[7]

After punishing the rebels Jahangir moved from Mirza Kamran's garden to Lahore fort and stayed there for about a year.

Then he planned to go on a hunting tour to Kabul. He left Lahore on March 16, 1607 and took up his headquarters in the Dilamiz Garden, which was on the other side of the Ravi, and stayed there for four days. Here he placed Lahore in charge of Qulij Khan who was asked to settle matters of administration in consultation with Miran Sadr Jahan, and Mir Sharif Amali.

Jahangir returned from Kabul to Lahore in November 1607 (3 Shaban) and stayed there till January when he left for Agra. During this period, he appointed Mir Qawam-ud-Din as Diwan, Shaikh Yusaf as Bakhshi and Jamal-ud-din as Kotwal of Lahore and presented each according to his circumstances with dresses of honour. Qulej Khan, the Subedar of Punjab was also the recipient of the role of honour of the prince.[8]

In the sixth year of his reign (April 16, 1611) of Jahangir, Ahdad invaded Kabul with a large number of horsemen and foot soldiers at a time when the governor of Qandhar Khan-i-Dauran Muizul Mulk had gone in the interior of Afghanistan. Admittedly, the inhabitants of Kabul under the leadership of the governor defended Kabul, yet Jahangir was not satisfied as he wanted to crush Ahdad absolutely. Accordingly, he made up his mind to assign the task to Khani-Khanan. But shortly after, when he sensed that Qulij Khan, Subedar of Lahore was annoyed at the duty of driving back Ahdad being assigned to Khan-i-Khanan, he changed his mind and assigned the task to

Qulij Khan. On September 21, 1710, Shaikh Farid Bukhari Murtaza Khan was appointed the governor of Lahore. The choice of Murtaza Khan was prompted by the loyalty and strength he had shown while dealing with the Khusro's revolt.

It may be presumed that Guru Hargobind's arrest by Jahangir was the result of the machinations of Murtaza Khan who was orthodox in religious views and being under the influence of Shaikh Ahmed Sirhind did not wish well of the growth of Sikhism. In 1613, Jahangir raised the Mansab of Murtaza Khan by 1000 so that it came to 6000 personal and 5000 sawar.

The grant of viceroyalty to Murtaza Khan was a high charge and a great honour for him.[9] In 1612, the news arrived about the death of Amir-ul-Umra from Burhanpur. He had caught the disease at Lahore. Sometime after his illness, his mental power gave way to insanity. His memory was lost. The illness took him to his grave.

On April, 4, 1615 (5th Rabi 1, 1024 A.H.) Murtaza Khan obtained permission to reduce the Kangra fort, the equal of which, according to Jahangir, "people could not point to in the hill country of Punjab or even all the habitable world. Raja Suraj Mal, son of Raja Basu, as his country was near the fort, was appointed to help Murtaza Khan" and his previous Mansab was raised by 500 personal and horse.[10] Murtaza Khan, however, died in 1616 before the fort could be captured. The death of Murtaza Khan came as a big shock to the Emperor. There is a reference to this in the Emperor's Memoirs.[11]

In 1616, Punjab was visited by a severe pestilence of which Lahore had its share. According to Mu'tamid Khan, the court historian of Jahangir, "This dreadful calamity arose in the parganas of Punjab. It reached Lahore, and a great number of the Muslims and Hindus lost their lives from it. It then proceeded towards Sirhind and throughout the Doab as far as Delhi and the surrounding places. It destroyed many villages and parganas in that part of the country."[12]

"In Lahore, its ravages were horrible. In one house ten, even twenty, persons died and their surviving neighbours, annoyed by the stench, were compelled to desert their habitations. Houses full of the dead were left locked and no person dared to go near them through fear of his life."[13] In this accursed year still one more bad news came from Punjab, Raja Man Singh, a loyal officer of Jahangir, was killed. He had been sent at the head of the army of Kangra. When he arrived at Lahore, he heard that Sangram, one of the Zamindars of hilly Punjab, had attacked his place, taken possession of a part of his province. Raja Man Singh went to drive him out. Sangram fled and hid himself in the difficult hills. Raja Man Singh pursued him there and in the fight that ensued, he was killed and his army was defeated and fled. Jahangir was grieved at the loss.[14]

Ghias Beg, the father of Nur Jahan, styled Itimad-ud-Daula, was appointed the viceroy of Punjab after the death of Murtaza Khan. In January 1617 A.D., Agha Fazil who had been appointed the deputy of Itimad-ud-Daula at Lahore was honored with the little of Fazil Khan.

Upon the recommendation of Prince Kharran, Suraj Mal was sent as superintendent of the expedition to Kangra. But he created trouble and revolted. Raja Bikramjit Singh was sent against him. Suraj Mal was defeated and fled to Chamba where he died. The forts were conquered and Nurpur area was given to Suraj Mal's brother, Jagat Singh.

Although from the very beginning Jahangir had endeavoured to capture the fort of Kangra, yet it had not been effected so far. In 1618, Khuram was assigned the task of reducing the fort to submission. The Imperialists assumed the offensive with full vigour. The siege of Kangra was pursued for weeks together; the supplies were cut off and the beleaguered garrison had to live on boiled dry grass. Death and starvation stared them in the face. After a prolonged siege of 14 months, when they saw no hope of deliverance, they surrendered on November 16, 1620.

When Itimad-ud-Daula was promoted to the post of Madarul-Mulk (Premier), on his recommendation Mir Qasim, Bakhshi of the Ahadis, who was son-in-law of Itimad-ud-Daula, was promoted to the government of Punjab on March 28, 1618. He was also bestowed upon by the Emperor a mansab of 1000 personal and 400 horse and the title of Qasim Khan. The post of the Bakhshi of Ahadis was given to Inayat Khan in place of Qasim Khan.[15] A year later when the Emperor halted at the fort of Rohtas on his way to Kashmir in 1619 A.D., Qasim Khan was received by him and was favoured with a horse and a sword.[16] He was promoted to the mansab of 2000 personal and 1000 horse in the year of 1620 A.D.

Since the conquest of Kashmir by Akbar, Kashmir had been the most favourite holiday resort. Jahangir in 1619 started for Kashmir. When he reached Sirhind, he went round the garden of the city which had very old terraces and was sufficiently charming, although it had lost the freshness and beauty it formerly had. The Emperor appointed Khwaja Waisi who was well-acquainted with agriculture and buildings as the Karori of Sirhind. He was specially instructed to improve the garden and repair and rebuild the old buildings.

Soon after when the Emperor reached the river Beas, Raja Bikramjit came from Kangra to pay his homage to him. He was given a jewelled dagger and dress of honour and he returned to Kangra.

The Emperor had sent Mansur Khan to complete the erection of the royal buildings at Lahore. They were almost complete by this time. But the Emperor had no time to visit Lahore. So he sent Khuram to see them and return within ten days. In February 1620, Jahangir reached Kalanaur and halted in a garden outside it. At Kalanaur the Emperor received Alam Khan who had been sent to Persia as Mughal ambassador. Out of many presents which Khan Alam gave to Jahangir, one was a painting portraying the fight between Sahib-i-Kiran Timur with Tuqtamash Khan, and his children and Amirs. The painting was extremely charming and gave minute details. It contained 240 figures in all and near each figure was written whose portrait it was. Khan Alam got it at Isfan. It originally belonged to the library of Shah Ismail the first where from it was stolen and sold by Sadiqi, one of the librarians. The painter was some Khalilmirza Shahrukh. The pictures were analogous to Ustad Bizads' paintings but he seemed to have been a pupil of Shahrukh. Bishan Das the court painter who had been sent along with Alam Khan to

Persia and had taken portraits of the Shah and his courtiers was given an elephant as a mark of honour. On the same day, Qasim Khan with the Bakshi and Dewan of Lahore had the good fortune to do homage.

While still at Kalanaur, Jahangir was overtaken by his desire to see Miyan Shaikh Muhammad Mir, who was a Darvish, a Sindhi by origin, very eloquent, virtuous, austere, of balanced temperament. As it was not possible for the Emperor to go to Lahore, he requested him to come to him. Miyan Shaikh Muhammad Mir acceded to the request and came to Kalanaur. The Emperor was impressed by his nobility and vast knowledge about spiritual affairs. He found in Mian Mir too high a spirit to be obliged by offering a gift. He simply offered him the skin of a white antelope after which he bade Jahangir farewell.

Some time in June 1620, Sheikh Ahmed of Sirhind who had for some time been placed in the prison on account of his orthodox views and immoderate language was summoned to the presence of Jahangir who released him giving him a dress of honour and Rs. 1000 for expenses, because he (Shaikh Ahmed) justly represented that the punishment had really been a valuable lesson to him, and that his desire was to wait on him (Jahangir).

On his return from Kashmir in November 1620 A.D., Jahangir fixed his court at Lahore. He gives the following account of the newly-built royal palaces at Lahore. "In one month after this stage (Jahangirabad) I encamped in the garden of Momin Ishqbaz, which is on the bank of the Lahore river (the Ravi) and has some lofty palm-trees and handsome cypresses. It is certainly a rare garden. On Monday, the 9th of the Divine month of Azar corresponding to the 5th Muharram 1030 A.H. (November 20, 1620 A.D.), mounting an elephant of the name of Indri, I went towards the city scattering coins as I proceeded. After three watches and two gharis of the day had passed, at the selected auspicious hour, having entered the royal residence I alighted happily and auspiciously at the building recently brought to completion and finished handsomely by the exertions of Mamur Khan. Without exaggeration charming residences and soul-exciting places had been erected in great beauty and delicacy adorned and embellished with paintings by rare artists."

"Altogether there had been expended on these buildings, the sum of Rs. 70,00,000 or 23,000 current tuman of Iran." "Qasim Khan was further raised to a mansab of 3000 personal and 2000 horse at the end of the sixteenth year of reign (1622 A.D.) and ruled over Punjab till 1623."

Next year in 1621, the Emperor again became anxious to visit Kashmir. Accordingly, he started in March 1621. En route to Kashmir, he was delighted to see the gardens at Sirhind. After sojourning at different places, when he reached Bahilwan, he decided to visit Kangra, the fort which had been conquered recently. But he had to delay his visit because of the sudden death of Itimad-ud-Daula about the end of January 1622. Then after condoling with the sons and grandsons of Itimad-ud-Daula, he betook himself to the fort of Kangra. He was accompanied by Qazi-ul-Qazat (Chief Qazi) and a few other learned men in Muslim theology who were supposed to celebrate the Emperor's visit to the fort by performing the requisite ceremonies.

On reaching the fort, Khutba was read in the name of the Emperor Jahangir and to mark the occasion, a bull was slaughtered in the fort. An order was also issued for a mosque to be built in the fort. After this, he paid a visit to the Durga Temple at Kangra and Jawala Mukhi.[17] The next place which Jahangir visited was Koh-i-Madar or the hill which as per Hindu mythology had served as the churn for the gods. The place was extremely delightful. A royal edifice was ordered to be raised at that place.

On the 4th of Aban (November) 1622 the Emperor entered the city of Lahore after visiting Kashmir. The mind of the Emperor at this time was pre-occupied with the anxiety to retrieve Qandhar from the Persians. He, therefore, addressed himself to the tasks of arranging provisions for the army of Qandhar. The services of Abdullah Khan, Khan Jahan, who had come post-haste from Multan, Mahabat Khan and Mirza Rustan Khan and others were requisitioned to do the needful.

Just at the time the two ambassadors of Shah Abbas, Haidar Beg and Wali Beg were accorded audience. They were presented with dresses of honour and their expenses after which they were permitted to leave for their country. They handed over a letter from the Shah of Persia to the Emperor detailing the reasons for his conquest of Qandhar which were not to the taste of Jahangir.

Jahangir henceforward stepped up the activities pertaining to the proposed conquest of Qandhar. Just as this juncture, news reached Jahangir that Khurram had gone on wrong path. The news greatly disturbed Jahangir who postponed his project of sending expedition to Qandhar, and began preparations to counter the menace of Khurram. He at once left Lahore and started for Agra, making sojourn on the way. Since Jahangir's march from Lahore was sudden and certainly not a pre-contemplated move, he was accompanied by only a few Amirs who were in attendance. The number remained small even when he stayed at Sultanpur (on the bank of the Beas) and Sirhind. After passing beyond it, great numbers of the army came in from all sides and quarters. At Karnal, Asaf Khan coming from Agra waited upon the Emperor. Nahazish Khan, son of Said Khan having arrived from Gujarat paid his respects. When Jahangir reached Delhi, a big force had come together. On the approach of the Mughal army, Khurram retired to the hills of Mewat then to Telugana. He then occupied Bengal and Bihar but ultimately, he surrendered and made submission to the Emperor.

On the 19th New Year's Day of accession (1624), Sadiq Khan was promoted to the governorship of the province. His mansab was raised to 4000 zat and 3000 sawar and he was given a dress of honour and a sword and an elephant.[18]

In 1625, when the Emperor returned from Kabul and halted at Lahore, he appointed Yamin-ud-Daula, Asaf Khan, the brother of Nur Jahan, to the government of Punjab province. He was also appointed Prime Minister and an order was issued that he would preside permanently over the administration of all affairs—revenue and political.[19] Punjab prospered under the munificent administration of Asaf Khan. His high taste for architecture was responsible for embellishing the Lahore city.

But a fresh trouble arose in the land of the five rivers. This time the trouble was stirred by Nur Jahan to humiliate Mahabat Khan to achieve her ultimate aim of securing the throne for her son-in-law Shaharyar after the death of her husband whose health was breaking down faster and the problem of succession had become the most immediate urgency. Her object was a well-calculated move. By 1625 the popular and charming Khusro had been in his grave for three years. The Khan Azam who might have sponsored the cause of Dawar Bakhsh had died at Ahmedabad in 1624. Shah Jahan was thoroughly humiliated, rendered utterly powerless and what was more important completely discredited in the Emperor's eyes.

But Shah Jahan was not the only claimant. Prince Parvez being the eldest living son also had a strong claim. Parvez enjoyed the friendship of his, Mahabat Khan, the boldest and most resolute man, the foremost captain, the ablest diplomat of the Empire. After his recent exploits, the whole Empire stood in awe of him, the entire Imperial army respected him and his own troops adored him.

Nur Jahan found it essential to undermine Mahabat Khan's power, if she was to attain her objective. Her brother Asaf Khan who had long been on the bitterest terms with Mahabat Khan, whom the latter had done his best to send into exile, and who had nothing to gain from the accession of Parvez, cordially supported her in her new venture.

As a first step they proceeded to separate Mahabat Khan from Parvez, to deprive him of the command of the forces which nominally belonged to the prince, and to prevent him from hatching any plans they got a fiat issued by the Emperor to act as its Subedar and Khan Jahan Lodi was appointed in his place as Vakil to Parvez. Parvez and Mahabat Khan both saw through the political game, and the prince declared himself unwilling to part with Mahabat Khan. But soon after he agreed, possibly he did not want to meet the fate of Khurram. Mahabat Khan had to assume the charge of Bengal.

Having thus achieved one great object, Nur Jahan and Asaf Khan next called upon Mahabat Khan to send to court the elephants he was said to have obtained in Bengal and Behar during the revolt of Khurram and to furnish an account of the large sums forfeited to the State from the dismissal of disloyal Jagirdars. An Imperial agent was despatched to him to fetch the elephants in question and to take an account of the disputed sum. In case the account was proved to be unsatisfactory, he was desired to deliver to him an order of recall to the court.

Mahabat Khan saw through the insidious attempt to vilify and humiliate him. He was shocked at the flagrant ingratitude shown to him so soon after he had saved the Empire from grave disasters. He knew fully well that his patron Jahangir was now an invalid and hardly likely to be able even to move his little finger to save his life and honour. From the character of Nur Jahan and Asaf Khan and the tenor of his own life-long relations with them he could judge that they would not stop until they had reduced him to nothingness.[20]

In the meantime, an incident occurred at the court which very clearly indicated how deep was the animosity which the ruling group bore to Mahabat Khan and what sort of treatment he had to expect from them. Shortly before, he had married his daughter to Barkhurdar, son of Khwaja Umar Naqshbandi, without first obtaining the customary royal permission. "He might reasonably have been called to account for this neglect but the ruling faction raised a hue and cry beyond proportion to the significance of the occasion and determined to capitalise upon it to inflame the Emperor against him. Jahangir, accordingly, was surcharged and he sent for the young noble and ordered that he should be severely humiliated. Mahabat's dowry to Barkandar was also forfeited to the state."[21]

This event and the general behaviour of the ruling faction in the court forced Mahabat Khan to take steps to redeem his honour. He took five thousand selected Rajputs with him and left for Lahore in a threatening manner to see the Emperor.

The Emperor had left Kashmir in September 1625, arriving at Lahore on October 12, 1625 and set out for Kabul in March 1626. He was encamped on the bank of the Jhelum when Mahabat Khan arrived in the vicinity of the camp. His appearance at the head of a Rajput force caused much consternation at the court. No one had the courage to disarm him; he was only forbidden to attend the court except on occasions when he might be summoned.

Shortly after the arrival of Mahabat Khan on the scene, the Imperial cortege began to cross the river Jhelum. Almost all officers, soldiers and domestics, the arms and the treasury were safely transported over the bridge. Jahangir, his family, Motamad Khan, Mir Mansur and few servants and eunuchs alone remained in the camp on the left bank to cross next morning. Mahabat Khan conceived the bold design of taking the Emperor captive. Taking advantage of the situation Mahabat entered the royal tents and took Jahangir to his custody.

But in the excitement of his extraordinary daring, Mahabat Khan neglected to take Nur Jahan into custody whom he had always considered more dangerous than anyone else in the court. When he realised his mistake, he came back to the royal camp but found that she had gone over to the other side of the river along with Prince Shaharyar.

Nur Jahan hurried a messenger to her brother Asaf Khan, and convened a council of all the principal Amirs and officers. She scolded them for their neglect and stupid arrangements. All the nobles were ashamed of it. Plans were suggested to rescue the king and it was finally decided to attack Mahabat Khan with a large army, punish him and rescue the Emperor. But when the king came to know of the plan, he was upset. He feared that he would be murdered. Accordingly, he sent Muqarrab Khan, Sadiq Khan Badakhashani and Mansur Khan asking them not to carry out the plan.[22] He gave them his ring to assure Nur Jahan, Asaf Khan and others of his safety. Asaf Khan was appraised of the views of the king; but he did not agree. Fidai Khan took his force and went to the bridge but found that the Rajputs had already burnt it. There was no way to cross the river. Six of his attendants were drowned in the attempt to cross it by horses. He himself along with seven others reached the bank but found it useless to risk his life. He quickly retreated and crossed back the river.

On March 11, 1626,[23] the Mughal forces led by Nur Jahan, Asaf Khan, Fidai Khan and others decided to cross the river. A route was selected for this purpose but unfortunately it proved most dangerous and difficult. The army could not remain organised, some landed at one place while others at some other place. Fidai Khan reached at one place while Sher Khwaja and Allah Yar Khan landed away from Fidai Khan. Mahabat Khan's men who were holding the other bank of the river Jehlum, took advantage of the enemy's a plight and made a vigorous attack on them. The royalists were thrown into utter disarray and helplessness; quite a large number of them were killed and many more were drowned. Nur Jahan fought energetically and riding on an elephant fighting and at the same time taking care of the daughter of Shaharyar Yar. Her eunuch attendants were killed and the elephant was wounded. The driver plunged the wounded beast into the deep waters, so that the Rajputs might cease to pursue him. The elephant, with great difficulty, succeeded in swimming across to the other bank. At this critical juncture, Khwaja Abdul Hassan advanced but his horse was nearly drowned when a Kashmiri sailor rescued him. Asaf Khan was advancing but was much bewildered. The condition of the army was precarious.

Even then Fidai Khan's party under the inspiration of their heroic leader performed some remarkable exploits. They reached the shore in discipline. After a fierce fight, they got the upper-hand and fought on to the house of Shaharyar where the Emperor was made to reside. Fidai Khan soon found that he could not succeed in reaching Jahangir, he retreated and re-crossed the river. Next day he fled away to the fort of Rohtas. Asaf Khan also lost courage. He with his son Abu Talib and 300 sawers left for Attack where his Jagir was. The Rajputs were victorious. They plundered the treasury and defeated the enemy. Khwaja Abul Hasan, after concealing himself for sometime, joined Mahabat Khan and swore fidelity. Iradat Khan and Motamid Khan also followed his example. Nur Jahan unable to bear the pangs of separation from her husband for long and fully realising that her cause was for the moment completely lost, voluntarily surrendered to Mahabat Khan and was allowed to join the Emperor.

Now Mahabat Khan was supreme. He assumed charge of the machinery of the government. He augmented his treasure by appropriating to himself the hidden wealth of his enemies. Simultaneously, he deputed his son along with a strong contingent to reduce the fort of Attock where Asaf Khan had taken shelter. Shortly after, Asaf Khan offered submission and was placed in Mahabat's custody.

Now Mahabat Khan made the Emperor resume the journey to Kabul in his company. On the way at Attock, Mahabat Khan got the formal permission of garrisoning the fort with his own men. At this juncture, Abdul Khaliq, nephew of Khwaja Shams-ud-din, Muhammad Khwaja and Tohammad Taqui, once the pay master of Khurram Jahan, were put to death on account of their close attachment to Asaf Khan. Similarly, Mulla Muhammad Tathi, the spiritual preceptor of Asaf Khan, was enchained. To secure Punjab, Mahabat Khan appointed Siddique Khan, a brother of Asaf Khan but having good relations with him, to the governorship of Punjab.

The royal camp reached Peshawar in May 1626. Mahabat up to now how had become supreme and authoritarian in his attitude. Asaf Khan and Nur Jahan were his captives; Khurram was not in a mood to move; Malik Amber had just died and no one in Deccan was in a position to challenge his authority. This was the reason that Jahangir showed much respect to everything that Mahabat Khan asked—so much so that he told him all the secrets of Nur Jahan and of others who were against Mahabat Khan. As a result of this, Mahabat Khan turned kind to the Emperor; he decreased the retinue and guard of the Rajputs on the king.[24] He allowed him to go a hunting almost everyday and even arranged a Qumargah for him. With Nur Jahan and other members of his family, he paid visits to saints, as they always had been found of doing so.

On the other hand, Nur Jahan had been continuously on the alert. She employed all the resources of her intellect to set a group of noble against Mahabat Khan. She cajoled the unwilling, she bribed the greedy, she strengthened the wavering; she held out promises to all. She enlisted the support of many humbler men as well and organised a great conspiracy. She sent Hushiar Singh, her eunuch in advance to Lahore who had succeeded in enlisting 2000 soldiers in her name. Fidai Khan raised quite a big army by getting supplies even from Parvez. Orias Khan had promised the Queen to bring her 5000 cavalry.

By this time the camp reached Rohtas, Nur Jahan found her position strong enough to take the offensive as her men had succeeded in surrounding all strategic places. The Emperor asked Mahabat Khan not to hold the usual morning parade of his forces lest some disturbance should take place and instead, he should move a stage away from the forces.

He professed to obey the Imperial order but in reality took to flight. He was careful enough, however, to take with him among others as hostages Asaf Khan, his son Abu Talib, the late Prince Daniyal's sons—Tahmuras and Hoshang and Lashhari, son of Mukhlis Khan, who was his surety. Now the Emperor was the master of his kingdom as independent as he was before his arrest.

The Emperor himself passed on to Rohtas where a regular Durbar was held. The Emperor regained his liberty on the bank of the river where he had lost it a few months before.

A little after, Mahabat Khan also released other eminent prisoners with him. Mahabat Khan was ultimately granted pardon and sent to Thatta as Subedar.

The royal camp after a few days reached Lahore. The reorganisation of the administration was taken in hand. The difficult task was entrusted to Asaf Khan who was appointed Vakil. He was also made the governor of Punjab. Abdul Hassain was appointed his Diwan. Mir Jumla was appointed Bakhshi being succeeded by Afzal Khan as Khan-i-Saman (steward).

Jahangir stayed at Lahore up to March 1627 after which fearing the scorching heat of the summer left for Kashmir, Nur Jahan, Asaf Khan, Shahryar, and Dawar Bakhsh accompanied him. Even the paradise on earth, as Kashmir is often regarded, could no longer do him good. His asthma took a dangerous turn and he had to return to Lahore because of its warm climate which was more suitable for the health of the Emperor.

While on the way back his illness became acute and he died on 28 Safar 1037 A.H. (November 8, 1627). The dead body was removed to Lahore where it was buried in a garden at Shahdara near Lahore. A tomb had already been erected there.

Jahangir's administrative structure in Punjab did not differ from that of his predecessor except on very minor points. The officials at provincial Sarkar and Pargana levels were the same. The objective and style of functioning of the administration also did not undergo any change. The administration was run to perpetuate the Mughal rule, strengthen it by suppressing all those who showed signs of refractorness and appropriate the surplus produce of the peasants. The king, being the sole source of political authority, the officers of the provinces always looked towards him for guidance and decisions, and in turn enjoyed great powers within the framework of the thinking of the Emperor. This being so, the government policies reflected the mood of the Emperor. When Jahangir occupied the throne, he as a matter of policy posed himself an orthodox king. This thing was immediately reflected in the execution of Guru Arjan Dev, and later on, in the imprisonment of Guru Hargobind in the Gwalior fort. But when after some time, he realised the soundness of the policy of Sulehkul (peace for all) of his father he shed off orthodoxy and adopted liberal attitude in his style of functioning not only in the religious sphere but also in almost all the spheres of his activities with the result that liberal approach became the hallmark of administration in the province. Under its impact, Punjab started taking strides on the road towards liberalism in religious sphere. The Muslims began to develop liberal tendencies systematically held and sustained by Sufis of liberal persuations. Mian Mir's influence became widespread. Jahangir himself met him in 1620 at Kalanaur.

Jahangir showed dislike for those who wanted to revive Islamic orthodoxy at the cost of inter-communities and intra-communities relations. People like Majaddud and others who were likely to exercise unwholesome influence over political affairs, were dealt with severely. He imprisoned Sayyid Ahmed of Sirhind in the fort of Gwalior. The Shaikh was head of Naqshbandi Silisila and was known for his ultra orthodox views.

Jahangir's respect for Guru Hargobind after he was released from the Gwalior prison is a positive proof of the liberal-mindedness of the Emperor.

Jahangir extended facilities to the people, particularly those activities which were conducive to the interests of the State. He encouraged trade at Lahore and in his time Lahore became a centre of trading activities in indigo and fine cotton goods of Masaulipatam and Gocunda. He took keen interest in the trade of horses. He sent Khan Daman to Kabul to purchase horses. Murtaza Khan got from abroad 30 Iraqi and Turki horses.[25] Guru Arjan Dev procured horse from Turkistan.

He built some new roads to give incentive to trade activities as also to facilitate movement of troops and people. A road from Agra to Lahore was built with a trees on both sides.

Jahangir forbade the horrible custom of Sati prevalent among some Muslim converts from Hindus who buried their widows with their husbands.[26] According to Beni Parshad, "the state fixed the coinage. It regulated trade and industry". Jahangir forbade the levy of cesses and tolls which the Jagirdars and imposed for their private gain. He ordered that the bales of merchandise were not to be opened on the roads as was sometime done, probably for purposes of octroi, with their permission.[27]

If no heir could be discovered to the property of deceased private persons, the effects were to be applied to the erection of school, inns, the construction of tanks, wells and repair of bridges.[28] The cultivation of Bhang was forbidden.

The Mansabdars were increased in number and their status began to be expressed in terms of far higher figures than what was the case during his father's time. This change put great burden on the royal exchequer. The burden was not too heavy during Jahangir's reign. But it was bound to be so if this thing was followed by Jahangir's successors. And this very thing happened. The succeeding emperors, Shah Jahan and Aurangzeb, appointed more Mansabdars and the extent of Paibaki land suffered constraction correspondingly with the result that the revenue assessment of each assignment was put at higher figure higher than the land could yield, much to the charin of the Mansabdars and to the agony of the peasants who were squeezed still more to cater to the financial demands of the Mansabdars.

NOTES

1. *Jahangir's Memoirs*, Vol. I, 52, 54, 55, 59 (Eng. Tr.), *Iqbal Nama*, pp. 9-10.
2. *Ibid.*, I, 62; *Iqbal Nama*, II K.K. I. 251.
3. *Ibid.*, Vol. I, 52-54, 57, 67 (Eng. Tr.).
4. *Ibid.*, Vol. I, p. 63.
5. *Iqbal Nama*, p. 20.
6. *Jahàngir's Memoirs*, Vol. I, p. 66.
7. *Ibid.*, pp. 72-73.
8. *Ibid.*, p. 135.
9. *Iqbal Nama*, p. 37.
10. *Jahangir's Memoirs*, I, p. 283.
11. *Ibid.*, I, pp. 224-26.
12. *Ibìd.*
13. *Ibid.*, 330; *Iqbal Nama*, pp. 88-89.
14. *Ibid.*, Vol. I, pp. 361-62.
15. *Ibid.*, II, p. 2.
16. *Ibid.*, p. 122.
17. *Memoris of Jahangir*, Vol. II (R&B), p. 25.
18. *Ibid.*, Vol. I, p. 97.
19. Mutamad Khan, *Iqbal Nama-e-Jahangir*, p. 278. Shahanwaz Khan, *Masasirul-Umara* (Eng. Tr.), p. 289.
20. Beni Prasad, *History of Jahangir*, p. 368.
21. *Iqbal Nama*, p. 253.
22. *Ibid.*, p. 180.
23. Elliot and Dowson, *History of India*, Vol. VI, p. 423.
24. *Iqbal Nama*, p. 192.
25. Surjit Singh Gandhi, *History of the Sikh Gurus Retold*, Atlantic Publishers, p. 373.
26. *Travancies*, pp. 207-24, Delhi, 2007.
27. *Jahangir Memories*, Regulations.
28. *Ibid.* (Regulation 1.8.)

Punjab Under Shah Jahan—Shihabud Din (1628-58 C.E.)

6

I

Khurram, better known to history as Shah Jahan, was born on the night of Thursday, 5 January 1592 at Lahore. His mother was a Rajput princess, Manmati or Jagat Gosain, whom Salim had married in 1586. She was daughter of the Kota Raja Uday Singh. Akbar was much joyed on the birth of his grandson. It was doubly welcome; it brought him the usual felicity, but more than that, it revived the drooping spirit of his childless wife Ruqiah Sultan Begam. An astrologer, Gobind, had predicted to her the happy event, and had advised her to adopt the child. So, when in accordance with the custom obtaining among the royal, on the sixtieth day after the birth of the child, Akbar was invited by his son Salim to give a name to this new-born baby. He christened him Khurram or Joyous and verily did he diffuse joy in the Imperial household. The same day he was handed over to Ruqiah Sultan Begam who adopted him, and henceforward until he reached the age of discretion, he grew up under the fostering care of his grandmother.

Punjab enjoyed not only the privilege of being the birth place of Shah Jahan, it also got the credit of contributing a lot towards the intellectual and physical growth of him. Besides learning a lot from various scholars of Punjab, he received lessons in varied weapons and different methods of warfare. In A.D. 1597, when Akbar was going for the last time to Kashmir, he left Shah Jahan at Lahore under the guardianship of Murad Juwaini. The Mir was to teach him archery and to perform daily before him Taslim-I-Qin. Within a short time, Shah Jahan became an expert shot, both with firearms and bows, an indefatigable rider, an excellent swordsman and a keen lover of all sports. On his return from Kashmir, Akbar stopped at Lahore for a very short time during which he decided to send Salim against the Rana of Mewar. Salim before his departure requested Akbar to let him take one of his sons with him but Akbar was not prepared to part with Khurram, nor did he consider it wise to send Khurram with him, though he had no objection to Parwez's going with his father. Shah Jahan remained a darling of his grandfather till the latter passed away. Akbar had complete faith in his grandson's ability and fidelity towards him. When Akbar's health began to decline, Shah Jahan spared no pains to serve his grandfather. He was devotedly attached to Akbar and would not leave his bed side even when there was a conspiracy to apprehend Salim and to seize him as soon as he left royal apartments.

Salim ascended the throne on October 24, 1605. Soon after this, his reign was disturbed by the outbreak of Khusro's revolt. In this connection Jahangir reached Punjab. The revolt came to an end within less than a month and Jahangir entered Lahore on May 9, 1606. He stayed here for some months. It was during this period that Khurram received his first military rank of 8000 zat and 5000 sawar, together with a tumanu-tegh, a flag and drums.[1]

About a week later, he was betrothed to Arjum Banu Begam, the daughter of I'tiqad Khan future Asaf Khan. Jahangir with his own hands put the ring on the finger of his prospective daughter-in-law, and the occasion was celebrated with great rejoicings. It was in the month of November of the same year that Jahangir on his return from Kabul assigned to Khurram Shah *jagir* in Ujjain,[2] and the *sarkar* of Hissar Feroza[3] and permitted him to pitch a red tent, a privilege generally conceded to the eldest prince. To crown it all, the Muhr Uzak[4] was placed in his charge and it was ordered that all the *farmans* and *parwanas* should bear his seal. Khurram during his father's homeward march from Kabul divulged the plot hatched by Khusro and his party men to kill the Emperor. As a result of this, Khurram rose even higher in the estimate on of his father. Khurram was assigned the jobs of subduing the Rana of Mewar and waging war against the Deccan states. Shah Jahan acquitted himself creditably in all these allotted tasks. He subdued Jam who held control over the northern coastline of Kathiawar.

Ever since 1615, operations with occasional interruptions had been going on against the famous fort of Kangra. Some cause or other had foiled the attempts of the Mughal to reduce it till in August 1618. Shah Jahan took upon himself the responsibility of carrying the campaign to its logical conclusion. He sent Raja Vikramjit to reduce the fort. The latter first isolated it and then pressed the siege vigorously and compelled the garrison to surrender. This victory enhanced the prestige of Shah Jahan all the more.

But then certain factors operated which brought about a turn in his career. He had to rise in revolt against his father to safeguard his interests against the machinations of Nur Jahan who wanted to make Shaharyar, her son-in-law, the successor of Jahangir. The revolt of Shah Jahan lasted until the end of Jahangir's reign.

The death of the Emperor in 1627 brought the question of succession to the fore. Nur Jahan, in expectation of the crisis, had for a long time been making almost frantic efforts to perpetuate her domination. She had withdrawn her support from Shah Jahan because she found his temperament too independent to admit of her control. She had adopted Shaharyar as her candidate to the throne because he was a pliable and worthless creature. But unfortunately when the critical moment came, he happened to be away from the scene.

Even then Nur Jahan made a bid to retain her power. She hurriedly sent a message to her son-in-law to prepare for the struggle. She even made an abortive attempt to imprison her brother Asaf Khan.

Shaharyar at once responded to her mother-in-law's call and proclaimed himself Emperor. He seized the entire treasure at Lahore and also the whole mass of artillery which Jahangir had left while going to Kashmir. Further, he confiscated the property of the Amirs, and imprisoned their women and children. By distributing money lavishly, he recruited a large army.

Asaf Khan worked for his own son-in-law, Shah Jahan. He proved too astute to fall a prety to the machinations of Nur Jahan. He refused to go to see her and with the assistance of his confederates began to mature his own designs of securing succession for Shah Jahan. First, he won over to his views the Mir Bakhshi Iradat Khan and then in consultation with him took a step which was meant at once to bridge over a constitutional difficulty and to create a crisis which would ultimately be to the advantage of his cause. Shah Jahan being far away in the Deccan, it was difficult to secure the allegiance to him of the rank and file, particularly when in those days, men were accustomed to fight for an individual, not for a cause. Moreover, a man on the spot claimed their loyalty first, and in the present case Shaharyar was nearer than Shah Jahan. So the problem before Asaf Khan was how to secure general sympathy in face of an imminent struggle with Shaharyar. He could not at this stage proclaim Shah Jahan as Emperor, because that would carry little weight, nor could he fight Shaharyar, because it would be tantamount to rebellion.

In view of this there was need for a formal constitutional head to lend a legal colour to his activities because it would fill a gap in the imagination of the people. He decided to proclaim Prince Dawar Bakhsh as the new Emperor. It was certainly an extremely politic move. The late Emperor had been for some time favouring this prince, and as the son of the deceased Khusro, his claims to the throne were better than those of Shaharyar who was the son of a slave girl, no matter that he was the son-in-law of the empress. With Dawar Bakhsh at their head, Asaf Khan and his party moved to Bhimbar where Asaf Khan won over more men to the cause of Shah Jahan. He also succeeded, with the help of Abul Hasan who was staying there, in extricating the three princes (Dara, Aurangzeb and Shuja) from the control of Nur Jahan. Next, he conciliated Sadiq Khan who was not favourably disposed to Shah Jahan and to convince him of the high degree of trust which he reposed in him, Asaf Khan placed the three princes in his charge.

Having done this, Asaf Khan moved to Lahore to deal with Shaharyar who had declared himself Emperor.

The rival forces met within three miles of Lahore. Asaf's troops, though not adequately equipped, consisted of experienced men who had seen many a battle. On the other hand, Shaharyar's army was almost a rabble, most of whom had never even heard the sound of a drum. On the very first charge, they broke up. Shaharyar, instead of rushing aid to his commander-in-chief, Bainanagar, fell victim to the artifices of Afzal Khan who was at this time in his camp and posed himself as his friend. So, when the former heard of the defeat of Baisanagar, he retreated to the fort and closed the gates. From the field of battle, Asaf Khan moved nearer to the fort. Here he was joined by Afzal Khan and a large number of adherents of Shaharyar. Access to the fort thus becoming easy, Iradat Khan and Shayista Khan entered it in the night and pitched their camp in the royal courtyard. In the morning, they occupied the fort and recovered Shaharyar who had hid himself in the seraglio. He was brought before Dawar Bakhsh and compelled to perform *kurnish* (bow). He was ordered to be imprisoned and shortly after Tahmur and Hoshang, sons of Daniyal, were also consigned to prison. Shah Jahan who was informed of the developments that had taken place in the wake of the death of Jahangir by Asaf Khan through his special emissary Banarsi, communicated to Asaf Khan to "put out the eyes of Shaharyar, Dawar Bakhsh, and his brothers Tahmur and Hoshang and to bring them to court if possible, otherwise to despatch them to their rightful abode". Asaf Khan acted as directed. He was richly rewarded for his services. He was raised to the mansab of 8000 zat and 800 sawar. He was also appointed wazir. At the same time he continued to hold the post of the subedar of Punjab. The administration of the province was, however, conducted by his deputy subedar.

II

Lahore seems to have enjoyed comparatively peaceful time during the reign of Shah Jahan. At least no major disturbance is mentioned during these thirty years of Imperial rule, and chroniclers have been busy recording events essentially of social and cultural importance. The carpet factory of Lahore, established in Shah Jahan's reign was highly praised for its fine products. "So soft and delicate are these that the carpets made at Kimran in the manufactory of the king of Iran, look like coarse canvas. These were made of Pashm and were priced at one hundred rupees a yard. All the rooms in the palaces were furnished with these beautiful carpets."[5]

In May 1632, the viceroyalty of Punjab was assigned to Wazir Khan with a view to tightening the administration which had become a little loose during the period of the deputy subedar Inayat Ullah Yazdi. Wazir Khan was a capable man. He was a resident of Chiniot, a city of Punjab. He possessed capacities of a higher order and is known as the ablest governor of Shah Jahan's reign. He gave peace and prosperity to the people. A great scholar of Arabic and philosophy, his accomplishments as a physician had much attracted the Emperor and the royal court.

In the seventh year of his reign (A.D. 1043-1633) Shah Jahan decided to come to Lahore from the Imperial capital. On his way to Lahore, as he was camping on the bank of the Beas, the eldest daughter of Dara Shikoh, died. This upset the prince to a great extent and he had an attack of fever also. As the court physician attending on the prince did not succeed in curing him of the malady, Wazir Khan, the Subedar of Lahore, was sent for. Wazir Khan arrived at the camp on 4th Shawwal, 1043 A.H. (April 3, 1634) and treated the prince, who got well quickly. On April 5, 1634 (6th Shawwal, 1043 A.H.) the royal camp moved to the tank of Khwaja Hushiar, which was in the environs of Lahore. On the 7th Shawwal, riding on an elephant the Emperor started towards the town of Lahore. His Majesty was received with great pump by Wazir Khan and the nobles of Lahore. Wazir Khan presented him with a nazr of 1000 ashrafis. The Emperor entered the palace in state after the first watch of the day. On the 9th, Wazir Khan presented his Majesty with jewels, gold and silver utensils rich stuffs and carpets, horses and camels, valued at four lakh of rupees, which he had collected during his viceroyalty in Punjab. The same day Said Khan, Subedar of Kabul, and Kulich Khan, the governor of Multan, presented themselves to Shah Jahan alongwith their nazars consisting of cash, jewellery, horses and camels. Shah

Jahan, in token of having recognised them, properly honoured them. Nijabat Khan, the Faujdar of Kangra, was also raised in rank. According to Abdul Hamid, "The whole of the presents amounted to ten lakhs of rupees."

Exactly on the sixth day after this, Shah Jahan visited the Mausoleum of Jahangir to pay his homage. On this occasion, he distributed ten thousand rupees among the poor, while another sum of five thousand rupees was distributed by the royal princes who accompanied him.

Shah Jahan, after this, paid a visit to Sain Mian Mir who was head of the Qadiri order of the Sufis and commanded respect among all sections of the people. Mian Mir spoke very little. He simply informed him: "It is the duty of just kings that they should remain vigilant about their subjects and dominions. To promote the prosperity of his subjects by seeking to populate new areas and bringing them under cultivation should be his foremost concern as it makes the soldiery contented and the treasury full. He considered the ruler to be a perfect specimen of humanity and the chief manifestation of the Almighty."[6] The notable thing about the visit was that the visit of royal personages including Shah Jahan, did not disturb him in the least and he remained engrossed in his own devotional exercises.

On 20 April 1634 A.D. Shah Jahan and the royal princes were sumptuously entertained by Asaf Khan in his new palace at Lahore. Asaf Khan had built this lofty and superb edifice in the direction of the Lahore fort on the boundary of the horse-market[7] plain where traders and merchants assembled daily in this city. The cost of construction of the building was twenty lakh rupees, and the period in which they reached completion was ten years. Asaf Khan on this occasion presented the Emperor with jewels, horses, rich stuffs and other curiosities valued at six lakhs of rupees exclusive of presents given to the members of the royal family.[8]

During his stay at Lahore, Shah Jahan also attended to the repair and reconstruction of royal palaces. He ordered the reconstruction of Ghusal Khana and Khwabgah (the bath rooms and sleeping apartments) according to the plans designed by skilful engineers. He also issued orders to rebuild Shah Burj or the regel tower, which had been built by Jahangir. The former work was entrusted to Wazir Khan while the latter project was left to the taste of Asaf Khan who had already displayed much tact and judgement in the embellishment of the Imperial court.[9]

The next occasion when the Emperor thought of visiting Lahore was when he was going to Kabul in the 12th year of his reign. The Emperor reached Lahore and received Ali Mardan Khan from Kandhar. His mansab was increased to 6000 zat and 6000 sawar and he was appointed governor of Kashmir. The Emperor visited his house with all sorts of ceremonies.

The Emperor returned from Kabul in 1639. Ali Mardan from Kashmir came to pay homage. The Emperor seems to have been very much pleased with Ali Mardan Khan. His mansab was increased to 7000 zat and 7000 sawar.[10]

Here it was reported in him that Wazir Khan, the governor of Lahore, had committed certain indiscreet acts, and was not pulling on well with the people. An order was issued for his transfer and Ali Mardan was appointed the governor of Lahore in his place. Ali Mardan was the son of Ganj Ali Khan who descended from the Kurdist tribe in Persia. In 1625, at the death of his father, Shah Abbas allowed Ali Mardan, his son, to inherit his honours and dignities and conferred upon his the title of Baba Sani (Baba the second, his father being the holder of the title 'Arjamand Baba'). The successor of Shah Abbas laid his hands heavily upon the supporters of the late regime and Ali Mardan was one of those who apprehended peril to their lives. Forthwith, he began to strengthen the fortifications of Qandahar in self-defence and opened negotiations with Shah Jahan. The Shah flew into a rage and resolved on his destruction. Ali Mardan solicited the Mughal protection and surrendered the fort of Qandahar as its price. The Mughals honoured him by conferring upon him the rank of 7000 zat and 7000 sawar. Since then he had been serving the interests of the Empire with utmost loyalty.

As a governor of Punjab, he conducted the affairs of the province efficiently. His talent shown more conspicuously in the field of civil administration than in the military one. During his period, Punjab witnessed extension of irrigation facilities and laying out of gardens. A sum of Rs. 1,00,000 was spent by Ali Mardan Khan for digging a canal from the village Rajpur near Nurpur to Lahore. The total length was 48 jarib kos. The author of *Ma'asir-al-Umara* says about Ali Mardan Khan, "One of his great deeds which will remain on the page of time for ages was his bringing a canal into Lahore which is the ornament of that city (Lahore)."[11]

In the 14th Regnal year, Said Khan Bahadur was appointed to the post of the governor of Punjab. He did his job for about three years. With his characteristic zeal, he addressed himself forthwith to seeing that the projects undertaken by his predecessor yielded fruit.

The canal after its completion was found to be faulty in its construction inasmuch as it did not ensure proper flow of water. A second attempt at deepending and levelling the canal was also not crowned with success. At last, it was decided to abandon the whole of the channel except 5 kos and dig a new one. It was 11 kos shorter than the original one and was completed by the 16th Regnal year of Shah Jahan's reign.[12] It now took off from the Ravi at Rajpur close to the hills and carried water in full quantity upto Lahore.

Three small canals were also dug at the same point to irrigate other areas. One of them ran to Pathankot, the other to Batala, while the third one irrigated the area of Patti Haibiat Pur. According to Sujan Rai Bhandari, they conferred great benefit on the cultivators. Besides another small canal was cut from the Tavi river and it watered the area upto Ali Mardan Khan's gardens at Sodhra near Wezirabad in the Upper Rachna Doab.[13]

Alongwith the excavation of canal, the work of laying out gardens was also undertaken. "His Majesty (Shah Jahan) ordered that a specious garden with chambers baths, reservoirs and fountains be laid on its banks near Lahore." Accordingly, the plan of Shalimar garden was prepared by Ali Mardan Khan who had a special taste for gardens which he had cultivated in

Persia. The work on the garden was started in the thirteenth year of Shah Jahan's reign on 3rd Ravi-ul-Awwal 1051 A.H. (1640 A.D.). Khalil Ullah Khan was entrusted with the execution of the work with the help of other servants of the state. Shah Jahan himself did the opening ceremony of the garden on October 31, 1642 A.D. exactly after one year five months and four days after the start of the work on the garden. Under the impulse provided by the example of the court, quite a large number of gardens came into being in and around the city of Lahore. These gardens were laid out primarily to provide resorts of recreation for the court and the king and his family.

The lay-out design of the Shalimar Garden displayed Persian influence which the Mughals had inherited and which formed an integral part of their racial consciousness. The Shalimar Garden comprised three tabaqas, out of which the highest was styled Farah Bakhsh (bestower of pleasure) and the other two lower tabaqas were named Faiz Bakhsh (bestower of plenty). In 1641, Asaf Khan, the father-in-law of the Emperor, died after a protracted illness due to chronic dropsy. He was buried in the mausoleum of the late Emperor Jahangir at Shahdara.[14] A dome was built over his grave.

After having settled the affairs of Kabul and Punjab, Emperor Shah Jahan decided to leave for Akbarabad (Agra) on 22nd Shaban 1052 A.H. (November 15, 1642). Four days earlier on the 18th Shaban 1052 A.H. (November 11, 1642) Said Khan Bahadur Zafar Jang waited upon the Emperor and presented a nazr of ashrafis on 21st Shaban 1052 A.H. (November 14, 1642). Zafar Jang was honoured with a Khilat-e-Khas and the viceroyalty of Punjab.

On the first of Muharram 1054 A.H. (March 10, 1644 A.D.). It was reported that Safdar Khan was not able to cope with the work of the government of the province of Qandahar. He was, therefore, removed and his place was filled with the appointment of Zafar Jang whose vacancy in its turn was filled by the appointment of Quilij Khan as the governor of Punjab on March 14, 1644 (4th Muharram, 1054 A.H.). On the 29th Shawwal 1055 A.H. (December 18, 1645 A.D.), Nur Jahan, the much loved widow of Jahangir, who was in receipt of two lakh of rupees per annum died at Lahore and was buried in a mausoleum which she had herself built close to the tomb of her brother Asaf Khan.[15]

A little less than four months after, the viceroyalty of Punjab again changed hands and this time it went to Jafar Khan (April 6, 1646; 19th Safar 1055 A.H.) His brother Bahram was appointed Bakhshi and Waqi-a-Nawis at Lahore and Sarandaz Khan, the Qiladar of Lahore. He was much esteemed for his being just and good at administration.[16]

As agriculture mainly depended on rainfall, the failure of rainfall caused a famine in Punjab in 1646. Shah Jahan took prompt measures to mitigate the sufferings of the people. By his order, ten kitchens providing free food were set up and run efficiently by the State Government. Sayyid Jalal was specially commissioned by the Emperor to distribute Rs. 10,000 daily to the poor and the destitute. Sold children were ransomed by the government and restored to their parents. In February 1647, Shah Jahan sanctioned another sum of thirty thousand rupees for relief measures in Punjab.[17] On May 29, 1647 A.D. (24th Rabi II 1057 A.H.), Jafar Khan presented to the Emperor one crore and 20 lakh of rupees and three lakh of ashrafis which Raja Jai Singh had delivered to him at Lahore, after bringing this money from the royal exchequer in Akbarabad. Jafar Khan was honoured with a khilat and was appointed Mir Bakhsi. Qazi Afzal was appointed the viceroy of Punjab in his place.[18] He was succeeded by Shaikh Abdul Karim (1651-55)[19] who was in turn succeeded by Khaja Muin[20] and Bahadur Khan[21] in 1066 A.H. (1655 A.D.) and 1067 A.H. (1646 A.D.) successively. Sayyid Izzat Khan was the last viceroy of Punjab of Shah Jahan's time who, having been appointed to his post in 1067 A.H. (1656 A.D.) continued to rule over the province till the time of Aurangzeb.

From 1649 to 1657 A.D., two important things happened. One of them was the three unsuccessful attempts to recapture Qandahar; while the second which was in the cultural field was the seven discourses with Baba Lal at Lahore (between November 22, 1653 and the middle of December 1653). The report of the discourses was said to have been formally composed in Hindi and later on re-written in Persian by Dara Shikoh's Mir Munshi, Chandra Bhan Brahman.[22] Such topics as 'an ascetic life', mystic problems and idol worship, etc. figured prominently in the discourses. The question which Dara Shikoh put to Baba Lal about Hindu mythology raised his intense desire to satisfy himself regarding the veracity of many problems, viz. Ruyat or vision of God, etc. which pressingly disturbed the minds of the Muslim mystics and religious thinkers. The answers which Dara Shikoh received from Baba Lal regarding *pancha bhuta* (five elements), *indriyan* (five senses), relation of *khaliq* (creator) with *makluq* (created), *Pramatma* (divine Soul), *jivatma* (human soul), *nidra* (sleep) and *mahapurkh* (perfect man) were fully drawn upon by him in his unique work Majma-ul-Bahrain which he later on wrote in 1654-55. Dara's discourse with Hindu saint course for others to follow—the process highly helpful to promote understanding between different religious sects.

Qandahar and Punjab

On February 11, 1649, the Persians retook the fort of Qandahar. The news of preparations on the part of Shah Abbas II had been pouring in the Mughal Court at Agra but so far these had been taken in a light manner. Shah Jahan now wished to move immediately to Kabul and save the situation. But his ministers who were afraid of the severity of winter in that area, counselled him against the proposal. However, the court left Delhi for Lahore to hear of further developments in Qandahar.[23] And what was further development? Loss of Qandahar, one of the two keyposts on the north-western frontier. Then three attempts, one after the other, were made to recover Qandahar and in all those, Punjab figured prominently. Immediately after the news of the Persian occupation of Qandahar, Aurangzeb and Said Ullah hastened from Punjab to drive out the invaders, but arrived too late to save the city owing to the inclement climate and mountain passes being covered with snow. The prince and the wazir invested the place for about four months at the head of 60000 horses and 10000 infantry but were foiled in their attempt to recover the city. Punjab supplied food and fodder in abundance during the course of the campaign. After a futile siege of three months and 20 days, Aurangzeb was ordered by Shah Jahan to withdraw from Qandahar. The departure of the prince was accelerated by the approach of winter and the news that a force, 20000 strong, was coming from Persia to the relief of the beleaguered garrison at Qandahar.

The second attempt to recover Qandahar was made in A.D. 1652. As early as August of the previous year (1651) Shah Jahan while returning from Kashmir issued orders to his officers to assemble for the projected campaign. Shah Shuja was asked to come from Bengal. Raja Jai Singh, Raja Jaswant Singh, Rustam Khan, Allah Vardi Khan, Raja Vithalda, etc. were ordered to reach the court by the 20th January of the following year, i.e. 1652. The Emperor held his court at Lahore in the beginning of 1652. Rustam Khan joined the Emperor at Lahore with two hundred thousand rupees. Shah Jahan left Lahore after celebrating his weighing ceremony and arrived at Kabul on April 14, 1652.

As on the previous occasion, so now, the campaign was led by Prince Aurangzeb and Said Ullah Khan, who were ordered to lay siege on May 2, 1652. The troops numbered between 50000 and 60000 of whom one fifth were musketeers and artillery men. The result was the same as it was in 1649. The prince, in spite of his best efforts, had to return to Kabul unsuccessful. Shah Jahan sent him as Viceroy to the Deccan.

Dara, the eldest son of the Emperor, now volunteered to make an attempt to conquer Quandahar. For that purpose the provinces of Kabul and Multan were also bestowed on him (he was already the governor of Punjab). He spent three months and some days at Lahore, preparing his army for Qandahar. He collected the guns which could use iron shots of 96 pounds and 112 pounds. Under orders of Qasim Khan, the royal Mir Atash, 3000 cannon balls, both small and big, 50000 maunds of gun powder, 25000 pounds of lead and 14000 rockets were prepared. Arrangements for the ration supply were made with grain dealers. At last with the permission of his Majesty, Dara started for Qandahar via Multan. But he did not fare better than his brother, Aurangzeb. At long last he too returned. This was the last attempt of the Mughals to recover Qandahar which was now lost for ever to the Mughal empire.

In April 1656, Allami Said Ullah Khan died. He was considered to be the ablest and most upright of the ministers India had produced since the days of the tolerant Akbar. On 16 April 1657, Ali Mardan Khan, universally regarded as the most talented officer both in field and court, died on his way to Kashmir and was buried in the environ of Lahore.

On the 8th Zilhijja 1067 A.H. (September 17, 1657 A.D.) the Emperor Shah Jahan was seized with illness at Delhi. His illness lasted for a long time and every day he grew weaker. The stage reached when he was unable to attend to the business of the state. This thing gave rise to the wildest speculation about the Emperor's survival which in turn intrigued his sons to embroil themselves in the war of succession in which ultimately Aurangzeb triumphed.

Rebellion of Raja Jagat Singh of Nurpur

In 1639, Rajrup, the son of Jagat Singh, the chief of Nurpur, a hilly state on way to Kashmir rebelled at the instance of his father who was stationed in the Bangash territory at that time. The main cause for this rebellion was that Rajrup stopped paying his own annual tribute and the tribute of other hill states in the lower valley of Kangra which he was expected to collect and remit to the royal exchequer. Jagat Singh very cleverly posed to have felt much upset at his son's unbecoming demeanour and requested the Emperor through his friends at the Imperial court in Lahore at that time that he should be permitted to proceed from Bajaur to Nurpur, so that he might punish his son and collect the tribute from the hill states of Shivaliks in place of his son and dispatch it to the Imperial Diwan. The Emperor acceded to his request and he was relieved of his post to enable him to leave for Nurpur.

When Jagat Singh reached his native state, he also rose in rebellion. Shah Jahan forthwith sent a strong army under the supreme command of Prince Murad Bakhsh. The Imperial forces led a vigorous attack on his three strong forts, Mankot, Nurpur and Taragarh. In this job, the Imperial forces were helped by the neighbouring chiefs especially the Raja of Guler among whom Jagat Singh was very unpopular.

Jagat Singh, after a few months of struggle, lost hope about his success against the Imperial forces and sued for peace. Prince Murad agreed to intercede with his father for him and sent a letter to Shah Jahan in this regard. The latter demanded absolute surrender of Raja Jagat Singh as the pre-condition of peace. Jagat Singh refused to surrender and therefore, fighting went on for sometime.

Completely exasperated Jagat Singh at long last surrendered without any condition (March 1642). He also agreed to the demolition of the fortification of Tara Garh, Mankot and Nurpur. On March 11, 1642, he accompanied the Imperial generals to the court in order to pay respects to the Emperor. He was pardoned and restored along with his son to his rank and position in the Imperial service.[24]

III

Changes in the Administrative Configuration of Punjab

The region of Punjab as it was divided into a number of Sarkars, grouped into several subas. While the trans-Sutlej Sarkars were incorporated in the subas of Lahore and Multan, the cis-Sutlej sarkars formed a part of the suba of Delhi. The suba of Lahore comprised almost the whole of trans-Sutlej region, except the sarkar of Dipalpur. The Suba of Multan which consisted of the sarkars of Multan, Dipalpur and Bhakhar was now reduced in size, for the latter was separated from it and incorporated in the Suba of Sind.[25] The cis-Sutlej sarkars included in the suba of Delhi were (i) the sarkar of Sirhind and (ii) the sarkar of Hissar Feroza. The sarkar of Narnaul which was created by Sher Shah Suri and included in the Suba of Agra of Akbar remained its part till the reign of Shah Jahan. It was now included in the suba of Delhi by Shah Jahan. Another notable change effected in the administrative units during the period was that some of the sarkars were called chaklas with minor territorial adjustments.[26]

Changes were also brought about in the functions of some government officials and in the state policy at provincial level regarding assignment of jagirs and mad-i-mash. The powers of Karori (Amilgazar or Amil) were reduced. Shah Jahan's Diwan

Islam Khan set up an Amin in every Muhal transferring the work of assessment from the Karori to his new colleague. The Karori hence forward concerned himself chiefly with collecting the amount which the Amin had assessed. Islam Khan's successor Sa'udullah Khan is said to have further reduced the powers of the Karori by putting an end to the practice of combining the offices of Karori and Foujdar (commandant) in the same person. A new administrative unit chakla comprising a group of Muhals (parganas) was introduced and an Amin Foujdar was appointed over it, the Karori becoming really a subordinate official. The tendency now grew that the provincial officials like their counterparts at the central level should be paid in lieu of their salary by means of land from which they were entitled to collect the land revenue and all other cesses imposed or sanctioned by the Emperor. One result of this was the reduction in the Paibiaqi land (such areas which were to be assigned but were for the time being managed by Imperial officers). This problem of assignment system began to raise its ugly head during Shah Jahan's period. Because of the policy of transfer of assignments with a view to countermining the local influence of the Mansabdars which they were bound to acquire if they were allowed to stay permanently. The Jagirdars began to take interest only in the collection of revenue and not in the welfare of the cultivators or in any improvement of agriculture. Moreover, the official assessment of the proposed collection was often more than what he actually collected (Hal-i-Hasal). This thing also irritated the Mansabdars. Some Jagirdars, especially the smaller ones, who did not possess enough resources to arrange for the collection of revenue from a distance started the practice of ijara or revenue farming. The farmers (ijaradars) after having obtained their job by offering the highest bids stopped at nothing in order to fulfil their pledge to the Jagirdars and to make a profit for themselves. Sadiq Khan, the historian of Shah Jahan's reign declares that this practice had become very common during Shah Jahan's reign and that its was one of the causes of the ruin of the peasantry.[27]

As regards the holders of the Mad-i-Muash revenue grants, Shah Jahan continued to follow in the footsteps of his predecessors.

In one respect, however, he differed. Shah Jahan got examined all the grants made till his times and resumed such of them as were held by persons found to be undeserving or had died or were found to have occupied land elsewhere using the same grant or had obtained the grant itself by fraud or forgery. In the time of Akbar and Jahangir, no regular provision seems to have been made for inheritance and the heirs had to apply for the renewal of the grant of which only a part was normally granted to them. Shah Jahan was the first to issue a regulation in this respect. By Shah Jahan's order of the 5th year, all grants of 30 bigha or less were to be wholly distributed among heirs on the deaths of grantees. If the grant was of larger area, half of it was to be distributed among the heirs and the other half resumed unless the heirs proved their deserts (Istihqaq) before the court and obtained sanad for this portion also.

Shah Jahan chose governors for Punjab from amongst capable officers who were at once gifted generals and talented executives. They were expected to be men of high character and integrity. Shah Jahan did not tolerate incompetence or abuses in provincial governments and never hesitated to remove men if they were found to be wanting in integrity and balanced outlook. He lost no time to remove Wazir Khan when he was found overstepping proper limits in dealing with the subjects. The officers were expected to help the peasants in extending the area under cultivation. Shah Jahan kept a vigilant watch over the government and his officials. Justice was quick and impartial.[28]

He expected his officers to give impartial justice to the people irrespective of race and creed throughout his empire. Abdul Hamid Lahori profusely praises this aspect of Shah Jahan's reign. He says, "His Majesty has often been heard saying that kings have been vested with authority and all people made their subjects by God for the sole purpose that the kings may pay their full attention to the maintenance of justice, which is the basis of the continuation of the world and human race. The purpose of punishment awarded by the king should be to prevent the cruel from oppressing the weak...the King should not kill large number of men for a small fault and on a small suspicion injure fellow-beings, who are a divine trust."[29] The evidence contained in the Mazhar-i-Shah Jahani, however, brings to light the fact that in spite of Shah Jahan's interest in the administration of justice and the Empire's prosperity, the subedar and other state officers did oppress people at least in the out-lying areas.[30] This was particularly true in the case of an officer who happened to be a relation of some high-up; he would be simply transferred and no serious action was taken against him.

Another notable change in the administration was the institutionalized form of nazar or offerings to the Emperor and high officials. This was instituted by Nur Jahan and was very popular in the reign of Jahangir, but under Shah Jahan it had become a compulsory obligation—so much so that the Emperor expected presents from his courtiers on every ceremonial occasion and the latter in their turn extorted them from their subordinates. It was a gilded form of bribery and practically all European travellers in the province made a note of it.[31] General laxity in administration was another evil stalking the administration of the province.

Shah Jahan's reign is marked for a swing towards orthodoxy in religion. His attitude towards non-Muslims, especially the Hindus, Sikhs and Christians, was far from that of Akbar the Great. The restoration of the orthodox calendar (Hijra instead of Ilahi) and Char Taslim in place of Sajda or Zaminbose were 'straws in the wind'. The return of orthodoxy was definitely portended by the destruction of temples at Benaras in 1633 and forcible conversion to Islam of some Portugese at Hugli in 1632 and of the Bundalas in 1635. The attacks of the Mughal forces upon the Sikh Guru Hargobind point to the same inference. There is no doubt that this policy of religious intolerance was not followed as vigorously as it was done under his successor and though liberalism in Muslim thinking was allowed to co-exist and flourish side by side with orthodox religious thinking, yet it had its effect on the social plane. As elsewhere in the Mughal Empire, so in Punjab certain happy trends concerning relations between the Hindus and Muslims suffered in their further growth. In certain parts of Punjab inter-marriages between

Hindus and Muslims were getting popular. These were now palpably discouraged. In Bhimbar and the neighbouring district of Gujarat it was a prevalent custom that the Hindu girls were married to Muslims and Muslim girls were married to Hindus and the Hindus cremated their Muslim wives on their deaths Shah Jahan did not like the idea of Muslim girls being cremated after their death and immediately ordered that if all Hindus who had Muslim wives, got converted to Islam, their Muslim wives should be remarried to them in the Islamic way. Otherwise the Muslim wives should be seized from them and restored to the Muslim community. This order put a stop to the growth of the institution of inter-religious marriages which could, if allowed to flourish, contribute towards building more harmonious relations and amity between the Hindus and Muslims. Irritants began to be introduced to mar the harmony between the two communities. Akbar and Jahangir did not permit cow-slaughter in towns and cities out of respect for the sentiments of the Hindus. Shah Jahan appears to have allowed it in the cities and towns where Muslim population was in majority.

Innovations and heresies among them were severely suppressed. In 1639-40, Ali Mardan Khan arrested faqirs in Lahore and sent them to Kabul prison. They called themselves 'Independents' (be-qaid) and had renounced prayer and fasting during the month of Ramzan and were the cause of various immoralities and debaucheries. As a matter of fact, the Muslims were forced to follow the Islamic shariat strictly and any deviation from it was looked upon as blasphemous.

Suraj Bhan Brahmin, the author of *Tazkira-i-Pir Hassan Taili* (f. 36 b) testifies to the aforesaid fact. If religious tension did not take grave form, it was probably because of the pantheistic philosophy which had made deep dents into the minds of the liberal religious leaders of the Muslims such as Mian Mir, Mullah Shah and others.

NOTES

1. *Naa'sir-i-Jahangiri*, p. 73.
2. *Jahangir's Memoirs*, translated by Rogers and Beveridge, p. 87.
3. The Sarkar of Bissar Feroza was assigned to him later, *ibid.*, p. 135.
4. *Qazvani*, p. 44.

5. Abdul Hamid Lahori, *Badshah Nama*, p. 448.
6. Saiyid Athar Abhas Rizvi, *Muslim Revivalist Movements in Northern India*, p. 341.
7. The place south of the Badshahi mosque was known as the Nakhas in the early years of this century and this presumably is the spot where the palaces of Asaf Khan were built. The place should not be confused with the Nakhas of later times on the site of the Sultan's Seraei outside the Delhi Gate near Shahid Ganj.
8. *Badshah Nama*, 1(2), p. 13.
9. Muhammad Salih Kamboh, *Amal-e-Salih*, p. 8.
10. Elliot and Dawson, *Badshah Nama*, Vol. 7, p. 67.
11. *Massir-al-Umara* (Eng. Tr.), p. 198.
12. *Badshah Nama*, II, pp. 168-69.
13. Irfan Habib, *Agrarian System of the Mughals*, p. 34.
14. *Badshah Nama*, II, p. 317; Nuhammad Salih Kamboh, *Amal-i-Salih*, II, p. 377.
15. *Badshah Nama*, II, p. 475.
16. Beale, *The Oriental Biographical Dictionary*, p. 126.
17. *Badshah Nama*, II, pp. 283-632.
18. *Badshah Nama*, II, p. 681.
19. Muhammad Salih Kamboh, *Amal-e-Salih*, III, pp. 138, 195, 202 as quoted on page 150 of *Lahore Past and Present* by Muhammad Baqir, University of Punjab, Lahore, published in 1938.
20. *Ibid.*, pp. 231, 239.
21. *Ibid.*, pp. 239, 267.
22. Edited by Cheranji Lal (Delhi 1885), edited by Bulaqi Das and published with Urdu translation.
23. Banarsi Das Saxena, *History of Shah Jahan*, p. 224.
24. B.P. Sexena, pp. 94-95 for further details.
25. *Mazhr-i-Shah Jahani*, Yusaf Malik, Ed. by H.U. Rashid (Karachi 1962), p. 14.
26. Irfan Habib, *op. cit.*
27. Sadiq Khan, *Shah Jahan Nama* (original) 174, II 10 a-b as quoted by M. Athar Ali in his book *The Mughal Nobility Under Aurangzeb*, p. 84.
28. I.H. Qureshi, *A Short History of Pakistan*, p. 99, Book III, University of Harachi, Pakistan.
29. *Badshah Nama*, I, pp. 139-50.
30. *Mazhar-i-Shah Jahani*, p. 177. Ahmed Beg Khan, the grandson of Itmad-ul-Daula whom Shah Jahan had raised to the rank of 2000 zat and 1500 sawar at the time of accession to the throne with the faujdari of Sihistan Sarkar in Sind initiated a reign of terror there. Since he happened to be the nephew of Asaf Khan, he was transferred to Multan, a better place.
31. Bernier Francois, *Travels in the Mughal Empire* A.D. 1656-68, Bombay, 1934 by *Archibald Constable.*

Punjab Under Aurangzeb—Muhiyud Din (1658-1707 C.E.)

7

I

Shah Jahan's illness led to a war of succession in 1656 among his sons. Punjab throughout the war remained faithful to the cause of Dara because firstly it was under Ghairat Khan, a loyal deputy of his and secondly the people here known Dara better because of his intimate association with Mian Mir and his being the viceroy of the province for some time past.

In view of this Dara after he was defeated at Samugarh (4 June 1658) thought it safe to leave Agra forthwith and to proceed to Lahore. He took with him a large number of gold coins, precious stones and other valuable property. His three wives, daughter, Jani Begam and Sipihar Shikoh also accompanied him. Besides, he was followed by about five hundred soldiers. Dara reached Delhi on 5 June 1658 and sent orders to the governor to make over the fortress to him.

Aurangzeb up to this time had traversed many miles on the road to his destination. He had succeeded in imprisoning Murad. Shuja had shown no activity after his defeat by Sulaiman Shikoh. Now he had only to deal with Dara in order to occupy the Imperial throne. Already, he had inflicted a crushing defeat on Dara in the battle of Samugarh and had occupied Agra.

When Aurangzeb came to know of the scheme of Dara to raise a fresh army, he at once won over the governor of Delhi who declined to comply with the orders of Dara and of Shah Jahan to handover the fort to Dara.

The hostility of the governor of Delhi coupled with the fall of Agra fort within five days of its blockade by Aruangzeb

(June 8, 1658) disconcerted the original plan of Dara to put up resistance to Aurangzeb with his own forces and those of his son, Sulaiman Shikoh, which were asked to join him soon.

Under the circumstances, Dara had to take resort to flight from Delhi to Lahore. Punjab, in fact, very much attracted Dara. He looked upon this province as the home of soldiers 'close to Afghanistan from where the hardest mercenaries could be enlisted'. Besides, the Lahore fort had vast assenal and magazine. No wonder, he made up his mind to march to Lahore sending instructions to Ghairat Khan to raise troops. Sulaiman Shikoh was also instructed to join him in Punjab. Letters were despatched to various chiefs and landlords requesting their help.

On 12 June, he left Delhi and started on his march into Punjab. Two weeks after, he reached Sirhind. Here he captured the property of the revenue collector who being hostile to him had fled from there. Then he crossed the Sutlej and destroyed all the boats found at the ferries to check the progress of Aurangzeb's army that was pursuing him. Here he was met by his faithful general Daud Khan who after leaving Sulaiman Shikoh had come hurriedly to help his master. Him he appointed to guard the ferry at Talwan and to oppose the enemy's crossing the river.[1] A second party under Sayyid Ghairat Khan and Musahib Beg was asked to guard the ferry at Ropar. After this, the prince reached the river Beas where he met Guru Har Rai. As the Guru had soft corner for him for his liberal tendencies, and for his being the disciple of Hazrat Mian Mir, he gave him his blessings and detailed a contingent of some of his followers to guard the ferry of the river Beas for him.

Dara reached Lahore on July 3, 1658. In short time, he succeeded in recruiting twenty thousand men. Some Imperial commanders such as Raja Raj Rup, the chief of Nurpur, and Khanjar Khan, the faujdar of Bhera, and Khushal also joined him. Dara also secretly wrote to Aurangzeb's officers and to Rajputs inciting them to rebel against Aurangzeb, but to no avail.

All along, Dara had been sustaining himself on the hope that Aurangzeb's forces would be utterly exhausted due to their long march from the Deccan and two severe battles and he would get time for consolidating and organizing his power. "But in hoping this he had counted without Aurangzeb's energy and strength of will, before which every obstacle, human or physical, gave way."[2]

Aurangzeb after a hurried coronation ceremony in Delhi started towards Punjab in hot pursuit of Dara. He took every step to expedite the pursuit and to this effect ordered his naval department to construct portable boats to cross the rivers of Punjab, for he knew that Dara must have destroyed the extant boats. The aim of Aurangzeb was not to allow enough time to Dara to regroup his forces.

This being so, Aurangzeb deputed Bahadur Khan, one of his generals, to reach the banks of the Sutlej. The general reached there on 2 August 1658. At Talwan, he found the opposite bank very strongly guarded by Daud Khan whose contingent had already been reinforced by another 5000 men sent by some friendly zamindars, had to rush to the ferry of Ropar, sixty miles upstream from Talwan which was very negligently guarded by sayyad Ghairat Khan and Musahib Beg whom Dara had sent from Lahore. He defeated Dara's men and crossed the Sutlej on the night of August 4, 1658. Daud Khan on hearing the news of this disaster retreated towards Sultanpur.

Another division of Aurangzeb's men, under Khalil-ullah Khan, made a forced march to Ropar ferry and crossed it on the night of 7 August. As a result of this, all the ferries of the Sutlej river, that were guarded by Dara's men, were evacuated.

Now the river Beas only separated Dara from his enemy. Dara sent immediate orders to Daud Khan to guard its western bank as strongly as possible and if the circumstances allowed, even give battle. Daud Khan, on finding that Bahadur Khan's forces had already been joined by those of Khalil-ullah Khan, did not think it advisable to risk a battle against such heavy odds.

At this critical juncture Aurangzeb himself reached the Sutlej at Rupar. He sent Jai Singh and Daler Khan with the artillery under Saf Shikan Khan to join Khalil-ullah Khan.

Aurangzeb reached Garh Shankar on August 18, 1658. In the meanwhile, Aurangzeb started using his cleverness and diplomatic skill to weaken the cause of Dara.[3] He wrote a tempting letter to Raja Rup Singh who had taken from Dara ten lakhs of rupees. The Raja deserted the cause of Dara. Another equally successful trick played by Aurangzeb upon Dara was that he caused a forged letter to be written in the name of Daud Khan making him say, "Your Majesty may rest assured that at the first opportunity I will do what I promised and never be false to my word." The letter had the desired effect on Dara who began to suspect Daud. Daud noting the change in his master's behaviour wrote to him: "If your Majesty has any doubt to my fidelity, order me to go and offer my life in the defence of your person and family".[4] The Dara revised his opinion about Daud Khan but only for a while. Another letter of this type from Aurangzeb totally destroyed his confidence in Daud Khan. So he ordered him never to appear in court and his appointment was cancelled.

Raja Raj Rup Singh had already deserted him. His hope that he would get aid from Kabul also did not materialize.

Under the circumstances, future looked bleak to Dara who naturally felt down-spirited. He at once recalled his son Sipihir Shikoh from the ferry of Goindwal and feeling unable to resist the troops that threatened him left Lahore with a force of 13000 or 14000 horses and took the way to Multan.

As per description of Manucci in his book *Storia-da-Mogor*, complete confusion prevailed at Lahore. The city remained absolutely unguarded. The whole of the army was taken away by Dara. Many were made to march even against their consent; others were forcibly enlisted in the army and compelled to march Manucci himself was seized by one Rumi Khan and ordered to start his march for Multan, and he with great difficulty managed to escape, although one of his friends was carried away against his will.

Aurangzeb who had by this time already crossed Sutlej sent his eldest son Prince Mohammad Azam to take charge of Lahore, and himself proceeded to Multan. Dara was betrayed. According to Mohammad Akbar, Aurangzeb after crossing the river sensed that Khalil-ullah Khan had slackened the pursuit of

Dara, due to some fear in his mind and therefore, decided to pursue Dara in person. But this seems to be a more conjecture. As soon as Khalil-ullah Khan received the news of Dara's flight, he sent a party under Tahir Khan to reach Lahore by forced marches in order to keep order in the masterless city, and to save Dara's abandoned property and government stores from being looted. Khalil-ullah Khan himself started towards Lahore and reached near the city soon after. He did not care to enter the city but set off towards Multan. Obviously, Khalil-ullah Khan rushed to Multan to pursue Dara, but since Aurangzeb was ultra cautious in case of Dara, he decided to pursue Dara himself.

Aurangzeb arrived at Multan and paid his homage to the mausoleum of Saint Shaikh Baha-ud-din, where he offered Rs. 1000 as a present. He assigned the responsibility of the pursuit of Dara to his generals and marched back to Lahore where he reached on the 24th of Muharram 1069 A.H. (October 22, 1658).

In this way, Punjab on which Dara had pinned his hope in his bid to gain the throne of Delhi, passed under the hegemony of Aurangzeb. Dara had been deserted by most of his followers and he now fled from post to post for his life and not for the throne. Aurangzeb was thus secure on the throne.

On reaching Lahore, Aurangzeb put up in the garden of Faiz Baksh on the road to Delhi. The following day he was visited in state by Prince Mohammad Azim from the city who was accompanied by Muhammad Amin Khan, Mir Bakhsh and other Omerahs. Aurangzeb in company with the prince made a minute inspection of the fort. Amin-ullah, the Qiladar of the fort, having paid his respects, the Emperor gave his verbal instructions regarding the arrangements to be made in the citadel. On his way back to the garden Farah Bakhsh, Aurangzeb read the prayer in the mosque of Wazir Khan with the congregation. Khalil-ullah Khan was appointed the Viceroy of Punjab, and as a reward for the services rendered by him, the Emperor was pleased to confer on him a jagir assessed at one crore of rupees. Lashkar Khan, the former governor of Kashmir, was appointed the governor of Multan. Khwaja Ismail Kirmani, having been appointed Dewan of Lahore, was honoured with a khillat. Darvish Mohammad was raised to the mansab of 500 horse and Sultan Beg to that of 1400 horses. On the day of the new moon, the Emperor marched to Delhi on October 28, 1658 (30 Muharram 1069 A.H.).[5]

Dara's faithful wife, Nadera Begam, the daughter of Prince Parwez, to whom he was much attached and who had been his faithful companion in all his travels, died of dysentery and vexation. The prince sent her corpse to Lahore in charge of a faithful servant to be interned according to the will of the deceased in the precincts of the mausoleum of Mian Mir. Gul Muhammad along with his seventy troopers escorted the coffin.

On February 8, 1662 A.D., Khalil-ullah Khan became very ill on his way to Delhi, as he went to see the Emperor Alamgir. He was ordered to take rest in his residence at Delhi and Taqqarub Khan and other state physicians were appointed to treat him. Khalil-ullah Khan, having become very weak, did not survive his illness and died on the Rud Rajab 1072 A.H. (February 21, 1662 A.D.). Ibrahim Khan was appointed viceroy of Punjab in place of Khalil-ullah Khan.[6]

In December 1662 the Emperor left Delhi for Lahore en route to Kashmir. On January 6, 1663, as the Emperor reached near Talwandi, Ibrahim Khan, the viceroy of Punjab, also arrived there to receive his Majesty. The Emperor with his court reached Lahore on 2 Rajab 1073 A.H. (February 10, 1663 A.D.) and put up in the gardens of Faiz Bakhsh for a week when he decided to visit the city on February 18, 1663 A.D.[7] (10 Rajab 1073 A.H.). On this day, the Emperor entered the city with Prince Muhammad Muazzam, both of them sharing the same elephant. On the following day, he entered the palace in the Lahore fort. This day being Friday he said his prayers in the mosque of Firoz Khan,[8] in the outskirts of the citadel close to the Hathipal Gate. On this occasion, he proclaimed that on all Fridays the congregation should continue to assemble there in this way to perform their prayers. During this month a sum of Rs. 20000 was distributed among the poor through Abid Khan, the Sadr-ul-Sadar.[9]

II

The court of the Emperor was held in high esteem by the different sovereigns of Asia and Africa and presents were exchanged. Budhak Beg, the envoy of Shah Abbas of Persia, who had visited the Emperor at Lahore was dismissed with presents valued at seven lakh of rupees for his Persian Majesty. Sayyad Yahyia, the envoy of the Sherif of Mecca, to whom six lakhs and thirty thousand rupees had been forwarded, came with a present of Arab horses from his master and was dismissed with a khillat with six thousand rupees.

In 1662, Aurangzeb had a massive embankment of brick work constructed for about four miles along the bank of the river Ravi which had been causing a lot of danger to the city of Lahore. As stated by a contemporary historian, "the quay served as Sad-i-Sikandri (or rampart said to have been built by Alexander to prevent the incursions of Gog and Magog) and not only was the city saved from ruin because stream now began to flow at a distance of one mile to the north."

After staying for 2½ months in Lahore the Emperor started for Kashmir but after crossing the Ravi by a bridge on the same day halted in the Bagh-i-Dilkusha where he held a grand entertainment.[10]

On the Emperor's return from Kashmir, the Emperor stayed for a few days in the garden of Dilkusha across the Ravi. Here he met the Lahore governor, Ibrahim Khan. He offered Rs. 10000 at the mausoleum of his grandfather Jahangir. On November 12, 1663 A.D. (11 Rabi II 1074 A.H.), a grand Durbar was held in the Shah Burj or the Regal tower which is praised "as the bestower of dignity on the highest heaven and as a house of wonder in attempting to see which the sun ascending the nine steps of heaven is itself exalted." The palace was beautifully decorated and looked splendid and magnificent. This being the 46th anniversary of the Emperor, he was weighed against gold, silver and other materials which were given away in alms.

The nobles of the court were honoured with dresses. Among the recipients were Ibrahim Khan, the governor of Lahore, who was the son of Amir-ul-Umera Ali Mardan, Haji Muhammad Tahir, Qiladar Feroz Khan, Faujdar of Dipalpur and Amir Khan, the governor of Kabul. Before leaving for Delhi, the camp was fixed for several days in the gardens of Faiz Bakhsh.

In 1667, Yusafzais revolted under the leadership of Bhagu. Hardly had they been suppressed when Afridis rose in revolt in 1672. They were soon followed by Khataks. The Mughal generals could not achieve success against them, rather some of them, as for instance, Amin Khan and Shujaat Khan met disaster. Aurangzeb now was convinced that a supreme effort should be made to restore Imperial prestige. He himself went to Hasan Abdal between Rawalpindi and Peshawar (7 June 1674) and stayed there for a year and a half directing the operations. During his stay there, he always kept vigilant eye on Punjab affairs. The provisions of food and ammunition were mainly provided by Punjab. Punjab officers such as Fidai Khan were also commissioned to conduct military operations against the turbulent Afghans. The growing popularity of the Sikh movement much upset the emperor who regarded it as a challenge to his authority. When it was reported by his intelligencers that Guru Tegh Bahadur during his tour of Malwa and Bangar had attracted large crowds especially composed of peasantry and the unprivileged classes, he read in it signs of a danger to the established authority. He, therefore, issued orders from Hasan Abdal to arrest Guru Tegh Bahadur and then put him to death at Chandni Chowk Delhi in full gaze of the public with a view to striking terror into the hearts of the people in general. Guru Tegh Bahadur was accordingly arrested at Malikpur Rangran near Rupar and put in one of the dingy cells of the fort of Sirhind where he was kept for about four months after which he was transferred to Delhi in the Kotwali of Chandni Chowk. On November 11, 1675, he was put to death after he declared unequivocally his decision of courting death instead of embracing Islam.

After his return to Delhi from Hasan Abdal the emperor did not pay any visit to Punjab because his attention was chiefly directed to the quelling the rising power of the Marathas in the Deccan and the rebellions of Rajput chiefs in Rajputana. Even then, he was always anxious that Punjab should be administered well. He took care to appoint very able persons to the governorship of the province.

Khalil-ullah Khan (1658-62 A.D.) was an experienced general having seen many actions during the reign of Shah Jahan. Ibrahim (1662-67 A.D.), son of Amir-ul-Umra Ali Mardan was equally experienced in war and administration. During his time Punjab was administered efficiently, a score of grand edifices were raised and law and order situation was comfortable. Muhammad Amin Khan (1667-69) was also a man of probity. Later on the emperor thought it prudent to appoint him as the governor of Badakshan and to solve the problem of tribal disturbances in the north-western frontier region. In this task, however, he totally failed. The Afghans inflicted a crushing defeat on his forces entrenched at Ali Masjid (21 April 1672) and he could escape to Peshawar with great difficulty. Aurangzeb degraded him for his failure which was largely because of his casual manner of conducting the campaign and his over-bearing haughtiness and sent him off to Gujarat as subedar.

After Amin Khan was relieved of his charge of governorship of Punjab, for about two years it is not clear as to who actually held the reins of the government in Punjab. Then Amanat Khan[11] (Sayyid Ahmed Khan) took over the government of Punjab on September 20, 1675. During one and a half years of his rule, he did not allow the administration of the province to grow lax. Quwammuddin Khan[12] (1678-80) succeeded him. He too exerted his utmost to administer the province efficiently. On the eleventh Shaban 1089 A.H. (September 28, 1678 A.D.) news was conveyed to the Emperor that Lahore was facing shortage of food stuffs and the prices had gone up. The Emperor ordered that an additional allowance of Rs. 20 a day be given to Balghur Khana (grain storage).

Towards the close of the year 1680 A.D., it was reported to the Emperor that Sayyid Ali Akbar, the Qazi of Lahore who was an honest and straight forward man, had died during the disturbance caused by the quarrel of his nephew Sayyid Fazil on one side and Quwammuddin Khan, the Viceroy of Punjab and

Nizam-ud-din, the Kotwal of Lahore on the other. Aurangzeb punished Kotwal Nizamuddin with the sentence of death and Quwammuddin Khan the Viceroy of the Punjab was transferred to Ajmer. Prince Muhammad Azam was posted in his place in Lahore[13] in 1680 C.E.

Mukarram Khan succeeded Prince Muhammad Azam Khan. Sipahdar Khan, the son of Khan Jahan Bahadur, took over from Mukarram Khan (November 2, 1686 A.D.). The agents of Prince Muhammad Azam managed the affairs of Punjab for some time after Sipahdar Khan was removed from this post. He undoubtedly possessed the qualities which make one a good administrator. He was followed by a galaxy of viceroys, such as Khan Jahan Bahadur (1690-93), Mahabat Khan Ibrahim (1693-96), Mukarram Khan (1696), Abu Nast Khan (1696-?), Ibrahim Khan (?-1699), Muhammad Muazzam (1699-?), Zabardast Khan (?-1704) and agents of Prince Muazzam (1704-07).[14]

III

Administrative Structure

In administrative structure practically no changes were introduced. The old machinery was allowed to exist and operate as it was in the reign of Shah Jahan. The evil tendencies in the administration that had surfaced in the reign of Shah Jahan went on gathering strength; nothing was done to counteract their adverse effects. The problem of assignments which had started during the reign of Shah Jahan became acuts and posed a serious crisis during the later half of Aurangzeb's reign. The area of crown lands was considerably reduced thus impeding the government to release more lands for assignments to Jagirdars. There was an enormous influx into the ranks of Mansabdars from the Deccan as officers of the Deccan kingdoms and the Marathas who had to be bought over in order, at least, to be neutralised. The number of mansabdars, as a result thereof, increased to such an extent that the existing jagirs could no longer suffice for their pay. In one of his letters Aurangzeb himself refers to the scarcity of Paibaki and the crowd of men claiming pay and declares that everything 'flesh and bone' has been assigned and no further demands for assignment could be entertained by the court. Ma'Mari and Khafi Khan have made similar statements. Large numbers, we are told, had become jagirless. Persons appointed to mansabs could not obtain jagirs for years and if a jagir was transferred from the hands of any one, he might not get another. The older nobility (called Khanzadan) were extremely indignant at the way their claims were disregarded to provide for the Deccanis. The small mansabdars who possessed neither money nor the influence to induce the officers of the court to assign them jagirs were the greatest sufferers in the crisis posed by the assignment problem. They were often made to wait for quite a long time to get their jagirs. Not unoften, the jagirs were assessed at higher level than the actual receipts from them, inducing jagirdars to adopt objectionable and unfair means to fill their coffers to the agony of the peasants. The assignments given as 'Madd-i-Maash' also increased in number and almost all Muslim saints and tombs were obliged by giving 'Madd-i-Maash' which were increasingly made hereditary by Aurangzeb during the course of his reign. These grants were invariably given to the Muslims. These assignments entitled the assignees to their share of the government revenue and not to the occupancy rights.

In the fiscal administration of the province there were significant changes. On 9 May 1667, the Emperor abolished the custom duty altogether on the case of Muslim traders while that on the Hindu traders was retained at the old level. The real loss to the state was likely to be still greater as the Hindu traders had now a strong temptation to pass their goods off as the property of Muslims, in collusion with the latter. An order of 1671 of Aurangzeb asked Punjab viceroy to replace his Hindu head clerks (peshakars) and accountants (diwanian), if possible, with Muslims. Under Aurangzeb Qanungoship on condition of turning Muslim became a proverbial expression; and several families in the Punjab still preserve his letters patent in which this condition of office is unblushingly laid down. In 1679, by an Imperial order, Jazia was reimposed on the 'unbelievers' "to spread Islam and to put down the practice of infidelity". The assessees were roughly divided into three classes according as their property was estimated (i) Poor—having not more than

800 dirhams as annual income; (ii) Middle—having between 800 and ten thousand dirhams as annual income; (iii) Rich—with income above ten thousand. Money-changers, cloth dealers, land owners, merchants and physicians were placed at the highest class, while artisans such as tailors, dyers, cobblers and shoe-makers were counted as poor. This last class paid only when the professional income left a margin above the cost of maintaining themselves and their families. Beggars and paupers naturally were exempted from the tax. The rates of taxation were fixed at 12, 24 and 48 dirhams per year for the three classes respectively (or Rs. $3^{1}/_{3}$, $6^{2}/_{3}$ and $13^{1}/_{3}$). On the poor, therefore, the incidence of the tax was atleast 6 per cent of their gross income, on the middle class it ranged from 6 to 6¼ per cent and on the rich it was always higher even than 2½ per thousand. In violation of modern canons of taxation, the Jazia hit the poorest portion of the population the hardest, and annually took away from the poor man the full value of one year's food as the price of religious indulgence. Akbar had abolished the tax and removed the individious badge of degradation from the majority of his subjects (A.D. 1564). Aruangzeb reversed this policy.

Aurangzeb's reign is marked for the ascendancy of Muslim orthodoxy in imperial policies. According to Lane Poole, "For the first time in their history, the Mughals beheld a rigid Muslim in their Emperor—a Muslim as sternly repressive of himself as of his people around, a king who was prepared to stake his throne for the sake of his faith."[15] "Exception apart of fermans occasionally breathing a qualified toleration, it cannot be gainsaid that Aurangzeb aimed at the establishment of Dar-ul-Islam which implied the eradication of heresy even among the Muslims and a calculated and sustained Jahad against the infidels. The destruction of temples (1669 onwards), the dismissal of the Hindus from the revenue department (1671), the reimposition of Jazia (1679) and so on, were but the alphabet of unmistakable bigotry."

This policy of bigotry in the religious sphere affected the social life very deeply. The Hindus and other non-Muslims in the State were completely demoralised. The Hindu peasantry and Hindu artisans apart from sharing the hardship which their counterparts among the Muslims also suffered because of the crisis of the mansabdari system and of the exploitative nature of the Mughal rule, had to suffer more because the non-Muslims had to pay Jazia and custom duties at a higher rate. The Hindus reacted differently to this environment. Many of them acquiesced in their fate, a chunk of them quietly nursed anger within the deep recesses of their hearts and quite a large number of them began to search for some alternative. Sikh religion provided a kind of alternative and no wonder the Hindus in a very large number embraced Sikhism because in it they found the hope for freedom from their sufferings.

The atmosphere of repression and suppression was choking indeed. Quite a few Hindu men of letters flocked to the court of Guru Gobind Singh at Anandpur and dedicated themselves to serve the cause of Sikhism through their pen and speech. They produced works of a very high quality to educate people to shed off passivity, cynicism and inertia. It is believed that their number touched the figure of 126.[16] They were liberally helped by Guru Gobind Singh.

The relevance of Sikhism to the contemporary phenomenon and its ideology having the potentiality to guide the people in future also gave impetus to the rapid growth and expansion of the Sikhs. The inauguration of the order of the Khalsa on the Baisakhi day of 1699 was a response to the problems current as well as those likely to emerge in future. The Khalsa was atonce a social pattern, a committed brotherhood and an instrument to promote the cause of social harmony and peace as against political tyranny and religious particularism of ruling classes, comprising mostly the Muslims.

The swing towards orthodoxy did not have healthy effect even on the Muslims. Many of them under its impact began to consider themselves as a privileged class born to get employment and high status thereby making them ease-loving and lazy. Besides, the process of evolving composite culture which was ushered in by Akbar suffered a serious setback. A Muslim was urged to look to Persia and Arbia for inspiration rather than Indian tradition. Even his civil criminal law must be derived from the writings of jurists and the decisions of judges in Baghdad or Cairo. The Muslims in India became, to all intents and purposes, intellectual foreigners.

Although they were still people among both the major religious groups, the Hindus and Muslims, as for instance the disciples of Mian Mir, etc. but their voice was almost inaudible in the din and noise of communal clangor. The orthodox section of the Muslim population became more assertive, more aggressive and many a time unreasonable. Their centre was Sirhind and their important religious movement was that of Nacshbandis. In Aurangzeb's reign, Sayyids, Shaikhs and Ulemas received great patronage. The Ihtisab department opened avenues for employment to a large number of Ulemas from whom Qazis, Muftis and Mahtasabs were drawn with the result that all those persons began to preach Islam in its orthodox form with special emphasis on 'Millat' and 'Jehad' a crusade against infidelity (shirk) and Biddat (innovation).

NOTES

1. Manucci, *Storia-de-Mogor*, Vol. I, p. 358.
2. J.N. Sarkar, *History of Aurangzeb*, p. 105.
3. Mannucci, *op. cit.*, p. 311.
4. M. Akbar, *Punjab Under the Mughals*, p. 182.
5. Munshi Muhammad Kazim, *Alamgir Nama*, p. 203.
6. *Ibid.*, p. 766.
7. *Ibid.*
8. The site of the mosque is not known.
9. *Mushi Mohammed Kazim, op. cit.*, p. 767.
10. *Ibid.*, p. 815.
11. Musta-id-Khan, *Maasir-i-Alamgiri*, p. 143.
12. *Ibid.*, p. 166.
13. *Ibid.*
14. The Deputy Governor was Munim Khan.
15. Lane Poole, *Medieval India*, p. 70.
16. Surjit Singh Gandhi, *History of Sikh Gurus Rotold*, Vol. II, pp. 1-138, Atlantic Publishers, Delhi.

8 Administrative Apparatus

The geo-political situation of Punjab has always posed administrative problems. The vulnerability of the province to foreign invasions through the passes of the mountains in the north-west frontier of the province has constantly stood on the nerves of the rulers of Punjab or India, thereby constraining them to concentrate their attention on the defence of the province. The root tendency of the tribal people in the north-west to be unruly, refractory and independent led them to take special measures to keep them under control and also to protect the people from internal disorder. The position did not differ during the Mughal rule. It always lurked in the minds of the Mughal emperors to have full control of the province. To do so, another factor which was non-existent during the period of sultanate but which became predominant during the Mughal rule and increased the importance of Punjab was that Kabul and Qandhar became part of the Mughal empire and the route connecting them with Delhi passed through the province. Moreover, the fertility of its lands and the sturdiness of its people added another facet to their outlook in Punjab affairs. In view of all this, the Mughal administration of Punjab came to possess some distinctive characteristics which were as under:

(i) That Punjab was always under strict vigilance of the Emperor who showed keen sensitivity to the problems cropping up in this province.

(ii) Special care was taken while making appointments of the subedars of this province. Often, the governors of this province were men of sharp intelligence, high personal merit and great administrative ability, and whenever, any subedar did not come up to the expectation of the Emperor, he was relieved of his administrative duties forthwith.

Territory of Punjab

The boundaries of Punjab extended and contracted from time to time. In the early Mughal period, Punjab extended from the river Sutlej to the river Indus, a distance of 180 kos, and its breadth extended from Bhimber to Chaukhadi, a distance of 87 kos. During Emperor Akbar and after, Multan was organised into a separate province and Kashmir was incorporated into the province of Kabul.

For adminstrative purpose there was no Suba of the name of Punjab. There was Lahore Suba. The Ain (1,539-49) groups Parganas of the Suba Lahore under five Doabs (tract situated between two rivers) namely, Sind Sagar Doab, Chan Hat Doab, Rachna Doab, BET, Jalandhar Doab)—each of the tracts constituted Sarkar and administrative unit of the province. The area not inclusive in the boundaries of the tract or falling into a Doab was treated as Birun-i-Punjab (outside five rivers) and could be administrated not necessarily from the nearest headquarters of a Sarkar. Each Sarkar comprised Parganas[1] (Mahals) whose number was different during different periods (I) of the Mahal rule. In areas where the means of communication were scantily, a further sub-division was made which was called Tapa.[2] It consisted of 327 Mahals (parganas) in 1759. The total area of the measured land was 24319-960 bighas and the total provincial revenue Rs. 15981111.

The divisions were made on the basis of the revenue assessment. Moreland, however, suggests that the administrative and fiscal divisions quite distinct from each other, his proposition being that the jurisdiction of the Faujdar extended over an administrative charge quite distinct and independent of the fiscal units of the Sarkar and parganah. In P. Saran's view, such a distinction did not exist. He holds the opinion that the administrative charge and fiscal jurisdiction of a Sarkar coincided. In recent times, the controversy has been taken further and an attempt has been made to establish "that the faujdari constituted an independent administrative unit and its territorial limits varied from place to place and from time to time". This amounts to re-asserting what Moreland had said earlier. Moreover, on careful scrutiny of the evidence available, U.N. Dey concludes that the regular divisions and sub-divisions were the "Sarkars and the Parganas and the example of faujdaris only referred to some exceptional cases among out of fiscal administrative considerations. It is also significant that the term faujdar and faujdari were also used in the Mughal administration just to convey the meaning of administrator and his charge."

Mughal Monarch was different from the Monarch of the Sultanate period. The Sultan as the Monarch during the Sultanate period was a recognised leader of the community—the status which evolved as Islam escalated. He was to act as the Chief of the Executive, Judiciary and other branches of administration. But he was to exercise his power or authority within the orbit of the Quranic injunctions, Hadiths and the sayings of the prophet. He possessed no divine rights. He was rather a choice of the community which came to be established either through election or nomination or by displaying extra-ordinary qualities. He was to recognise the authority of a Khalifa, which he did by reference on the coins or in the Khutba to Khalifa or by definite acts of allegiance.

The Mughal monarch on the other hand considered himself all-powerful, free to exercise his power and authority in all spheres of administration. He seemed to have carved his position on basis of Changezian and Tumurian traditions interpersed with the traditions built up by the Safvi dynastic rule in the contemporary Persia. His authority was un-restricted in the sense that he had not to refer to Quran, or Hadiths for guidance like the Sultan. He himself was Imam-i-Adil (Chief Judge) as well as sole arbiter during disputations on the interpretations of Quranic or Hadiths texts. Like Changez "he asserted that the external heavens had delegated to him a divane mission designating him only legitimate ruler of the world and transmitting that soverignty to the descendants. He was Khalifa himself in his territory and did not recognise any Khalifa whether of the Abbasids or Umayyads as it was done during the Sultanate period by the Sultans.

Akbar's Vazir Abu Fazal Allami (d. 1602) author of the celebrated *Akbar Nama* and the *Ain-i-Akbari* based on the Turmuride/Chingised precedent developed a fabulous Quranic mythology for the most beloved Emperor, tracing the divine light which penetrated the legendry Mughal Queen Alankuva and which sustains the universe to the emperor's bloodline to finally become manifest in him. This was intended to justify the divine right of the Mughal King. In a sense, as Michel Foucault argues, the king could always know every thing because he was the one who determined (as god's representative on earth) the truth.

Such a status or position of Mughal Emperor was continued to be the preserve of all the Mughal Monarchs with a little difference and that too of emphasis. Even the monarch such as Aurangzeb who openly proclaimed his sponsorship of Islamic orthodoxy did not fundamentally change the concept as well as action-model as configured by *Akbar Nama*. Unlike Akbar to a great extent and to a small extent Jahangir and Shah Jahan, he did not subscribe to electicism or religious pluralism and took pleasure in bolstering up Islamic unitarianism. Yet he did not adopt that part of Islamic polity which recommended devolution of authority among ulemas or Muslim people. The Mughal King, therefore, sat at the pinnacle of the empire and the power and authority to manage what has been described as a patrimonial bureaucratic imperial state by Bonniec Wade in his book *Imaging Sound,* p. 4, To achieve this objective, he was assisted to a great extent by the Persian model of the organisation of bureaucracy which has based on gradations, from the lowest point to the highest. The Mansabdari system which determined the nature, rank of bureaucrats was the creation of this type of thinking.

The whole territory under the Mughal Monarch was divided into provinces each under a Subedar under whom worked a team of officials at Sarkar, Pargana and village levels. Subedar was selected carefully by the Mughal Monarch and was to hold that position as long as the Mughal Monarch wished. The loyalty and submission to the emperor were the two most important qualifications for the Subedar to retain his position. He was not a replica of Mughal Emperor as Ishwari Prasad has held, he was just a member of the bureaucracy which was designed on the bases of relationships between different members of a family. In view of all this, it is not difficult to surmise that Subedars in the provinces enjoyed no autonomy except in minor and local-level cases.

This perhaps is the reason that no important creative initiative is in evidence at provincial level which could add new vistas to the prevalent administrative or social structures to stimulate society to galvanise itself to become a progressive force.

The Subedar, in fact, was an instrument in the hands of the Emperor to serve and advance his designs. The prosperity of the province depended directly upon the quality of monarch. The concepts such as human rights, freedom of expression and rule of law, soverignty of the people, etc. which had started influencing the polity in some European countries was a far cry in the Mughal Punjab. Despite limitations within which, Subedar had to work, subedar had importance of his own because the success of provincial administration depended on his efficiency, his capability to execute orders of the monarch quickly and precisely, and his tact to handle day-to-day challenges.

Suba Administration

The head of the province under Akbar was officially called Sipahsalar. Under his successors, he was designated Nazim; but, popularly, he was known as subedar or simply Suba. He was vicegerent of the monarch and held the over-all responsibility of the provincial administration. Next to him in official status was Dewan, but he was, in no way, subordinate to the Subedar. In the provincial government Dewan was responsible for the revenue administration, civil justice and general supervision over the department of the Sadr. The Subedar was responsible for the executive, defence and criminal justice and exercised over-all control. The other important officers attached with provincial government were Bakhshi, the Sadr, the Qazi, the Waqinawis, Bayatut and the Censor.

Principal Provincial Authorities

The Subedar's appointment was effected through Imperial farman called Farman-I-Shahi. The provincial Dewan was appointed through the farman called Hasb-ul-Hukm and the sanad appointing him bore the seal of Diwan-i-Ala (Chief Diwan). The provincial Bakhshi who also often worked as Waqi Nawis was appointed through the office of Mir Bakhshi under his seal. The provincial sadr was appointed on the recommendation of Sadr-us-Sadar by an Imperial Sanad, which bore the seal of Sadr-us-Sadar. The Qazi of the Subah as well as those of the towns and parganas were appointed under the seal of the Sadr-us-Sadar by imperial Sanads, to be obtained from the office of the Sadr of the Subah and not directly. The provincial Sadr often acted as the Muhtasib of the province as well as of the towns where he was hosted. The office of Muhtasib of the province as also of the towns was filled in by the Imperial Sadr.

Duties and Functions of the Subedar

Subedar (provincial governor) was assigned the duties of maintaining peace and order, general supervision of all the departments working under him, to ensure the smooth and successful collection of revenue, and to execute the royal decrees and orders sent to him. He recommended officers for promotion and imperial honours and collected the tributes due from the local feudatory chiefs and remitted these to the Imperial treasury. He kept the Emperor informed of what was happening in the province and carried out the orders he received from the Emperor. He could conclude peace but the terms were subject to ratification by the Emperor, who could modify them or reject them.[3]

Moreover, he was to administer justice. In connection with this business, he was instructed to dispose of the cases expeditiously. In trying cases, he was not to rely on witnesses and oaths but to investigate the matter personally. In giving punishments, he was to be forgiving and mild, and not to discriminate between persons of different status. He was not authorised to inflict penalty of death on any one. He, however, was expowered to send such cases to the Imperial court along with a full account of them. But if he, however, feared imminent risk of sedition by sending bad characters to court, and felt immediate action necessary, he could apply the last remedy of the law. He heard appeals against the decisions of Qazi and Mir-i-Adal.[4]

His next duty was that of vigilance. He was expected to keep intelligent men in the secret information service and use them with firmness and tact and also to appoint reliable and dutiful persons for the country police. Besides this, he was to devote attention to the comforts and prosperity of the people and encourage agriculture and works of irrigation, roads, sarais, gardens and hospitals, wells, reservoirs and other similar works. Furthermore, he was to inspect the soldiery and not to let them become too expensive and wasteful. He was to report all important matters to the imperial court. To facilitate the work of the governor, the principal jagirdars and other officers were ordered to obey and cooperate with him so that under his guidance, prosperity may prevail in the province. Any jagirdar who defied his orders or acted contrary to the expected norm of the administration could be punished by him.

"The governors, however, were not allowed to assume royal aigrettes in the Imperial darbar in the exercise of those powers which were the special prerogative of royalty."[5] In the sixth year of his reign, Jahangir circulated that "the provincial governors should not show themselves in Jharokha, nor to ask their officers to keep guard or salute them, nor to inflict punishment of blinding or mutilation of any limb, nor force Islam on anyone, nor to confer titles on servants, nor order royal servants to do *kornish* or prostration, nor force singers to remain in attendance as in the Imperial darbar, nor beat drums when they went out, nor to seal anything they wrote."

Dewan

The provincial Dewan was the next most important officer in the province but he was not directly subordinate to subedar, rather his rival in the province. He was selected by the Diwan-i-Ala and was appointed directly by the court. He acted directly according to the orders of the Imperial Dewan and was in every way responsible to him. In the year 1596, Akbar issued an order that all provincial Dewans should report their proceedings to him in accordance with the suggestions of the Chief Dewan Khwaja Shams-ud-din.[6] He was instructed to report to Diwan-i-Ala twice every month the occurrences of the Subah with a statement of the cash balance with him.

The Dewan, being the head of the civil and revenue department and the officer-incharge of the finances, had manifold duties to perform. According to P. Saran, his duties were "the collection of the revenue from the Khalsa mahals and keeping the accounts of the balances and the receipts and supervising the lands assigned for charitable endowments, the allotment and disbursing of salaries to officers of the province according to their ranks (grades) and administering the financial business in relation to the jagirs assigned according to the royal sanads in the Khalsa Sarkars. All the aforesaid transactions were to bear the seal of the provincial Dewan. Besides this, his agents in different parts of the province realised sales tax, Rahadari dues, octori and whatever other taxes were levied by proper authorization for the purposes appointed by the Emperor or the Imperial Dewan".[7]

Furthermore, the dewan was to strive for the growth of agriculture and keep strict watch over the treasuries. He was to see that no official should extract the forbidden cesses. He was authorised to convert payment of revenue from one form into another for convenience of the cultivators. The Dewan was sometimes invested with the auditor's office also. He exercised full control over the allocation of expenditure to different departments.[8] He kept the following records:

(i) Records dealing with the executive department together with separate files of the revenue of the mahals of the Khalsa under the seals and signatures of the Qanungos and Zamindars and the estimates, realizations and expenditure together with Roznamchas and Awarijas under the seal of the Karori (Collector).

(ii) Records pertaining to the department of the Mahals of the jagir lands in the order of the amount of salaries granted by the Emperor.

(iii) Records dealing with the departments of Inams, lands, commissions to Headmen, Qanungos and Muqaddams.

(iv) Records of the deposits in the treasury under the seals of Karories and Fatohdars.

(v) The Roznamcha of the income and expenditure.

In short, in the Daftar Khana or record room of the Dewan, papers pertaining to all items in which some finance was involved were preserved. The copies of these records were prepared and sent to the Diwan-i-Ala. Sometimes the copies were preserved and the originals were sent. "However, the item that received his special attention was the revenue accounts of the mahals, and whenever there was any transfer of some mahals, a due note and return was prepared and sent to the centre under his seal."[9]

The duties of the Dewan being varied and vital, he was allowed quite a big secretariat which consisted of officers to be appointed by the centre as well as those appointed locally by the Dewan of the province. Peshkar (secretary or personal assistant), Darogha (office superintendent) who was also a mansabdar, Munsif and treasurer were appointed by the centre. On the other hand, Munshi of the Dewan's court (kachehri), Hazur Niwas, Muharrer-i-Khalsa, Muharrar-i-Daftari-i-Tan and Muharrer for weighing and measuring—all these officers were appointed by the Dewan himself.

The provincial Dewan enjoyed a unique position in the Mughal administration. Since he was to be appointed, promoted and dismissed by the centre, he was responsible to the centre wherefrom he received directly his orders and to which he submitted his accounts directly and regularly. In financial matters, he enjoyed the same position as was occupied by the governor in executive matters. Thus, there were two parallel and mutually independent organizations in the province. The

Diwan was the head of a large number of services on the revenue side from the Amalguzar down to the Patwari.

The purpose of creating two parallel organizations was to create a check on the highest officials of the province. The Subedar and the Diwan kept a jealous watch over each other's activities and reported them to a headquarters. But from this it does not follow that the centre wanted to create a perpetual rift and clash between the two officials; rather mutual co-operation and collaboration were anxiously sought for. In case, they failed to co-operate with each other, the centre transferred or recalled[10] one or the other or even both of them. Where there was a difference of opinion between the Subedar and Dewan, the matter was to be referred to the centre.

Even then the status and rank of the Dewan was lower than those of the governor who being high mansabdar and the head of the executive commanded much greater prestige and honour in the eyes of the people.

Sadr

Another important officer of the provincial government was Sadr. He was appointed by the centre. His primary duty was distribution of the stipends and other financial assistance to Ulemas to encourage them to promote learning. He was also to settle the disputes arising out of succession to these grants. The judicial department of the Subah was under the Qazi of the province. However, at the provincial level, quite often a person who was appointed as Sadr was also entrusted with the work of judiciary or in other words he acted as the provincial Qazi as well in which capacity he recommended names for the appointment of the Qazis at the district level. At more than one place in Mughal records, he is also called Mir Adil. "This we find that the three offices i.e. those of the Sadr, the Qazi and Mir Adil though mentioned separately in some records, in actual practice often seem to have been entrusted to the same person. But existence of instances of different persons holding these offices indicate that the three officers had not been amalgamated into one."[11] He governed Sayurghal the lands for religious and charetable purposes. The revenue of such lands, according to Muslim Law was one-tenth of the produce. It was called the Ushr.

Bakhshi

The organisation of the army and mansabdari system had considerably increased the importance of the office of Mir Bakhshi[12] at the centre. Because of the posting of the mansabdars and the army in different provinces, it was essential that a counterpart of the Mir Bakhshi should be created in the provinces to act as a link between the centre and the province. No doubt, the provincial Bakhshi served as a link. The chief duties of this official were:

(i) recruitment of soldiers,

(ii) maintenance of troops in good order,

(iii) holding periodical inspections of the troops of Mansabdars in the province, and

(iv) enforcing branding regulations, inspecting horses and other animals belonging to the army and passing the pay bills both of the Mansabdars and their soldiers.

At the time of an expedition it was the duty of the Bakhshi to see that all the Mansabdars and other officers were summoned to take part with their quotas of men and horses. He had to report to the Emperor all that happened in the province as a result of the expeditions and the progress of the work of the various departments in the province. By virtue of this position, he could report provincial matters to the Emperor[13] without referring to the governor of the province.

The office of the political remembrancer was also attached to that of the provincial Bakhshi. In his capacity as Waqia Nigar, he appointed his agents in Parganas, in Sarkars and in the offices of the Nazim, the Dewan and in the courts of justice, in fact, in almost all the branches of administration. The duty of the agents was to regularly report the incidents of those places. The Bakhshi prepared abstracts of all that he considered relevant or useful and passed them on to the provincial Darogha of Dak (Postmaster General) who despatched them to the Imperial court along with other dispatches.

It was also the function of the bakhshi to prepare the list of the properties of a diseased mansabdar, but often news reporters in the pargnahs were entrusted with this task and they reported directly to the provincial Dewan.[14]

The provincial army consisted of three different kinds of forces. First, the contingents which every high official from the governor downwards had to maintain in accordance with his mansab. This was, of course, part of the regular standing army of the empire. It was maintained more for the general service of the empire than for that of the province. At first, it was paid usually by assignments made carrying an income equal to the salary of the assignees. Later on, the system of assignment was discouraged by Akbar and disbursements of salaries were made directly from the Imperial treasuries.[15]

The second category of the provincial army consisted of the contingents of certain minor zamindars which were attached to the provincial governors to assist them whenever called upon.

The third and the most important class of local or provincial forces consisted of the members of cavalry, infantry and other arms mentioned in the Ain in the accounts of the subahs as the quotas of Sarkars and Mahals. According to P. Saran, the army was really in the nature of a militia and not a regular army. Nor was it a part of the zamindar's levies. The figures given in the Ain represent, in reality, the general estimate of sort of a militia or a fighting man-power, which, each province, Sarkar or Mahal, was expected to be able to raise and supply to the government in time of need or whenever demanded to do so. The proporation of the contribution of cavalry of each locality was determined more by the martial qualities than by the mere numerical strength of its population and that of infantry more by the numerical strength than by the martial qualities. Lahore was rated only next to Ajmer in cavalry contribution. Bengal combined with Orissa led in the infantry contribution.

Diwan-i-Bayutut

Diwan-i-Bayutut was the representative of Khan-i-Saman in the province.[16] He looked to the comfort of the emperor while he was on tour. He supervised Imperial stores and other state workshops. He registered property of the deceased persons in order to secure the payments of the dues to the state. He made provisions for the karkhanas (factories) and fixed prices of the articles manufactured. He also looked after roads and buildings.

Secret Services and Harkarahas

As time passed on, the waqia or legal remembrancer began to be suspected of collusion with the local officers. In view of this, a new set of officers, viz. sawani-nigars (who were called khufia nawis also) were appointed. They were to remain secretly in all important places and transmit news not only about the government officials, but also about all other happenings. Like the system of waqia-nigars, the agents of the secret reporters were also appointed to watch the conduct of the governor and other departments and through them were conveyed the farmans and orders from the headquarters, concerning the attachment of the jagirs of the deceased, of the discharged and of the mansabdars, fallen in the estimation of emperor or concerning other administrative business. With the passage of time swan-i-nawises who began as a secret branch of the intelligence department became established as an open parallel organisation of reporters with the waqia-nawis who were more of the nature of the office recorders and reporters.

According to P. Saran, the transformation of the secret service into an open service necessitated the creation of another secret service. These were named the harkaras. They were appointed from the office of the chief superintendent of the harkaras. Like the agents of waqia-nawis and swani-nigars, their agents also used to sit in the court of the governor and other officers. They reported all happenings in different localities to the governor as also to the Imperial court.

This department of intelligence took some time to be organised into a vigorous and effective machinery under Akbar. It has been recorded by Jahangir that the department had been fully re-organised by his father who had made a rule that events of the subahs be reported according to the boundaries of each and news writers for this purpose had been appointed. The system brought inestimable advantages to the empire. It brought the news of different happenings in different parts of the province thereby enabling the competent authority to take requisite steps in time. In 1578, Akbar in the course of his tour was informed of a case of encroachment on the maddi-mash land. The Emperor redressed the grievance forthwith. Even such occurrences the death of a traveler on the road by a sudden storm was reported to Jahangir.

Sarkar (District) Administration

For administrative convenience, the province was divided into sarkars which were further sub-divided into Parganas or Mahals. The territorial division of the province into sarkars was mainly done on revenue-assessment basis. Each sarkar had a set of officers whose duties and functions are described below.

Faujdar

He was the executive head of the sarkar appointed directly by the Mughal Imperial authority by farman-i-sabti, although he worked under the general supervision of the Bakhshi. His primary duty was to maintain peace and order, to keep the roads free from robbers and thieves and to enforce the Imperial regulation in his area. He was required to give assistance to the Amil in the collection of revenue and to guard the frontiers and the royal areas of his sarkar. He had a small military contingent at his disposal obviously to maintain law and order and also to see that the government officials discharged their duties without any interference from outside. Furthermore, it was his duty to keep the army fully equipped and in readiness for action. He also worked as kotwal of the rural areas which had no kotwal of their own.[17]

But he had no authority to interfere in the revenue and judicial affairs, nor he did exercise the magisterial powers which were entrusted to other officers of the Sarkar.[18] In fact, in the Sarkar he only represented the executive functions of the Sipahsalar or Subedar of a province.

Later on, sometime during the period of later Mughals, the Faujdar began to exercise judicial authority also.[19]

Amil or Amilguzar

Next to the faujdar, the most important officer in the sarkar was the Amil who functioned under the supervision and instructions of the provincial Dewan. He was responsible for controlling the lower revenue officials such as surveyors, assessors and others. He, after the completion of assessment, was required to send a copy of the abstract, within fifteen days to the Imperial Dewan's office who could approve of this report or could depute a commissioner to investigate and ascertain the accuracy of the report.

The Amil was also responsible for the collection of revenue in the Khalsa land and for depositing it in the treasury. When the amount touched two lakh dams, it was remitted to the central treasury. He was also required to inspect the sayurghal tenures and send copies of the same to the registry office to be compared with the copies kept there. It was his duty to ascertain the correctness of the Chaknamah and to resume the share of the deceased granter or one who was an absentee.[20] He was paid from Imperial treasury, the abstract of his salary being endorsed by the seals of the kotwal and Diwan-i-Subah.

The obligations and powers, according to Dr. Saran, can be stated under a few broad heads, viz. (i) watch and ward, (ii) control of the market, (iii) care and legitimate disposal of heirless property, (iv) vigilance over the people's conduct and prevention of crime, (v) prevention of social abuses such as sati, and (vi) regulation of the cemeteries, burials and slaughter houses.[21]

For the successful performance of his first duty, the Kotwal was asked to divide the whole town into wards and appoint a headman for each ward who should answer for all untoward happenings in his ward. For thefts and robberies committed within the town, the Kotwal was responsible for making good the losses. It appears that the idea was only to make the Kotwal feel his responsibility seriously, but the Kotwal, perhaps for fear of undergoing loss, in case robberies are not traced out punished even those persons who were unconnected with the crime. The effectiveness of supervision by the Kotwal has been borne out by the remarks of Manucci and Thevonat. In addition the town Kotwal had to regulate markets which he did by examining weights and punishing those who kept short weights.

Moreover, he was to guard the property of persons dying suddenly or without heir, prepare an inventory of all such effects and report the matter to the court so that they might be handed over when a legitimate heir might appear.

Furthermore, he was to prevent manufacture as well as use of spirituous liquors. He was also to see that the prostitutes and public women lived in separate quarters outside the town. Besides this, the Kotwal's duty was to prevent forcible sati, and also to prevail upon those, who willingly desired to become sati, to desist from the act.

He was also to prevent circumcision under twelve and prevent infanticide. The control of slaughter-houses was also in his charge. He was to take care that on certain days animals were not butchered. He was also to locate the cemetery outside the town at such a place that it might not be detrimental to health.

The kotwal of the Sarkar towns also acted as a senior criminal magistrate[22] over the shiqdar of a parganah and if his headquarter town happened to a custom post, he also acted as custom officer and magistrate.

As the functions enjoined upon the Kotwal were too varied and vast, he could appoint assistants to carry out the various duties incidental to his office.

Qazi

The main function of the Qazi was administration of justice but he also performed certain non-judicial duties. He controlled the funds for religious purposes and the department to providing clothes to the poor in the Sarkar. Payment of madadi-mash sanctioned by Sadr-us-Sadr required his concurrence.

Under Aurangzeb, the Qazi was also required to collect jaziya and zakat and was provided with a separate staff for this work. Besides this, he was required to look after the public mosques within his jurisdiction. The marriages of the Muslims were solemnized before him.

"These non-judicial functions atonce made the Qazi a very important officer in the Sarkar and at the same time provided him with ample scope for corruption. Aurangzeb recognised this aspect and on account of this, he gave the following instructions: Be just, be honest, be impartial. Hold the trials in the presence of the parties and at the court houses and seat of the government. Do not accept presents from the people of the place where you serve. Attend not entertainments given by anybody and everybody know the poverty to be your glory."[23] The Qazi was assisted by Mufti and Adil.[24]

Parganah Administration

Each Sarkar was divided into parganas or Mahals, the lowest fiscal administrative unit. It had a Tehsildar in-charge of the collection of revenue. It was at the parganah treasury that the land revenue was actually paid to the state by the Muqaddams. Sometimes the peasants directly paid revenue into the treasury. The Tehsildar was helped by a staff of clerks. One controlled the treasury, another kept the account of the money realised from various sources and the third, recorded all the areas which were due.

Principal officers at the parganah level of administration were as under:

Shiqdar

The executive head of the Parganah was the Shiqdar who discharged the functions which were divided in the Sarkar between the Faujdar and Kotwal. He was in-charge of law and order, the criminal justice in the parganah and the general administration by virtue of being the executive officer of the parganah. He was to take note of the arrivals and departings of dangerous men and not to allow anyone to reside in the town who had no ostensible means of livelihood. One of his primary duties was to assist the amil in the realisation of revenue, whenever force became necessary for the purpose. With some limited powers, the Shiqdar also acted as criminal magistrate.

Amil in the Parganah had the same duty as the Amilguzar had to perform at the sarkar level, i.e. he was to deal directly with the peasantry in his work of assessment and realisation of revenue. Besides this, he assisted the Shiqdar in the maintenance of law and order and punishment of miscreants.

Qanungo

The Qanungo was an old official and perhaps the one officer whose association with the Pargana has continued since very early times down to our own day.

He was the head of the Patwaris of the Parganah. He kept records for the Parganah as the Patwaris had to keep for the village. Formerly, the Qanungos were paid by means of commission of one per cent, which was changed by Akbar and thenceforth they were paid cash salaries from the public treasury besides an assignment for personal maintenance.

Three grades of Qanungo existed in the time of Akbar. The first group consisted of those who received Rs. 50/ per mensum; the second and third groups comprised the Qanungoes who received Rs. 30/ and Rs. 20/ respectively.

Village Administration

A Parganah consisted of a number of villages. Each village was recognised as a unit by the Mughal government. The village as an autonomous institution in which the villagers transacted their affairs themselves had come into being very early in Indian history. According to R.C. Majumdar, "the village was treated as a concrete unit of the state possessing distinct rights and duties and accountable to a supreme power for the dual discharge of the trust".

The village life was not disturbed by the Muslim rulers, perhaps out of the political expediency and foresight. But it does not mean that there was no control, whatsoever, over the village affairs. No doubt in the normal tenor of the life of the village, no interference was attempted by the Mughal government, yet the villagers' representatives were invariably answerable for crimes of serious nature such as murder, dacoity or treasonable activities. In disputes of all kinds—civil, criminal, religious or social in which the decisions of the local body failed to give satisfaction to either party, appeal could be made to an ascending hierarchy of the judicial officials of the government. In spite of the different stages of control mentioned above, the village administration under the Great Mughals was well-nigh the same. The provincial government kept itself in touch with the villages by means of:

(i) the Faujdars posted to the sub-divisions who always lived in the district towns;

(ii) the lower officials of the revenue department who did the actual collection from the peasantry;

(iii) the visits of the Zamindars to the Subedar's court and

(iv) the tour of the Subedar.

The contact was not very intimate and the villagers were left pretty much to their own devices.

The following were the important functionaries in the villages:

(i) *Headman*

The headman of a village was known by the name of Muqaddam.[25] The headman exercised general supervision, settled disputes, performed policing duties and collected revenue from his village. In cases of robberies or murder of a traveller, he was obliged to produce the culprits and the amount stolen. The poor people of the village were much afraid of their Muqaddam as he, if he so wished, could get any one punished simply by naming him as a robber or a murderer. According to Irfan Habib, "Here was another weapon which the Muqaddam could use to cow down the poor section". Moreover, he had a say in allotting the uncultivated land. This right was implicitly recognised by the authorities when they entrusted the task of setting new villages. The taqavis were also conveyed through him. With these powers, he naturally began to consider himself as some one superior to peasants.

"The distance that grew up between the headman and the ordinary peasants and the considerable power that he wielded over the village seem sometimes to have led to his claiming or acquiring certain rights indentical with those of the Zamindar".[26]

The position of the Muqaddam in the village of a Zamindari was that of a servant holding this office at the latter's pleasure.

The office of the Muqaddam was hereditary but could be bought and sold. He could also be deposed by revenue authorities if he failed to discharge his obligations. Revenue authorities could nominate him for new villages or fill up the vacant office.

As regards his remunerations, he received a commission equal to $2^1/_2$% of the total amount collected either through deduction at his level or through the revenue-free land. Besides this, he was allowed to get the amount known as Khurk in order to meet his boarding expenses whenever he had to go out to conduct his village business.

Patwari

Next to him was the village Patwari. He maintained revenue records and agricultural statistics of the village or the villages assigned to him. After the kharif harvest inspection, it was the duty of the *Patwari* to give the Muqaddam a list known as the *fard dhal bachh* showing the demand due under different heads from the owner of each holding. The Patwari was bound to help the Muqaddam by maintaining accounts and by writing, if required, the receipts to be given to the shareholders. But he was forbidden to have anything to do with the collection of revenue.[27] In the administration of Akbar, he was assigned a commission of one per cent on the revenue of his village.[28]

The organisation of the village and the observation of the accepted codes of conduct were regulated by the village Panchayat which looked after morals, education, sanitation, and relief work. It also arranged festivals and settled disputes in the village.

Land Revenue

From 1526 to 1540, no change was effected in the agrarian system of the province. There is nothing in the contemporary records to indicate that either Babur or Humayun made any alteration in the existing system. In fact, both the Emperors accepted what they found. We read of Babur distributing assignments among his followers very shortly after the battle of Panipat. Humayun confirmed the assignments which had been given by his father. Khondamer's account of the reconstruction of the central administration suggests no change in the actual work of the ministry. The few months in 1555-56 which constituted the second phase of Humayun's reign afforded no opportunity for the introduction of any change in the system.

Akbar also could not do much immediately after his accession to the throne. It took him quite a long time to effect reform in the revenue administration. According to Moreland, this long reign (of Akbar) falls into two divisions: upto the 24th regnal year (1579-80) the revenue administration may be described as a series of experiments, and the period from 1580 onward during which the stability of a system had been attained.

The start was made by continuing Sher Shah's system which has been described by Abul Fazl in detail in Ain.[29] According to this system, a greater part of Hindustan was brought under a system of measurement which probably was carried out every season. The area of the crops having been ascertained, certain scheduled crop rates were applied to them and the revenue realised accordingly. The schedules of crop rates were prepared by dividing all kinds of crops into three broad classes, good, middling and bad, and striking the average produce by taking one-third of the sum of all the three. In this way, the average produce per bigha of each crop was worked out and one-third of this average was the state demand. The share of the state was then commuted into cash at the current rates which were naturally different in different localities, depending upon the productivity of the area, the market conditions and various other factors but in view of the absence of any realiable data as also the apparatus to determine the price level, it was fixed arbitrarily.

Upto the eighth year of Akbar's reign, the revenue system practically remained the same. The schedule of crop rates of Sher Shah continued to be the basis of state demand although attempts were made to make them conform to reality by determining them on the basis of the average yield worked out separately for each locality. The revenue was fixed in cash, not in kind: price schedules were framed by experts and applied for conversion of kind into cash with the prior sanction of the Emperor. No doubt, the Emperor took care that prices were not fixed at deliberately pegged-up rates; yet the system in operation suffered from serious snags. The government had to experience a lot of inconvenience because every year the officials had to prepare price schedules every year. Moreover, the system offered great allurement to the officials to whom it gave a rather free hand to fill their coffers by oppressing the people by manipulating rates of commutation.

The first step towards improvement was taken up in the 8th regnal year (1563). In this year, Etmad Khan was appointed to organise the Khalsa land. He instituted an enquiry into the holdings of the Jagirdars. As a result thereof, he detached the land over and above the jagir lands. So far as the process of the assessment of revenue was concerned, it continued to operate as in the past using for the entire kingdom the schedule of rates prepared under Sher Shah. The crop rates being valued at prices fixed by the orders of the Emperor.

The annual Dasturs for the various crops from the 6th to the 9th year were, more or less, the same. This shows that in the beginning there was not only a single rate for the empire but also for all practical purposes, a single price schedule applied each year in all the regions with only small modifications. Since the Jamas had no relevance to the reality, it would be difficult to imagine how these uniform rates could have at any time been imposed upon the peasants.[30] Abul Fazal recognizes that much distress used to occur from the promulgation of the Dasturs in the early years of the reign and immediately goes to explain that Jama or general assessment at that time known as the Jama-i-Ragani was greatly inflated and in individual cases the assignments were either greatly over or under-assessed. Moreland who is fundamentally correct in his appreciation of the nature of this Jama does not appear to see any direct connection between it and the Dasturs. But unless Abul Fazal's reference to it in the context of the Dasturs is an irrlevent digression, it would be natural to suppose that the Jama was inflated to some extent precisely because it was based on these unreal cash rates. Akbar's administration must have inherited some record of measured areas from the archives of the Surs and the Dasturs could have easily been multiplied by these to yield the Jama for each locality. But since the Dasturs themselves were uniform and bore little relation to local productivity or price fluctuations the revenue paying capacity of the peasants and the Jama, at which the assignments were made to the Jagirdars. Moreover, it seems the area statistics could be manipulated, for Abul Fazal says the Jama could be increased by a stroke of the pen in order to meet salary claims.

The absence of enforceable revenue necessitated some steps which were effected by Muzaffar Khan and Todar Mal in the 11th year of the reign. "They obtained the local area and revenue statistics (Taqsims) of the country from the Qanungos. Leaving the Mahsul (produce or revenue) to appraisment and estimate, a fresh Jama was brought into being. It seems that it was this summary way of determining the actual yield or crop rates that was responsible for the defects of the new Jama, which is said to have been still 'far away' from the actual revenue received (Hasil).

In view of this, certain changes were effected in Jamas. According to Irfan Habib, "A change is noticeable from the tenth year onwards in the nineteen year tables of the Ain. The difference among the rates of different provinces and among the rates of the same province in different years became very pronounced. Not only that, the rates are often expressed in two maximum and minimum figures, representing the range of divergence in rates promulgated within the province for different localities. It seems certain that new local crop rates had now been worked out and that henceforth the price schedules were drawn up afresh every years, separately for each locality. It may be assumed that these changes were the result of the measure undertaken by Muzaffar Khan to work out new revenue rates for instituting a new Jama."

As the Dasturs approached closer to actual conditions, the administration probably was to enforce them to some extent for determining the revenue demand upon the peasants; but still there were many other things to be done to end the gap between assessment and actual realisation. The framing of cash rates was the dire necessity. Abul Fazal's comments in this connection are pertinent. He says that peasants were highly distressed by the annual commutation of the kind rates into cash rates. The Empire had greatly expanded and long delays used to occur in the sending of the local price reports to the courts and the sanctioning of the rates of the year. As a result, sometimes the peasants complained that more had been taken from them (in the interval) than was ultimately sanctioned and sometimes the Jagirdars protested about the balances of revenues left unrealised owing presumably to the delay in receiving the approved rates. Moreover, it became notorious that some of the price reporters had deviated from the path of uprightness.

In the thirteenth year,[31] Muzaffar Khan who was incharge of both the general and revenue ministries was relieved, for the Emperor realised that the two duties were too heavy for him, and in his place Shihabuddin Khan was appointed. During his time, the practice of annual measurement was replaced by a form of Nasq in the Khalsa lands. He based his assessment in the previous records of measurements and schedule of crop rates. He did all this with a view to avoid larger expenses which measurement involved and reduced the chances of embezzlement which quite a good number of surveyors were likely to get. In the 15th regnal year, when the Wazarat fell to Muzaffar Khan and Todar Mal, once again the practice of annual measurement was resumed for purposes of assessment.

In the 19th regnal year, however, Akbar introduced new reforms. Till this year, the land was measured by Jarib made of twisted hempen ropes which became shorter or longer according to the dryness or moisture of the atmosphere. Now it was replaced by a Jarib made of bamboos joined by iron rings which was no more subject to variations, and the relief to the public was felt everywhere, while the hand of dishonest greed was shortened. Besides this, with a view to putting an end to the corruption that had crept into the assignment system and to effect as extensive measurement as possible just for once or for a period of years and then use it as the basis for a workable *Nasq* and for compiling the new general assessment the Jama-i-Dahisala, the Ain-i-Dahsala (Zabti) was introduced.

The new revenue collectors (Karoris) were reputed to be charged especially with the task of extending cultivation, and it is not improbable that this was associated with the detailed agricultural information they were required to supply.

The collection of the revenue data and other connected reforms introduced in the 19th regnal year yielded sufficient information so as to enable the Mughal government to introduce fresh reforms in the 24th regnal year. The whole scheme of reforms and the necessary regulation had been worked out jointly by Raja Todar Mal and Khwaja Shah Mansur, but the Raja had to proceed to eastern provinces to deal with an uprising and the burden of carrying out the reform fell on Shah Mansur. These reforms were collectively called Ain-i-Dahsala.

According to this system, final Dastur-ul-Amals[32] giving cash rates per bigha were prepared for different localities by adopting a double process. First a crop rate or rate was prepared locality-wise based on an average of actual rates for the harvests for previous ten years and then the average of the cash rates of the previous ten years was also prepared. On the basis of this average cash price, the crop rates were converted into cash rates for all and thereby eliminating the necessity of annual commutation of revenue rates into cash. The state share during Akbar's reign was 1/3rd.[33] We are told that information for the 20th year to the 24th year was obtained by way of actual knowledge (Tahqiq) and (of) the five preceding (years) (15th-19th) from the representations of truthful men.

The Dasturs prepared in the 24th regnal year were made permanent but Irfan Habib suggests that some revisions had to be made from time to time and the final Dasturs preserved in the Ain are not exactly those prepared in the 24th year but as they stood on about the 40th year.

Each Dastur related to the circle that came into being as a result of grouping together of certain areas having homogeneous agricultural conditions.

In preparing the Dasturs for cash crops, a different process was adopted. According to Abul Fazl, "the revenue on the high-grade (Jins-i-Kamil) crops was also fixed; they took the year when it was greater." Irfan Habib takes this process to mean 'no Dastur had been prepared for such crops as Indigo, Poppy, Pan turmeric, hemp, etc. for which the revenue rates had been directly formulated in terms of cash. In addition, the thick or pounda sugarcane seems to have been omitted from the rate list. Perhaps the yield of these crops was liable to such fluctuations for every harvest that no crop rate could be fixed that might be of any practical use. What Abul Fazl means is probably, that in determining the permanent Dasturs for such crops, no attempt was made to fix the local rates by the process of averages, the method adopted being simply to choose certain good seasons and accept the revenue rates determined for them.[34]

The adoption of the Zabti system seems to have necessitated the classification of land on the basis of continuity or otherwise of cultivation. Accordingly, the land was classified into four divisions. The first class of land was polaj, which was annually cultivated while the second, pranthi was left fallow to recoup fertility. The third class, known as chachar, was the land kept fallow for three to four years. The fourth class was the banjar land which remained uncultivated for more than three or four years. In the 27th regnal year of Akbar, Raja Todar Mal introduced fresh reforms. In case of land which had to be kept fallow for four years (*chachar* of the Ain) only half of the stipulated rent should be taken for the first year, three-fourths in the second and in the third year, the peasant should be responsible for the full rent. In case of uncultivated land, they were to be allowed to keep back a small amount of grain so that their lands might become capable of yielding revenue.[35] In 1586, Illahi Gaz was substituted for Iskandri Gaz for measuring the land. The former consisted of 41 digits while the latter was that of 32 digits.

The system was applied to the whole of the Lahore Subah, the larger portion of Multan, and to the area interposing Delhi and the Sutlej—then forming part of the province of Shah Jahanbad. This system did not apply to the hill states, the trans-Indus areas and Kashmir—then forming parts of the province of Kabul.[36] In Kashmir, Nasq and Batai were adopted as the measure of assessment. According to U.N. Dey,[37] Kashmir was one where Nasq of crop-sharing was the method of assessment and the land revenue was expressed in terms of ass-load of rice which was never paid in cash. In Thatta, an adjunct of the

Subah of Multan, the Batai (Ghalla Bakhshi) the crop sharing system was adopted as the mode of assessment.

The pattern of land revenue system as spelt out above remained the same under the successers of Akbar with the difference that the area of land given as assignment[38] expanded particularly under Aurangzeb because of his keenness to accommodate the large influx of the Deccani Nobles and the efficiency decreased owing to the general lethargy of the bureaucracy, the long absence of the Emperor from the capital and his obsession to appoint the revenue staff from amongst the Muslims to satisfy his religious-cum-political fads.

Nasq Crop-sharing and Kankut

Side-by-side Zabt, another method of assessment known as Nasq was also in vogue. In the Ain, many references to Nasq can be gleaned. When we put all these references to Nasq together, the first thing which strikes us is that Nasq is often not treated as an independent method of assessment but only as a hand-maid of other methods. In Punjab as elsewhere, where there was Zabt, it appears as a subordinate of the Zabt. In Kashmir, it was subordinate to crop-sharing. We may say, therefore, it was a method or procedure which could be adopted, whatever be the basic method of revenue assessment in force. Zabt consisted of two things, the fixed revenue rates and the measurement of land. If the revenue official was to accept the presumably fixed area, increasing it presumably by estimate and did not actually measure the land, it means he was applying the system termed as Nasq. According to Irfan Habib, Nasq standing in these passages (of Ain) as an alternative to annual measurement under Zabti, signified the use for revenue assessment in successive years of the same area figures previously determined by actual measurement. Abul Fazl speaks of Nasq under Zabti as Nasq-i-Juzvi (partial Nasq). There are other forms of nasq also, as for instance, Nasaq-i-Ghalla Bakhshi, etc. but behind this diversity of forms there is one essential feature that is common to them all—the whole or a part of assessment once made being repeated year after year. It did not matter how the initial assessment had been made or what was repeated—

area figures, amounts of cash, quantities of grain, or perhaps number of ploughs. Any avoidance whatsoever of the process of actual assessment by acceptance of something previously worked out or determined was Nasq.

After the introduction of Zabt, in the 24th year of Akbar's reign, people brought more land under cultivation or some land must have gone out of use. In such cases, Nasq was applied. On the basis of the earlier assessment the state share was estimated. If in some cases the peasant was not satisfied, he could ask for actual measurement which the revenue officials must do.

This system continued to exist all through the Mughal period. The author of *Khulasatus Siyar* written in Punjab near the close of Aurangzeb's reign vouchsafes the the general prevalence of assessment based upon area, whether actually measured year by year or maintained by Nasq. Indeed the area under Nasq recorded by the author is generally considerably in excess of that in Ain. On banjar land it was left to the option of the cultivator to pay in ready money or by kankut or bhaoli.[39] Sharing of crops as the mode of assessment was resorted to where the cultivable land was not measured but in Lahore Suha the quantity of this type of land was just meager.

Rural Taxes and Exactions Other Than Land Revenue

Besides land revenue, the peasants had to pay other taxes. These were divided into Jihat, taxes on certain trades, and Sa'ir Jehat, market and transit dues. In practice, however, the distinction between the two seems to have been obscure. In one list that we have for example the Sa'ir taxes cover almost all the major taxes apart from the land revenue. There were in addition exactions and perquisites appropriated by officials personally and by Zamindars and accordingly excluded from the Jama. These were known as Fannat but more commonly as Ikhrajat and Abwab and Habubat.

The two major objects of taxation in an ordinary village apart from the cultivated fields were the cattle and the orchards. The Ain lays down that if a man kept land otherwise liable to land revenue (khiraj) under pasture, a tax of 6 dams per buffalo and 3 per cow should be imposed upon him. But a cultivator having up to four buffaloes, two cows and one buffalo to each plough was liable to be exempted. Moreover, the Gaushalas where the cows were kept for religious purposes were exempted from this tax. This exemption continued to stay till 1634. In the times of Jahangir, the orchards were exempted from taxation even when land previously cultivated was planted with fruit trees. But this tax was reimposed by Aurangzeb.

Another source of revenue was the property of those who died without heirs. Besides, the peasant had to pay a levy of one dam per bigha known as zabitana.

Jaziya on non-Muslims in 1679 by Aurangzeb meant an important increase in the burden of rural taxation. A separate organisation of collectors (Umana) was created for this purpose. The tax was directly collected from individual subjects in the cities. For the villages, it was first ordained that a flat rate of Rs. 100/ upon 100000 dams (of the Jama presumably) should be realised from the non-Muslim peasants by the government officials in Khalsa lands at the authorised rates. A manual compiled in the later years of Aurangzeb shows, however, that detailed lists of the men liable to pay this tax were prepared in both towns and villages. The specimen accounts reproduced in it show that the incidence was not light by any means. Out of 280 males in a village, 185 were held assessable and of those 137 paid the minimum rate of Rs. 3 and Rs. 2 per annum, which at that time would have meant a month's wages for an unskilled urban labourer. As a tax, Jaziya was extremely regressive and highly burdensome for the poor.

In addition to the taxes itemized above, there were some illegal exactions to which the peasants were subject. Among such forbidden exactions were customary gifts like Salami and Bhent; fines and bribes collectively called Bala Dasti payments expected on the performance of certain definite acts by the officials, e.g. Pattadari, when permitting the crop to be cut and Tehsildari when presumably accepting the payment of revenue and finally Kharaj-i-Sadir expenses to meet the needs of the officials during their visits. There were other exactions still. The exact rates for these cases cannot be ascertained; in any case they could hardly have been uniform. But together they could have sometimes amounted to pretty large sums.

Although begar or compulsory labour was not part of the fiscal system, yet it continued to be there; labour continued to be forced to carry the baggage for touring officials, to provide services to cut down the jungles, to clear paths and to carry camp baggage and the killed animals.

Medium of Payment

The peasants of Punjab as also of Northern India with the exception of Kashmir and Orissa and isolated parts of Rajputana, paid revenue in cash. In the Mughal periods, the methods of assessment, chiefly used in Hindustan, namely Zabt and the form of Nasq based upon it involved the direct statement of the revenue demand in terms of cash. No provision is on record for allowing a commutation of cash into kind in any circumstances. When the methods of crop-sharing and kankut both of which set the demand in terms of the produce, were used, commutation into cash was permitted at market prices. In case it was not burdensome for the peasantry. In fact, cash nexus was finally established in almost every part of the Mughal Empire. "Its prevalence meant simply that the peasants were normally compelled to sell, in not a few cases, the larger portion of their produce in order to meet the revenue demand. Demand in cash introduced and increased the share of another class in the surplus produce, namely the village money-lender and the rural merchant."

Collection of Land Revenue

The collection of land revenue took place invariably at the time of harvest. The revenue collector (Amalguzar), says Abul Fazl, should begin the collection for the Rabi (season) from Holi (the festival falling in March) and that of Kharif from Dussehra (falling in October). It was laid down that he should collect the revenue upon the crop which is being harvested and not delay it for another crop. In the Kharif season, the harvesting of different crops was done at different times and the revenue had accordingly to be collected in three stages. The Rabi harvest was all gathered within a very short period and the authorities seem to have usually anxious to get the revenue collected before the harvest was cut and removed from the fields. Out of this anxiety grew the practice of preventing the peasants from reaping their field until they had paid their revenue. This was obviously a coercion and quite a good number of examples of this kind can be gleaned from the revenue records of the 17th century. The practice was at the same time the mark of a well developed money economy for it would have been impossible to attempt it unless the officials expected that the peasants would pay up by pledging their crops beforehand to grain merchants or moneylenders. The revenue was paid into the treasury usually through the Amil or revenue collector though Akbar's administration sought to encourage the peasants to pay it direct. The peasants or rather their representatives or village officials were entitled whether they paid directly or indirectly to obtain proper receipt for their payments; the treasurer on the other hand was also asked to get the village accountant (Patwaris) endorsement in his register to establish the amount of payment. "These regulations were largely in the nature of precautions that the administration took to protect itself and incidentally perhaps the revenue payers from fraud and embezzlement."

The latest studies conducted in connection with the determination of the share of the gross produce of the peasantry which they were able to keep for themselves have shown conclusively that the peasant was left with about half of the product, the rest was appropriated by the Sirkar, Sirkar's local guards, pariahs tilling the land, Brahmins and accountant (Patwari), etc.

The example of Gujarat amply testifies what we have said above.[40] From a maund of rice, one pound went to the Chief, one to the weigher, I to the guard, ½ to the carrier, and ½ to the village administration. In addition every cultivator gave laigesse from his crop, 5 pounds to the temple, 20 to the Muslim Divines, 10 to the Manager's cook and to cover the Chief's travelling expenses-5 pounds. After all these shares were paid one half of the remainder went to the land owner. Thus, 7% of the crop went into services and 48% to the land owner, so that the landholder kept 45% of the rice crop. This share is duly reduced when the deductions are taken into account. This was equally true when the agricultural production consisted of cash crops.

Revenue Assignments

The different forms of assignments, each yielding a certain estimated revenue, constituted a very important and peculiar feature of the Mughal administration. The bulk of these assignments were made by way of payment to the salaries to most of the officials of the government. The next largest share of the assignments was made by way of payment for charitable purpose both to individuals and institutions, and these assignments were called Suyarghals. Assignees had no control over the assessment of the revenue. The fact that jagir was assigned to a particular officer as his pay or allowance shows that every such jagir was estimated at a particular value, and the assignee was not expected to realise from it more than his due or what the jagir was officially expected to yield.

In A.D. 1583, Raja Todar Mal issued instructions for the guidance of the revenue officials which support the above view. The cardinal point in these instructions was that the collectors of the crown lands and the jagirdars should collect the rents and taxes in accordance with the Dastur-ul-Aml. "If from wickedness and tyranny, they took from the cultivators more than the agreement, the oppressors were to be fined and the complainants were to be compensated."[41] Closely connected with the abstract of these instructions, there is another fact that in the 19th year when the Karories were appointed, the Amirs were asked to appoint Karories in their respective jagirs.[42] From this we may safely conclude that assessment of both Khalsa and Jagir lands was made according to the government regulations and the work of the collection in jagirs was carried out by the jagirdars through their own agents.

The Jama figures according to which the assignees were expected to collect in many cases differed from the actual receipts, sometimes because of the variations between the actual conditions and the conditions taken into account at the time of preparing Jama, sometimes because of over assessment and sometimes because of natural calamities. The actual receipts increased over and above the Jama, because of the good administration of an assignee. Akbar increased the rank of the assignee corresponding to the increase in his receipts. But later on the ratio between the receipts and the standing assessment was worked out for each Mahal and expressed in terms of month proportions. Thus, where the current receipts (Hasil) equaled the Jama, the Jagir was styled twelve monthly. Where it was half six monthly (Shashmaha) and so on. As a natural corollary, the system of month proportion was initiated for the payment of emoluments in cash as well. Since Mansabdars holding the same ranks but cash emoluments of different month ratios would have widely different incomes, the military obligations were also laid down separately for each month ratio so as to make an allowance for these differences.

If the Jagirdars complained very strongly of the inflated nature of the Jama, a reduction in it, known as Takhfif, was sanctioned by the court. For this amount, the Jagirdar was admitted to have a claim (Talab).

The Jagirs (excepting those which were named Inams and Watans) were constantly transferred after short periods so that a particular assignment was seldom held by the same person for more then three or four years. Akbar seems to have in his own view decisively established this practice when in his 13th regnal year he dislodged the officers of the Atka family from their Jagirs in Punjab. From that time to the end of our period of study this practice continued to be followed although during the later years of Aurangzeb's reign the assignees began to assume the character of hereditary Jagirdars.

Generally, the administrative structure of an assignment bore close resemblance to that existing in the case of Khalsa lands as for instance in both cases there were officers such as Amils, Amins, and Fotdars. But there were variations also. A small assignee might saddle Amil with the work of Amin and of the treasurer. Sometimes, a single person being appointed to the duties of the Amin, Shiqdar, Karkun and Faujdar of the Mahals of the Jagir, leaving only the treasurer as his colleague.

In actual working, the Jagirdars exacted pledges from their agents concerning future collections as was the case in Khalsa. But they generally took in addition a certain amount termed,

Gabz, in advance and it was apparently common for one person to displace another as the Amil of a Jagirdar by offering a bigger Gabz to the latter. On the other hand, it was sometimes extremely difficult for the Jagirdars especially if they were serving in some other province to keep a check on their Amils and prevent embezzlement of the revenue due to them. Many of the assignees, therefore, found it simpler to farm out their assignments. This practice called Ijara was regarded as a source of great oppression, for the farmers after giving high bids for the farms to get contracts would still seem to make handsome profits by extorting money from the peasants by every imaginable means. Although the custom of Ijara was not officially recognised, yet it got on. An illustration of this is provided in the court news of Aurangzeb's reign. It was reported to the Emperor that the Mansabdars who had Jagirs in Kashmir were giving them on farm to local men who were extremely oppressive. Aurangzeb, thereupon, ordered that the Diwan of the province should prohibit this practice and insisted that the assignees send their Amils to collect the revenue.

Assignees assigned part of their Jagirs to any of their officials or troopers and there was nothing to prevent this tendency. The government, since the times of Jahangir, took care that the Amils should not develop family ties with the local gentry. Jahangir on his accession issued an order which is clearly designed to prevent these officials (the Amils of the Khalsa and (of) the jagirdars) from forming family ties with the local gentry.[43] The local element was, therefore, almost entirely excluded from the assignee's administration. The local element was, however, represented by two officials who were in dependent of the assignee, but were indispensable for them. These were the Qanungo and the Chaudhri.

Provincial Revenues

The province was left only local and inferior sources of income. The reason was the principle on which the services in general were organised which left very little financial burden on provincial government. According to P. Saran, with the exception of the clerical and subordinate staff in offices, nearly all other services were paid on the 'Mansabdari system', with the result that the provincial and local administrations were relieved from having directly to deal with the major portion of the disbursements and other administrative expenses. The important provincial sources of income were as under:

(i) Income from public works such as gardens.

(ii) Octroi.

(iii) Duties on various markets in large towns.

(iv) Duties on internal transit.

State gardens brought to the government good income which was utilized for their upkeep and the maintenance of the garden servants. If it fell short, it was supplemented from the provincial treasury. Octroi was another source of income. Regarding this realisation Dr. P. Saran says, "There is no direct evidence of the levy of octroi duties on goods entering a town for consumption, but the taxes raised from sales in the markets were perhaps reckoned as octroi. The taxes on cloth market, pan market, and jewel market also formed the important part of the provincial exchequer. There was a regular staff of police and revenue officials to guard and protect the markets and raise taxes from them." Manucci informs us that the Kotwal of Lahore collected a weekly tax from six thousand houses of ill-famed among these there were dancers and singers also who paid tax to the king.

Though the administrative expenditure was incurred directly or indirectly by the central government under its control, yet there were certain items of local expenditure which were certainly met from the provincial treasury. Part of the expenditure incurred on local works such as canals, embankments, Sarais, etc. was often charged from the local treasury. Expenditure on hospitals, kitchens and charity houses for the distribution of blankets and other clothing to the poor was also incurred by the provincial government. Possibly some local schools and mosques also received aid from local treasury.

Ownership of Land

The ownership of land under the Mughal Rule vested with the cultivator who could sell, mortage or give away lands in gift. Land passed from father to son like all other property. The state had an interest in the landed estates of the cultivator who ran away after defaulting in payment of the revenue. There is no substance in the assertion of some scholars that the Mughal Emperors treated the land as their private property. However, when land changed hands, elaborate rules safeguarded the claim of the state to the revenue. If an heir or a buyer had time enough for cultivating it after acquiring his title he paid the land revenue. If the heir or the buyer did not get enough time to cultivate the land, the revenue was remitted. The leased or mortgaged lands also paid land revenue under similar conditions.

JUDICIAL ADMINISTRATION

The law courts under the Mughals were organised on the administrative pattern of the Empire consisting of villages, Parganas, Sarkars and Subas.

Pargana Adalat

Each Pargana was provided with an adalat (court) which was placed under a Qazi who decided civil and religious cases. Shiqdar who represented the Kotwal's magisterial functions and the general executive and police functions of the Faujdar tried cases of a purely secular criminal category. To expedite the disposal of the cases or in view of the rush of work, more than one Qazi were appointed in each Pargana. According to P. Saran, "A network of Qazis was spread over the Parganahs, each parganah being divided into very small judicial circles. The Qazis also kept charge of mosques and even did teaching work".

Sarkar Courts

The chief court was that of the Qazi of the Sarkar where cases involving civil, common and criminal law were heard, and applications from the Pargana Qazis' courts were filled here.

The executive head of the Sarkar (mostly the Faujdar) also exercised judicial authority and in his court cases concerned with disturbances and security were heard and decided. The Kotwals in the Sarkar and in the various towns also decided petty cases.

According to P. Saran, "The Kotwal and Qazi shared the whole business of justice in the Sarkar between them. The Kotwal was a magistrate, prefect of police and municipal officer rolled into one. As magistrate, he took cognizance of criminal cases of the whole Sarkar, while in other respects his jurisdiction was limited to the headquarters towns of the Sarkar. There is no clear classification of cases which came under the authority of the Qazi and the Kotwal, but from the known cases, it is quite easy to comprehend that the secular type of criminal suits went to the Kotwal and the religious ones, such as inheritance, marriage, divorce and civil disputes, went to the Qazi's court."[44]

The court of the Amil dealt with revenue cases and heard appeals from the Pargana courts. The appeals from this court went to the court of the Dewan. The Sarkar Qazi had to perform multifarious duties which were not directly connected with the administration of justice. He was the official visitor of the jails within his jurisdiction and was given power to inquire into cases of prisoners confined therein. He could review the proceedings in the cases of convicted prisoners and release on bail persons under trial.[45]

Courts at the Subah Level

At the provincial level we have four categories of law courts. They were (i) Nazim's court, (ii) Qazi-i-Subah's court, (iii) Dewani-i-Subah's court and (iv) Sadri-i-Subah's court.

The Nazim's Court

The Nazim's court was both an original and an appellate court and he, being the representative of the Emperor, received appeals from all the courts situated within the province, including the court of Qazi-i-Subah. In original cases, the Nazim usually sat as a single judge, and appeals from his judgement went to the appellate courts at the centre. When he heard appeals, he sat on a bench of which the Qazi-Subah was invariably a member, unless the appeal was from the court of Qazi-Subah. Even appeals of land revenue cases could be filed with him, though normally this was the work of the court of Dewan-i-Subah.

Qazi-i-Subah

The court of Qazi-i-Subah was original as well as appellate, i.e. it could try cases involving civil and criminal issues, and act as court of appeal at the provincial level. His judicial powers were co-extensive with those of the governor and he had a permanent seat on the bench of the governor's court. The Qazi-i-Subah was consulted by the governor in the cases where the use of sovereign's prerogative came into question.

Court of the Diwan of the Province (Diwan-i-Subah)

The appeals against the Amil's orders or decisions were filed in this court and appeals from his court lay with the Diwan-i-Ala. The Emperor or the Nazim as his representative, however, had jurisdiction over the entire administration and could entertain appeals from the Diwan-i-Subah's court.

The Qazi-i-Askar

There were separate Qazis for the army. In the time of Akbar Qazi Tawias (upto A.D. 1567), Qazi Yaqub (1567-77) and Qazi Jalal (1577) held this post in succession. In the 30th year of his reign, Akbar appointed Qasim. Beg Tabrizi[46] to the post of the Qazi of the camp. Mulla Shukr-ullah Shirazi held the post of Qazi during the Shah Jahan's reign. "This post was not new like so many others. Qazis of the army existed even under Sher Shah."[47] "In addition to the above regular courts, important and complicated cases chiefly those in which government officials were involved were investigated and tried by special commissions."[48]

Vakil-i-Sharai or Vakil-Sarkar

The Mughal Emperors fully re-organised the principle of representation through lawyers who were called 'Vakils'. The statement of Moreland that there were doubtless learned students of both Muslim and Hindu texts, but there were no advocates or pleaders practicing in the courts is not correct in view of the finding of Bashir Ahmed who has cited many cases where the Vakils argued the cases.[49]

During the periods of Shah Jahan and Aurangzeb, Vakils (lawyers) were appointed as whole-time employees by the state in all the Sarkars and were called Vakil-i-Sarkars or Vakil-i-

Shariat. Their duty was to defend the state in civil suits and also to provide assistance to the poor with free legal advice. "The Vakils had to file vakalatnama (power of attorney) in the court for every individual case and a client always retained the right of canceling the vakalatnama (power of attorney) in the court."

Islamic law was applied to Muslim in all civil cases. Criminal law and the Muslim law of evidence and contract was the same for the Hindus and the Muslims. In cases of inheritance, marriage and the like, a Hindu law was followed and for this purpose a Pundit was attached with the court. The Mughal Emperor recognised the religious character of the Hindus and never tried to alter or codify the law of the Hindus on the lines of Fatwa-i-Alamgiri.

Certain aspects of the Mughal penal code deserve notice. It made distinction between first offenders and habituals. It sometimes gave the accused an opportunity for confessing his crime and expressing repentance for it. The persons who did so were treated leniently. The sentences on convicts were of a more appalling nature that was customary in India. Capital punishment after torture was prevalent. The mode of execution included impalement, trampling by elephants, crucification, beheading, etc. For minor crimes, mutilation and whipping were resorted to. The death punishment had usually to be confirmed by the Emperor. Akbar drew the lines at the old Mughal practice of flaying alive and was disgusted when the horrible punishment was inflicted. Babur had ordered it without scruple. In the reign of Jahangir even when that order was stated to have been abrogated, one found provincial governors carrying it out on their own.

A CRITICAL APPRAISAL OF THE MUGHAL JUDICIARY

The Mughal judiciary was fairly organised. From Parganah to the capital of the Empire, various types of courts were provided and this being so, the remarks of J.N. Sarkar that "there was no system, no organisation of the law courts in a regular gradation from the highest to the lowest nor any proper distribution of courts in proportion to the area to be served by them,"[50] are unfounded. Trials were quick and so the decisions.

However, there were certain serious defects in the judiciary. The chief defect lay in the quality of these courts as has been rightly pointed out by Ibn Hasan, that the judicial department stands in a marked contrast in organisation, in status and dignity to other department of the central government which were highly organised. Another great weakness was the corruption[51] of the Qazis who never hesitated to accept bribes. Abdul Wahab Borah, the first Chief Qazi of Aurangzeb's reign, amassed a fortune of 33 lakh of rupees in cash, besides much jewellery and other valuable things within a period of sixteen years during which he held office.[52]

Another major defect of the Mughal judiciary was the arrangement for imprisonment. Life in a prison was worse than that of a beast. The length or period of imprisonment does not seem to have been defined by definite rules. The Qazi had a right to send any one to prison for an offence or crime for which such a punishment could be awarded.[53] Ibn Hasan remarks: "The object underlying imprisonment could be both detention and reformation but in the former case there ought to be some period fixed for it and in the latter some practical steps to reform the prisoner during his term of imprisonment." But the Mughal government provided neither, the lack of one weighed heavily upon the prisoner while the lack of the other placed in the hands of the executive a most dangerous weapon of oppression.[54] According to Ibn Hasan, the account recorded by European travelers as well as the scattered cases in the chronicles show that there were neither jails in the modern sense nor proper arrangements for keeping criminals and political offenders in custody. P. Saran states: "there was an elaborate arrangement of prisons and that besides forts and central prisons of the capital towns, there were prisons also at the headquarters of the Sarkars and Parganahs".[55]

Justice was done according to the law, whatever it was. The primary aim of the courts was to maintain the existing structure of society and even help its maintenance and continuation. The government did not use the judiciary as an instrument of progress or made any change in it during their long rule to respond to the social or economic changes. During the times of Aurangzeb courts were used to buttress the cause of orthodoxy of which Aurangzeb claimed to be a great champion.

NOTES

1. | Year | Number of Paranas |
|---|---|
| 1594 | 232 Mahals |
| 1665 | 314 -do- |
| 1695 | 316 -do- |
| 1700 | 458 -do- |
| 1720 | 329 -do- |

2. W.H Moreland, *India at the Death of Akbar*, Macmillan & Co. Limited, London, 1920.
3. Ibn Hasan, *The Central Structure of the Mughal Empire,* p. 330.
4. Ishwari Prasad (Tr.), *The Mughal Age*, p. 521.
5. P. Saran, *Provincial Government of the Mughals*, p. 188.
6. *Ibid*., p. 189.
7. B.S. Nijjar, *op. cit*., p. 109.
8. P. Saran, *op. cit*., p. 191. Dr. Saran has prepared the list on the basis of British Museum Manuscript—add. 6588 Vols. 72 to 73b.
9. U.N. Dey, *The Mughal Government* (1556-1707), p. 77.
10. P. Saran, *op. cit*., p. 195.
11. U.N. Dey, *op. cit*., p. 79.
12. *Encyclopaedia of Islam*, Vol. I, p. 600.
13. *Ain-i-A•kbari*, Vol. II, Jarret, pp. 41-42.
14. P. Saran, *op. cit*., p. 197.
15. *Ibid*., pp. 259-65.
16. Ibn Hasan, *op. cit*., p. 96.
17. *Ain-i-Akbari*, Vol. II, Jarrat, pp. 43-44.
18. Saran, *op. cit*.
19. U.N. Dey, *op. cit*., p. 80.
20. *Ibid*., p. 84.
21. P. Saran, *op. cit*., p. 233.
22. U.N. Dey, *op. cit*., p. 87.
23. M. Bashmir Ahmed, *Administration of Justice*, pp. 153-55.
24. Ishwari Prasad, *The Mughal Empire,* p. 324, Chugb Publications, Lucknow, 1974.
25. The term Rai for the headman was frequently used in hill states of Punjab and that of Chaudhari in the territory now forming Haryana.

26. Irfan Habib, *Agrarian System of the Mughals*, pp. 133-36.
27. B.S. Nijjar, *op. cit.*, p. 117.
28. Irfan Habib, *op. cit.*, pp. 133-36.
29. *Ain-i-Akbari*, p. 297.
30. Irfan Habib, *op. cit.*
31. *Ain-I-Akbar*, II, 333 (Tr), II, p. 488.
32. It is not clear whether the figures under the years 15th to 24th in the 19th years tables are the actual Dasturs promulgated from year to year or those determined retrospectively in connection with the Jama-i-Dahsala. But there are some indications that favour the latter alternative. From the 15th year (and in some cases the 14th year); the variations between provincial and annual rates become much more pronounced and many new crops appear on the schedules. The introduction of the bamboo measuring rod in the 19th year was officially assumed to have increased the size of the bigha by 15th per cent, but there is not hint of a proportionate rise in the rates under the 19th or 20th years. This can be explained best if we conceive the figures to have been those worked out in the 24th year, when a uniform size for the area would have been assumed.
33. Irfan Habib, *op. cit.*, p. 210.
34. *Ibid.*
35. These rules were later on modified as will be found from the account given in *Ain*.
36. Refer to Olaf Caroes book, *The Pathans*, Chapter xiv, "Akbar and the Tribes".
37. Refer to Athar Ali's book, *Mughal Nobility*.
38. Assignment of the area did not entitle the assignment holder to make changes in the revenue system; he only was allowed to collect the revenue.
39. *Ain-I-Akbari*, vol (Jannet), pp. 74-75.
40. We have gleaned this information from V.I. Pavlov's book *Historical Premises for India's Transition to Capitalism*.
41. P. Saran, *op. cit.*, p. 321.
42. *Ibid.*, p. 322.
43. Irfan Habib, *op. cit.*, p. 287.
44. P. Saran, *op. cit.*, p. 353.
45. M.B Ahmed, *Administration of Justice in Medieval India*, pp. 156-58.
46. P. Saran, *op. cit.*, p. 350.
47. *Ibid.*
48. *Ibid.*

49. As quoted in M.B. Ahmed, *op. cit.*, p. 190.
50. J.N. Sarkar, *Mughal Administration*, p. 98.
51. *Masir-al-Umara* (Tr.), pp. 75-76.
52. In the latter part of Shah Jahan's reign and thereafter considerable corruption and demoralisation had gradually crept into judicial administration. The post of the Qazi became for all practical purposes hereditary.
53. U.N. Dey, *op. cit.*, p. 237.
54. Ibn Hasan, *op. cit.*, p. 336.
55. P. Saran, *op. cit.*, pp. 390-92.

Economic Landscape

9

Industry

Punjab was not industrialised in the modern sense, yet it had varied industries the study of which, by and large, shows that its industrial pattern was not different from the one in vogue in European countries during the medieval age. The process of production was purely domestic and certainly neither capitalistic nor controlled by state. Most of the industries were manned by caste groups, as, for example, cotton industry and leather work, etc. were controlled by Julahas (weavers) and Chamars (cobblers) respectively.

A detailed study of the state of industry in Punjab under the Mughals is not possible but still some idea may be had in regard to that. A few of the important industries are described as under:

Cotton industry was one of the premier industries. Varieties of hand made cloth are legion but the most important ones were khaddar, lungis, pataks, Kheses and ghabroon.[1] The important centres of this industry were Lahore, Bajwara, Sultanpur, Gujarat, Multan, Ludhiana, Mianwali, Sialkot, Hoshiarpur, Jalandhar, Gurgaon. According to Munshi Sujan Rai, "Bajwara near Hoshiarpur was famous for its cloth, especially for the Deriah, Panch Tolia, Jhona, white chera and gold embroided clothes of a fine order especially Baftas, Chariah Fotas, Sozani, Adoka, table cloths, tray covers and small tents and weapons such as the Jamdharas, Katar and lance." Gujarat was famous for embroidered clothes. Multan was famous for lungis and it exported its lungis to other parts of Punjab and its Susi to Kohat, Bannu and other places in the north-west frontier province.[2] Ludhiana was renowned for its lungis and patkas.[3] Jullundur and Hoshiarpur also manufactured lungis and exported them to Ludhiana for sale. Coarse khes cloth was produced at Nakodar, Khushal Bhera, Amritsar, Sialkot and Shahpur. The industry was mainly run by Julahas who included a small proportion of recruits from the lower orders of the population such as Barwalas, Churas, Chamars, etc. A sprinkling of high-caste Hindus and Sayyads, Khokars and Pathans and Mirasis was also found playing the weaver's shuttle for their livelihood in Jhang and Multan.[4]

Silk industry was another industry, which employed quite a large number of workers. Silk garments were widely worn by the upper classes and the fashion of the time prescribed an extensive wardrobe for anyone who desired to move in high society. The manufacture of silk included four operations: (i) the preparation of the yarn; (ii) dying; (iii) weaving; and (iv) embroidering. The chief centres of silk industry were Amritsar, Jalandhar, Multan and Lahore. Akbar who had a special liking for silk established an imperial workshop at Lahore.

Carpet industry was centred at Lahore, Amritsar and Multan. Shawls of special texture were also made at Lahore. Carpets were made of pure wool and of wool mixed with cotton. There were more than a thousand workshops of shawls in Lahore only.[5] Pottery was an important craft of the Mughal times. There was hardly any village where this handicraft did not exist. The coarse pottery of the country was too well-known to need description. The village potter made it for local consumption in every town or village of the country on his Chak or wheel, as he had done for thousands of years in the past. This industry supplied pots for Persian wheels. Different types of clay such as yellow clay, fire-clay or simple clay were made use of in making different articles of pottery. Glazed wares were also made. A glaze was transparent vitreous coating applied to any kind of earthenware to render it impervious to liquids, or to serve as a means of decoration. It usually consisted of a composition of lead, horaz and crude glass, often coloured with mineral dyes. The best centres of this industry were Gujranwala, Gujarat and Sialkot.

Enamelled pottery, like that of Sind, was not a native art and was brought by the Mughals from China by way of Persia. Multan was the chief centre of this art and famous for providing enamelled tiles of light and dark blue colour with geometrical patterns and pious Arab inscriptions.

The enamel was made with limestone and soda, the best colours used being dark blue from cobalt, and a very fine turquoise from copper violet. Brown, green and other colours were introduced but with less success. Boat-making was done at Wazirabad.

Paper was made by hand. Sialkot was famous for good paper, especially the Mansinghi paper and silken paper of very good texture, white, clean and durable. These products were exported in all directions. The boats used in the Indus and other rivers of Punjab were made at Lahore.

Oil pressing and cotton ginning were carried by the primitive methods still in vogue in villages. Spirits were widely distilled from sugar by age-old methods in spite of the repeated edicts issued by the Mughal Emperors. Iron mongery was limited by the high cost of the metal and wood work by the small demand for furniture. Leather-work was not a prominent industry, shoes being not so commonly worn, Suddles were mainly made of cloth halters of rope.[6]

Gur (molasis) was extracted from sugarcane in village furnaces of the type which are still generally prevalent in Punjab. The neighbourhood of Lahore produced a costly form of gur known as candy. The preparation of flour and wheat was in general a purely domestic undertaking.

Ship industry was also known to Punjab. In *Akbar Namah*, there is a reference to the construction of two ships, one was constructed in 1594 and the other in November 1596.[7] Lahore was famous for manufacturing swords, bather saddles and shoes.[8] Steel was the famous manufacture of Sullanpur.[9]

Technology and Production Skills in the Crafts

The state of productive forces in the handicrafts in the period under consideration was characterised by simple and even primitive tools and implements, although they were handled by craftsmen with a fair degree of productive experience. As an example of the proficiency of craftsmen, we can refer to the quality of carpets, silk cloth and gold ornaments. These articles amply bear out the high standard of the skill of our craftsmen. But the tools they used were primitive and simple. The high proficiency of the craftsmen of Punjab was owing to their hereditary specialization. Marx wrote about the Indian weaver: "It is only the special skill accumulated from generation to generation and transmitted from father to son that gives to the Hindu...this proficiency." That the standard of tools did not make any advance was due to many reasons. The technical progress was constrained by poor remuneration of Indian artisans, especially high-skilled craftsmen whose income differed little from those of the ordinary artisans, and who because of this could not invest to bring about improvement in their tools.

Moreover, the skills of the Indian artisans handed down from generation to generation were scarcely subjected to conscious experimental improvements. That is why the technology which had once taken shape and which had been tested by ages of experience was usually converted into a kind of production ritual which was sacrosanct in every details.

Besides this, there was very limited division of labour. In fact every manufacturer, every artisan working on his own account, conducted the whole process of his art, from the formation of his tools to the sale of his production. As the division of labour often induces specialization and also technical progress, its absence or limited range naturally affected the pace of improvement in technique adversally.

In the period under consideration there was sufficient capital available in the province but in spite of this, the economy of the province did not make the necessary leap to start the capitalistic process. The reason for this is detailed as under:

(i) Agriculturists were drained off by the state and others to such an extent that they were left with no more than was warranted for their subsistence. To express it in technical language, the surplus product (product over and above the subsistence-product) was appropriated by the state and others. This being so, the peasantry was unable to produce commodities for marketing.

Whatever little, especially in cash crops, they could turn out for sale, that too could not be sold as they wished. In most of the cases in cash crops, the peasantry had taken money in advance or had entered into a deal with some merchants before the crop was actually harvested, so that moneylenders would come in and take the charge of the crop against their previous advances. The crux of the matter is that the agricultural sector was not allowed to develop fully. Besides this, there was only a one-way trade between the towns and villages. Villages sent their agricultural products to the towns while they got very little from the towns because of the self-sufficient nature of village economy.

Artisan population was, no doubt, very large in the province, but they too were not in a position to start independent factories. Most of them functioned as a limb of the village socio-economic system, and they served the needs of the village population and got in return the share in the crops of the landholders in kind, which was sufficient for them only to subsist. Moreover, the production of non-community articles by the artisans conformed to the needs of the feudal lords in villages and of the Mansabdars in the court. These articles were luxury goods, and were not meant for mass consumption and thus mass marketing. Moreover, the artisans producing such articles worked either in government karkhanas or as labourers of some merchants or feudal lords. They did not work independently taking into consideration the demand and supply factors of the articles thus produced. Merchants, in quite a good number of cases, had accumulated capital and could start factories making at least the pre-capitalistic productive experiment; but they did not do so. They always tried to hide their wealth from the eyes of the ruling lords and this being the case, they did not invest the money like their counterparts in England. The issue of insecurity became acute as the time slided towards the eighteenth century. In this connection Orme's evidence is pertinent. He observes, "that the artisan was not personally free which is why he had extremely limited opportunities for accumulating capital and extensive production.

"The mechanic or artificer", Orme insisted, "will work only to the measure of his necessities. He dreads to be distinguished, or to become too noted for having acquired a little more money than others of this craft, because that will be taken from him. If conspicuous for the excellence of his skill, he is seized upon by some person in authority, and obliged to work for him night and day on much harder terms than his usual labour acquired when at liberty." Merchants for fear of being extorted by the ruling people did not muster courage to establish factories, which alongside the mark of large-scale production and division of labour, also backoned to the riches of merchants. Thus, because of the subsistence cultivation of the peasantry, the inability of artisans to produce articles in an atmosphere of personal freedom and covetousness of the authorities—all these factors did not allow the economy to forge ahead and develop into a capitalistic model.

Trade in General

Punjab had a fairly large foreign as well as local trade. In quantum it was far larger than it was during the Sultanate period. The reasons are not difficult to identify. The foremost reason was the peace and stability that Punjab enjoyed from the time of Akbar. Secondly, the obstacles created by the Portuguese for Indian merchants on the seas gave rise to the increase in caravan trade with Persia. The caravan routes that cut right across the country from Bengal to Lahore and from Gujarat to Kashmir via Punjab also served to promote long-distance internal trade.

Furthermore, Afghanistan depended in large measure on Punjab because it lay nearest to it, and this thing also stepped up the trade of the province. The policy of the government also helped the growth of trade. According to Irfan Habib, "A series of Imperial orders issued by Akbar and his successors declared all such imposts—known indiscriminately as Baj, Tamgaha or Zakat—abolished either entirely or with exceptions." There is no doubt that despite these orders, the dues continued to be collected by Jagirdars and officials, of course illegally, yet the sympathetic policy of the state contributed a lot towards providing a stimulus to trade.

Punjab had trade connections with Kabul, Badakhshan, Turkistan, Khurasan, Iran and Tibet and different provinces in India, as for instance, Sind and Agra.

Situated on the high way between Kabul and India, Lahore was great commercial centre and regulated most of the foreign trade. From here many roads branched off to different countries, the chief of which were: (i) Lahore to Sind, (i) Lahore to Fatehpur, (iii) Lahore to Kabul and (iv) Lahore to Srinagar. Obviously, by these roads, Lahore was linked with the commercial centres of Asia and Hindustan. Musk melons were imported from Kabul, Badakhshan and Turkistan. Valvet and Silk came from Herat, Badakhshan, Turkey and Khurasan. Musical instruments, pictures, curiosities and from 1600 on wards tobacco were brought from Europe. Punjab export trade mainly consisted of brocades valvets, silk, shawls and carpets. Awan[10] in the Sind Sagar Doab was a good breeding ground for horses while Hazara and the country around Nagarkot were famous for cattle and sheep. These animals were also exported in Jahangir's time. Brisk trade in fine cotton goods of Mausaulipatam and Golcunda flourished in Lahore. Moreover, white cotton goods, both of Bengal and Golcunda, ivory of Multan, quick silver, vernmilion, coral, turbans, girdles, silk goods from Ahmedabad, silk from Patna, Lac, paper and drugs were sent outside in every large quantity.[11]

The province of Multan being on the route to Qandhar and Persia and having the three rivers, Indus, Ravi and Jhelum close to it carried on trade with Lahore easily. Lahore received sugar from Multan for local consumption and export to Sind. The horses mostly came from Afghanistan and Persia to Lahore through Multan. The Sikhs often bought horses from there and sold them in Punjab. Jahangir himself sent Khan Dauran to bring horses from Kabul.[12] These horses were in demand in the whole of India both for the royal stables and for individual soldiers. Murtaza Khan sent 30 beautiful Iraqi and Turki horses for the royal use from Lahore.

Gujarat, founded by Akbar and famous for swords Jamdhars and embroidery exported its products to other places. Kheora salt mines produced salt which was exported to places outside

Punjab. Bajwara in Hoshiarpur district was well-known for weaving and the manufactures were sent to all parts of India.[13]

Local Trade

By local trade we mean trade between town and country. It is impossible to read the sources of the period without gaining the impression that there was a very large urban population. The multitudes of artisans and servants found in the towns provide a frequent topic of comment to foreign observers. In Akbar's Empire, we are told there were 129 big cities and 3200 townships, each having under it from a hundred to thousand villages. The largest city in the 17th century was Agra, with a population estimated at 5,00,000 and 6,60,000 in the days when it contained the court. Lahore in the days of Mughal glory has been described as second to none either in Asia or in Europe.

Whatever data regarding urban population is available one thing at least is clear that the ratio of urban population to rural population was quite high, not exceeded till very recent times.

The towns had not only to be fed by the countryside but also to be supplied with raw materials for their manufacturers. Since there is no evidence that villages depended, in any way, upon urban industry, the raw materials brought into the towns were probably confined to those required for the luxury trades "for the ultimate use of urban population". All the same these together with the provisions needed for such large numbers could not but have comprised a fairly large proportion of the total agricultural production and few villages could have been left un-affected by the pull of the urban market.

If, then a large portion of the peasant's produce was ultimately put on the market, his own relations with it are naturally worth investigating. Sometimes, he parted with his own portion in lieu of land revenue and in such cases it was the potentates—the Jagirdar or their agents who must have arranged for its sale. But in most cases, the peasant was as a rule obliged to pay the revenue in cash and then he must have had to sell his produce himself. This he might have often done by carting his produce to the local market or the town; or, in the case, at any rate, of a high-grade crop he might be approached in the village by merchants interested in the trade. But it is possible that a very large number of peasants were not able to reach the open market at all being compelled to sell on constrained terms to their creditors. Whether the creditors were merchants or money-lenders, the result was always to depress the price received by the peasant. However, it was not as if the peasants not bound in this manner, were able to obtain anything like a fair return. Their urgent need for cash to pay the revenue and keep themselves alive, forced them to sell as soon as the harvest came into their hands, while the merchants could usually afford to wait. On the way to and in the market again the peasants might be obliged to pay various dues and perquisites. In the process of sale, they were probably commonly defrauded in the weighing of their produce and in the cash paid out to them.

Finally, there was the scourge of monopoly. Although it was prohibited officially and denounced by moralists, yet monopolists did flourish at certain places obviously with the collusion of corrupt government officials. When it was a case only of a few persons cornering the stock. It was not the peasant but the townsman who suffered from it. But often in order to establish a monopoly local authorities prevented the peasant from selling his produce to anyone except one buyer or group of buyers so that he was victimized. Such local monopolists seem to have been a common place phenomenon though it is possible that being disapproved of at the court it could not ordinarily have been carried beyond certain limits. In 1633, an indigo monopoly was established with Imperial aid and sanction covering the whole empire and due to run for three years, but it was abandoned in the second year, perhaps, because the indigo cultivators rooted up their plants in protest.[14]

Trade, whether it was long-distance or local was backed by a well-organised system of finance and credit. The case of hundis or banker's drafts and bills of exchange was widespread and the rates, considering the times, were certainly moderate. There was, besides, an organised system of insurance, not only against risks of loss in transit but also against the incidence of taxes.

Means of Transportation

There were different means of transportation used in the country. Small caravans carried articles of higher value; but where the bulk was concerned as it was in the case of food grains or sugar, banjaras did the job. They led a nomadic life and lived in Tandas (camps) consisting of 600 or 700 souls having a large number of bullocks and camels which they used for the purpose of the transportation of goods. The cost of transport by this method was lower, the necessity of finding fodder or grazing lands along the routes must have severely limited the benjaras operation during the summer and the dry tracts.

Small carriages were also used for transport but they could carry only small quantities of merchandise.

Rivers offered very cheap rather the cheapest means of transport. Lahore and Multan were river ports from where rather smaller craft went down to Thatta. The cost of transit by boat from Multan to Thatta in 1639 was nearly twice the Ain's price of wheat but only about 1/6th of its price of white sugar. From this it can be adduced that there was huge divergence in price levels at different places at one time. There were no permanent bridges on the rivers. Wherever they existed, they were temporarily floating. Stronger and more permanent were built on the Kishen Ganga river when Jahangir was going to Kashmir. The absence of permanent bridges was great hurdle to the transportation of goods. Dara Shikoh when he fled from Lahore to Multan sent his goods by the river. Jahangir helped the merchants by building some new roads, but generally the condition of roads was wretched. A road from Agra to Lahore was built with a pillar at every kos and well at every three kos and with trees on both sides.[15] This so impressed Coryat that he was led to think that a like of it did not exist on the surface of the earth. Jahangir got the road from Poonch to Kashmir repaired.

The most important routes in Punjab through which the merchandise passed and human traffic took place were (1) Delhi to Lahore, (2) Lahore to Attock via Jehlum and Hassan Abdal,

(3) Jehlum to Attock via Rohtas, (4) Lahore to Multan, (5) Multan to Bhakkar and (6) Multan to Dera Ismail Khan. This route led to Qandhar.

For the smooth passage of human traffic and trade goods, there were a number of Mughal masonary bridges in the Central Punjab, out of which a number of such constructions were done by a religious personage. Shah Daula Bridges over the Ayak River at Sialkot, over DEG river near Eminabad, over Black Bein near Sultanpur Lodi over the white Bein between Nakodar and Sultanpur built by Akbar had a crucial role in facilitating movement of goods to and fro.

The most important ferries were at Nilab, Dhan got and Chopara. From Lahore there was continuous navigation down the river to Thatta, the sea port of Sind Ravi river being shallow at many places and very low in winter was only navigahle between March to October and the flat bottomed boats playing on it were of a burden of 60 tonnes or upward with a carrying capacity of 1000 to 2000 maunds (33 to 60 tonnes) in weight.

Mining

Silver, copper, zinc, brass and lead were among the principal minerals which were found in Punjab.[16] Gold was obtained from the Indus and Jhelum rivers by washing its soil.[17] Silver and lead mines existed in northern mountain in Lahore Suba.[18] Gyprum was found at Bhera. Salt rocks were at Kalbagh and Kheora were an important source of salt.[19]

Agriculture

Agriculture was the mainstay of the people of Punjab during our period. The soil of Punjab was rich as it is now, but it could not be exploited fully because of uncertain rainfall and inadequate irrigation facilities. The mode of cultivation was as old as ever. The implements used by the peasants were old and hackneyed. They used ploughs made of wood to which iron blades were fixed. Whether wooden or iron implements in general cost the peasant more or less is a question which cannot be answered in terms of figures, but the difference either way was very small: Wood was easier to get than now, but iron was certainly much more expensive in terms of grain while the cost of manufacture measured in the same currency was probably very little, and, on the whole, the quantity of produce required to maintain the supply of the necessary implements cannot have altered materially during the last three centuries.

To make up for the inadequacy of water supply, irrigation facilities were provided by wells primarily up to the death of Akbar.[20] Babur, writing early in the sixteenth century, comments on the absence of artificial canals in India, and hazards the explanation that water is not absolutely requisite, the autumn crop being nourished by the rains while "spring crops grow even when no rain falls". In Akbar's time, there were some inundation channels and also the remnants of the aqueducts constructed by Feroz Shah to supply the gardens and cities established by him, but the value of these works was essentially local, and the country as a whole depended either on wells or on minor streams which were utilized by means of temporary dams.

The canals in Punjab were of a later origin. In 1630, Ali Mardan Khan, the governor of both Punjab and Kashmir, got a canal dug by an expert, and for this Shah Jahan gave him one lakh of rupees. Munshi Sujan Rai writes: "near Shahpur has been taken out of this river (the Ravi), a royal canal which goes to the garden of Shalimar in Lahore, a second canal which goes to the Parganah of Pathan (Pathankot), a third which goes to the Parganah of Batala, and a fourth which goes to the Parganah of Biar Patti (Haibatpur Patti)."

A small canal was cut from the river Tavi to irrigate the Ali Mardan Khan's garden at Sodhara near Wazirabad in the upper Rachna Doab. The presence of canals in the Multan Sarkar is indicated by an order appointing a Mir-i-Ab (canal superintendent) for the area which has survived in a collection of administration documents. It requires the appointee to dig new channels, clear the old channels and create bunds on flood torrents and see the equitable distribution of canal water among cultivators. The most southernly position of the present Sind Sagar Doab lying in the Baluch country was reputed for its fertility which Aurangzeb attributed to well irrigation. The area is, indeed, full of abundant river channels but tradition also suggests that the present reach of the Indus above Mithankot was originally a man-made canal which the Indus absorbed into its own bed in the 19th century.

The land was cultivated by smallholders, the substantial capitalist farmer being practically non-existent. Agricultural labour was generally immobile because of its poverty, scanty means of transportation and venues for employment. There were also a large number of landless labourers who were practically serfs tied to the land, in a condition of periodical slavery to the cultivators who fed and clothed them in return for their labour.

In view of the poverty of the peasants, Akbar and his successors directed their revenue officers to advance money to needy cultivators, although the amount thus advanced could only meet a very little part of their total demand, thereby constraining them to fall victim to moneylenders.

Crops

There were two harvests. The Rabi or spring which was sown mostly in October-November, and reaped in April, May and the Sawani (Kharif), which was sown between the months of June and August and reaped from early September to the end of December. The principal Rabi crops were wheat, barley, poppy, saffron, linseed, mustard, muskmelon, peas, onions and carrots. Under the category of autumn crops, sugarcane, cotton, rice, pulses, jawar, lohiya, indigo, hemp, toriya, watermelons and betels were included. Muskmelons could be had throughout the year.[21] Under the fostering attention of the Mughal emperors, new experiments in the cultivation of the choicest products of Turkistan, Persia and Hindustan were made with brilliant results. Vetches of Kabul and Muskmelons of Persia were among the chief foreign crops which were given trial here.[22]

The Currency System

Previous to the Mughals, especially in the reign of Muhammad Tughlaq, the system of currency was in a chaotic condition. Akbar reformed it into a well-regulated system. Uptill 1577, the mints were controlled by the chowdharies but in the year 1577, mints were put under the control of Imperial officers, such as Muzaffer Khan, Todar Mal, etc. The chief features of the coins during Akbar and his successors were the purity of metal, fullness of weight, artistic design, absence of any effigy,[23] and a vast variety. The coins were struck in gold, silver and copper. "There were 26 varieties of gold coins of different weights and value, varying from Shanash weighing 101 tolas, 9 mashas and 7 Surkhs, to Muhar (91 tolas and 8 mashas) to Aftab and llahi equalvalent to ten rupees. The dam was the common copper coin and weighed 5 tankas; the chief silver coin was called rupee, weighting 11½ mashas and contained 172.5 grains of pure silver." Silver (rupee) mints existed in Lahore, Sirhind. While copper mints functioned at Lahore Sialkot, Bhera, Kalanaur and Sirhind.

Wages

In Punjab of our period, the subject of wages had relevance to town life rather than to country life. According to Moreland, "The labour market in Akbar's times was exclusively an urban phenomenan." The agricultural labourer was ordinarily a serf, receiving in return for his work an amount of commodities determined by custom, and about sufficient to keep him and his family alive. The village artisan was also supported by customary payments. Accordingly, it was only in towns and cities that men were hired to work and rates of wages could be said to have existed. This view does not imply a complete separation between the urban and rural population; there was, in fact, a drift from the villages towards the army and the cities composed partly of the natural overflow of population, and partly of men who had abandoned cultivation under stress of bad seasons of an environment unfavourable in other ways. This particular trend was stronger under Aurangzeb than under Akbar. The statement made by Terry that men stood to be hired in the market place, as they may be seen standing in some cities these days, indicates that a labour market did exist. But very little information regarding its working appears to be on record, and apart from the particulars given by Abul Fazl, we come across only a few incidental notes of the rates at which travellers and merchants engaged domestic servants. Even the facts related by Abul Fazl are of limited importance. He did not attempt to make a record of current rates of wages but in describing the various departments of the Imperial household, he noted the rates of pay which had been approved by Akbar, or what would now be called the sanctioned scales of the establishment. The rates applied primarily to expenditure in the Imperial camp. A few of the wage rates as given by Abul Fazl are as under:

ordinary labourers	2 dams per day
superior labourers	3 to 4 dams day
carpenters	3 to 7 dams day
Builders	5 to 7 dams day

The sanctioned wage rates rendered Akbar's workman better off than many of the workman in India of 1961. According to our estimate which has been hazarded comparing the purchasing power of the wages in Akbar's time and in 1961, the lowest paid urban worker could have bought as much of cereals as and more of milk products than a relatively low-paid worker in 1961.[24] The table in proof there of is under:

Commodity	Unit	Physical Equivalent in Akbar's time	Physical Equivalent in 1961
Jowar	9.4	11.1	8.0
Wheat	6.2	9.3	5.7
Milk	3.0	4.5	2.0
Ghee	0.8	1.1	0.4
Oil	1.0	1.4	1.2
Gur	1.4	2.0	5.3
Sugar	0.3	0.5	2.4

Even so, the condition of skilled artisans in Mughal Punjab was not good. Artisans were either skilled labourers or independent producers. In both the cases, their lot was far from satisfactory. For instance, in case of carpet industry, as a skilled labourer, he was given only those wages which were just sufficient to keep him attached with a particular work-house and the whole surplus was appropriated by the employers. Even when he worked independently, he conducted sale as well as production under great strain because for money and sale he had to depend upon others.

NOTES

1. *Ghabroon* is really a species of *Khes* with checks or stripes and with a double warp and weft of different colours.
2. S.M. Latif, *The Industrial Punjab*, p. 5. Also refer to the *Atlas of the Mughal Empire* by Irfan Habib, p. 42.
3. Latif, *ibid*.
4. Latif, while surveying the industry, says in his book *The Industrial Punjab*. "In the eastern districts, the *Julahas* constitute a real caste, but further westwards distinctions of caste tend to disappear. Khokars and Pathans, Mirasis and Rajputs and even needy Sayyads are found playing the weaver's shuttle for their livelihood in Jhang and Multan."
5. *Ain-i-Akbari* (Tr. in English), p. 22.
6. M. Akbar, *Punjab Under the Mughals*, p. 232.
7. *Ibid*.
8. Manucci, *Punjab Under the Mughals*, p. 424.
9. Sujan Rai, *Khulasat-ut-Twarikh*, p. 66.
10. *Ain-i-Akbari*, I (Tr. in English), p. 95.
11. *Ibid*., II, p. 323.
12. *India and Jahangir*, p. 31.
13. *Jahangir's Memoirs*, Vol. II (Tr. in English), p. 61.
14. *India of Aurangzeb*, p. 83.
15. Dr. Irfan Habib, *Agrarian System of the Mughals*.
16. *Jahangir's Memoirs*, II (Tr. in English), p. 100.
17. *Ain-i-Akbari*, II (Tr. in English), p. 312.
18. *Ibid*., p. 121.
19. Sujan Rai, *Khulasatut-Twarikh*, p. 79.
20. *Ibid*., p. 77.
21. J.N. Sarkar, *India of Aurangzeb*, pp. 104-05.
22. *Ain-i-Akbari*, II, p. 82.
23. *Ibid*., p. 312.
24. Itching of effigies was prohibited by the Quranic law, *Ain-i-Akbari*, p. 28.

Society and Culture

10

The people of Punjab were divided into two classes. The upper class to which the ruling group belonged consisted of the superior sections of the Muslims and of the Hindus. The Sayyads, Mughals, Iranies, Pathans and Shaikhs formed the superior class among the Muslims and Rajputs, Brahmins, Kashatriyas and Kayasthas among the Hindus. The Sayyads and the Brahmins formed the non-military wing of the ruling class. In fact, the Mughal state was an upper class state of which the army and services were the two pillars. Both were monopolised by the military section of the upper classes—Mughals, Iranis, Pathans and Rajputs. The Sayyads were given employment in the judicial department, for they belonged to the class whose occupation was learning and teaching. Similarly, the Brahmins were employed to assist the Quzis in the dispensation of justice.

The persons belonging to this class were paid high salaries, most of which were spent on luxuries and pleasures. They were not trained or encouraged to practice thrift, rather they were encouraged to spend lavishly. This was the logical result of the escheat system which had a very grave effect upon the morality of the nobles and sharpened their propensity of extravagance. This made these nobles to live in an indescribable luxury. They indulged in every kind of pleasure and lived in grand havelis (palaces). They married three or four wives and sometimes more.[1] Drink was the common vice and many died of excessive drinking.

The Hindu and Muslim groups which constituted the vast majority of the population were engaged in pursuits which were regarded as unworthy of the higher classes—agriculture, industry and trade. They were the unprivileged subjects of the state and had no part or say in the administration. Naturally, they showed little interest in the affairs of the state and were indifferent to its trades. The Muslims of this category were mostly converts from Hinduism. Even after embracing Islam they could not shed their old castes. On the other hand, the Hindu masses not only observed their traditional caste-lines but also made them still more rigid. In fact, in the liberal atmosphere which the Great Mughals with the exception of Aurangzeb created, the Hindus by and large, instead of effecting reforms in their religious attitude and behavioural patterns, harnessed their energies to strengthen the old Brahmanical social organisation. Tara Chand remarks, "Evidently the spirit of the Hindu social organisation pervaded the working of the empire, for the idea of caste had taken deep root among the Muslims and was the basis of the administrative structure of the Empire. In the Hindu system, the Kashatriya was the protector and systainer of social order, so much so that he claimed even to determine and alter the status of the other castes."[2] The Brahmins were ministers of religion. They were not the guardians of the social system. The Mughal Emperors were like Kashatriya Kings whose duty it was to uphold the social order. The Ulemas and Sayyads played the same part as did the Pandits or heads of different orders or sects played. Since these people were educated and small in number, they commanded great influence as well as respect. The Brahmins alone were authorised to interpret the Hindu scriptures. In practice, even the interpretation of the sacred books of the Muslims was confined to the learned class which consisted largely of the Sayyads or Ulemas. In the same way, the lower classes of the Muslims (workers, labourers, craftsmen, clerks and slaves) had their counterparts in the lower classes of the Hindus.

This comparison, however, does not go very far. In the Muslim society, inequalities were ignored, tolerated or occasionally denounced; on the other hand, in the Hindu society inequalities or groups were sanctified.

The vast majority consisted of professional men, scholars, lower officials, merchants and traders and the masses including slaves. In Dr. Laet's view, professional men, scholars, lower officials, merchants and traders led quite a comfortable and peaceful life; although it is too much to expect that they led luxurious life.

The masses, however, were the real sufferers. They comprised the workmen, labourers, farmers, petty shop-keepers and domestic servants. Their life was a little better than that of slaves. They lived on a plane hardly above that of animals. They had scanty clothings, poor food and dirty huts without any furniture. Their houses were dirty and insanitry. Their food was little dry bread, and their clothes were very scanty. Most of them remained bare-footed. Their children uptil the age of twelve remained naked except a loin cloth or a chain round their waist. The workers were victims of low wages and oppression by the officials.[3]

The condition of the slaves and eunuchs was also miserable. Slaves were bought and sold like a commodity. They were continuously recruited from among the prisoners of war, persons unable to pay the government taxes or those who in times of famines sold themselves or were sold by their parents for bread. Slavery was a recognised institution in Mughal India. The eunuchs, however, were better off than the slaves, since they were the personal and Haram attendants of the nobles, governors and Mughal Emperors.

Position of Women

Even after two centuries of the Mughal rule, the position of women did not improve. They wielded no independent status. The norm of the Hindu society as recorded by *Manu Smriti* that a woman, when unmarried should remain under the supervision of her father, when married under that of her husband, and on her husband's demise under that of grown-up sons, remained unaltered. In a broad way, even in Muslim society, this norm was not excluded. In fact, since majority of the Muslim consisted of Hindu converts or their descendents, it was well-nigh impossible for such Muslim women, to get rid of this feeling and therefore they did not enjoy better position than their Hindu counterparts. In spite of the emphasis of Islam on social equality, Muslim women were denied respectable status. Not only this, they had to tolerate their polygamous husbands.

As any free-horn Muslim could marry at least four wives at a time, no woman in Muslim household could claim to be the mistress of her house. Although polygamy was not the sacred rule in Hindu Dharm, yet certain princes did marry more than one wife and to that extent, Hindu ladies also suffered a serious handicap.

Fidelity to husband and chastity in respect of sex were two things whose breach was not tolerated by the society. Sexual wrong-doing on the part of women was considered an unpardonable sin, perhaps because sexual life which on its positive side is a very personal matter and on this account should be free from all taboos and restrictions, except those imposed in the interests of the society, especially the weak and the young, was regarded an integral part of the social organisation. On the other hand, adultery on the part of a husband was passed over as a trifle. If the wife was bitter and complaining, the husband adopted the high and mighty attitude that his happiness was more important than all such petty morals.

This double standard was partly due to the inbuilt faith of the male that he held ownership of woman as a property and partly to the appropriation of excelusive rights which the husband acquired over the wife over the years.

Parents, with the exception of those of the royal ladies, were never assiduous and sincere in their efforts to educate their daughters. Restrictions were imposed on their social mobility and their free mixing among themselves, much less with the members of the opposite sex. Purdah excellently served the purpose of theirs.

The custom of purdah was as much prevalent among the Hindus as it was among the Muslims; although the factors and the motives giving rise to the custom and then its perpetuation were different. In India the origin of custom can be traced to the division of persons into high and low and the desire on the part of the aristocracy to make it a hallmark of their class. According to N.C. Mehta, seclusion of women could be traced to all ancient communities and it was particularly so among the aristocracy during the palmy days of Hindu civilization. During the Muslim period, two other factors encouraged purdah system: one was the anxiety on the part of the Hindus to protect their women from the lustful eyes of the Muslims and to maintain the purity of their social order and second was the tendency to imitate the ruling classes.

That the women of the ruling classes also observed purdah is clear from the contemporary records. The Muslims had got their own views regarding purdah, which they had borrowed from the Iranians in common with several other institutions.[4]

Respectable ladies went about in litters, called dolies which were carried sometimes by two and sometimes by four kahars (doli bearers) accompanied by their maid servants and eunuchs which covered their heads and bodies to their anklets.

The position with peasant women was different; they moved freely without any veil. They did not live in seclusion and observed only ghungat. But so far the status was concerned, they were no better than their counterpart. The word Hajab (meaning veil or screen) occurs seven times in the text of the *Quran*. The *Quran* enjoins modesty, however, instructing women in Suraff 24, Alanur (the light) at verses 30-3, to lower their gazes and be mindful of their chastity women should not display their beauty and ornaments, but should draw their head covering over their bosoms except in the presence of their immediate family (Sura 33, Al-Lahzab at verse 59). Among some of the ladies even from amongst the Hindus, Hajab was welcome as distinguishing a woman as a member of the wealthy and privileged elite, a concept that reaches back to the historical distinction in dress between wives and slaves.

In the system of marriage too, women were assigned the inferior place as compared to men. Parents had to give dowry in the marriages of their daughters. This thing positively was a great burden on the parents. For some parents who were economically hard-up, it was extremely difficult to procure even a wedding outfit for their daughters—let alone the grand dowry. In its social implications, this evil had its varied ramifications. It epitomised the low status of women. It constrained many parents from arranging marriages for their daughters. Since to arrange marriage for the daughter was one of the most important religious as well as secular duties whose fulfillment involved financial burden, social hardships and unnecessary inconvenience, certain parents considered it better not to have daughters at all. This thing led to the evil of female infanticide which during the period of our study was in vogue, particularly among the Rajputs and Gakkars.

There was, however, one outstanding development in the Mughal period. The Sikh Gurus espoused the cause of women and openly preached for a dignified status for them in the society. Guru Nanak protested against any consideration as considered woman inferior to man. He declared unequivocally that women should be fully respected. Female infantitude was denigrated as the most un-ethical, and the persons indulging in infanticide were to be excommunicated and those having any social relations with them were termed Tankhaya punishable. According to Sikh code of conduct (Rehayat Maryada), "Sikhs were prohibited even in dream, the relationship with those indulging in female infanticide." In one of his fiats the Sikh Guru Gobind Singh made infanticide is unpardonable sin and enjoined upon them not to regard. The persons indulging in it as stated in Guru Bhai Prahlad Singh's Rehayat Name (Sikh code of conduct) were sure to meet disaster: "He who is a Sikh and deals with one indulging in female infanticide would be led to disaster ultimately."

In order that the evil of sati self immolation on the pyre of ones deceased husband on the part of women. Self immolation may be eradicated completely and the widows should not be sentenced to the life of isolation and self-abnegation, the Gurus allowed the remarriage of widows. Guru Nanak in *Gauri Rag* recommended that the widow ought to have the right to exercise her option for re-marriage. The custom of sati had been prevalent since long in the Punjab as well as in other parts of India. Herodotus describes it as practised by the ancient Scythians and Thracians. Rig Ved and Athur Ved also refer to it. Strabo reports that the custom prevailed in India in the time of Alexander. In Hindu literature especially that which came into existence during and after the Epic period, it was accorded religious sanction.

Likewise, wearing of veils was also discarded by the Sikhs. Whatever historical reasons for this practice to emerge and take root, it impinged on the freedom of women. In view of all this, Dorothy field remarks, "The most notable social improvement was the emancipation of woman, many of whom found salvation through the Gurus' teachings." The fact is significant in the context of the attitude of the people in general. The women in the eyes of the Sikh Gurus were co-partners of men in this world on equally. Guru Amar Das appointed ladies as preachers and assigned them Manjis (missionary centres) to carry on preaching work among women.

The status of woman in Sikh family is as respectable as that of a man. Both wife and husband form a coherent growing/ harmonious whole marching in togetherness toward the highest ideal displaying their commitment to strengthen social relationship in spirit of love and harmony.

Marriage

Marriage was considered as 'one of the greatest felicities of human life'. The Muslims followed the edict of the prophet that every Mohammadan should marry. Abul Fazl writes: "If there be no marriages, then the fountain-head of humanity shall become choked and the stream of divine benevolences shall sink into the Sand." For the Hindus also it was a must because male offspring was necessary for their salvation. Marriage among the Muslims, however, was not made in heaven but is contractual.

The general tendency both among the Muslims and the Hindus was towards early marriage. According to Abul Fazl, it is held expedient that the bride should be under eight and any age over 10 is thought improper. An enlightened king like Akbar was concious of the dangers inherent in such early marriages and issued orders that the boys were not to marry below the age of sixteen and girls not below the age of fourteen.[5] It was the duty of the Kotwal to verify and note down the ages of the couple before giving his consent to the marriage.[6] The order was, however, not rigorously enforced nor renewed by later Emperors.[7]

Inter-caste marriages among the Hindus were out of fashion. No such restrictions existed among the Muhammedans. Barring a few close relations such as mother, grandmother, sister, niece, aunt, mother-in-law, step-daughters and granddaughters, there was complete freedom of choice.[8] But, in spite of this, marriages between Shias and Sunnis, Turks and Indians were very rare. Marriages between near-relations were common among Muhammedans. Akbar, however, considered it improper to enter into matrimonial alliance with near and dear ones.[9]

Monogamy was observed by the generality of the Hindus who would take to a second wife only if the first wife was sick or proved barren or the children dies.[10] A free-born Muslim could marry at least four wives at a time, but the common Mohammedan, it appears, preferred to have one wife. Akbar favoured monogamy, and considered it highly detrimental to a man's health to have more than one wife. He passed orders that a man of ordinary means should not have more than one wife. The wealthy people had several wives—sometimes exceeding the limit prescribed by the prophet. According to Chopra, there were many discussions over this controversial issue in the Ibadat Khana and the final decision reached by the Ulemas was that a man might marry any number of wives by mutah but only five by nikah.

Gay marriages were strictly prohibited in all sections of Indian society.

Islam, Hinduism and Christianity being male-dominated religions rooted in ancient patriarchal traditions from a more premitive age. Woman was not accepted as equal to his male partner. Although this prejudice has been existing since long, there is no solid and specific evidence of its justification. Though in Islam women gained economic rights as individuals to own their property, free of interference from their husband, yet their status was far from being equal to their husband. Under Islam women could give evidence in court but in some cases the word of two women was required to match the gravitas of a single male witness. Strict rules were developed for the exclusion of women from prayer or even touching *Quran* during menstruation.

Among the Hindus, the status of women was a sterio type of what Manu had delineated. The Sikh Gurus, however, were very vocally preached perfect equality between bride and groom in all spheres of social and political activities.

Re-marriage of widows was not common among the Hindus as it was among the Muslim except Sayyads, Pathans, and Rajputs. Among the jats, a widow generally married her husband's brother. Those persons who had come under the influence of the Sikh Gurus did not observe any inhibitions of widow-remarriage. Divorce was common in the hills.[11] "Among the Sikhs divorce was discouraged."

The selection of a match was left solely to the discretion of the parents. The boys had little say while the girls, excepting those of the upper class, had none at all. Usually, marriages among were contracted through the mediation of Brahmin match-makers. Guru Nanak's marriage was arranged through the mediation of a family prohit. A liberal king like Akbar wished that consent of the bride and the bridegroom and the permission of the parents should be sought before the confirmation of a marriage.[12]

The custom of sati according to which a Hindu widow[13] burnt herself alive on her husband's pyre, whether she was willing or not, was rampant. Guru Nanak preached against this detestable custom. Akbar prohibited this inhuman custom through a royal farman.[14] Jahangir made this practice a capital offence. Shah Jahan also prohibited sati. Similarly, Aurangzeb issued an edict in 1664 forbidding this practice. The Mughal government did not succeed completely in its aim. Nonetheless, it exercised considerable check over it. Bernier, a European traveller, who stayed in India for twelve years, has given a vivid picture of this evil practice in these words: "the Mohamedans by whom the country is governed are doing all in their power to suppress the barbarous custom. They do a part of their polity to leave idolatrous population, which is much more numerous than their own, in the free exercise of its religious but the practice is checked by indirect means. No woman can sacrifice herself without permission from the governor of the province in which she reside and he never grants it until he shall have ascertained that she is not to be turned asides from her purpose and to accomplish this desirable end, the governor reasons with this widow and he makes her enticing promises; after which, if these methods fail, he sometimes sends her among his women, that the effect of their romances may be tried."[15]

Social Etiquettes and Manners

The statement of the writer of *Mirza Nama* that "social calls have never been in vogue" is only partially true. People did visit one another on various occasions such as births, marriages, sicknesseses and funerals, etc. but that the frequency of such visits was not much due to two reasons: the prevalence of caste system and purdash system, and the inability of women on account of restrictions imposed by society to attend to male guests or to talk familiarly with them.

Even then, social living, might it be on a restricted scale, caused social etiquettes and manners to emerge which on analysis, were found to be mainly inspired by Indian cultural ethos and to some extent by the Perso-Arabic group-living.

Formalities for Receiving a Guest

Visitors were received with many formalities during the Mughal days. Whenever a visitor arrived, it was customary for the master of the house to receive him at the gate. In case he was an elderly or spiritual person, it was usual in a Hindu home to wash his feet. In case there was no information, the housekeeper would rise up in his seat. The visitor was then taken to the drawing room which in case of a rich family was well-decorated spread over with beautiful carpets and having velvet cushions so arranged as to enable the visitors to incline and rest. In ordinary homes, a cot and a mat would serve the same purpose. Chairs were rarely used.

While sitting, all care was taken that legs or feet were not visible and the persons who let their legs or feet be seen were considered to be devoid of manners. Nobles and governers usually received their visitors in their daily durbars held in the Diwan-khana richly decorated with handsome rugs and costly tapestry. The visitors took their seats on his either side according to their rank or dignity after the usual salams (salutations).

The Punjabi manner of conversation was informal, frank and polite but not modest. While talking to the elders or superiors, the people were very careful and shirked using the language unpalatable to them. Religious teachers, Brahmins and the Quzis were specially cared for and respected. Babar who calls the Pathans rustic and tactless, says, "Biban waited on me, this person sat, although Dilawar Khan, his superior in rank, the sons of Alam Khan who are of royal birth, did not."[16]

The decorum maintained in places of worship was exemplary.[17] The people made no gestures and were never indecent in their discourses with one another. In religious assembles held whether at Shivala or Gurdwara, the behaviour of the people was that of devotion and affection for one another.

Manucci describes five types of salutations prevalent among the Hindus in Mughal days. Ram-Ram, the most popular form of greeting among equals has been referred to by many travellers. Often the palms of the hands were folded and raised upto the stomach as a mark of respect to an elderly friend. A person of higher status was greeted by raising the folded hands above the head. Greater respect was paid to an elder, father, mother or spiritual teacher. The younger would greet an elder by bowing down touching his or her feet and raising the hand to his head. He would even prostrate himself before his teacher. The votaries of Guru Nanak returned salutation with the words 'Sat Kartar'. The Mohammedans greeted each others with the word 'As-Salam-Alekam', the other responding 'Wa-Lekum-as-Salam'. Kurnish and Taslim have been mentioned by Abul Fazal as the recognised modes of salutation to the king. Kurnish consisted in placing the palm of the right hand on the forehead and bending down the head. While in Taslim, the person placed the back of his right hand on the ground raised it slowly till he stood erect, touched the breast and then he put the palm of his hand on the top of his head. Babur related that it was the custom to kneel thrice before the king upon taking leave or upon presentation, or upon receiving a mansab, a jagir, or a dress of honour or an elephant or a horse but only once on all other occasions.[18] This mode of worship became common and if we are to believe Ovington, Akbar issued orders that Taslim should be repeated thrice. Akbar, the founder of Din-i-Ilashi, introduced another salutation called Sijdah which consisted in bowing down the forehead to the earth. But soon, this custom was discontinued in Darbar-i-Am because it was looked upon as tantamounting to man-worship. Aurangzeb forbade even Taslim and recommended only Salam-Ale-Kum.[19]

Charity

Charity, being the very important element of both the religions—Hinduism and Islam—was considered a great virtue by the people. Zakat, the annual legal alms[20] of five things, viz. money, cattle, grain, fruit and merchandise was obligatory on every Mohammedan.[21] The building of temples and mosques had its own merit among the Hindus and Mohammedans respectively. Guru Nanak, who lived during the period, said, "The wealth of those who have not given alms shall slip away". Though no line can be drawn, yet the Hindus preferred to give away edibles like rice, corn, grain, etc. in charity while Mohammedans believed in offering garments, blankets sheets and shoes.[22]

Abul Fazl admires the Indians who were ever ready to extend help to anyone, may be a strange on someone in distress and would grudge neither property and life nor reputation in his cause.

Inspired by the spirit of charity, tanks and rest houses were built at various places. Rai Goverdhan Suraj Dhwaj who flourished during the reign of Jahangir is said to have built serais and tanks on the road from Delhi to Lahore. Guru Amar Das got built a Baoli at Goindwal. Guru Ram Das got excavated the tank known as Amritsar and Santokhsar. Guru Tegh Bahadur is said to have inspired the people to spend their charities on sinking wells to supply water to the travellers and others. The Hindus, being strict believers in the theory of transmigration of souls, were particularly charitable towards birds and beasts.[23] In Sikhism charity or giving to the needy was recognised an act of high spiritualment.

Furniture

Furniture did not undergo any radical change. It was as old as over. Chairs were considered superfluous because the Indian mode of sitting did not necessitate it. But it does not imply that chairs were non-existent. Several contemporary paintings depict

Mughal kings and even their nobles sitting in chairs having arms and high backs. The seats, sometimes cushioned, were always wider than they are today. The legs of the chairs were sometimes carved out and the feet were connected by wooden planks. Some of the chairs were covered with ivory. Couches usually made of precious wood or even metals were well-cushioned with costly carpets and rugs.

Stools were often used for sitting purposes. Khatt or bedstead was the most common article of furniture used by the rich and the poor alike. These bedsteads woven with cords or braids of cotton or silk according to the owner's means, had their legs often painted or glassed. Gilded beds have also been mentioned by Bernier. The bed clothes of the rich were costly and comprised coverlets which were sometimes made of silk and embroidered. Ordinary beds were made of cotton. Good mattresses were much in demand in those days. Carpets were the most important furnishing articles in the drawing rooms of Diwan Khanas. Akbar caused great improvements to be made in the carpet-weaving industry as a result of which wonderful varieties and charming textures were produced. Lahore and Kashmir carpets were particularly famous. Another item in the furniture was the fan. During the Mughal days, the common people used fans made from the leaves of the palm and coconut trees. But the rich had broad fans, made of soft leather or even of ivory.[24]

Drinking

Drinking was a common habit and many people died of intemperance. Murad and Danyal, sons of Akbar, died of excessive drinking. Jahangir, though himself a hard drinker, knew the evils of drinking and endeavoured to check this evil when he came to the throne and to this end he issued edicts prohibiting the sale of wine and 'Bhang', but it appears, much success could not be achieved in this respect. By the time, Shah Jahan occupied the throne, people took wine like water.[25] Shah Jahan tried, like his father and grandfather, to check the evil but he did not succeed in imposing prohibition. Bhang was also used by the people but generally on festive occasions.[26] The use of betel was not common in Punjab. Opium and poppy seeds were also consumed.[27]

Ornaments

The use of ornaments was as popular as ever in India. A few ornaments, however, became popular only with the advent of the Muslims. Males wore anklets, bracelets and armlets. Kamarband, an ornament of the waist, was commonly used by both the sexes. The nose ring was the Muslim contribution. Beside this, the Muslims made ear-rings much lighter but more brilliant and valuable than before. The children of the rich wore gold or silver bells and chains round their waists. The necklaces, collars, girdles, ear-rings, anklets, rings and bracelets were the most important ornaments of the women of Punjab.

The use of betel or pan to colour the lips as well as to sweeten the breath and of henna to colour the palms, nails and finger-tips of hands, as well as nails and soles of the feet were common among women. The henna was also used to dye grey beards, moustaches and hair. The shoes of the nobles were of valvet or red leather. The people in general wore shoes made of ordinary leather prepared by the village shoe-makers, commonly known as Chamars or Mochis.

Food

The nobles took very rich diet. A large number of dainty dishes were taken both at lunch and dinner. Meat of different varieties and tastes was prepared daily. Fresh ordinary fruit was commonly used by them and there are references that the Mughal nobles used to procure dry or fresh fruit from Kabul and Kashmir. Sharbat or sweet drinks were also commonly served. The food of lower classes, particularly of workers and peasants was very poor. It consisted of dry bread which was taken either with cooked pulse or vegetables or butter and milk. "When they eat it, they stir it with the ends of their fingers in melted butter. Wheat is the usual food of the soldiers and poor people", says Travernier. The use of butter-milk (lassi) was also common. The Hindus were mostly vegetarians while the Muslims were rarely vegetarians. The high-ups of both Muslims and Hindus had no inhibitions in regard to wine and meat diet.

Amusements

There were many kinds of amusements in which both the nobles and people took lively interest. Chaugan, Kabutar Bazi (pigeon flying), hunting, gladiotorial combats, elephant fights, and swimming were quite popular outdoor pastimes. Chandal Mandal was another outdoor pastime and even the women joined their men in revelry with freedom. Of the indoor games, Shatranj (chess) and Chaupar, the game played with dice or kowaries (sheels) on a piece of cloth or board, were very popular with the aristocrats and commoners alike. Gambling was also a source of recreation. Music and dancing were other indoor means of entertainment. Qamargah was the greatest amusement of the Mughals. In Shah Jahan's period, female dancers and public women enjoyed great liberty and existed in a large number. They were called on all festivals. The nobles kept them in their harems for amusements. The Hindus on certain auspicious days celebrated innumerable religious festivals. The Beas, the Jhelum, the Chenab, the Ravi and the Sutlej were regarded as most sacred by them. Nagarkot was one of the most important places where people from far and near assembled every year to observe the religious rites.

Display of fire-works was one of the exciting amusements of the ladies. Manucci writes: "Their amusement at night is generally to have large torches lighted on which they will spend more than one hundred and fifty thousand rupees."

Dress

Dress occupied a fairly prominent place in the life of the ladies of royalty and nobility. In the days when the upper class ladies had limited occupations and their physical charms was the only pass-port of royal favour, most of them devoted their almost entire attention to their dresses. Women of royalty and nobility took pleasure in putting on elegant and costly dresses.

The material used in the dresses was usually silk, doria (stamped cloth) and muslin. Sometimes the dresses consisted of Zarbaft (cloth woven by golden thread), Tiladoz, Makkeshkar, Kimkhwabs (varieties of cloth made of gold) and Kalbattu (golden trackets). The dresses were embroidered with gold and silver. Laces were added to make them graceful. The difference between the dress of nobility, royalty and that of the middle class lay mostly in the quality of the material and the price rather than in style.

The dress of the ladies during the time of Babur and Hamayun bore resemblance to the practice followed in Persia and Khurasan to which most of them belonged. They were trousers which were wide and loose. They covered their upper parts with shirts which were fastened at the back. Another garment with a V-shaped collar was also used. In addition to them, an upper garment named Yallek was also in vogue. It was buttoned in front, had a deep neck and had either half sleeves or full sleeves. Some other garments used in those days were poston, Ulbeg, Baniach and Tarhat. They also used Pishwaz (gowns).

In course of time, Indian patterns began to fascinate Muslim women of the upper classes. The reasons were not far to seek. Firstly, the climate of Punjab affected the dress-pattern. Secondly, the liberal policy of Akbar created an atmosphere of unity and harmony wherein the Hindus and Muslims met one another in a spirit of friendship.

New costumes emerged from the time of Humayun. Princesses put on dresses resembling those of Turkish women. They dressed their hair in the typical Hindu way. They no longer left their hair loose and parted but twisted them into different shapes. Towards the end of Humayun's reign Turkish ladies started using the ornaments which the Hindu women usually wore. As regards the head-dress of the Mughal ladies, the Taj-i-Kulah which was the favourite head-gear of queens and princesses upto the 15th century, began to lose popularity and Tagi, a high crested cap, began to take its place. The married girls wore Tagi with a veil hanging called Lachak or Qasabad.

Rajput ladies wore Angiya, a high fitting bodies. It could be half-sleeved or full sleeved. Below the Angiya Lahanga was worn. To the ends of Izarband (bending cord) were attached bunches of pearls to add elegance and beauty to the dress. Finally to complete the set, Odhni was used.

Like Hindu ladies, the Muslim ladies also used Dupatta. Nurjahan introduced various new dresses of brocade and gowns, famous among them being 'Nur Mahali', Do Dami, Panchtolia, Ordhnis (veils), Badlah (Brocade), Kinari (lace) and Farshi-Chandini (carpets of sandal wood colour). An elegant item of female dress called Jammu female dress appeared during this period. It consisted of a tight fitting kurti (small shirt), hanging down to knees. It was decorated with frills in the front and was worn along with short Angya. In the lower part tight-fitting trousers were worn. The material used for trousers was silk either printed with flowers or striped. Light thin cloth was used for veil.

During the reign of Shah Jahan, the same dress continued except one change. The kurti grew in length and reached upto the ankle. The ladies wore heel-less slippers called popash. They were of various patterns.

The dress of common Muslim women consisted of a shirt and a trouser. The shape of their trousers varied. Hindu women generally wore choli which was a small jacket worn around the chest. Below it they wore sari.

The upper class males had a special taste for silk and cotton, as they preferred these fabrices to flimsy gauze-like stuffs which were in fashion with the aristocracy. The nobles bound their beards with a scarf called 'Romali'[28] and they tied around waist a cubit long white cloth with a red border. They also wore a white wrapper above that salwar and shirt as upper and lower garments were in vogue. Gown was also worn over the shirt. The attire of the males of the poor class was made of coarse cloth. In the case of labourers and ordinary menl included a piece of cloth for the head and a string tied round the waist with a cloth about the size of a napkin (langoti) hiding the private parts. Women upto twelve had not much to wear like boys. They tied their hair on one side. They pierced their ears to wear ornaments. They used petty coats and dhotis. Purdah (Hajab) was often observed among the Urban Muslim ladies.

NOTES

1. De Laet, *Empire of the Great Mughals* tr. by Hoyland and Bannerjee.
2. There were quite a number of instances in which the Rajput Rulers of the Hill States in Punjab had raised or degraded the status of individuals and groups.
3. Both Bernier and Tavernier say that at the end of Shah Jahan's reign official tyranny was prevalent to a large extent.
4. B.S. Nijjar, *Punjab Under the Great Mughals*, p. 140.
5. P.N. Chopra, *Social Life During the Mughal Age*, p. 16.
6. *Ibid*., p. 17.
7. *Ibid*., p. 18.
8. Herklots, *Islam in India*, p. 56.
9. P.N. Chopra, *op. cit*., p. 23.
10. B.S. Najjar, *op. cit*., p. 161.
11. *Ibid*.
12. P.N. Chopra, *op. cit*.
13. V.A. Smith, *Akbar the Great Mughal*, pp. 131, 133.
14. A.L. Srivastav, *Akbar The Great*, Vol. III, p. 65, Shivalal and Aggarwal Co., Agra, 1973.
15. Bernier, *Travels in the Mughal Empire*, pp. 306-07.
16. A.S. Beveridege, *Babur Nama*, p. 466.
17. Referring to the assembles Palsaert writes: "It is more like a school of wise and virtuous philosophers than a gathering of false infidels."
18. A.S. Beveridege, *Babur Nama*, pp. 183-84.
19. P.N. Chopra, *op. cit*., p. 67.
20. *Ibid*., p. 71.
21. Herklot in his book, *Islam*, pp. 113-14, says that the legal alms may be given to the following classes of pilgrims who are unable to defray the cost of their journey, faqirs and beggers, debtors unable to pay their debts, champions in the cause of God, travellers who are without food, proselytes to Islam.
22. M.A. Macauliffe, *Sikh Religion*, VII, p. 14.
23. P.N. Chopra, *op. cit*., p. 72.
24. *Ibid*., p. 119.
25. Manucci, Vol. I, p. 5.
26. M. Akbar, *The Punjab Under the Mughals*, p. 253.
27. *Ibid*., p. 254.
28. Refer to the evidence of Babur in his *Memoirs*.

Architecture and Painting

11

During the early years of the Mughal administration, the country was too unsettled to produce any construction work of distinction, but gradually a form of a building art emerged which in the course of time developed into one of the most important architectural styles in India. According to Percy Browne, "The type of building thus evolved was no provincial or even regional manifestation. On the contrary it was an imperial movement affected only in a moderate degree by local influences as it displayed the same uniformity in its architectural character as well as in its structural principles in whichever part of the empire it was introduced."[1] The factors responsible for this remarkable development were the wealth and power of the empire itself, the relatively settled conditions that prevailed in most parts of the country and the aesthetic nature of the Mughal rulers themselves.

Babar relates in his Memoirs that a considerable amount of building construction was undertaken at his orders chiefly in the form of ornamental gardens and palaces, but as these projects were of a secular nature, they have been allowed to fall into decay leaving only the barest traces of their existence. There are, however, two mosques which have survived and have been attributed to this ruler: one, Kabuli Bagh at Panipat and the other, a Jama Masjid at Sambhal. These are fairly large structures but do not possess any distinctive architectural character. Humayun, because of the vicissitudes of his reign, could not do much in the domain of architecture. The two mosques which remain of the buildings erected during his reign in a ruinous condition—one at Agra and the other at Fatahabad—

speak very little of the style or the design. But both Babur and Hamayun affected the course of architecture in another way. Babur, the most dynamic personality in the history of Asia, brought certain architectural traditions from Samarkand and Persia. Similarly, Hamayun as a result of his stay at the court of Shah Tehmasap, brought into India some of the architectural traditions of Persia. So Persian influence did affect the architecture of the Mughals as it developed in India. Babur brought some pupils of Sinan, the celebrated attomon architect Yusaf, a pupil of Sinan is said to have built palace at Delhi, Agra and Lahore during Akbar's period.

According to Percy Browne, "The traditions did not reveal themselves within Humayun's life-time but matured after his death and are found in this monarch's mausoleum at Delhi, the earliest building of note to be erected during the Mughal rule. This building was built under the supervision of Mirza Ghiyas of Persia and represents an Indian interpretation of Persian conception, as while there is much in its structure that is indigenous, there is at the same time much that can be of Persian extraction."

Akbar did not adopt the ready-made Persian styles of building, nor did he want to superimpose Persian styles or designs on the Indian way of building. He selected the style which fulfilled his own purposes. "Such a course was typical of this monarch's policy as a whole, the first principle of which was the encouragement of the indigenous system of his subjects, and only when these proved ineffective, did he lay under consideration the experiences of other countries."[2] In the sphere of the building art too, Akbar found the artisans of India still maintaining the living tradition of their craft. The style of building that evolved under this ruler's patronage was chiefly executed in red sand-stone readily available in these parts, with insertions of white marble not infrequently introduced for purposes of emphasis.

In principle, the construction was of the trabeate order although the arch was often used but mainly in its capacity as decorative arcading; as a matter of fact in its appearance but not in structure, the style was arcuate and trabeate in almost equal proportions. It is also possible to see by its character that it was not far removed from a wooden origin, a method of construction that was still practised in the more northern parts of Hindustan as may be observed in the secular architecture of Punjab at such places as Lahore, Chiniot and also in Kashmir. During this early Mughal period, the dome was of the Lodi type, sometime built hollow but never technically of the true double order. The pillaı shafts were usually many sided and the capitals were almost invariably in the form of bracket supports. As to the ornamentation carved or boldly inlaid, patterns were common while painted designs were often produced on the interior walls and ceilings."[3]

These main elements of Akbar's style of architecture were typified in the fort of Lahore in Punjab as also in that of Agra. The Lahore fortress was similar in style to that of Agra as it is made in red sand-stone with the combination of beam and bracket forming its principal structural system. Yet the workman engaged at Lahore while employing the same methods appear to have been more imaginative in their ornamental conceptions than their fellow craftsmen at Agra, as if by a technical process different from those which had preceded it, so that these later Jahangiri buildings not only mark a change in the architectural style but also in the method of decoration. Hitherto the inlaid work had been of the kind known as open sectile, a marble in tarsia of various colours, from now onward the art took the form of that called pretra duara in which hard and rare stones such as Onyx, Jasper, Topaz, Cornellian and the like were embedded in the marble in graceful foliations.[4] The most important monuments of this period are the gateway to a Sarai at Jalandar, and the Jahangir's mausoleum at Shahdara near Lahore most of which was probably constructed after his death under the orders of his remarkable consort, Nur Jahan Begum. The former is a small but attractive structure, although somewhat of the precious order, as the designer has aimed at a nicety of details rather than breadth or strength. Jahangir's tomb, as was becoming the custom of the Mughals, occupies the centre of an immense garden which was square and on the old bank of the

Ravi river. The tomb also is a square in plan and of 325 ft side. It is a structure of one storey only having handsome octagonal minarets in four stages rising up from each corner to a height of 100 feet above the ground level.

"No capacious interior effect was aimed at in this mausoleum, it was evidently to be regarded more as a monumental reliquary than a mortuary hall. The internal arrangements, therefore, consist of a corridor leading to a range of rooms continued right around the outer sides of the building, and a series of compartments, one leading from the midst of each side to the tomb chamber in the centre of the whole.

Architecturally speaking, the building except for the four minarets, is not distinctively impressive. It strikes only because of applied colour decoration distributed freely over all its surfaces. In doing so, several processes were called into requisition, fresco-painting, in-lay and mosaic tiles. Viewed as a whole, there is in its speciousness and its setting something of the character of the nature-loving monarch whose remains it enshrines, his preference for wide terraced gardens glowing with flowers and brilliant colouring generally recalling similar qualities in his famous ancestor Babur both of whom seem to have been as much interested in the works of nature as in those of man."[5]

Besides this, the Khwab Gah and Moti Masjid, are two other monuments of Jahangir in Punjab. The former is a marble sleeping pavilion, which stood within a large quadrangle enclosed on three sides by a colonnade of red stone pillars, intricately carved with bracket capitols consisting of the figures of peacocks, elephants and griffins. In the centre of the fourth side which overlooked the river stood a pavilion in the Mughal style of architecture and on either side at the point of contact of the colonnade with the outer wall were two chambers with verandahs of elaborately carved pillars supporting a sloping Chhaja in the Hindu style.

Moti Masjid was got built at a cost of 3 lakh of rupees. It is an instance of supreme perfection of art continued with simplicity.[6] Formerly, it was a private chapel royal of the ladies of the Imperial Harem.

With the reign of the Emperor Shah Jahan, we reach the period when the Mughal glory was at its height. It had its effect on the style of architecture which grew to be of exceptional splendour in the sphere of buildings. It was an age of marble, this material in most refined form taking the place of the sand-stone hitherto largely employed, so that architecture received a new impressiveness during this regime.

Such a change in the substance of the building art brought with it many changes in its temper and treatment. Marble, especially of the textual quality, provided its own decorative appearance owing to its delicate graining and any ornamentation required to be most judicially applied; otherwise the surfaces become fretted and confused. The forms, therefore, of this style were essentially marble forms, while the decoration was only occasionally plastic, such enrichment as was considered essential being obtained by means of inlaid pattern in coloured stones. With this change in technique there ensued a change in the larger architectural elements of the style. Particularly noticeable is the alteration in the character of arch, the curves of which were now often foliated, usually in each case by means of cusps, with the result that white marble arcades of engraved arches became a distinguishing feature of the period. The dome also assumed another form, as the Persian type bulbous in its outlines. Other developments were: (i) introduction of pillars with tapering or bluster shafts, voluted brackets, capitols and foliated bases, (ii) structural and ornamental elements of curvilinear order, (iii) the fluidity of line and form, sensuousness generally reflecting the exalted conditions that commonly prevailed when a ruling power has attained its greatest elevation.

The preference of Shah Jahan for buildings of this kind is too apparent to need any detailed treatment. He caused many of his predecessors' sand-stone edifices dismantled with the sole object of replacing them with more polished type. In the Lahore fort, a number of Akbar's sand-stone structures were swept away to make room for pavilions of a more elegant type. In their places rose most of the buildings towards the northern side of the enclosure such as Diwan-i-Am, Khwab Ghah, the Shish Mahal, the Shah Burj, and the Naulakha. The introduction of marble structures into the sand-stone fortress was a preliminary procedure, a preparation for the magnificent architectural schemes undertaken by Shah Jahan which gave distinction to the Mughal reign under Shah Jahan.[7]

In Punjab, side by side this development, another architectural style was becoming manifest. The focus of this independent development was the city of Lahore; but examples of it are found in some other places in Punjab as well, where for some time, it was a regional mode. This phase of architectural expression took the form of structures composed of: (i) brick masonry with an occasional insertion of sand-stone for additional strength, (ii) exterior decoration covering most of its surfaces with patterns in brilliantly coloured glazed tiles. "Such a technique in construction and ornamentation was the result of two factors, firstly the geological conformation to Punjab, and secondly the proximity of this part of the country to the powerful empire of Persia with which the northern frontier was contiguous. The first factor can be accounted for because in the alluvial plain comprising much of this region, a stone outcrop is rare and so the natural tendency of the people, throughout their history, was always to build in brick and wood. The influence of the architectural style of Persia is responsible for the second of these factors, as for considerable periods, Punjab had learned to look to the north-west and beyond for its cultural inspiration. And at this particular time, the influence was usually strong, as during the first half of the seventeenth century, the Safavid art of Persia had attained its meridian, and Punjab came under its irresistible spell. Not that the brick buildings at Lahore and elsewhere reproduced exactly the style of those incomparable structures that Shah Abbas a few years earlier had set up in his new capital at Ispahan, but they were in the same tradition, and above all, they depended largely for their appearance on the brilliant rural decoration executed in a like technique."[8]

The most important example of this phase of architecture was Wazir Khan's mosque in Lahore which was built in 1634; other buildings representing this mode of architecture being the gateway of Gulab Singh, Chaburji, the tomb of Ali Mardan Khan and of Sharaf-u-nissa, the Shalimar Bagh and mosque of Dai Anga. The mosque of Wazir Khan has been critically examined by Percy Browne who says, "In the mosque of Wazir Khan this style is represented in its expansive and colourful mood. But its chief attraction lies in the fact that every portion of its structure, both inside and outside, is enriched with a variegated scheme of colour either by means of floral patterns painted in tampera, or panels of more conventional design executed in lustrous glaze."

After the death of Shah Jahan, the Mughal architecture deteriorated rapidly, mainly because of the indifference of Aurangzeb towards the subject of building construction. The architectural productions of the Mughals during the later half of the seventeenth century were less numerous and of a lower standard than those executed under any previous ruler of the dynasty. This tendency is clear from Jama Masjid in Lahore. This large mosque was erected in 1674 by Aurangzeb's master of ordinance, Fidhai Khan. In spite of the fact that the Badshahi Mosque in its architectural character retains much of the strength and solidity of the style at its meridian, it displays at the same time evidence of the change that was taking place in the spirit and substance of the building art. The defect is noticeable in the sanctuary facade which, though in good proportion, lacks that touch of vitality that spirited play of surface and contrast of light and shade that is the hallmark of all good architectural efforts.

After the death of Aurangzeb in 1707, the collapse of the empire was only a matter of time, and the few buildings in the Mughal style that were erected after this date are a melancholy proof of the decadent conditions that then prevailed.

Mansions of the Nobles

No uniform pattern was followed by the nobility in the construction of their houses in various parts of Punjab because the design of a building is conditioned by the climatic conditions in a particular region, the availability of materials and the taste of the builder. Even then the Muslim art of building was the dominant feature of the buildings of the nobles.

A house, however, in a country like India which is in the tropics was considered to be beautiful if the situation be airy and exposed on all sides to the winds. Many of the houses were built high and flat on the top whence fresh air was taken in the cool hours of the day. There were for warming purposes no chimneys attached to the houses for they never used fire.

In their upper rooms they had doors and windows to let in the air but used no glass.[9] An ideal house situated in the middle of a flowery garden would have courtyards, trees, basins of water. The tanks attached with these houses were filled with water drawn by oxen from wells. The roofs were generally kept flat so that the dweller might be able to enjoy the evening breeze. Khas Tatties (latrines) were also used but only in the summer.[10]

Houses of the Masses

Excepting the temples, a palaces and fortresses, the houses of the commoners were built of earth and wood. The floors were of pounded earth covered with cowdung. No Hindu ate without spreading cowding. The roofs were generally of SAR and earth supported with strong timber and coated with plaster. The purpose of the common people was to have a resting place and a cover against the inclemencies of weather. No aesthetic ideals were involved while raising a building.

Branches of trees, ropes and grasses of various kinds formed the main building materials of the houses. "Due to the frequent changes in the course of the river Jhelum, the people in Multan had their houses built of wood and grass."

Houses of the Middle Class

The houses of the traders, merchants and petty Umras were modest in their appearance as compared to those of the nobles. Some of them were built of bricks, burnt tiles and lime while others were of clay and straw. The attached rooms were supported by long, handsome pillars of wood. In the villages, the well-to-do zamindars had a several huts grouped together.

Sikh Buildings

Apart from the buildings mentioned above, another set of buildings, Sikh temples, represent a phase of architecture in themselves. In its social ideology, the Sikh movement stood for harmonious relations among all sections of people and particularly between the Hindus and the Muslims. This ideal was a welcome message to the people lacerated by narrow religious or other prejudices. Hence, it became a great moving force and its impact found expression in Sikh temples. The most important of these was 'Hari Mandir', built in the centre of a tank. Its foundation was laid by Guru Arjan Dev. The present building structure dates from 1764 while the greater part of its architectural appearance was added as late as the beginning of the nineteenth century. Yet it is almost sure that the builders while erecting the building did not alter it considerably because their motive was to revive the edifice as their Guru had raised. In its basic outline, there was no change and the foundation of the time of Guru Arjan Dev was not disturbed. The only approach to the shrine was through a causeway across the water which is over 200 feet long.

The idea of placing the temple in the middle of a sheet of water was conceived with a view to isolating the shrine in the metaphysical sense from its earthly environments, as also to add to its aesthetic aspect. The temple is a square building of some 50 ft. side situated at the centre of a square platform of 60 ft. side. It has four doors, symbolising its principle of equality of all people irrespective of caste, creed, clime and birth.

In architectural design it drew upon the Mughal and Hindu traditions and the local designs and styles. Its domes show the influence of Mughal architecture while its general outline, its cupolas and its lattices indicate the influence of Hindu temples. The location of a temple at the centre of a tank is something which can be descerned in both Hindu and Muslim buildings. The circumabulatory paths around the temple and the tank are also not new to Hindu architecture. The single hall of the temple partakes of the Muslim design of mosque building. The Sikh Gurus adopted the Muslim design in this respect, which well served the congregational mode of worship. Moreover, the hall gives the impression of a Buddhistic chaitya hall.

Although one can discern elements of Hindu, Muslim and Buddhists styles of architecture in the edifice of Hari Mandir, yet it was not done to emphasise any particular style. The ultimate purpose seems to be of adopting a design, distinctive and different. It was not representative; it was revealatory revealing harmony among all sections of people through the meditation in the sacred name of God.

Painting

No specimens of the art of painting of the Sultanate period are available, probably because of the Quranic prohibitions, this art was shunned by the Muslim rulers, the Muslim nobility and the rank and file. With the Mughals, however, a change in the attitude occurred. Humayun brought two painters Mir Sayyid Ali and Abdul Samad from Tabriz.

In the Sultanate period, it was believed that a painter who painted the figures of living beings imagined that he was giving life to the object of his painting and hence rivalling Allah (God) who alone is the giver of life. In view of this, the art of painting, at least of living beings, was considered irreligious by orthodox Muslims.[11] Akbar, on the other hand, held that painting made the artist feel humble before God because he could not give life.

On account of the former tendency, the early Muslim artists confined themselves to the painting of inanimate objects such as trees, rivers, water and fire, etc. Under Akbar the art of human portraiture developed. Akbar gave extensive patronage to the pictorial art which made considerable progress during his period. Khwaja Abd-al-Samad from Sheraz enjoyed special savour of Akbar.

Jahangir had his aesthetic faculties trained and developed to a remarkable degree, and he extended lavish patronage to different painters. This being so, the art of painting reached its highest water mark under him. The picture galleries at Lahore representing the Imperial family and the nobility, have been ranked among the finest in the world. That the pictorial art touched new heights can be seen from the picture of Guru Hargobind, drawn by an unknown artist and procured by Mr. Randhawa from amongst the leaves of Adi Granth at Kartarpur.

Shah Jahan was more interested in architecture than in painting, but he never discouraged painting. The paintings of his time were characterised by graphic colouring and ornamental borders. Under Aurangzeb this art suffered a decline in the

Mughal court, although it flourished in the Kangra, region of Punjab and the courts of the Rajput Princes.

The art of painting of the Great Mughals was full of softness and sentiment for chivalry and romance. Scenes of love-making, Laila and Majnu, Shirin and Farhad, Youths and Maidens dallying in gardens by the side of a stream, of gorgeous receptions of foreign ambassadors in royal courts, of feasts and festive functions where wine passed freely, where dainty dishes were served and were depicted equally well and in plenty. Then like every age of romance, conquest and mystery, this age was greatly interested in the super-natural and the marvelous. Genii, goblins, monsters and fairies moved amidst men as common well-known familiar figures. They were the stock-in-trade of the story-teller and the painter.

Gardens

The Mughal emperors and the nobles, by and large, had special fondness for gardens. The interest in laying these gardens was not confined to the males alone, some of the ladies were also interested in them. Among them were Bika Begam, the grandmother of Akbar, Mariam Makani, the grandmother of Jahangir, Shahar Banu Begam, and Maryan-uz-Zamani; Nur Jahan had the credit of having designed and inspired so many lovely pleasure spots. The garden called Shahdara which was built at her behest near Lahore is a fitting memorial to her aesthetic sense and taste for gardens. Jahan Ara Begam owned many gardens such as Bagh-i-Iishhad Bagh-i-Nur-Darshan, Bagh-i-Safa in Kashmir and a garden at Ambala.[12] According to Percy Browne, the idea of these retreats the Mughal emperors imbibed from Persia whose poets were for ever singing of their beauties. As for instance, Firdausi took particular pleasure in describing the garden of Afrasiab. Babur was so much obsessed with the things of nature that he commemorated the victory over Ibrahim Lodi in A.D. 1527 by laying out a large garden called as Kabali Bagh at Panipat. In addition to the part like enclosures surrounding most of the principal architectural projects of the Mughals, especially their tombs, spacious gardens were also created as pleasure resorts. The latter type of gardens were the famous gardens of Kashmir, among which the Shalimar and the Nishat Bagh are the best known. The Shalimar Bagh of Lahore also falls in this category. It was laid out by the Emperor Shah Jahan in 1637. Its layout plan is the same as we find in other cases. It is formed by means of a series of rectangular terraces arranged in descending levels with the object of maintaining a continuous flow of water throughout the entire system. In all instances the layout is conventional and axially symmetrical. There is a pattern in the conception but as a rule it is too geometrical to be rhythmic. The style belongs to the school of the formulists and not to that of the naturalists, the aim being to discipline nature and not to immitate it. Roshan Ara, Shah Jahan's daughter, had a great love for flowers and falls of water in the gardens.

The Panjaur garden was another famous garden of the Mughals. Fidai Khan, the foster brother of Aurangzeb, was a man of taste and laid out a beautiful terraced garden in imitation of the Shalimar Garden of Lahore and built magnificent mansions the glory of which is still evident. The garden was known for its red roses. A canal was dug at the foot of the neighbouring hills and led to the garden to irrigate its numerous grass plants and flower-beds and to feed its springs which added grandeur to the place.

NOTES

1. Percy Brown, *Indian Architecture*, p. 95, D.B. Tara Pore Vala Sons and Co., Bombay.
2. Percy Browne, *Indian Architecture* (Islamic Period), p. 95.
3. *Ibid.*
4. To find the difference kindly refer to the details given by Parcy Browne in his book *Indian Architecture* in regard to the tomb of Itmad-ud-Daulah at Agra.
5. Percy Browne, *op. cit.*, p. 103
6. S.M. Latif, *History of the Punjab.*
7. Percy Brown, *op. cit.*, p. 110.
8. *Ibid.*, p. 109.
9. P.N. Chopra, *op. cit.*, p. 73.
10. *Ibid.*, p. 74.
11. B.S., Nijjar, *op. cit.*, p. 184.
12. Rekha Misra, *Women in Mughal India*, p. 112.

Religious Configuration Through Period of Great Mughals

12

The religious configuration during the Mughal period underwent quite a number of changes. Many new contours appeared while a number of contours either lost their sharpness or simply obliterated under the impact of vicissitudes, fresh urges and impulses.

Sunni variety of Islam made much headway. Other prominent sects as for instance. Shias Quarmatians and Ishmailies also continued to flourish, although much less than Sunni variety. The religious elite both of Sunni Islam and various other, sects were as circumspect and hypocritical as they were when the Great Mughals established themselves in the Punjab. They were also as interfering in the affairs of state as they were earlier, although in periods of the Mughal emperors like Babar. Humayun and Akbar, they never domineered the state. Islamic Unitarianism which has been the faith of Sunni Muslims since long and according to which, they wanted to convert the whole of India into Dar-ul-Islam (land of Islam), also lost its crusading elan because of the eclecticism of the Mughal emperors, especially of Emperor Akbar. Under such circumstances, some of them whether out of self-interest or real concern for Sunni Islam were perturbed, thereby feeling impelled to rearrange themselves both polemically and organizationally. Certain new religious formations and formulations emerged while the old ones began to be reappraised. In the process rivalry between the Shias and Sunnies sharpened leading to violent clashes. In 1585 one Mirza Fallad Beg Bartas managed to get Mulla Ahmed, the Shia, on some pretext out of his house at midnight and stabbed him because he had reviled the companions of the prophets.

After burial of Mauled Ahmed, Faizi and Abul Fazul set guards over his grave, but despite this, people of Lahore exhumed his dead body and burnt it. Such clashes were not uncommon doing the whole of Mughal period, of course a little less during Babur through Akbar. During Aurangzeb, certain state fiats were promulgated to put restrictions on the Shias with a view to humiliating and degrading them because Shias did not conform to Sunnism as understood by Aurangzeb in particular. Ismailies and Qarmathians, the heterodox sects of shias were also scorned although the scorn rarely turned into violence. The main stream Sunni Islam besides facing opposition from mainstream Shias and its sects had to face challenge from certain other sects and movements which emerged in the sub-continent of India under Mughal rule.

One of them was the Roshnias. This was founded by Mian Bayazid born at Jalandhar in the Punjab in the year 1542-43 in the reign of Humayun. The sayings of Bayazids quoted in Dabistani-Mazahib expressed sound reason, pure morality and fervent piety. They had set aside the Holy Quran and believed that nothing existed except God, who filled all space and was the substance of all forms. The divinity despised all worship and rejected all mortifications. Prayers were allowed but there was no particular quarter to which they should turn because wherever you turn, you turn towards God. Religious bathing in water was not essential, for, as soon as wind blows upon us the body is purified in as much as four elements are equally pure. Bayazid himself and his son Jalal aggressively preached their convictions and recognized even robbery and docoity if the proceeds thus collected were to be distributed among the poor. Even they practised high-way robbery and deposited one fifth of their booty in a store-house to be given away to the needy. Roshanias never flaunted or claimed their identity separate from Sunni mainstream, but still the most orthodox of the Sunnis did not take them kindly especially when they questioned the utility of certain customs and modes of worship long cherished by the Sunni Muslims.

Mahdavi was another movement within mainstream of Sunni Islam. Its founder was Sayyid Mohammed of Jaunpur who claimed to be the *Mehdi* (the last Muslim prophet) who would restore Islam to its pristine vigor. He insisted that the Shariat should be followed strictly. The movement led by dedicated workers soon spread amongst all classes of people as it stressed the special historical mission of Islam to uphold truth to the world. A large number of people were affected by the Mahadvi doctine which brought about a greater adherence to the Shariat. In the Punjab Mahadavi movement was started by Sheikh Abdulla Niazi a famous disciple of Sayyid Mohammad of Gujarat who chose to settle in Sirhind. In 1565 C.E., at the time of expedition of Attock. When Akbar reached Sirhind, he granted him land as Maddi-Mash.

Sunni Islamists, however, were hostile to Mahadavis because they believed in the advent of Mehdi which bore witness to the Shia belief that their last Imam would appear to emancipate the suffering humanity, although Mahadavis themselves never considered themselves as Shias. Perhaps piqued at the questioning of heterogeneous sects or impelled by some inner impulse nurtured by the Naqshbandies of Central Asia. Sheikh Ahmed Sirhindi of Sirhind commonly known as Mujadd-id-Alf-i-Sani, the reformer of second millennium took upon himself, to revive Sunni Islam by purification from within and by protecting it from outside. He was born at Sirhind on 26 June 1564. He received his early education at home and later went to different teachers of renown to acquire knowledge of Hadies. Tafsir and rational science. He was initiated to Chishtia and Suharvardi silsalas and later joined the Naqshband Silsala under the discipleship of Khwaja Baqi Billa. He laid emphasis on (i) submission to laws percepts and traditions (ii) distance from innovations (Rafi-i-Bidat). He reproved the use of reason in matters of faith and held the opinion that "if reason were sufficient the great philosophers who had adopted reason as the guide should not have fallen in the melting pot of error." He believed the prophet as the vehicle of God's command, obedience to him is equivalent to obedience to God and hence true believers must conform in thought, word and deed to the injunctions and practices of the prophet. It was on this ground that he condemned all types of innovations. Sheikh's condemnation of innovations was all-inclusive and known no exception. Shi-ism was innovation which was worse than infidelity. He was fiercely hostile to the Hindus and considered nothing more pleasing than their humiliation. He was unhappy over the Muslims adopting Hindu manners and customs. He declared them wholly reprehensible and worthy of rejection. He held that purification of faith through Quran and Hedith as interpreted by the just and right-minded Ulemas. A strict adherence to law and abandonment of all innovations were the main principles of Islam which it was the duty of all Muslims to follow. He denounced Akbar's vagaries and efforts to weaken orthodox Islam as also the laxity of the Ulemas and upper classes and heterodoxy of the Sufis. He condemned the eclecticism of Akbar. In one of his letters to his disciple Farid Bukhari he expressed. "The monarch is to the world (state) as the heart to the body if the heart remains pure, it helps the body to be pure as well. The purity or impurity of the state depends upon its ruler...in the Akbar's reign) the infidels forced Pagan practices on the Muslim land and the Muslims were prevented from observing their religions commandments." He worked hard to propagate his views. He corresponded extensively. His correspondents included Khan-i-Khanam, Sikander Khan Lodhi, Mahabat Khan, Khani-Azam, Murtza Khan, Sheikh Farid Bukhari, Khana-i-Jahan, Qulich Khan. Sadari Johan *et. al.* His contact with high-profiled personalities made his creed very popular and orthodoxy gathered strength with the result that non-Muslim as well as all those owing allegiance to heterogeneous Islamic sects began to be considered despicable, some of them to be hated, humiliated even eliminated. Guru Arjan Dev and quite a number of Sufi saints such as Sarmad, etc. had to undergo sufferings, even executions at the hands of those who were either prodded or ordered by bureaucracy steeped deep in orthodoxy.

Side by side the strengthening of Sunni ideology and practices in spite of its challengers in the form of sects within Sunni mainstream as well as in the mainstream of Shias, it had to face the Sufis who claimed to be Islamist par excellence but were at variance with Sunnes especially in terms of approach to the ultimate destination. During the Mughal period, their influence had escalated considerably. According to Abul Fazal, there were fourteen orders of the Sufis out of which Chisti, Suharwardi and Qadirya orders played a crucial role in the Punjab.

Baha-ud-din Zakariya was the first to establish Saharwardi centre at Multan. Shaikh Yusaf in the beginning of the Lodi period and his grand-son Sheikh Bahud-din- at the end were at the helm of affairs. Ajodhan (Pak Pattan) was the most important seat of the Chisti order. In the early sixteenth century. Sheikh Ibrahim was the head of this seat. He was very popular and people called him Farid-Ganj or the second Farid. It was believed that one of the important factors to influence the state to be tolerant and accommodative to the non-Muslims during Jahangir and Shahjahan was Mian Mir and other Sufi saints, especially of Chisti order. The Qadiri Silsilah was founded by Shaikh Abdal Qadir Jilani (1265) of Baghdad. It was introduced in the subcontinent by Naim-ut-allah and Makhdum Mohammad Jilani towards the middle of the fifteenth century. Some of the most renowned Qadiri saints were Shaikh Dad Kirmani, Shaikh Abul Maali of Lahore, Hazrat Mian Mir and Mulla Shah Badakshi. Jahangir, Shah Jahan and Dara Shikoh held Mian Mir in high esteem. It is believed that Jahangir under the influence of Mian Mir stopped implementation of that part of his order according to which Guru Arjan Dev's properly was to be confiscated. Dara became disciple of Mulla Badakshi alongwith his sister Jahan Ara and the latter wrote a short biography of saints known as Manis-ul-Arwah. Dara in his Sikinat-ul-Auliya gave a detailed account of the life of Mian Mir and Mulla Shah and some of their disciples. Almost all the Sufi orders had full faith in Quran and Prophet Mohammad, singularity of God and his transcendence. His all powerfulness, but they differed from the Sunnis in their approach to realize him within oneself. According to M. Akbar they were pious rebels and words like fasts and pilgrimages were interpreted differently. Fast implied internal purgation of man, the Sign of Hilal (the crescent moon) brings to the inner mind a vivid picture of the eye-brows of the perfect spiritual guide. Id is knowledge of God. Kurbani (sacrifice) is the annihilation of the brutal spirit. Harmony, love or all, hatred towards none was the most important element of their social behaviour. They were both tolerant and respectful towards all religions and groups. They had a distinct catholicity of mind which had great appeal even to the Emperor Akbar not to speak of general public. Sheikh Mubarak, Sheikh *Faizi,* Dara Shikoh and Abul Fazal were the great exponents of Sufi philosophy. The Punjab did not remain unaffected by the fermentation of the electic ideas. The Sufi saints like Shaikh Ishaq-i-Kaka, Qazi Sad-ud-din, Shah Hussain, Shah Suleiman, Shah Inyat Qadari, Sheikh Wali Shah were prominent Sufis who worked hard to cement the relations between Hindus and Muslims as also between different sects among Muslims.

The overall social effect on the Punjab was the lessening of inter—communities and intra-sect bitterness and endengering of an impulse to harmonise relations on individual and social levels, Din-i-Ilahi was an epitome of that impulse.

From the facts detailed above it is not difficult to surmise that among the Muslims a sort of convulsion within the Muslim community had taken place. Inter-sects contradictions had emerged, each sect claiming its superiority to all others and considering its approach to non-muslims, unchangeable. A sort of new religious ferment had been created which foreboded certain vital changes. The state religious policy professed Sunni, yet it had been under stress and vacillated between liberalism and orthodoxy. Akbar was the champion of Islamic liberalism while Aurangzeb was a great proponent of Islamic orthodoxy and strove to bolster up Sunni Islamic beliefs, even through force, Many of his edicts amply demonstrate that he was hell-bent to revive. Sunni variety of Islam at all costs. In this process, he was not amenable to the liberal influences of Sufis and was unwilling to accommodate non-muslims as it was done in the time of Akbar.

Auragnzeb's fanatical allegiance to the Sunni Islam not withstanding, the Punjab religious landscape happened to be dotted with variety of contours.

The Hindu religion like the Muslim religion also underwent changes, generally speaking. The sects which existed on the eve of the inauguration of Mughal rule continued to exist although in their zeal and effect there was distinct alteration. The authority of the Vedas was recognised by almost all the Hindu sects though the position of the vedas as revealed knowledge was unique, Purans enjoyed the great popularity. Shaivism, Vaishnavism and Shaktism—the Major Sects of Hinduism, all had their respective following among the Hindus. Shaivism was more popular. The main reason of its popularity was its monastic order. According to Sujan Rai, the categories of Sanyasies were quite numerous, all of them were extremely ascetic in their practices, underwent hard penances and shunned the pleasure of senses. Vaishnavism and Shaktism both had ceased to enjoy that status which they had enjoyed earlier. In the Punjab deeper meanings of any sect were not followed equally by the masses and the practices. The Vaishnavites were satisfied with the worship of Vishnu and his various incarnations, visits to temples raised to house the icons of deity and of reading or listening to the Vaishavavite texts. The bairagies and Sanyasies who claimed to be committed to the spread of Vaishnavism freely indulged in malpractices and loose morals. Vaishnavism did not attack caste-system and empty Brahminical ritual system. Shaktism also suffered decline during the Mughal period. Its social stance was marred by the emergence of left handers as its branch, whose supreme ideal was idealization of the individual soul with the super-soul which could be attained through complex practices in which sexual union was accorded a very important place. Matsuya— fish, Mausa—flesh, maithuna—coitation, madhya—wine became extremely important to the Vamcharyas. The ritual indulgence in meat, wine and mathuna smacked of debauchery and naturally such a religion could not serve any social purpose.

Like Shaivism Vaisanavism and Shaktism, Jogism did exits but it began to loose creditability during the Mughal rule. Quite a number of Yogies met Guru Nanak during his itineraries. Guru Nanak's debatation with the Jogies then on sumer mountain has been recorded and texualised in Guru Granth Sahib under the title "Sidhi Ghost", Bhai Gurdas has also recorded the Guru's encounter with them in Achal Vatala. In Guru Nanak Parkash authored by Bhai Santokh Singh, Guru Nanak has been shown as deliberating with Machhinder Nath, Charpat, Gopi Nath, etc. who according to Dr. Kirpal Singh, the builder of the edited text of Guru Nanak Parkash were in fact their successors, who had assumed the names of their predecessors with a view to emphasizing that they embodied their techniques and instructions. The Jogies had twelve orders while the Sanyasies had ten according to Guru Nanak. Their influence had waned to a considerable extent because of their faith in otherworldliness.

The advent of Islam in India and new discoveries of the fifteenth or sixteenth centuries could only marginally move the Hindus society. Brahmanism continued to remain dominant feature of the religious life of Hindus in the Punjab.

During the reign of Akbar which was marked for religious liberalism, the Hindu society instead of salvaging itself from the dross that had engulfed it engaged itself to restructure its past traditions, beliefs and social structures with the result that Hindu revival was not a rebirth with new vitality but re-establishment of the past configurations which were a mis-match with the new needs of the society. Tulsi Dass literary Magnum Opus 'Ram Charitar Manas' was an eloquent testimony to this trend.

However, there were radical Bhaktas, notable among them being Namdev from Maharashtra, Ravi Dass and Kabir from Uttar Pradesh who conceived of Hindu religious life to be based on unpolluted spirituality, social equality, cosmopolitanism, unencumbered by meaningless rituals. These Bhagats/Sants had quite a large number of followers in Punjab committed to the belief system which accorded no recognition to icon-worship, caste-system, rituals and hegemony of the Hindu priestly class. From the aforesaid profile of different religious streams, the following conclusion edges out:

(i) That the religious landscape underwent a lot of changes.

(ii) That the traditional understanding of both the mainstream religions viz. Islam and Hinduism began to be questioned equally by their respective sects and people in general.

(iii) Traditional spiritual and social targets of both the mainstream religions began to be questioned, sometime vitrolically, sometime violently, resulting in conflicts sometime destructive, sometime creative but engendering impulse to search for fresh models of spirituality, polity and social morphologies, which might lead the people to realise their fresh aspirations, inspired partly by their own experiences and partly under the impact of the fresh geographical discoveries of the 15th and 16th centuries and the rise of mercantilism which suggested dismantling or modifying of the prevalent religious and cultural boundaries.

Sikhism—A Challenger and an Alternative

13

As it is made clear in the foraging narration that Punjabi Society by and large had turned sick with no elan left to cure it. Its major segments—Hindus and Muslims had been rendered bereft of any vitality to shed murk and dross because of their indulgence in wrong notions of spirituality, society and polity and incapacity to fashion suitable responses to the crises gripping it. True, there were certain positive responses as for instance Sufism among the Muslims and Bhakti movement among the Hindus. But they were on a small scale and could affect at best just a fringe of society. Further, they were framed in a setting which being almost similar to the one prevailing earlier was unlikely to give a push to the society to forge ahead.

Sikhism, however, provided a response which was quite new and fresh and was forged in the prospective which could release forces which could lead the society upward. It was not a religion in the traditional sense, rather it presented a blue print for the holistic development of individuals as well as society, rejecting all artificial barriers of caste, creed, wealth, status, etc. Its coverage was the whole mankind. It carried in its stock the requisite solutions to problems both at micro and macro levels. It was the vision and strategy to initiate process to bring about not only reconciliation between Hindus and Islamic civilizations but also to found a new model of civilization in the form of Sikhism on bases of the principle of equality, harmony and integrated development of society in all its aspects including economic one.

The medieval Hindu society was in the grip of an awful social malaise. It looked like a person on the verge of death, crying and shrieking for survival. It had lost its elan vital without which no society is able to respond to different challenges which it is bound to face from time to time. The Brahmins or others whom the social structure had assigned the job of fashioning creative responses to different challenges and to carry the masses along with them had ceased to play their historical role, rather they had circumscribed their activities to safeguard, sustain and promote their own interests, and naturally all their activities centred round this purpose.

Sikhism was the product of the historical situation that had thus been created. It was an attempt to meet the social and religious challenges involved in that situation. It originated with Guru Nanak[1] (b. April 1469, d. 1539). He was followed by a continuous line of nine successors who for about two centuries guided the destiny of Sikhism. The line of the Gurus ended with the death of Guru Gobind Singh in 1708.

The ultimate objective of Guru Nanak was to regenerate the individual and the society and to achieve this object he evolved a programme of action. He advocated strict monotheism which was different from that of Hinduism. The monotheism of Hinduism is expressed through plurality of deities, whereas Guru Nanak believed in no gods and goddesses, nor even in reincarnations of God. His God was infinite, beyond time and space, and self-existent. He never dies nor is he even born. Nanak disapproved of the worship of idols because people tended to look upon them as God. Nanak believed that God is Sat (Truth and Reality), fearless and enemity-less. This being so, Guru Nanak not only made God a spiritual concept but also based his principles of social behaviour on his concept of God. Since he is truth and beyond fear and enemity, to speak untruth, to nurse enemity and to act like a coward is irreligious. A good Sikh, therefore, must not only believe that God is one and the only one, omnipotent and omniscent, but also conduct himself in such a way towards his fellow beings that he should not look untruthful, filled with prejudice or enemity towards any one and he should always be merciful towards his fellow beings, ever ready to forget and forgive.

Nanak believed that the power that is God cannot be defined because God is Nirankar[2] (formless). All of his descriptions of God are consequently admissions of inability to define him:

> Thou hast a million eyes, yet no eye hast Thou.
> Thou hast a million feet, yet no feet hast Thou.
> Thou hast a million forms, yet no form hast Thou.
> Thou art without feet, yet no feet are without Thee.
> Thou art without odour, yet millions of odours emanate from Thee.
> With such charms, O Lord, hast Thou bewitched me.
> Thy light pervades everywhere. (Dhanasri)

Nanak had a variety of names for God, such as Father (Pita), Lover (Pritam), Master (Khasam), the Great Giver (Data). Nanak did this to show human dependence on God rather than invest him with anthropomorphic qualities. Although Nanak used both Hindu and Muslim nomenclatures for God—Ram, Govind, Hari, Murari, Rab, Rahim and Karim, etc., yet the attribute he usually ascribes to Him was of the True Creator (Sat Kartar) or the True Name (Sat Nam).

According to Nanak, the Guru's help is essential for the realization of God. But who is the Guru? Nanak uses the term Guru in three senses: (i) The Guru is God; (ii) The Guru is the voice of God; (iii) The Guru is word, the truth of God. How to reconcile these three senses of the term Guru? Apparently these terms do not reflect any identity; but on probing deep into the matter one would find the basic identity which these senses possess. The Guru in the sense of a perfect man who has realized God answers to all these different connotations of the term. He is the voice of God, the word of God, indeed God Himself. Such a perfect man's guidance is indispensable for any progress on the road to realization of truth.[3]

The ultimate object of man is to be God-like. For this he must imbibe all those qualities which emanate from truth, such as love, humility, honesty, compassion, contentment, truthfulness, etc.

The greatest enemy of man is *Haumai*[4] (self-centredness) which involves him in worldly attachments and does not allow him to seek truth. All the activities of an unregenerate man are guided by *Haumai*. Even that which man calls right or good is done only if it accords with his *Haumai* and if it is not in keeping with it, it is rejected. Without getting rid of *Haumai* the path to ultimate realization cannot be recognised.

The mind of the unregenerate man expresses itself in the evil impulses which are as follows: kam (lust); karodh (anger); lobh[5] (greed); moh (attachment) to worldly things); and Ahankar (pride).

To him the best course to conquer these evil forces was to practise *Nam*—ever remembrance of God—realization of His presence everywhere and in all objects, inanimate and animate. *Nam* is the remedy for the sick or diseased world. *Nam* is a realization, the coming of God's grace within oneself which obliterates the sense of the other and makes one not only be himself, but be a portion and link of God.

In order to realise the *Nam*, one will have to observe its discipline, that is to say, he must lead an ethical life, offer prayers, live the company of holymen (sangat) and develop an attitude of selfless service. The person who realises *Nam* makes no difference between the individual and the universal; he becomes *Gurmukh* who always does good to human beings. He does not abjure the world, he lives in it but lives like a lotus in water. He is a *Panch*, Plato's philosopher King, a Brahm Giani—one who has realised God and has acquired Divine knowledge. Such a person does not fear anybody. The Panch is ideal man of the Guru. His qualities have been described by Nanak in his composition *Jap*. He is a saint in religion, a true statesman in polities—all his actions are guided by *Bibek Budh* (sense of discernment). He is *Jiwan Mukt*—enjoying perfect release while living in the world. He attains perfection in virtue and happiness. Although the limitations of the body and the world are there, yet they do not restrict his perfection which is more of the soul than of the body. Perfection for him does not come after death. It is attained while the *Panch* is alive. He overcomes the idea of *Haumai* and feels one with the universal in nature. This type of person, always operates within God's *Hukam* (Divine Order). Guru Nanak did believe in the traditional theories of *Karma*, rebirth and transmigration of soul. But he also believed that the bondages of *Karma* are capable of being conquered or surmounted through self-exertion and divine grace.

Guru Nanak preferred a householder's life to the life of a recluse. The Guru himself led a householder's life and impressed upon the people to emulate him because this life is not an obstacle on the pathway to bliss, thus bringing out clearly the importance of living a full-blooded life in the world.

The compositions of Guru Nanak are replete with vitriolic criticism of meaningless superstitions, Brahmanical rituals, caste prejudices, untouchability and religious exploitations. The society which the Guru envisaged stemmed from his personal experience of the unity of mankind and oneness of God. The bases of his social philosophy were *kirt karo, Nam japo* and *wand chhako*. *Kirt karo* means that the people shall earn their livelihood by honest creative labour. *Wand chhako* signifies that one must share the fruits of one's labour put in honestly. By *Nam japo* was meant that people should meditate on *Nam*, i.e. they should not lose sight of the cosmic process and the divine will permeating everything in the world.

Besides this, if the society is to endure successfully the stress of different challenges, it is imperative for its members to be ethical in their attitude and behaviour at all levels. The Guru roundly condemned the unethical attitude of the people.

With creative thought alone, changes cannot be brought about. Requisite institutions have to be created to give a local habitation and endurance to it. Guru Nanak created institutions such as *Sangat*, *Pangat* and *Kirtan* for the further promotion of his cause. *Sangat* was an assembly of like-minded people engaged in the pursuit of truth. This organisation was open to all persons irrespective of their social status and caste-affiliation, etc. The Guru made it an instrument to shape the Sikh psyche and to promote the Sikh ideals of a casteless, classless and egalitarian society. It was also to be an organization to knit the Sikhs together to give them a corporate character. *Guru Ka Langar* (community mess) was another important institution created by the Guru. This institution possessed the potentiality of being a valuable instrument of social reform in a setting where caste taboos prevented people from sitting and eating together. Hence, from the very outset the institution of *Langar* was integrally associated with that of *Sangat*. This institution was of great significance. It went in a big way towards erasing social and economic inequalities; for everyone, irrespective of caste and creed, social status, sex and birth was to sit and eat, along with others, the same food. Hence, it served as a medium of social integration between the high and the low thereby levelling a mighty blow to the caste system and untouchability. The *Langar* was run with the help of voluntary contributions made by the Guru's devotees.

Kirtan as an institution also carried great significance. By *Kirtan* is meant recitation of the compositions of the Guru in accompaniment with musical instruments and in musical measures. *Kirtan* was held both in the early morning and in the evening following the conclusion of the day's work. This institution contributed a lot in chiselling the thinking of the disciples and inducing them to work for the causes as preached by the Guru.

Guru Nanak, with a view to familiarising the people with his teachings, undertook extensive tours in the North, South, East and West and visited important centres of the Hindus, Muslims, Buddhists, Jains and Jogis and met people of different races, tribes and cultural patterns. His travels covered a period of nearly thirty years.

In his first *Udasi*[6] (long tour) he traversed (in terms of the modern political geography of India and Pakistan) Haryana, Delhi, Uttar Pradesh, Behar, Bengal, Orissa, Madras, Kerala, Mysore, Andhra Pradesh, Maharashtra, Gujarat and West Pakistan. The most important places visited by him were Kurukshetra, Panipat, Hardwar, Joshi Math, Gorakh Mata, Gola, Ayudhya, Prayag, Banaras, Gaya, Patna, Dhubri, Dhampur, Gauhati, Shillong, Silhet, Decca, Puri, Cuttuck, Guntur, Kanchipuram and Tiruchhirpalli. From Tiruchhpairpalli the Guru sailed down the Kaveri river and reached Nagapaṭnam, a very old part of South India. From there he proceeded to Ceylon where he visited such places as Betticola, Katargam and Sita Waka. The last named place is also called Sita Ellya from the tradition of Sita having spent here period of captivity. At the time of Guru Nanak's visit this place was in the Kotte kingdom of Raja Dharma Prakarma. The inscription discovered by Dr. Karuna Ratna[7] in the museum of Anuradh Pura furnishes a brief account of the encounter of Janakacharya (Nanak) with the Buddhist Bhikshu Dharma Kirt-Sthavira. This inscription also informs that the Raja Dharma Prakrama had promised to embrace Nanak's creed if he won in the debate. Nanak won. But before he could embrace Nanak's creed, the Brahmins very cleverly got arranged another public debate, this time between Nanak and Dvaja Pandita and manoeuvred the result in favour of the latter. In this way, they did not allow the ruler to fall under the influence of Nanak. At Mannar, the Guru left Celyon and sailed for Rameshwaram where from he proceeded to Trivandrum. On his way back to Talwandi, the Guru visited important places such as Bidar, Nanded, Baroach, Somnath, Dwarka, Girnar Rocks, Jagannath, Ujjain, Ajmer and Mathura, Sirsa, Pak Pattan and Talwandi.

The second tour took the Guru into the interior of the Himalayan region where he visited the Kangra valley, the Spiti tableland, Western Tibet, Ladakh, Kashmir and Punjab (Pakistan).

Images of Guru Nanak are said to be present in some of the temples of Tibet and Ladakh. There is a class of people living in this area who have substituted or added[8] the Mantra Om Aham, Bhadra Guru Parm Sidhi Hum, to the usual Buddhist Mantra, Om Mani Padmi Hami and it is these men in whose temples the image of Nanak is given a permanent place. Kargal, Amar Nath, Pehlgam, Mattan, Anant Nagar, Sri Nagar, Bara Mula and Hasan Abdal were visited by the Guru. After that, en route to Talwandi, Tilla Bal Godai and Sialkot were visited.

The Guru undertook his third missionary journey to the Muslim countries of west Asia wearing the dress of a Muslim devotee. Some prominent places connected with this tour of the Guru were Multan, Uch, Hinglaj, Mecca, Medina, Baghdad, Mashad, Herat, Kandhar, Kabul, Para Chinnar, Gorakh Hatri (Peshawar) and Saidpur. From Saidpur the Guru proceeded to Talwandi and from there to Sultanpur. On the way, he came to the spot on the bank of the river Ravi where he founded the new settlement named Kartarpur (City of the Creator) where he lived a normal householder's life for 18 to 20 years.

Even during this period, he undertook short tour in Punjab. One of them, according to Bhai Gurdas, was his visit to Achal Vatala and the other to Multan and Pak Pattan. At the latter place, he met Shaikh Ibrahim while at Multan he was accorded hearty welcome by Mukhdoom Bahauddin. During his tours, he gave his message to as many people as possible. His message was meant for all irrespective of region, country, clime, caste or creed. He had a cosmic vision and earnestly desired to build a global society on the basis of faith in the oneness of God, unity of mankind, dignity of labour and sharing of the fruits of labour with others.

Before Guru Nanak breathed his last, he selected his successor and commissioned him to carry on the work he had started. The nomination of Angad to the Guruship was, in the words of Indu Bhushan Bannerjee, "A fact of the perfoundest significance". Trumpp writes: "The disciples of Nanak would no doubt have been dispersed and gradually disappeared as well as the disciples of many other Gurus before Nanak, if he had not taken care to appoint a successor before his death."

Guru Angad (g. 1539, d. 1552)

The period from Guru Angad Dev (Guruship 1539; d. 1552) the immediate successor of Guru Nanak, to Guru Arjan Dev, fifth in the line of succession, formed the first phase in the development of Sikhism. During this period, A.D. 1539-1606, it made rapid strides organisationally as well as in numbers and developed into a distinct community. Guru Angad during his ministry did his best to consolidate Sikhism. Guru Nanak had concerned himself more or less with the fundamentals and had left the details to take care of themselves. Guru Angad took care to interpret and re-emphasize the message of Nanak in unambiguous terms and in a down-to-earth manner. He successfully met the challenges of the Udasis, a sect founded by Sri Chand, eldest son of Guru Nanak. Baba Sri Chand held strong belief in asceticism and renunciation (udas) of the world as the correct path-way to eternal bliss and quoted Guru Nanak as the progenitor and upholder of this view. The view of the Sri Chand was obviously a mis-statement of the Guru's gospel; but Sri Chand's impact on the masses was quite deep because of his being the son of Guru Nanak and the natural tendency of the Indian people to put premium on asceticism. Guru Angad, therefore, took prompt steps and made it clear in unequivocal terms to his disciples that Sikhism was essentially a religion of householders.

He collected the hymns of Guru Nanak and committed them to writing. The anthology of Guru's hymns provided a focal point of piety and doctrine for the Sikhs. He made Punjabi language in Punjabi script as the vehicle of his thought and preaching. Some traditions ascribe the invention of the Gurmukhi script to him but Guru Nanak's composition 'Patti' Akhr composed in the form of an acrostic shows that the alphabets already existed as Gurmukhi which however were polished and refined by the Guru. The renaming of the existing Takri script and the instruction that it should be used in the copying of the Guru's hymns may well have been Guru Angad's decision. The significance of the adoption of the script and of extensive use of Punjabi lies in this that the Guru rejected the foreign Persian script and emphasised that unless the people adopted a script which was their own and which suited their language, their culture could not grow. It gave a severe blow to the Brahmans who through their manipulated monopoly of the knowledge of Sanskrit had given currency to the belief that their superiority or prestige was ordained by God or gods.

Guru Angad continued to impress upon his disciples the utility of *Sangat* and *Guru ka Langar*. Both these institutions gave a sense of unity and identity to the Sikhs. Another step, building the city of Goindwal also played a great part in promoting consciousness of distinctiveness among the Sikh.

In the city of Goindwal no separate ward was marked for low castes or for any particular community. It was indeed a picture of Sikh values of social equality and relegions. The city of Goindwal did a lot to shape the Sikh psyche and to propagate the Sikh ideology.

Guru Amar Das (g. 1552, d. 1574)

Guru Angad nominated Amar Das as his successor in 1552. He was then seventy-three. He held his ministry for twenty-two years untill he expired in 1574. From 1540 to 1552 he had been in the company of Guru Angad Dev and had fully grasped the Sikh mission and the challenges threatening its existence.

During the time of Guru Amar Das, it began to be felt that the Sikhs should have their religious centres so that they might stop going to Hindu *tiraths* (holy places). Their visits to Hindu tiraths made them vulnerable to Hindu influences. The Guru, therefore, built a *Baoli* at Goindwal. This was a well with eighty-four steps leading down to the surface of the water.

The *Baoli*, apart from catering to the need of the people for water, had deep effect on the psychology of the people. The Sikhs started visiting the place in a large number and this thing afforded an opportunity to the Guru to come into close contact with the Sikhs. Out of this close contact sprang the devotion for the Guru which proved to be a strong bond to bind them to Sikhism.

The Guru also chose the site for a new religious centre where the construction work was started by the Guru himself under the supervision of Shri Jetha, his son-in-law which ultimately became the site for the city of Amritsar.

The institutions of *Sangat* and *Pangat* received still greater strength at the hands of Guru Amar Das who had issued a fiat: "First eat together and then meet together" (*Pehle Pangat Peechhe Sangat*). The fiat was implemented rigidly. When Akbar paid a visit to Guru Amar Das at Goindwal, he could not see the Guru without first taking food in *Guru ka Langar*. The *Guru ka Langar* was made a means of emphasising the unity and equality of mankind.

The Guru preached vigorously what he stood for. He wrote a large number of hymns and exhorted his followers to recite them and told them that whosoever imbibed their essence would acquire godly qualities. In quite a number of verses, he emphasised that the Guru's *shabad* was superior to everything else and the Sikhs were advised to use only the Guru's *shabad* in worship. He added his compositions to the compendium which he had received from Guru Angad Dev and which contained compositions of his predecessor Gurus. The reason de'etra was to preserve the message of God as revealed to the Gurus. With each Guru upto Guru Arjan Dev, the codex expanded as it included the hymns composed by each of them.

Guru Amar Das maintained the tradition of Guru Nanak's social reforms. He condemned the caste system, untouchability and the customs of *sati* and *purdah*. All these prevalent Hindu social customs were dehumanizing and at best catered to the interests of only a particular class. He advocated equality in terms of gender, creed and caste on the basis of universal brotherhood of man. He encouraged inter-caste marriages and widow re-marriages.

The birth and death rites current among the Hindus were abandoned. They were too many and too costly, but the worst thing about them was that they were against the Sikh concept of death and violated the very spirit of Sikhism. The Guru advised his followers to abandon these rites and in their place prescribed a simple ceremonies which mostly consisted of recitation of holy hymns from Guru's compositions.[9]

The upshot of all the measures was that Sikhism began to emerge as a distinctive entity. In the accomplishment of his task, the Guru received great assistance from the liberal character of Akbar's policy. The orthodox sections both among the Hindus and the Muslims did not take kindly to the teachings of Guru Amar Das. The Khatries complained to the Emperor Akbar more than once against his unorthodox ways. At one time they even led a deputation and submitted a lengthy memorandum to the Emperor levelling a series of charges against him. The Guru had to depute his most trusted follower Bhai Jetha to the Emperor's court to answer the charges. The complaint was ultimately dismissed. A few years later, the Emperor personally waited upon the Guru at Goindwal and even ate in his kitchen. The tradition goes that he also made a land grant in the name of the Guru's daughter Bibi Bhani before his departure from there. All this gave a boost to the Sikh people and for the rest of the reign of Akbar all adversaries of the Sikhs were silenced.

The liberalism of Akbar's religious policy helped the Guru in yet another way. Muslim orthodoxy had to keep a low profile spirits during the period because Akbar had withdrawn his patronage from it. Therefore, Sikhism under Guru Amar Das, and in fact for many years long after, experienced no difficulty from the side of the Muslim orthodoxy. Some trouble was, no doubt, created by a few Shaikh families settled at Goindwal and at their instance, a group of young boys caused harassment to the Sikhs wanting to fetch water from the river Beas for the Guru's kitchen. But it was a localised affair, probably the outcome of some local quarrel of a mundane nature.

The growing number of the Sikhs needed sustained guidance, coordination and some sort of system. To this purpose the institution of Manjis was established. The word *Manji* literally signifies cot or *chorpoy*, a nomenclature for Indian bedstead. But here it denotes a responsible religious position conferred by the Guru upon a prominent devotee of his, or a seat of his delegated authority. The Guru appointed 22 missionaries to carry on the work of proselytisation. According to Macauliffe, Indu Bhushan Bannerjee, Kirpal Singh Narang and Hari Ram Gupta, Manji has been taken in the sense of some sort of a territorial unit which is incorrect.

Only man of recognised piety and sterling integrity were awarded the distinction of holding *Manji*. Their essential qualification was that they correctly understood and practised the teachings of the Sikh Gurus. They conducted their missionary work individually and also through congregations (Sangats). They maintained their connection with the Guru at the centre by means of periodical visits, more often on the annual Baisakhi fair when it was started at Goindwal. Some of them besides their preaching work, taught Gurumukhi script to the people and wrote *Pothis* of the Guru's hymns to be distributed among the people. Another important function performed by the *Manjis* was to initiate fresh people into the fold of Sikhism. The method adopted was the same as was being used by the Guru at the centre. This was known as *Charnamarit*, meaning 'nectar of the foot'. This was nothing but pure water sanctified by the washing of a toe of the Guru in it. Anyone who desired to become a Sikh was administered a palmful of this sacred water. But this device, though simple and inexpensive, presented one great difficulty. Since it was directly linked up with the person of the Guru, the initiation could be performed only where the Guru was personally present. Naturally, there was a great constraint on missionary work. This problem was solved by empowering the grantees of Manjis to get new entrants into the Sikh fold through the administration of their footwash (*Charnamrit* or Charan Pahul). The Sikhs thus enrolled were named *sehling*, meaning associates.

Guru Amar Das, with his clarity of vision and his determined policy to lend a distinctive entity to the Sikh people not only stablised the Sikh community and saved it from a possible relapse into Brahmanical Hinduism but also paved the way for its rapid strides in future. The danger of the Sikhs yielding to the pressures of Hinduism or of falling under the spell of ascetic practices was largely warded off. Then there was also a great deal of expansion in their ranks.

Guru Ram Das (g. 1534, d. 1581)

Guru Amar Das was succeeded by Guru Ram Das. Originally called Jetha, he was born of a Sodhi family of Chuna Mandi, Lahore on September 24, 1534. While serving along with other Sikhs in the construction of the Baoli at Goindwal, he attracted the attention of Guru Amar Das, and received the hand of his daughter Bibi Bhani in marriage. Thereafter he stayed with his father-in-law, and was closely associated with his ministry. He put on record many incidents connected with the struggle which his Master had with his opponents, and as such his writings are a mine of information about the period. He had made himself so indispensable that his choice for the Guruship was a forgone conclusion.

In order to avoid any possible unpleasantness with the relatives of Guru Amar Das, he shifted his residence to the present site of Amritsar which had been chosen by Guru Amar Das and where some construction work had already been done.

During his ministry he further consolidated the institutions of *Sangat* and *Guru ka Langar* and *Kirtan*. He also saw to the planning and construction of the new city of Amritsar. He caused Amrit Sar (Lake of Nector) and Santokhsar (Lake of Patience) to be excavated. He appointed Masands who performed the dual role of Sikh missionaries and collectors of devotees voluntary offerings. Each Masand was allotted a definite area to preach and to collect the offerings. Masand is a distorted form of the word 'Masand', shorter form of Masand-i-Ala or his 'Excellency'. The exact number of Masands and their respective areas are not known, still this much is certain that many Sikhs famous for piety and integrity were asked to act as Masands. In Guru Ram Das's time, the Masands were known as Ram Dasias; it was only in the time of Guru Arjan Dev that they began to be called 'Masands'. In keeping with the policy of his predecessors the Guru asked his follower to avoid singing filthy songs on the occasions such as marriage, child birth and instead he composed hymns which were akin to folk songs such as Ghori, Alahanian, etc. He composed four hymns known as Lawan in Sulti Safhi and asked the Sikhs to recite them to solemnize marriages as 'Lawans' embody a lesson for the pair to develop true love for each other and lead a life of equipoise. In this way a distinct social code of the Sikhs began to emerge which went a long way to make them feel that they were separate from the Hindus as well as Muslims.

Guru Arjan

Guru Ram Das had three sons, out of whom he considered the youngest, Arjan Mal, the most suited to succeed him. This aroused the ire of the eldest, Prithi Chand. Nevertheless, when the Guru saw that his end was near, he asked Bhai Buddha to invest Arjan Mal as the fifth Guru. Ram Das expressed that as one lamp is lighted from another, so the Guru's spirit will pass into him and dispel the darkness in the world. Guru Arjan's path was beset with many pitfalls. Akbar's liberalism instead of being utilized by the Hindus to fashion new responses to new challenges was used to rehabilitate or perpetuate the orthodox Brahmanical beliefs and caste-ridden society. Understandably, the protagonists of Hindu orthodoxy were unhappy with Sikhism.

Besides, the bulk of the Sikh people who had come into the fold of Sikhism as a result of the efforts of the earlier Gurus were mostly drawn from the commercial classes dwelling in towns. These people possessed, in ample measure, intelligence, wealth, organising ability and practical knowledge of the world. During the time of Guru Amar Das and later the Jats in large number entered the fold of Sikhism. It became imperative for the Guru to frame programmes to harness the intelligence and organising of enterprising spirit and their proverbial energy in the interest of the Sikh community and the ideals it stood for. But it was no ordinary task because to strike harmony between the mercantile class and the peasantry was a baffling problem in view of two factors: (i) the Jats were men of war-like habits; (ii) there was wide divergence between the respective outlooks and interests of the two groups, peasants and business people.

However, unbaffled by the complex nature of the problem and notwithstanding the trouble fomented by his brother Prithi Chand, Guru Arjan Dev addressed himself to the task of further consolidation and extension of the Sikh Panth. His approach to the problem was institutional, social and psychological. Like his predecessors he built up new religious centres to serve as a cohesive force. He completed the unfinished work of excavating two great tanks—Santokhsar and Amritsar. The side walls of the Tank of Nectar (Amritsar) were made *pucca* with the collective efforts of the Sikhs. Having completed this tank, he decided to build the central Sikh shrine, Sri Harmandir. Instead of building the shrine on a high plinth as the Hindu architectural custom was, Guru Arjan had it built on a level lower than the surrounding land, so that the worshippers would have to go down the steps to enter it. And, unlike Hindu temples, which had only one entrance, the Guru provided four doors on the four sides of the temple. These architectural features were intended to be symbolic of the Sikh faith which aimed at building a brotherhood which does not recognise any distinctions on the bases of caste, creed, wealth, rade and climate, etc.[10] In due course a floursહing city called Amritsar after the name of the tank grew up around this Sikh temple. The Guru himself played no meagre role in the growth and development of this city.

Another religious centre was established at Tarn Taran. In 1590, the Guru chose the site for building this new town in the heart of the Majha, or mid country lying between the Beas and the Ravi. Guru Arjan excavated a tank and built a temple there, which formed the nucleus of the new town. The tank was named Tarn Taran, round which the city developed which also began to be called Tarn Taran. In 1594, another city Kartarpur was founded in the Jallandar Deoab. A Baoli at Dabbi Bazar Lahore was also built by the Guru.

The Guru undertook extensive tours of the Majha and Doaba regions of Punjab. He visited Sarhali, Bhaini, Khanpur, Khanna, Kartarpur, etc. The Guru also preached in the Dakha region. He visited Khem Karan, Chunian and many other places. The Guru also paid a visit to the shrine of Guru Nanak at Dehra Baba Nanak. From there he proceeded to Barath to meet Baba Sri Chand, son of Guru Nanak. The Baba received him with great warmth and urged him to continue his mission with vigour. The Guru had started his religious travels in 1588 and completed the same in 1594.

Because of these steps of the Guru the ranks of the Sikhs swelled fast. To integrate them and also to collect funds for his building works the Guru reorganized the Masand system. The Masands already appointed did not suit him as many of them had shown loyalty to Prithi Chand or were unfit to carry on the work expected of them. The Guru gave a new dimension to the system. He issued specific instructions to the Masands so that they, henceforth, would look after both the secular and spiritual affairs of the Sikhs. They would foster among the Sikhs keen interest in trade, industry and other avocations and at the same time endeavour to keep them together as members of the Sikh Panth. They were also required to collect Daswandh which the Sikhs were enjoined upon to contribute to Guru's treasury (*golak*). Daswandh was levied for the maintenance of the Sikh church and to undertake works of public welfare. It was the duty of the Masand to submit the amount thus collected to the Guru regularly and procure a receipt against that. It should however, be remembered that the Masands were not permitted to touch a penny out of these offerings. Masands were required to pay visits to Amritsar at the annual Baisakhi fair and in this way a regular contact was maintained between the Guru and the Masands. At certain places, where the number of the Sikhs was too large, the Masand was allowed to appoint his agents called Sangatia or Masandia or Meora.

The Masand system as an institution trained the Sikhs in secular affairs and introduced a sort of order to which the Sikh masses became habit.

On June 14, 1595, his only son, Hargobind, was born at Vadali near Amritsar where the Guru retired for a while to avoid clash with his brother Prithia. The birth of a son, however, increased the hostility of Prithi Chand who now saw no chance for his own son, Manohar Das Meharban. Many passages in the writings of Guru Arjan show that there were a number of attempts made on the life of his son who, however, was providentially saved to grow up a worthy successor of his father.

The greatest work of the Guru Arjan was the compilation and editing of the holy *Granth Sahib*, the central scripture of the Sikhs.

Many factors impressed upon the Guru the necessity of taking up this step. Sikhism is essentially a religion of the *Nam*. Its most obvious religious trait was the recitation or singing of the Guru's hymns to the exclusion of all other ceremonies or rituals. Seeing the importance of this practice, many clever persons had begun to mix up spurious writings with the true compositions of the Gurus. In 1594, when Guru Arjan Dev returned from the religious tours of the Majha tract of Punjab, he discovered that Prithi Chand had not been idle in his absence and had begun to compile an anthology of sacred writings in which he was inserting compositions of his own. The Guru who was responsible for the organisation of Sikhism on a sound basis had to ensure unity of belief and practice and to this end he prepared an authentic compilation of the writings of the Gurus including his own Guru Amar Das had left definite instructions in the 33rd and 34th *pauries* of Anand Sahib that the real hymns of the Guru alone should be accepted and reverenced by the Sikhs. Besides, if the distinctive identity of the Sikh people was to be established, it was essential that they should have their own scripture. The Sikhs had been given a script and a language of their own and now there was a genuine need that they should have a separate religious book which should occupy for the Sikhs the same position as the *Vedas* do for the Hindus, the Bible for the Christians and the *Quran* for the Muslims.

While the Guru was busy with his work, a report was sent to Akbar that Guru Arjan's sacred anthology under preparation contained passages denigrating Islam. Passing through Goindwal,[11] the Emperor stopped en route and asked to see the work. Bhai Buddha and Gurdas brought a copy of the existent manuscript and read some of the hymns to Akbar. The Emperor found nothing objectionable and expressed his satisfaction by an offering of fifty-one gold Mohars to the sacred text besides giving robes of honour to the two disciples and sent one for Guru Arjan Dev.

At the Guru's request he also remitted[12] the annual revenue of the district to ameliorate the condition of the peasants who had been hard hit by the failure of the monsoon.

In August 1604, the work was completed and the *Granth Sahib* was formally installed in the temple at Amritsar. Bhai Budha was appointed the first Granthi (reciter).

The 'Granth' thus prepared was an enormous volume consisting of 6000 hymns. The major contributions included therein were of the first five Gurus including Guru Arjan Dev. Afterwards, Guru Gobind Singh incorporated in it 65 *Shabads* and 57 *Shalokas* of Guru Tegh Bahadur. Besides, the Granth Sahib includes the hymns of fifteen Bhaktas and Sufis and eleven Bhatts. In addition, the Granth Sahib includes the Ballad (Var) of Satta and Balwand, Sundar's elegy popularly known as *Ramkali Sadd*, and one hymn attributed to Mardana, the Muslim companion and disciple of Guru Nanak. The compilation of the Sikh scripture was a major step forward. It became the most powerful factor in spreading the teachings of the Gurus among the masses. More than anything else, it created the community consciousness among the Sikhs. It contributed immensely to the emergence of the Sikhs as a separate religion with a distinct ethos of its own.

Under Guru Arjan Dev Sikhism made great headway but this was not to the liking of the Muslim orthodoxy. So long as Akbar was alive, his favourable attitude not only saved Sikhism from the fury of the Muslim orthodoxy at a time when it was just an infant needing protection, it also provided the necessary conditions for its quick progress.

The electicism of Akbar led to a sharp reaction among the conservative sections of the Muslim population. They viewed the Emperor's policy towards the non-Muslims as extremely dangerous both to their creed and state because it was feared that it would give encouragement and strength to the Hindus besides diluting Islamic ideology. In their opinion any step which benefitted the Hindus was anti-Islamic. The Rajput policy of the Emperor was resented for the reason that it boosted the enemies of the Muslim establishment. The emergence of the religious activity among the Hindus was regarded with suspicion. Similarly the rise of the Sikh movement was to them a case of dangerous heresy which needed to be nipped in the bud.

Gradually, the conservative reaction gave birth to a powerful Muslim revivalist movement with its headquarters at Sirhind. It was started by a Muslim divine, Shaikh Ahmed Sirhindi Mujaddad-i-Alaf Sani to whom even a slight concession to the Hindus was an act of hostility to Islam. He advocated the view that the glory of Islam consists in the humiliation of the infidels. About the *jazya* taken from the infidels, he held that its real purpose was to humiliate them and this humiliation should reach a stage where owing to the fear of *jazya*, they should not be able to wear good clothes, and enjoy any peace of mind and be in constant dread and fear of the king's taking away their property. His views about the Muslim Shariat were very rigid, and he poured abuse upon everything that he did not understand or which could not fit into his ideology. He was thus the antithesis of Abal Fazal and was akin to Badauni in the desire to imprison the mind in the narrowest ideological vision. Naturally, he was a severe critic of Akbar's policy of tolerance towards the non-Muslims. He writes of the miserable conditions of the Muslims under the Emperor and calls him "an enemy of the Faith of Islam".

But the orthodoxy could not influence the policy of Emperor Akbar. The accession of Jahangir, however, brought about a change in the situation, in the beginning at least in favour of those who had assailed the liberal trends in Akbar's policy. There were some powerful people at the court of his father who were opposed to his accession and favoured his son Khusro in preference to him. Even Akbar at one time had shared the same view, feeling sore as he did at the unfilial and rebeleous conduct of Jahangir. The orthodox detractors of his father's enlightened liberalism came to Jahangir's rescue and smoothed his way to the throne. Thus, when he ascended the throne, he not only did not have his father's prejudices against the Muslim orthodoxy but was also in a frame of mind to oblige them, should an opportunity arise.

The much awaited opportunity appeared when in 1606 Prince Khusro, goaded by his frustrated ambition, rose in open revolt against his father, Jahangir, and hastened towards Punjab in a bid to mobilize support for his cause. On the way, he paid a visit to Guru Arjan Dev at Goindwal. The Emperor gave the rebel prince a hot pursuit and reached Lahore post-haste where the unfortunate Khusro was produced before him tied in chains by the commander of the pursuing army, Murtza Khan. The occasion was marked by the award of exemplary punishments to the supporters of the rebel. At this juncture on or about 23 May 1606, the enemies of the Guru, possibly the followers of Mujaddid-i-Alaf Sani, managed to connect the Guru with Khusro. They poured into the ears of the Emperor Jahangir that during the short halt of Khusro at Goindwal, Guru Arjan Dev had blessed him with a saffron mark on the forehead. This was considered as a gesture of blessing in favour of the rebel and the Guru was ordered to be arrested. No enquiry was made, and no trial held. Jahangir simply says, "I fully knew his heresies, and I ordered that he should be brought into my presence, that his houses and children be made over to Murtaza Khan, that his property be confiscated and that he should be sentenced to a torturous death Yasa-o-Siyast."

In the game of prodding Jahangir against the Guru, the role of Khatris, the leading elites of Hindu conservatism was notorious. They as a class did not relish the emergence of Sikhism because in their reckoning, it had a potential to destabilise Hindu society especially its social system which accorded a privileged status to them. When they observed that the Mughal government was ill-disposed to the Guru and intended to implicate him in Khusro's revolt, they went whole hog to lend their support to the government. Tradition goes that Chandu Shah, perhaps the most influential among them, even offered to pay a huge amount for taking the Guru in his custody. He had ulterior motive in doing so. He intended to provide cover to the government's misdeed in one hand and to wreak viengenence upon him for his refusal to accept his proposal to marry his son to his daughter on the other.

While giving an account of this affair in his Memoirs, Jahangir has advanced two reasons in justification of his action. First is the popularity of the Guru as a religious and worldly leader amongst the Hindus and the Muslims. The second is the visit of the rebel prince Khusro to Goindwal, whom the Guru is said to have blessed with a saffron mark on his forehead.

Of the two reasons, the second one has no foundation. The accusation was made practically a month after the Guru was alleged to have blessed the prince and some twenty-seven days after the Emperor himself had crossed the Beas at that very place. This makes the whole thing a puzzle and throws a very serious doubt on the genuineness and authenticity of the report. The fact that for twenty-seven days from April 26, when the Emperor appears to have crossed the Beas at Goindwal and was encamped at Jhabal on May 23, there is no reference whatsoever in Tuzak-i-Jhangiri in any way involving Guru Arjan in the affairs of Prince Khusro or of any of his accomplices, is an important factor to be taken into accounts. If the Guru had met and blessed Khusro at Goindwal, it would certainly have been reported to the Emperor on the spot or in its immediate neighbourhood where it could have been easily verified and authenticated by eye-witnesses and the Guru would have been arrested and carried a prisoner with him to Lahore. But in fact nothing came to the ears of Jahangir for as long as a month. In fact, the details contained in the report are not historically correct. The Guru was not a politician to be in any way interested in the rebellion of Prince Khusro against his father Jahangir.

As far as the *Qashka* or *teeka-mark* of saffron by the Guru on the forehead of the prince is concerned, it is on the face of it, a pure and simple concoction of some conspirator's fertile imagination to prop up the emotions against the Guru. Never in the whole history of the Sikh Gurus there has been any occasion for any Guru to anoint anyone Sikh or non-Sikh, with a teeka.

According to Mahma Prakash of Sarup Das Bhalla, the Guru took pity upon the prince in misery and provided him with food, obviously from the 'Guru ka langar' (free kitchen) open to all way-farers (Sakhi No. 143-1-4). He makes no mention of any teeka or financial help. In view of all this, the allegation against the Guru that he was involved in propping up the cause of Khusro falls flat as historically unsound.

From the above discussion, one thing clearly emerges that the Guru's so-called participation in the rebellion was merely a pretext devised for his execution. The reality seems to be that some one amongst the revivalists lodged the complaint with Jahangir implicating the Guru in the Khusro affair with a view to prompting the Emperor to take action against the Guru. The Emperor immediately after his accession to the throne was in the frame of mind to please his orthodox friends who had a stood by him first in his rebellion against his father, then against the group of Aziz Koka and Raja Man Singh who were at one stage bent upon putting the crown on Khusro. He readily believed the complaint and issued the order for the execution of the Guru which took place on May 30, 1606 as per *Yasa*.

Religion in Revolt

Guru Arjan Dev before departing for Lahore in response to the summons of Murtaza Khan nominated Hargobind as his successor. At that time, Hargobind was only eleven years old. He had been carefully trained for the high office.

Guru Hargobind had to work under great strain. The martyrdom of Guru Arjan was a big shock to the people who started pondering over the issue and asking themselves the question: 'Was it right to knuckle under the evil instead of combating it?'

Psychologically, the moment was crucial. Danger there was that the Sikhs might feel exasperated and revert to escapism and asceticism thus abjuring faith in Guru's philosophy of an active and he purposeful life committed to truth and righteousness. The courses were now open to the Sikhs; either to take it lying down and submissive or to take a bold line and face up to all dangers manfully. The Guru decided in favour of the latter course and adopted a full-fledged programme of militarisation.

Guru girded round his waist at the investiture ceremony two swords, one to symbolise spiritual power and the other temporal power. It was in a way a declaration to re-emphasise that the Guru's guidance and protection would cover both spiritual and temporal affairs.

To implement his programme he sent a circular[13] letter to his Masands to ask the people to bring in future arms and horses as part of their offerings. He strengthened the defence of the city of Amritsar by putting up small fortress called Lohgarh. In front of the Harimandir, he built Sri Akal Takhat (the throne of the timeless God), where the congregation heard ballads, extolling feats of heroism and besides listening to religious discourses discussed secular problems. Guru himself sat here to tander advice to as also to issue ordainments to his followers, etc.

The construction of Akal Takhat was, in fact, a proclamation of the concept of double sovereignty. The essence of which is that a man of religion must always owe his primary allegiance to truth and morality and he must never submit to the exclusive claim of the secular state to govern the bodies[14] and he/she had the right to challenge if the secular states took measure to snuff out truth and morality.[15]

He enrolled a body of 52 stout Sikhs, who formed the nucleus of his future army. Five hundred youths came from Majha, Malwa and the Doaba to offer their services in defence of their religion. They did not demand any pay. The Guru gave them each a horse and a few weapons and formed a little army comprising them.

Such programme of the Guru created a stir in official quarters. The Emperor felt alarmed. He summoned the Guru to his presence. When the Guru met him, he was sent as a state prisoner to the fort of Gwalior, where some other ruling chiefs were also serving their terms of imprisonment. The Guru's life in the fort was arduous.

The Guru's total stay in the fort of Gwalior was possibly three to four years, from 1608 to 1611/1612. There were two causes which prompted Jahangir to release the Guru; firstly he realised that without recourse to liberal religious policy, it was not possible for him to maintain stability and tranquility in his vast empire, and secondly, it appears that the Emperor was greatly moved by the phenomenon of batches of devout Sikhs making regular trips to the fort to pay homage as also to lodge mute protest.

The tradition goes that the Guru refused to be released until the 52 princes incarcerated with him were allowed to come out, each holding a part of his garment, which had been specially prepared to have fifty-two hems. Jahangir agreed at long last. For this act the Guru is remembered as *Bandi Chhore* or 'The Deliverer'.

It is believed that the efforts of Mian Mir were also responsible for bringing about a change in Jahangir's attitude towards the Guru.

Jahangir lived for several years after this but be never gave any trouble to Guru Hargobind. Rather he tried to befriend him.

Being left in peace, the Guru addressed himself wholeheartedly to the further progress of Sikh religion. During the period he was in prison, the strings of discipline had loosened and several selfish Masands had arrogated to themselves powers that were never vested in them. The Guru thought it high time to penalise them and make a lesson of them.

Like Guru Nanak he decided to tour extensively to spread his religion. He went as far as Kashmir in the north and Nanakmata near Piliphit in the east. He made many converts to Sikhism. At Gujarat, a very interesting incident occurred when the Guru was passing through that place. Shah Daula whose shrine is still revered by thousands remonstrated with the Guru, saying "How can a Hindu be a Faqir? How can you be a religious man, when you have a wife and children, and possess worldly wealth?" The Guru replied, "a wife is man's conscience, his children perpetuate his memory, and wealth gives him his sustenance. As for a Faqir, he is neither a Hindu nor a Musalman." He visited the places connected with the previous Gurus, and put up memorials there. He made arrangements for holding regular services in Sikh temples.

Jahangir died in 1627, and Shah Jahan succeeded him. The accession of Shah Jahan to the throne was an event of great significance in the history of the development of Sikhism. Shah Jahan's religious outlook was narrow as compared to that of his father who after 1611 had reverted to the policy of Akbar—so much so that he even imprisoned Shaikh Ahmad Sarhindi, head of the Naqshbandis. Shah Jahan prohibited the conversion of the Muslims and ordered the demolition of many temples. This brought him into conflict with the Sikhs who were determined and were particularly annoyed at the desecration of their famous Baoli at Lahore, which was built up by Guru Arjan Dev and a mosque erected on the site of the free kitchen attached to it.

With a view to avoiding any chance of an open clash with the Mughal Government as also to continue his missionary activities peacefully, the Guru established a new settlement at Kiratpur in A.D. 1627. The land was donated by the ruler of Kahlur (Nalagarh). The Guru sent Baba Gurditta, his eldest son, for the foundation laying ceremony. The Baba took Baba Sri Chand there and had the ceremony performed by him. This new headquarters suited the Guru very much, firstly, because it was not far off from the plains of Punjab, and secondly, it was outside the administrative jurisdiction of the Mughal officials. The Kahlur state was an independent state at that time. Still the tension surfaced between the Guru and the Mughal authorities. Guru Hargobind's decision to leave Ramdaspur temporarily and visit the Malwa region did not help. On his return the Lahore administration engaged the Sikhs in a series of battles, one in the neighbourhood of Amritsar (1634), second at Lohira Maharaj (1635), the third at Kartarpur (1635), and the fourth near Phagwara in village Palahi.

Guru Hargobind, during all the four battles, which were inflicted by Shah Jahan on the Guru fared well. This purpose had always been only defensive; he did not acquire even an inch of territory. There was something far greater involved in this warfare than a mere dispute over a hawk or a horse. A new heroism was rising in the land, of which the object, then simply seen, was to create the will to resist the mighty power of the 'Turks' as to replace it with the government of the concept of Sikhism.

To avoid further clash with the government and to carry out his plans of consolidating and spreading the influence of Sikhism, he shifted to Kiratpur, and continued to stay there till his death. During his stay he asked Baba Gurditta to appoint Almast, Phul, Gonda and Baba Hasna as head preachers. Baba Gurditta invested them with udasi robes. Almast and Baba Hasna were allotted the areas of East India and Pothohar respectively. Phul and Gonda were assigned the area of the Doaba to carry on the missionary work. All these four persons established in their allotted area preaching centres which were named as Dhuans or 'hearths', symbolising the flame of Sikhism. Besides this, the Guru sent Bidhi Chand to Bengal. Earlier Bhai Gurdas had been sent to Kabul and then to Benaras to enlighten the people on the Gospel of the Gurus.

The Guru's arrangement worked very nicely and produced good results. The Guru acquired great influence over the hill people and the hill rulers alike. The number of the Sikhs increased. All this the Guru achieved notwithstanding a series of domestic tragedies. Within a few years five member of his family, including three of his sons, died one after another. The most grievous of these deaths was that of Baba Gurditta in 1638. To add to his sorrow, Gurditta's son Dhirmal, turned against his grandfather. For a long time, Hargobind could not make up his mind about his successor. He had two sons living, Suraj Mal who showed little interest in Sikh affairs and Tegh Bahadur who was too much withdrawn to be entrusted with the leadership of the rapidly growing community. When the time came Hargobind chose Gurditta's second son Har Rai to succeed him as the seventh Guru.

Guru Har Rai (b. 1638, d. 1661)

The Guru shared his grandfather's views regarding the need of military preparedness and maintained a body of people well trained in the use of arms. Having been convinced of the deterioration of the Masand system, he set up Bakhshishs, new missionary centres, and for their control and management appointed, (1) Suthrashah, (2) Sahiba, (3) Sangata, (4) Mihan Sahib, (5) Bhagat Bhagwan, (6) Bhagat Mal. Of these Bhagat Gir, originally a Baraigi, was converted to Sikhism along with his followers. He was renamed Bhagat Bhagwan and appointed to carry on preaching work in the East, where he with the help of his followers established 360 seats for the propagation of Sikhism.

The Bhai families of Kaithal and Bagrian were made responsible for missionary work in the land between the Jamuna and the Sutlej. Bhai Pheru acted as the Guru's Masand in the Lamma region between the Beas and the Ravi. As the Masands or missionaries appointed by the earlier Gurus became more and more corrupt, this new order of preachers attained more prominence and was specially useful in preaching Sikhism in distant and difficult places.

Guru Har Rai undertook extensive tours of the Malwa and Doab regions of Punjab, and due to his efforts a large number of people of these areas embraced Sikhism. During his tenure of guruship, some notable conversions were made among the landed families of the Malwa. The ancestors of the ruling houses of Patiala, Nabha and Jind were first converted to Sikhism during this period. According to Dr. Fauja Singh,

"Once the chaudhries of some leading families of the Malwa were converted, the ground was well set for the rapid spread of Sikh faith in the region. The pace of progress in this direction was greatly accelerated during the periods of the ninth and tenth Gurus.[16]

The closing years of Guru Har Rai's pontificate were marked by the revival of Mughal interference in the affairs of Sikh community. There are two possible explanations of this development. First, Aurangzeb won the war of succession and ascended the Mughal throne in 1658. He was a staunch Sunni Muslim who thought that the resurgence of non-Muslim movements in the country was dangerous to Islamic rule and needed to be curbed forthwith. Secondly, the new Emperor was angry with Guru Har Rai for the latter's open support to his elder brother and rival, Dara Sikhoh.

The latter, being of Sufi persuasion, sought the company of saintly men of all denominations, and it was in this way that he had come to have some intimacy with the Sikh Guru. It has been mentioned by Sujan Rai Bhandari that when Dara Shikoh after his defeat at the hands of Aurangzeb fled across Punjab. Guru Har Rai, responding to his appeal for help, gathered the Sikh force estimated 2200 strong and tried to cover up the retreat as against Aurangzeb's pursuing troops. This aroused the ire of Aurangzeb who, on the conclusion of hostilities, summoned Guru Har Rai to Delhi to explain his conduct. The Guru instead of proceeding personally to the capital sent his eldest son; Ram Rai, to answer the queries of the Emperor. The old charge which had been levelled in the time of Guru Arjan and dismissed by the Emperor Akbar as totally unfounded was now revived, alleging that the Adi Granth contained derogatory references to Islam and its founder Prophet Muhammad. Ram Rai failed to show firmness of character and distorted facts with a view to keep to the Emperor in good humour.

Aurangzeb, on his part, used the opportunity to win over Ram Rai. He was the elder son of Guru Har Rai and was likely to succeed his father. In winning him over, therefore, the Mughal ruler cherished the hope of bringing the prospective Guru under his thumb. Guru Har Rai disapproved of Ram Rai's conduct and disowning him appointed his younger son, Har Krishan to guruship after him. By acting as such the Guru indeed dashed the hope of Emperor and his fanatical ulemas. At the same time, he rendered Ram Rai incapable to legitimately lay any claim to Guruship or to emerge as even a cult-leader.

Guru Har Krishan (b. 1656, g. 1661, d. 1664)

The appointment of Har Krishan by his father as his successor was fully in conformity with the succession practice as observed since the time of Guru Ram Das. Prior to Guru Ram Das, succession was open to the entire Sangat and a successor was chosen irrespective of whether or not he belonged to the family of the Guru in office. From Guru Ram Das onwards the guruship assumed a hereditary character, as all such institutions in those days would tend to do. Though the choice henceforward was limited to the male member of the family of Guru, yet that member was to be of proven ability to guruship. Guru Ram Das selected his youngest son, Arjan Dev. Guru Arjan Dev had no difficulty as he had only one son. Guru Hargobind had fives sons out of whom three predeceased him. The remaining two were passed over in favour of a grandson (younger son of the deceased Baba Gurditta). Guru Har Rai, as we have seen, selected his younger son, Har Krishan, in preference to Ram Rai, his elder son. Guru Har Krishan later on selected his grandfather's brother, Guru Tegh Bahadur, as the next Guru. Despite the fact that guruship went to the most deserving, certain members obsessed with the prevalent law of primogeniture or misconceived notion of their capability did not hesitate to organise Splinter groups, within the ranks of the community, such as the Minas and the Dhirmalias. The Minas were descendants of Prithi Chand, the eldest son of the fourth Guru, whereas Dhirmalias were the descendants of Dhirmal, a grandson of Guru Hargobind. Both Prithi Chand and Dhirmal were disappointed claimants to guruship and had endeavoured to set up rival gurudoms of their own. Now a third splinter group was in the process of formation. This was to be known as Ramrayas after the name of Ram Rai. Ram Rai was very sore over his supersession in the matter of succession. Being at the Imperial court and having good relations with the Emperor at that time, he thought that he could turn the tables upon his younger brother through the support of Aurangzeb, and thus made an appeal to the Emperor for his intervention. The Emperor was willing to help Ram Rai because who for his own reasons, preferred a man of his own choice and thought that a puppet Guru would most suit his interests.

Guru Har Krishan was then summoned to Delhi. The Guru went there in 1664 accompanied by twenty Sikhs and his mother. On reaching Delhi the Guru put up at the house of Mirza Raja Jai Singh (situated at the present site of Bangla Sahib). The Emperor was in no hurry to announce his arbitration. He was content to have both the claimants under his surveillance. According to Dr. Ganda Singh and Teja Singh, "The Emperor was convinced that the choice of the last Guru was not wrong, and he dismissed the claim of Ram Rai." It is also possible that this hesitation on the part of Aurangzeb was due to his realisation of the futility of imposing an unwanted Guru on the Sikhs.

Shortly afterwards, Guru Har Krishan was stricken with small-pox. But before he died, he declared that his successor would be his 'Baba' living at Bakala and in token thereof he entrusted the spiritual regalia (five paise and a piece of coconut) to Diwan Durgah Mal. According to Bhat Vahi· Talauda Pargana Jind and Guru Kian Sakhian by Sarup Singh Kaushish, the Guru did not leave any vagueness in his statement and actually mentioned the name of Tegh Bahadur as his successor and commissioned Diwan Durgah Mal to take the articles of spiritual regalia to Bakala and personally offered them to the new Guru.

Guru Tegh Bahadur (b. 1621, d. 1675)

Guru Tegh Bahadur was the fifth and the youngest son of the sixth Guru and was born on April 1, 1621 A.D. As a child he was brought up with utmost care and attention. Bhai Buddha and Bhai Gurdas gave him lessons in Sikh religion and philosophy respectively. He also studied History,[17] Arithmetic, Metaphysics, Logic, Theology, Six Philosophical Systems, classics like *Bhagwat Gita*, *Mahabharta*, *Ramayana* and the basic principles of

Islamic philosophy. He also became a great musicologist. He also received military training and grew to be an expert swardsman and nine-skilled horseman.

In the battle of Kartarpur (26 April 1635) when the Mughal forces under the over all command of Kala Khan and Painde Khan attacked Guru Hargobind, Tegh Bahadur fought valiantly in the rear of the Guru's army. His father Guru Hargobind was so much pleased that he changed his name from Tayag Mal to Tegh Bahadur, meaning 'Hero of the Sword'.

Immediately after the passing away of Guru Hargobind, Tegh Bahadur along with his wife and mother, Nanaki, shifted to Bakala where he stayed from 1556 to 1664. During this period, he undertook a tour of different religious places—Kurukshetra, Hardwar, Kashi, Mukteshwar, Sarram, Gaya and Allahabad, both to feel the religious pulse of the people and preach Guru Nanak.

In September 1664, when he had returned to Bakala in Punjab, he was invested with Guruship.[18] Twenty-two pretenders, however, asserted their claims to Guruship and posed as the legitimate successors. The most vociferous and conspicuous claimant, however, was Dhir Mal who was the first to pitch the camp at Bakala to flaunt his claim. Soon the imposters were completely exposed by Makhan Shah and his men. Even then, Dhir Mal did not change his ways. He hired one Sihan to assassinate Guru Tegh Bahadur but the attempt failed.

On November 22, 1664, the Guru left Bakala for Amritsar to pay homage to the sacred place. The ministers of Hari mandir who owed allegiance to Harji Mina shut the doors against him, and he was not allowed to enter the holy precints. They feared that once Guru Tegh Bahadur and his adherents entered Harimandir, they would never leave it and drive the priests of the Minas out of it.

The Guru thought it advisable to return to Kiratpur. Leaving Amritsar, he decided to spend some time touring the Majha and Malwa regions of Punjab before proceeding to Kiratpur. Accordingly, he visited Khadur, Goindwal, Tarn Taran and Khem Karan where Chaudhari Raghupat Rai presented a mare to him. In Malwa, the most important places he visited were Talwandi Saboke, Maur and Maisarkhana. The Guru also visited a large number of places in Bangar, the most important being Dhamtan, where Bhai Daggo, the local Masand, was asked to raise a building with a well for water supply. The Guru reached Kiratpur in May 1665. On May 13, 1665, he attended the Satarvin (a ceremony performed on the 17th day from death) of Raja Dip Singh of Bilaspur. The Guru stayed at Bilaspur for three days during which the Guru expressed that he would like to build a new settlement somewhere near Kiratpur and proposed to buy a suitable place of land for the purpose. Dip Chand's wife, Rani Champa, offered to donate the site of Makhowal; but the Guru succeeded in prevailing upon her to accept a token amount of Rs. 500.00. On June 1665,[19] the new settlement was founded. It was named as Chak Nanaki after the revered name of the Guru's mother. In course of time, the beautiful town of Anandpur grew up around it.

He did not stay at Makhowal for long. He set out (August 1665) on his travels eastwards through the Malwa and Bangar areas.

En route, the Guru visited Saifabad where he was accorded hearty welcome by Nawab Saif Khan. From here the Guru reached Dhamtan where he was arrested by Alam Khan Rohilla as per Imperial order from Delhi. According to Badshah Buranji, the Emperor had issued the order of arrest on the complaint of some orthodox Ulemas[20] and Brahmins who were feeling much upset over the new awakening which had dawned upon the people under the impact of the Guru's teachings.[21]

Through the intercession of Raja Ram Singh, son of Mirza Jai Singh of Amber, the Guru was released and allowed to resume his tour.

During his eastward journey, Guru Tegh Bahadur passed through some major centres of Hindu religion such as Mathura, Allahabad, Banaras, Patna, etc. At Patna, he left his family and proceeded further to Bengal and Assam.

The Guru reached Dacca at the end of October 1665 A.D. passing through Godgari and Gopalpur. The Guru received great respect from the people of Dacca, whose association with the Sikh faith was as old as Guru Nanak. Bhai Bulaki, the local Masand and Bhai Natha, the disciple of Almast, did all that they could do to make the stay of the Guru comfortable. It was here that the Guru received the welcome news of the birth of his son at Patna on December 26, 1666. He wrote a letter of thanks to the Sangat of Patna for taking care of his wife and other numbers of his family.

From Dacca the Guru left for Jaintia a hills and Sylhet (early in the year 1667 A.D.) where he established a missionary centre known as the Sylhet Sangat. Therefrom he moved towards Chittagong and Sondip. During his stay at Chittagong, he established a large religious centre of his faith. From there he reached Dacca in A.D. 1668. There Raja Ram Singh who had been sent by Aurangzeb to oust the Assamese Ahom King Chakradawaj from Gauhati which he had recently captured, met Guru Tegh Bahadur and asked him to accompany him. The Guru who had already wished to have a tour of Assam accepted the request. Another factor also impelled the Guru to accede to the Raja's request was that the Raja had a deep reverence for the house of Nanak. In 1669, the Guru stayed at Dhubri while Raja Ram Singh went ahead and camped at Rang Mati, the Mughal out-post near the frontier of Assam.

Soon after, the war between the Mughals and the Ahoms started. The Guru prevailed upon the contending parties to arrive at a negotiated settlement. According to which terms[22] the old boundaries were to be maintained. The Guru invited the soldiers of both armies to help raise a mound at Dhubri in memory of Guru Nanak's visit to the place to mark complete harmony between themselves.

The Guru left Assam in the year A.D. 1670 and hastened back to Punjab. On his return journey, he paid a flying visit to Patna. The reason for the haste was that during this period Emperor Aurangzeb had adopted a much stiffer attitude towards the Hindus. On April 8, 1669, he had (according to Ma-asri-Alam Giri) issued order to the governors of all provinces to destroy with a strong hand the schools and temples of the infidels and to put an entire stop to the teaching and practising of idolatrous forms of worship.

On the way back, he was arrested by the Kotwal of Agra but was soon released when it was made clear that the earlier order for the arrest was no longer valid because of the intercession of Raja Ram Singh. Having visted Delhi, Lakhanaur, village Malla, the Guru reached Bakala where he was joined by his family. Some time after, he proceeded to Chak Nanaki.

With the return of the Guru to Punjab began the period of his crowning glory. Refusing to sit idle at his headquarters, he resolved to move among his people. About the middle of 1673 A.D. the Guru left for an extensive tour of the Malwa and Bangar Des. According to Santokh Singh of Suraj Parkash, Gyan Singh of Tawarikh Guru Khalsa and Sakhi Pothi, the Guru visited twenty places, but a recent survey conducted under the supervision and guidance of Dr. Fauja Singh, the number of places visited by the Guru is much more. The Guru's important halts were Saifabad, Mulowal, Dhilwan, Khiva, Samana, Bhikhi, Khayale, Maur, Tulwandi, Bhatinda, Backhona, Gobindpura, Bangar, Dhamtan. The tour lasted till the end of A.D. 1674 when the Guru with his large train of followers returned home.

During his travels the Guru preached what may be called the ideology of Dharma which in the context of social and political reconstruction meant social responsibility, validity of moral values, social equality transcending narrow considerations of creed, caste, clime, sex and colour and rejection of hereditary principles as the basis of social order or ethics. The principle of justice formed an important feature of this ideology. The concept of justice figures prominently in the thinking of the Gurus. The scientific definition as it developed in the west in the 19th century and as we understand it today was not known then but justice as a principle of human relationship was well known and was by Guru Nanak and his successors strongly advocated. In fact, their close identification with the lower and downtrodden classes and their constant endeavours for their welfare emanated from their commitment to social justice. The exploitation of the poor by the rich was held inhuman and unjust. But if it was bad for the strong and the rich to exploit the poor; it was equally bad for the poor and the weak to compromise with injustice and tyranny.

These ideas presented good opportunities to the so-called lower classes like Jats, artisens and shoemaker, etc. to improve their social status. The result was that the Sikh movement grew rapidly in both numbers and resources. The growing popularity of the movement alarmed both the Muslim rulers and orthodox Muslims. The Mughal Government prompted by the Muslim orthodox sections, began to view the Sikh movement with deep suspicion.

Like other non-Muslims, the Sikhs too experienced the impact of the fanatical policy of Aurangzeb. Mirza Inayat-ullah Ismi tells us in *Ahkam-i-Alamgiri* that in compliance with the orders of the Emperor and with the consent of the local Qazi, the Sikh temples in the town of Buriya in the parganah of Khizrabad of the Sarkar of Sirhind were demolished and a mosque raised on its site. Sayyid Zafar Darvish was appointed in charge of that mosque to guide prayers. Some Sikhs attacked the mosque and killed the Darvish. The Emperor rebuked the Qazi and his father who was the head of the police. According to Hari Ram Gupta, such incidents had become a common occurrence.

The Emperor with this frame of mind could hardly bear with the growing influence of the Sikh religion under the inspiring leadership of Guru Tegh Bahadur.

But how did the clash come to surface? Knowing the mind of Emperor Aurangzeb, the news writers sent exaggerated and distorted reports about the large gatherings and money laundering on a large scale. The Emperor, busy as he was in quelling the pathan rebellion in north-western frontier, had neither the time nor the inclination to make enquiries about the proceedings of the Guru. He was already suspicious of the Sikh movement. He, therefore, readily believed all the reports of his intelligencers and wrote to the governor of Lahore to arrest Guru Tegh Bahadur and ordered that he might be detained in prison.

Some historians have given the impression that the cause of the execution of Guru Tegh Bahadur was the response which the Guru made to the request of the Kashmir Brahmins on May 25, 1675. A deputation of sixteen Kashmiri Brahmins headed by Kirpal Ram, son of Arhu Ram of Mattan, waited upon the Guru at Chak Nanaki. They told him how they were being hard pressed to embrace Islam and the Guru moved by their tale of woe, told the Brahmins to go homes and tell the authorities that they would have no objection to changing their religion if Guru Tegh Bahadur was first prevailed upon to embrace Islam.

From this the conclusion has been drawn by not a few scholars that the Guru made up his mind to suffer martyrdom for them or for the Hindu religion alone. The advocates of this view quote Guru Gobind Singh in their support: "Guru Tegh Bahadur did a miracle in the Kali Age by protecting the frontal mark and sacred thread of the Hindus." But this view is unfounded. To regard the appeal of the Kashmiri Brahmin as the sole cause of the Guru's execution is to lose sight of the whole historical background which preceded this event. The truth is that the case of the Kashmiri Brahmins only precipitated the matter.

The Lahore governor passed on the Imperial order for compliance to Dilawar Khan, the Faujdar of Sirhind who, in turn, asked the circle Kotwal of Rupar, Nur Muhammad Khan Mirza, in whose police jurisdiction lay Anandpur, to arrest the Guru. The order, however, was kept secret.[23]

The Guru apprehending trouble conferred guruship on his son on 8 July 1675, and proceeded towards Delhi, probably to meet the Emperor and plead the case of non-Muslims with him, and in the event of the Emperor's unfavourable reaction,[24] suffer the consequences. The Guru along with his three Mati Das, Sati Das, Dyal Das devoted followers who were accompanying him was arrested at Malikpur Ranghran near Ropar by Mirza Nur Muhammad, the Kotwal of Rupar on July 12, 1675 (*Sawan 12, 1732 B.K.*) and sent to the Faujdar's headquarters at Sirhind where they were kept in prison for about four months until he received a fresh order from Aurangzeb from Hasan Abdal saying that they should be dispatched to Delhi. They reached Delhi and were kept in the Kotwali, Chandni Chowk, Delhi.[25] They were charged with seditions activities. They were offered a choice between Islam and death and on their spurning conversion, for about eight days to Islam. Bhai Dayala and Bhai Mati Das were boiled and sawn alive respectively on the 10 November 1675. Sat Das was wrapped in cotton and roasted. The Guru's turn came at the end. According to Muhammad Ahsan Ijad, he was asked to embrace Islam and when he refused to do so, he was executed on November 11, 1675 A.D.

Guru Gobind Singh (b. 1666, d. 1708)

Guru Gobind Rai, called Guru Gobind Singh after the creation of the Khalsa, was only nine years old when his father was martyred at Delhi. The situation which he was called upon to face was very grave for the Sikh Panth. The immediate effect of the execution of Guru Tegh Bahadur was terrific and stunning for the Sikhs.

The intensity of the shock of Delhi executions was greatly enhanced by the absence of unity and cohesion in the ranks of the Sikhs about this time. Minas, Dhirmalays and the Ramrayyas had intensified their activities and were engaged in an all-out campaign of vilification of the mainstream Sikhism.

Another important factor to be taken into account by the Guru was the character which the Sikh movement had acquired over the decades. Since the time of Guru Hargobind the concept of Miri in Sikhism had taken deep roots. In consequence, the movement had assumed some distinctly militant secular tendencies. This thing confused many of the Sikhs because some of them could not understand Sikhism in its true import while some others were opposed to it because they thought that Sikhism was not treading the road as recommended by Guru Nanak.

The situation, indeed, was complex and was challenging. Fortunately, Guru Gobind Singh was a great organiser and had the vision and imagination of a great leader. Regarding the mission of his life the following words of Bachitar Natak are significant:

> I came into the world charged with the duty to uphold the righteous at every place and to destroy the wicked and the evil minded. O ye holymen, know it well in your hearts that the only reason I took birth was to see

> that the righteousness may flourish; that good may live and the tyrants be torn out by their roots.

The Guru passed the first ten years of his Guruship at Anandpur, the next three years (1685 to 1988) at Paonta and the next sixteen years again at Anadpur.

In order to fulfil his mission, the Guru repeatedly and emphatically impressed upon his people that to cling fast to the cause of righteousness even at the risk of their lives was an act explicitly divine, for, God is Asur-Sanghar (smasher of the wicked). Guru Gobind Singh himself took up the role of a saviour committed to destroy the wicked and to uphold the cause of the righteous.

Guru resumed the programme of militarization of his grandfather, Guru Hargobind, with great vigour. He issued Hukamnamas (circular letters) to his people to present to him all kinds of weapons. He himself wore and bore arms and induced others to practise archery and musket-shooting. He collected around himself many followers with martial instincts and those whose forefathers had fought in the army of his grandfather (Guru Hargobind) or had formed the bodyguard of Guru Har Rai.

The Guru got prepared in March 1680 a drum under the supervision of Nand Chand, his trusted Dewan. The underlying objective of the Guru was to make use of it as an aid in military training as well as in generating a sense of discipline among his followers. However, it caused a lot of misgivings among the hill chiefs as well as Mughal officials who looked upon it as a symbool of Guru's assertion of sovereignty. Since in the contemporary political parlance, the beating of drum was considered the prerogative of an independent chieftain. The name of the drum Ranjit Nagara (a heralder of victory) was also deemed to be suggestive of Guru's political ambition.

The Guru ransacked the old Indian literature with the help of a number of poets and scholars living at his court and brought out the heroic tradition enshrined therein. As a result many new compositions were produced, which may now be found in *Dasam Granth*. Among these compositions the "Chandidi Var, "Ram Avtar" and "Krishan Avtar" are the most significant. "Chandi-di Var" deals with the exploits of Goddess Chandi or Durga in extirpating the tyrants, while "Krishan Avtar" and "Ram Avtar" relate to the heroic deeds of Lord Krishna and Lord Rama.

These and many other measures generated a new force, a new response, and a new consciousness transforming his followers radically ever ready to pursue righteousness even at the risk of their lives. The adoption of the militant demeanour by the Guru caused concern to Raj Bhim Chand of Bilaspur in which Nanki Chak was situated. He began to view the activities of the Sikhs dangerous to his sovereignty. He had strained relations with the Mughal Faujdar of Sirhind. The Guru's headquarters lay on the border of his state and were in the vicinity of Hindur and the Mughal territory. The Raja apprehended that the Guru might join hands with his enemies and harm his interests. Any way, he insisted on the Guru recognising his authority in a manner that was both shabby and insulting. He not only demanded tribute which none of the Sikh Guru had paid till then but also haughtily asked for things which the Guru rightly refused to give. Considering the refusal as a challenge to his authority, he attacked the Guru but was beaten back. The Guru now decided to leave Anandpur[26] for some time. He proceeded to Nahan where he was accorded a warm reception. Shortly after the Guru fixed up his headquarters at Paonta on the bank of the river Jamuna, also in the state of Nahan Whose ruler Raja Medni Parkash was very anxious that the Guru should stay on in his state. The probable reason was that he needed his support against his rival, the Raja of Garhwal, Fateh Shah.

Soon a Sikh township grew up at Paonta. The Guru lived there for three years from 1685 to 1688. It was here that he went through the whole gamut of epic literature in Sanskrit. He himself wrote "Var Sri Bhagauti ji ki", popularly known as "Chandi di Var" in praise of the daring deeds of the goddess. Goddess Chandi's battles were, in the eyes of the Guru, fought in defence of righteousness. He also completed here his compositions entitled "Shastar Nam Mala" and "Krishan Avtar" in 1687 and 1688 respectively. In "Shastar Nama

Mala", the Guru describes the functions of various weapons and invests them with divinity. "Krishan Avtar" was written in heroic poetry. The most significant portion of this composition, however, was the last verse in which the Guru explicitly stated that he had written "Krishan Avtar" out of his love of "Dharam Yudha" (Struggle for Righteousness).

Besides Guru Gobind Singh gathered around him a galaxy of 126 literary luminaries from all parts of India. According to S.S Gandhi, there were men of parts including writers and poets who gathered.[27] With the help of these writers and poets a vigorous drive was made not only to re-write and reinterpret the old Puranic and other literature but also to produce such original literature as could prepare the people to imbibe the true spirit of the heroic traditions of ancient India. Though we have no detailed account of the literary compositions of the various poets, yet some works are available indicating the spirit which these works wanted to generate. Sainapat rendered Chanakya Neeti from Sanskrit to Brij Bhasha. Bhoj and Lakhan translated "Panj Tantar", Nand Lal composed Bandgi Nama, Amrit and Lohari gave live interpretation to Sabha Parv of Mahabharat. The common note of these compositions was the emphasis on heroic struggle to be waged against evil forces.

Realizing that his Sikhs could best understand Sikhism if they first understood the classical Hindu philosophy, the Guru sent thirteen chosen Sikhs to Pandit Raghu Nath for learning Sanskrit, but when he refused to teach them because none of them was a Brahmin, the Guru sent those very Sikhs to Banaras to study under the guidance of Pandit Sada Manak. These Sikhs—Ram Singh, Sobha Singh, Karam Singh, Ganda Singh and Vir Singh Dharam Singh, Gian Singh, Gaja Singh, Chanda Singh, Gaina Singh were later on initiated into the order of the Khalsa through the baptism of the sword. They founded an organisation known as 'Nirmal Panth' which in course of time, rendered meritorious services to the cause of learning and scholastic pursuits among the Sikhs.

Ram Rai who had at one lime conspired with the help of Aurangzeb to get Guruship for himself came from Dehra Dun and waited upon Guru Gobind Singh at Panta. This ended the long-standing opposition of Ram Rai to the mainstream of Sikhism.[28] Pir Budhu Shah (1647-1704) a renowned Sufi Saint, and his followers also developed fescination for the Guru.

The Guru continued his military exercises and hunting excursions at Paonta. The Guru recruited new warriors from amongst his disciples. He also enlisted 500 Pathans at the suggestion of Pir Budhu Shah, not only to utilise their services as military instructors but also signalling that in the struggle for upholding righteousness any one irrespective status, caste, and creed could take part.

The Guru's stay at Paonta has been considered a watershed in his career. It was here that the Guru enjoyed comparative calm and found time to mature his ideas and frame plans to be implemented in future for the regeneration of the people. But all was not smooth. Paonta was cut off from the rest of the Punjab and this being so, the Guru could not keep himself in full touch with the Sikhs with the result that the work of the spreading of Guru's message suffered considerably and the Masands who were in charge of different dioceses became awfully indifferent to their duties. Besides this, the inflow of money to the Guru's treasury could not match the swelling expenditure of the Guru. The Masands kept the offerings with themselves instead of sending them to the Guru.

Battle of Bhangani and the Guru's Returns to Anandpur

In September 1688, the Guru fought the battle of Bhangani against Fateh Shah and his allies. The reason was that with the passage of time, the relations between Sirmur and Garhwal got very strained.[29] Fateh Shah wanted to bring all the disputed territory between the two states under him by force. As a first step in getting an upper hand over Nahan, the Garhwal ruler marched towards Paonta which was so close to the border and was so strategically placed that Fateh Shah considered it essential to capture it. In this project, Fateh Shah was helped by the chiefs of Dadhwal and Jaswal, Gazi Chand of Chandel, Gopal and Hari Chand. According to later Sikh chroniclers the number of chiefs who joined Feteh Shah was fifiteen.[30]

The Guru, however, forestalled Fateh Shah and checked the invading army at Bhangani—six miles to the north east of Paonta. Just on the eve of the battle, the Pathan mercenaries under their leaders, Hayat Khan, Najabat Khan and Bhikhan Khan who had been in the Guru's pay mutinied and joined the Hill Chiefs. Only Kale Khan with his one hundred men remained loyal to the Guru. The armed Mahants with the exception of their leader Kirpal also left him.

The Guru's army emposed of 2000 soldiers was thus reduced to 1000 soldiers while the allies' forces numbered 10000, ten tonnes more than the Guru's. Even then the Guru was unnerved. His forces fought so gellantly and skillfully that the hill Rajas had to suffer defeat.

The battle of Bhangani brought into focus many aspects of importance. It bolstered up the morale of the Sikhs. It highlighted that all was not well with internal organisation of the Sikhs. The Masands as a group had gone corrupt beyond corrigibility raking the question whether the Masand system should be scrapped or maintained as such.

The battle was significant from another point of view. Nearly, fifteen hill rulers combined their military strength to attack the Guru. The combination of so many chiefs and that too within a record time was indeed astonishing for the Guru who had done nothing to provoke them. The Guru was not a ruler and as such did not possess any principality. To engineer such an attack was obviously uncalled for. The Guru, therefore, was constrained to think that the hill chieftains including Fateh Shah of Garhwal were motivated by certain ulterior designs which could possibly he the annihilation of Sikh Panth which in their reckoning had the potential of destabilising their socio-political system they had nursed and loved for such a long time. The Guru had to be wary of the hill chiefs while formulating his plans especially when even the ruler of Sirmrur who had always admired the Guru preferred to remain aloof from the battle which in fact was more against him than the Guru.

Guru Gobind Singh discouraged the wild schemes of his excited men to cross the Jamuna and march into the Garhwal territory. On the contrary, he took his victorious army to

Sadhaura and then to Laharpur. From there he returned to Anandpur.

Guru Gobind Singh used the changed circumstances to build his headquarters at Anandpur with remarkable boldness. He renewed his contacts with his disciples in the Malwa, the Doab and Majha regions. He built a chain of forts around Anandpur and garrisoned them with his men. He reorganised his Durbar and rapidly increased the strength of his army.

Two years after Guru Gobind Singh's return to Anandpur, the Guru had to take part in the battle of Nadaun—this time as an ally of the hill chiefs who had combined under Bhim Chand to defy the overlordship of the Mughals by stopping paying annual tribute. The Guru did so because he beleived that the Rajas, battling against unjust Mughal Emperor Aurangzeb, was a case of *Dharam Yudh*.

Alif Khan and his men fled but despite the victory, the hill chiefs decided to come to terms with the Mughal commander. Guru Gobind Singh refused to enter into these discussions. After spending eight days at Nadaun, he returned to Anandpur. The Guru was now convinced that he could not hope to trust the friendship of the hill chiefs. He addressed himself more vigorously to build up his strenth. The rapidly growing military strength of the Guru and his large congregations unnerved the Kangra Faujdar as also the majority of the hill rulers.

Accordingly, the Faujdar Dilawar Khan sent his son, called Khanzada in Bachittar Natak, to curb the power of the Guru. The attack having failed, an expedition under Hussain Khan was sent to chastise the refractory hill chiefs and destroy the Sikh centre of Anandpur. Even he could not gain any success. Similarly, Jujhar Singh and Chandel Rai were defeated in their purpose by the Guru's friend Raja Gaj Singh of Jaswal before they could harm the Guru.

The result of the defeat of the Imperial forces was that the Mughal administration in the Hill areas fell into disarray, the Sikhs became hardened in their attitude towards the Imperial authority and many of the Hill Rajas defied the Mughal authority and hesitated to pay their annual tributes. This thing caused anxiety to Aurangzeb who realised that something drastic had become absolutely necessary and accordingly he sent one of his sons, Muazzam for the restoration of order in the Hills. The prince deputed his general Mirza Beg to teach a lesson to the Hill Rajas. The General quickly reduced the hill chiefs to subservience.

The Guru, no doubt, passed through troubled times but he was left unmolested. The reason is stated to be the successful intercession on the Guru's behalf, of a Khatri named Nand Lal, who possessed some influence with the prince. Sometime after, the Guru himself had to fight an action. Two hill chiefs, Alam Chand and Balia Chand, fell upon the Guru when he, with only a handful of soldiers, was sporting in the Dun area. Timely help from Ude Singh decided the issue in the Guru's favour. Alam Chand lost his right arm while Balia Chand got seriously wounded. Both of them fled the field.

Creation of the Khalsa

In such a situation of formidable challenges, the Guru realised the urgency of improving the Sikh organization. He for long pondered over it and then decided to create a compact brotherhood of saint-warriors. This new body was called the Khalsa.

Early in 1699, he sent Hukamnamas to his followers asking them to visit Anandpur on the Baisakhi festival. He specially exhorted the Sikhs to come with their hair and beards unshorn. On the appointed day after the morning service, the Guru appeared before the congregation, drew his sword out of the scabbard and demanded a few human heads for sacrifice. After some trepidation, one rose to offer himself. He was taken into a tent. A little later the Guru reappeared in front of the assembly with his sword dripping with blood and asked for another head. In this manner one by one, five men were taken for 'sacrifice'. These five men were Daya Ram, a Khatri from Lahore; Dharam Das, a Jat from Delhi; Mohkam Chand, a washermen of Dwarka, Himmat, a cook of Jagan Nath and Sahib Chand, a barbar of Bidar. Then the Guru came out with these five Sikhs, who were believed to have been sacrified. He declared that they were his *Panj Pvaras* (five beloved ones) who were to be the nucleus of the new community he would raise which was to be called the Khalsa, the Pure.

The next thing was to baptise them in a manner which was unknown before. A special nectar was prepared for the ceremony. The Guru took water in an iron vessel and stirred it with a double-adged dagger (*Khanda* in Punjabi parlance) to the recitation of five holy compositions from the Sikh scripture, namely Japji, Jap Sahib, Anand Sahib, Swayyas and Chaupai. Sugar crystals called Patashas were put into the water. The nectar thus prepared was administered to the five beloved ones from the same bowl to signify their initiation into the casteless fraternity of the Khalsa The Guru gave each of them five palmfuls of this nectar (Amrit) to drink. He also sprinkled it five times on their hair and their eyes and caused them to repeat "Wahguru Ji Ka Khalsa. Wahguru Ji Ki Fateh". At this the Guru gave them the appellation of Singh (lion). Then the Guru offered to take the same baptism from the Panj Pyras. This earned him the title of "Aape Gur Chela", meaning that he was both Guru and disciple. After this thousands of people assembled there were baptised.

The baptism symbolised a rebirth for the initiates who were considered to have become Kritnash (free from the bonds of previous occupations), Kulnash (free from the bonds of family ties), Dharamnash (free from the bonds of previous faiths) and Karmnash (free from the bonds of previous actions). From now onwards, Guru Gobind Singh was their Father, Sahib Kaur their Mother and Anandpur their residence. They were to have a unique uniform. They were always to keep Kes (long unshorn hair), Kangha (comb), Kirpan (sword), Kara (steel bangle) and Kachh (shorts). These emblems made the Sikhs quite distinct from the Hindus and the Muslims. In addition to the five emblems the initiates were required to observe six rules of conduct (Rehat). Firstly, they were not to cut any hair on any part of their bodies. Secondly, they were disallowed to smoke, chew tobacco or take alcoholic drinks. Thirdly, they were not to eat an animal which had been slaughtered in the manner followed by the Musalmans. Fourthly, they were to tie turban and not to wear cap. Fifthly, the Guru enjoined upon the Khalsa to be strictly monogamous.

The creation of the Khalsa was the crowning event of Guru Gobind Singh's life. It represented a model fraternity in which tribe or caste affiliation had no room, nor were superstitions, demeaning ceremonies and empty rituals given any recognition. The Khalsa stood for righteousness, social equality, immaculate spirituality, honest labour, sharing of earnings with others and repudiation of all types of exploitation. It was also a brotherhood of saint-soldiers committed to a ceaseless fight against tyranny; a body of the elect (Guru's own or God's own) charged with the sacred duty of holding aloft the banner of righteousness (dharma).

The creation of the Khalsa was not merely an endeavour to integrate the members of the community, it was also a powerful bid to carry to completion his predecessors' programme of revolutionary reforms in the field of social and religious life. Besides, the Guru invested the Khalsa with the dignity and status which he himself commanded. This thing instilled into the body social of the Khalsa a unique confidence and henceforward, they acquired a new level of consciousness which imparted to the Sikhs a rare sense of fearlessness, commitment and a mission.

Organisationally, the creation of the Khalsa completely eliminated the need of the order of the masands and instead made the sangats realise they were directly under the protection of God and they should seek guidance from the Khalsa who was to be represented by any five baptised Sikhs duly selected and committed to the ideology of the Gurus. The existing system of three tiered authority comprising the Masands, the Guru and the sacred scripture was dissolved in favour of new authority vesting in Panth and the sacred scripture.

The establishment of the order of the Khalsa was received with mixed feelings. Khatris and Brahmins who were privileged people in the Hindu social organisation did not like the new form of baptism in which all people regardless of caste were made to drink nectar from the same vessel.

According to Koer Singh,[31] the Khalsa became the movement of the hitherto neglected and downtrodden classes in the social organisation of the Hindus. The people belonging to the scavenger class rejoiced in this august body. The Guru also felt proud of them and called them his sons (*Rangreta Guru ka Betta*). The members of the Khalsa underwent a remarkable change in their psyche. Teja Singh and Ganda Singh have observed that even those people who had been considered dregs of humanity were changed, as if by magic into something rich and strange. According to Gordon, "the dry bones of an oppressed peasantry were stirred into life, and the institution of the Sikh baptismal rite at the hands of a few disciples anywhere—in a place of worship, in a house or by the roadside brought about the more full and wide-spread development of the new faith."

The immediate effect of the creation of the Khalsa was to strike consternation among the hill chiefs who saw in the activities of the Guru a potent threat to their own religion and power. The Guru, wanted peace for his new-born Khalsa to grow and to organise; but the Hill chiefs found in the Guru's mission and reforms something fundamentally opposed to what they held dear as a member of Indian civilization. So was the case with the Mughal officials who considered the ideology and organisation of the Khalsa a veritable challenger to Islamic civilization.

The hill rajas, particularly the Raja of Bilaspur, got extremely nervous. He consulted his fellow hill chiefs who agreed that the Guru should be ejected from the hills. The hillmen encircled Anandpur and stopped supplies of food- grains. The Sikhs, led by Gobind's eldest son Ajit Singh, who was only a lad of fourteen, broke through the cordon more than once but eventually the Guru decided to move out of Anandpur to a small village called Nirmoh near Kiratpur. The Raja of Bilaspur tried to ambush his forces but was defeated and paid the price of having several of his villages plundered in retaliation.

Then the hill chiefs got help from the Emperor. Mughal forces from Sirhind and Lahore joined the hillmen and invested the Guru at Nirmoh. The Khalsa held them at bay, and after twenty-four hours of continuous fighting, broke through the besiegers and shifted to Basoli. The Raja of Bilaspur made one more attempt to crush the Guru's force but badly beaten, made terms with the Guru, and the Khalsa retunred to Anandpur.

The hill rajas again approached the Emperor for help against the Guru. The Emperor ordered the Mughal authorities of Sirhind and Lahore to extend help to the hill rajas. The combined forces of the hill rajas and the Mughals besieged Anandpur. The stock of food in Anandpur ran out and the attempts to move out of the town were frustrated. The Sikhs held on firmly until the besiegers were as wearied of fighting as they. At this juncture the Mughals offered the Guru safe passage if he evacuated Aandpur. The Guru wanted to hold on to the place but most of his men were in favour of evacuation. So the Guru evacuated the forthwith his family and a small band of soldiers (5/6 December 1705). He had not gone very far when contrary to their solemn oaths, the Imperial forces and the hillmen came running in pursuit. Skirmishes commenced from Kiratpur onwards. Realising the impending danger, Guru Gobind Singh gave a band of 50 men to Bhai Udai Singh and charged him with the responsibility of checking the enemy's advancement. Bhai Udai Singh fought at Shahi Tibbi a bloody battle with the enemy with a handful of his men; all of them perished fighting, covering themselves with imperishable glory.

When the battle of Shahi Tibbi was in progress, the rest of the party including Guru Gobind Singh had reached the bank of the Sirsa river. It was now almost the day-break. About this time, the news arrived that a contingent of enemy troops was fast approaching. Bhai Jiwan Singh, a prominent Rangretta Sikh, was given a band of 100 warriors and ordered to encounter the pursuers. With the rest of his people, the Guru plunged into the flooded waters of the Sirsa. The flood was so fast that many of them were drowned and many more scattered, including members of Guru Gobind Singh's own family. Besides, there was a heavy loss of literature and property. It was from here that the Guru's revered mother Gujri and his two younger sons Zorawar Singh and Fateh Singh, got separated and proceeded to Saheri, the village of their domestic servant, Gangu Brahmin, who later handed them over to the police at Morinda to be carried to Sirhind. As regards the Guru himself, he was able to reach, accompanied by his two elder sons and a small number of veteran Sikhs, the village Ghanaula on the other side of the Sirsa. After this, the Guru reached Kotla Nahang Khan wherefrom he proceeded further to Machhiwara and Rai Kot. On the way when he reached Bur Majra, he got the news that a large body of Sirhind troops were chasing him. Immediately, the Guru decided to face the enemy from within the Garhi of Chamkaur and hurried towards it. The Guru at this time, had his two elder sons, Ajit Singh and Jujhar Singh, and forty devotees with him, an infinitesimally small number in comparison with the huge host that had encompassed it. The Guru's provisions consisted of the little goods that he could manage to procure during the short interval before the arrival of the Imperial troops. It was under such conditions that the siege of Chamkaur started. The faithful little band of forty plus his two sons, with only a mud wall to protect them, fought against thousands to the last. The two eldest sons of the Guru, Ajit Singh and Jujhar Singh, and three of the beloved ones (Piaras) were killed. When only five Sikhs were left, they asked the Guru to leave the place. The Guru had to agree to their plea as he himself had promised at the time of the creation of the Khalsa that the authority of the Five Beloved ones was higher than even that of the Guru. Accordingly, the Guru slipped out of Chamkaur through the ranks of the enemy. Sangat Singh who resembled the Guru put on the Guru's clothes. The enemy was duped and they concentrated their attention on Sangat Singh. This enabled the Guru and his three prominent Sikhs (Piaras)—Daya Singh, Man Singh and Dharam Singh to get away. Since it was not possible for all of them to travel together, each went his own way.

The Guru after two nights on the way at last reached the village of Machhiwara. During his travels he had nothing to eat but tender leaves of the Akk plant and nothing but only a clod of earth to rest upon. While he was asleep in a garden outside Machhiwara, three of his devotees Dharam Singh, Man Singh and Daya Singh came up and rejoined him. Also joined them two devoted Pathan brothers Ghani Khan and Nabi Khan. They together made a plan to dodge the pursuing Mughal solders to enable the Guru to reach a safe place in the mean time. Bhai Daya Singh was disguised as a holy man and seated in a palanquin while Man Singh, Dharam Singh, Ghani Khan and Nabi Khan served as carriers. When the commandant of the Mughal contingent closed on them, he was told that the person seated in the palanquin was a high priest from Uch (now in Pakistan) and not Guru Gobind Singh. In the meanwhile, the Guru reached Alamgir, where he belessed Ghani Khan and Nabi Khan with Hukam Nama (letter of authority).

From Alamgir, the Guru went to Rai Kot. The chief of Rai Kot, though a Muslim, was a devotee of the Guru. At the Guru's behest, he sent Nura Mahi to Sirhind to fetch news about what had happened to the other members of his family. In the meanwhile, the Guru marched towards Lamma Jatpura. It was here that he learnt about the execution of his two remaining sons, Zorawar Singh, aged nine and Fateh Singh, aged seven and the death of his mother from shock. The Guru received the news with amazing courage and equanimity. "What use is it to put out a few sparks when you raise a mighty flame instead", the Guru exclaimed.

Nura Mahi also conveyed to the Guru that there was a rumour that Nawab Wazir Khan would soon send a force to attack the Guru. Realising that the territory around Rai Kot was not a suitable place for meeting the enemy's challenge the Guru directed the Sikhs to move towards the Jungle Desh, the land of Brars. On the way he passed through the villages of Manuke, Mehdiana, Chakkar, Takhtupura and reached Dina. It was here that the Guru wrote 'Zafarnama', a letter in Persian verse addressed to the Emperor, making a bold protest against the attitude of his local officials. The latter was in fact, a reply to the letter already sent by the Emperor. After leaving Dina, the Guru again visited many places. Ultimately, he chose Dhab Khidrana to give a battle to the army of Wazir Khan.

Meanwhile, a large number of followers had collected around the Guru. But the number certainly did not swell to twelve thousand as Muhammad Latif would have us believe. The tank of Khidrana being dry, the Sikh soldiers entrenched themselves in a forest in the neighbourhood of Khidrana and awaited the advance of the troops of Wazir Khan. Contending forces clashed with each other on the 29 December 1706. The brunt of the attack was borne by the forty men of Majha who had deserted the Guru's ranks during the siege of Anandpur but taunted by their women folk who would not let them enter their homes, had come back to reinforce the Guru's small army and agonised by their sense of remark. All of them died but not before they had struck terror into the hearts of Mughal soldiers. In view of the strong resistance offered by the Sikhs, as also due to the scarcity of water and provisions in this area, the attackers decided to return without clashing with the main body of the Khalsa under Guru Gobind Singh.

At the close of the battle, the Guru blessed each one of the forty as they lay dead or were dying and called them Muktas—Emancipated ones. On the request of one of them, Mahan Singh, the Guru tore up the paper on which they had written their disclaimer while deserting the Guru at Anandpur. The village was renamed Muktsar (the Pool of Salvation).

The Guru spent almost a month in the country around Muktsar. Then the Guru moved to Telwandi Sabo now called Damdama Sahib or Takht Dam Dama Sahib. The palce appealed to the Guru for its calmness and difficult accessibility. The Guru stayed here from January 17, 1706 to October 30, 1706.

The stay at Damdama was put to utmost use by the Guru. He utilized the time in laying abiding foundations of Sikhism in the Malwa tract.

Many old and hereditary Sikhs were given Pahul and brought more thoroughly into the Khalsa. Dalla, the chief of Talwandi, Tiloka, the ancestor of Nabha State and Rama, the ancestor of Patiala State, were outstanding examples.

It was at Talwandi Sabo that the Guru brought about a new recension of the Adi Granth. The order of Nirmalas was also created here with a view to giving the community a band of the Sikhs exclusively devoted to the study and preaching of the Sikh faith. Quite a large number of learned people who wanted to lead a life of independence also took shelter in the court of the Guru. Possibly it was because of all these things that Dumdama soon acquired the fame of Banaras, the ancient educational centre of India.

It was on October 30, 1706, that the Guru decided to proceed towards the south to see Aurangzeb in response to the Emperor's invitation which he had sent having received the letter entitled Zafarnama. The Guru's purpose in seeing the Emperor was to impress upon him the justness of his cause.

When the Guru reached the neighbourhood of Baghaur in Rajputana, he heard that Aurangzeb had died in the camp at Ahmed Nagar in last week of February 1707. The Guru left for Delhi.

Thereafter, there ensued a war of succession between the sons of Aurangzeb. Prince Muazzam (Bahadur Shah after accession to throne), who was the eldest son, hurried down from Peshawar to oppose his brother Azam who had proclaimed himself emperor in the Deccan. On June 8, 1707, a battle was fought at Jajau near Agra, where Muazzam was victorious. In this connection the sympathies of the Guru were with Bahadur Shah and he is said to have helped him with a detachment of his men in the battle of Jajau. This drew him close to the new Emperor, who invited him to Agra and presented him with a rich dress of honour and a bejewelled medallion worth 60 thousand rupees. The Guru was pleased with the interview, and saw in it the possibility of ending the long-standing differences with the Mughals.

While the negotiations were still in progress, Bahadur Shah marched into Rajputana against the Kachwahas of Jaipur and thence to the Deccan to suppress the insurrection of his brother Kam Bakhsh. The Guru accompanied him for his own purpose, and occasionally separated himself from the royal camp to preach his mission to the people. Seeing, however, that there was no prospect of the Emperor agreeing to any proposal for the redress of the wrongs, he broke off with the Emperor and came to Nander in the beginning of September. Here he met a Bairagi Monk Madho Das, whom he converted to his faith and re-named him Gurbakhsh Singh, popularly known in history as Banda singh Bahadur. Banda, shortly after, was asked to return to Punjab and renew the struggle against the tyrant Wazir Khan. Almost about that very time the Guru was stabbed by Gul Khan alias Jamshed Khan and his brother Ata-ullah Khan who in all probability had been deputed by Wazir Khan to put an end to the life of the Guru in the full knowledge of Bahadur Shah. The Guru put the assailant to death immediately. His flying companion Ata-ullah Khan fell under the sword of the Sikhs who had come up hearing the noise. The Guru's wound was immediately stitched and in a few days it appeared to have healed up. But when the Guru tried to bend a stiff bow, the imperfectly healed wound burst open and caused profuse bleeding. Suddenly on October 7, 1708, a couple of hours after mid-night, he roused the Sikhs from sleep and bidding them farewell breathed his last.

"The Gurus had led the Sikhs from generation to generation in the practice of qualities which make a great nation, and now that the task was over and the last of them merged his personality in the ranks of his disciples. All Sikh history had been moving towards this divine event. There was to be no personal Guru in future. The whole Sikh community in its organised form called the Panth, was to guide itself in the light of the teachings of the Gurus as incorporated in the Holy Granth called Guru Granth after the death of Guru Gobind Singh.

Guru Gobind Singh's period is marked for many a milestones on the highway to the development of Sikhism. Sikhism reached its culmination, as its various concepts, organisational structure and goals became clear and concrete. The Guru did recognise elevating role of Sikhism for the individual and in fact laid no small stress on the importance for him of such spiritual values as love, faith, truth and purity. But he did not subscribe to the view that it should begin and end with individual or that its only social function should be to carry on peaceful propaganda of its essential principles. Such a religion, to say the least, is an inadequate instrument for social progress or welfare. Not unoften, it happens that its peacefulness is misconstrued as submissiveness which is then exploited to the detriment of the whole social system. In a situation like this, religion degenerates into a convenient tool in the hands of the state to befuddle, as with opium, the rational faculty of the masses. The Guru, therefore, emphasised that if it was to discharges its ministry truly and for the good of the society, it must always have a revolutionary social role; that not only it must never have a truck with the anti-social forces, it must also take upon itself the positive role of eradicating such force. As this is not always possible without the aid of the force, militarism is inevitably commended as an essential auxiliary of the revolutionary functions of religion. Naturally heroism and dexterity in the use of weapons are applauded. Lest force should become brutal, qualification is added that the use of force must be only for the righteous cause. As to what is the righteous cause, the Guru says it is 'that one which aims at the eradication of ignorance and evil' and integrates the society on a higher level of consciousness.

The Khalsa of Guru Gobind Singh did not merely mark the culmination of the development of Sikhism under the ten Gurus of the Sikhs; it also ushered in a new phase in the evolution of the Sikh community. By creating the Khalsa the Guru had brought forth a new force which was bound to make a mark in the near future. The community was in fact on the threshold of big political changes when the Guru breathed his last at Nanded in the Deccan in 1708. And the big changes came within two years of the Guru's death when his chosen lieutenant Banda Singh Bahadur carved out an extensive sovereign Khalsa state in the Punjab east of Lahore. The struggle for mastery of Punjab which began in 1708 continued until in 1765 the Khalsa became a well-established political power.

NOTES

1. Puratan Janam Sakhi, Sodhi Meharban's Janam Sakhi; Lirowal Wali Janam Sakhi; Surjit Singh Gandhi, *History of Sikh Guru's*, p. 658.
2. Suiti ASA I (3) *Adi Granth*, p. 750.
3. Sujit Singh Gandhi, *History of Sikh Gurus*, p. 128.
4. In Haumai he comes and in Haumai he goes,
   In Haumai he is born and in Haumai he dies,
   In Haumai he gives and in Haumai he takes
   In Haumai be acquires, in Haumai he casts away.
5. My adversaries are five and I am but one,
   How shall I defend my house Oman!
   Daily they attack me and plander me
   To whom shall I cry? (Var Magh, send 2 Pauriz, *Adi Granth*, p. 147).

6. According to Maharban Wali Janam Sakhi, three vdasis were undertaken by the Guru. In the first udasi the Guru travels the places in the East and in the South of India. In his second udasi the northward and westward journeys have been combined while in the third udasi, the Guru visits the places in Punjab. Puratan Janam Sakhi makes mention of five journeys or udasis. According to its the eastword and southward journeys were covered by two separate udasis the Janam Sakahi regards the Guru's visits to different places within Punjab as the fifth Udasi.
7. Museum Register M. 111.
8. Sewa Ram Singh, *The Divine Master*.
9. Refer to *Ramkali Sadd*, a composition of Sundar, Guru Granth Sahib.
10. The teaching is for all the four castes—Brahmin, Kshatriya, Shudra, and Vaishya (*Suhi*, M. 5).
11. *Akbar Nama* (Persian), Vol. III, p. 801.
12. Surjit Singh Gandhi, *History of the Sikh Gurus*, p. 220. Also refer to Khula-sat-ut-Twarikh.
13. Macauliffe, *The Sikh Religion*, Vol. IV, p. 21.
14. Surjit Singh Gandhi, "Struggle of the Sikhs for sovereigntly" p. 465. Also see *Gurubilash Padshahi Chlvin* by Sohan.
15. Sarjit Sing Gandhi, *History of the Sikh Gurus*, p. 334, Gurdas Kapur and Sons.
16. Fauja Singh, *Sikhism*, Punjabi University Publication, p. 4.
17. Surjit Singh Gandhi, *History of the Sikh Gurus*, p. 342.
18. Koer Singh, *Guru Bilas Padshahi*, 10, p. 22. According to the author, many Guruships were set up.
19. Sarup Das Kaushish, *Guru Kian Sakhian*.
20. S.K. Bhuyan, *Badshah Burunji*, Sakhi, 116.
21. Fauja Singh, *Sikhism*.
22. E.A. Gait, *History of Assam*, p. 155.
23. Irivine, *Later Mughals*, p. 79; Muhammad Ahsan Ijad's *Ferukh Siyar Nama*, p. 31a.
24. The Emperor at that time was in the north-west frontier. Considering the difficulties of communication in that age, it is not surprising that the Guru had no idea about the exact whereabouts of the Emperor. The normal expectation was that he would be at his capital Delhi.
25. Sarup Das, Kaushisn: *Guru Ke an sachi*.
26. After this I left Anandpur and reached the city of Paonta (a place in Nahan state) situated on the bank of Jamna and saw and partook various activities.

27. Refer to Guru Gobind Singh ji De Darhari Ratan by Piara Singh Padam, pp. 4-6. As we understand they formed only the nucleus and in fact there were a larger number of poets and writers.
28. Macauliffe, *The Sikh Religion*, Vol. V, p. 21.
29. Surjit Singh Gandhi, *History of the Sikh Gurus*, pp. 409-14; J.N. Sarkar, Vol. III, pp. 563-65.
29. Gain Singh, *Twarikh-i-Guru Khalsa*, I, p. 190.
30. Koer Singh, *Gur Bilas Padshahi* 10, Chapter IX.
31. We are not sure whether direct representation was made; but it is fairly certain that the emperor had sent orders to the Mughal officials, notably to Wazir Khan, the Faijdar of Sirhind. Mirza Mohammad Harisi's Ibrat Nama.

Appendix

Subedars of Lahore

Mir Yunas Ali	-1530 C.E.
Mirza Kamran	1530-1540 C.E.
Haider Mirza	1540 C.E.
Shah Abdul Mali	1555-1556 C.E.
Kaizr Khwaja Khan	1556-1557 C.E.
Hussain Khan	1557-1560 C.E.
Shams-Ud-i-Din Mohammad Khan Atka	1560-1561 C.E.
?	1516-1564 C.E.
Khan-I-Kalan-Mir Muhammad Atkah	1564-1568 C.E.
Khan Jahan Husain Quli Khan	1568-1575 C.E.
Shah Quli Khan Mehram	1575-1578 C.E.
Said Khan	1578-1583 C.E.
Raja Bhagwan Das	1583-1586 C.E.
Ismat Khan	1586 C.E.
Raja Bhagwan Das	1586-1589 C.E.
Qulij Khan	1589-1592 C.E.
Khwaja Shamshed Din Khwafi	1592-1600 C.E.
Momin-	1600 C.E.
Qulij Khan	1602-1605 C.E.
Said Khan Chagtai	1505-1607 C.E.
Qulij Khan	1607-1610 C.E.
Murtza Khan	1610-1616 C.E.
Itmadud Daula (Ghias Beg.)	1616-1618 C.E.
Qasim Khan	1618-1623 C.E.
Sadiq Khan	1623-1625 C.E.
Asaf Khan	1625-1628 C.E.

Khaidmat Prast Khan	1628 C.E.
Asaf Khan	1628 C.E.
Qulij Khan	1628-1629 C.E.
Inayat Ullash Yazdi	1629-1632 C.E.
Wazir Khan	1632-1639 C.E.
Mutamad Khan	1639-1642 C.E.
Said Khan Bahadur Zafar Jang	1642-1644 C.E.
Qulij Khan	1644-1647 C.E.
Jafar Khan	1647 C.E.
Qazi Afzal	1648-1651 C.E.
Sheikh Abdul Karim	1651-1655 C.E.
Khwaja Muin Khan	1655-1656 C.E.
Bahadur Khan	1656 C.E.
Sayyad Izzat Khan	1656-1657 C.E.
Khalil Ullah Khan	1658-1662 C.E.
Ibrahim Khan	1626-1667 C.E.
Muhammad Amin Khan	1667-1669 C.E.
?	1669-1675 C.E.
Amanat Khan (Sayyad Ahmed Khan)	1675-1676 C.E.
?	1676-1678 C.E.
Qawwa Muddin Khan	1678-1680 C.E.
Prince Muhammad Azam	1680 C.E.
Mukarram Khan	1685 C.E.
Sipahdar Khan	1685 C.E.
Agents Of Prince Mahammad Azam	1690 C.E.
Khan Jahan Bahadur	1690-1693 C.E.
Mahabat Khan Ibrahim	1693-1696 C.E.
Mukarram Khan	1696 C.E.
Abu Nazir Khan	1696 C.E.
Ibrahim Khan	1699 C.E.
Mahammad Muazzam	1699 C.E.
Zabardast Khan	1704 C.E.
Agents of Prince Muazza (Deputy governor Munim Khan)	1704-1707 C.E.

Bibliography

Persian

Abdul Qadir Badauni, English Translation S.A. Ranking.

Abdul Rasul Maulvij Twarikh-i-Maazzam, Rampur Library.

Ahluwalia, Jasbir Singh, Metaphysical Postulates of Sikhism, Goodwin Publishers, Chandigarh, 1976.

——, *Sikhism Today*, Guru Gobind Singh Foundation, Chandigarh, 1987.

Ahmed Shah Batalvi, *Twarikh-i-Punjab*, Tr. by Gurbakhsh Singh Punjabi University, Patiala.

Ahmed Sirhindi Sheikh, *Muktubat-i-Imam Rabbani*, Punjabi University, Patiala.

Akbar Nama. Eng. Trans. by A.H. Beveridge, Calcutta, 1897.

Akhbarat-i-Darbare Mualla, preserved in the Old Historical Record, Jaipur.

Al-Badauni-Muntakhabu-T-Twarikh, Tr. by S.A. Ranking. Babur, Nur-ud-din Muhammad, *Babur Nama*, Tr. by A.S. Beveridge in 1921 from the original text, Bakhat Mal-Twarikh-i-Sikhan.

Ali, Athar, *The Apparatus of Empire*, Aligarh Muslim University.

Ashraf, K.M., *Life and Conditions of the People of Hindustan*, Manohar, Reprint, 1970.

Bannerjee, A.C., *The Sikh Gurus and the Sikh Religion*, Munshi Ram Manohar Lal, Delhi.

Bannerjee, Indu Bhushan, *Evolution of the Khalsa*, 2 Vols., Calcutta, 1947.

Beale, T.W., *An Oriental Biographical Dictionary.*

Bhandari, Sujan Rai, Khulas-at-Twarikh, completed in C.E. 1696.

Bute Shah; Twajcikh-i-Punjab (Persian) Chaturman; Chajbar Gulshan completed in 1759. Dara Shikhh; Sakinat-ul-Auliya.

Clark, Archer J., *The Sikhs in Relation to Hindus, Muslims, Chrishtian and Ahmadyas*, Princeton University Press, 1996.

Cunningham, Josheph, Dev, *A History of the Sikhs*, Reprint, S. Chand & Co., Delhi, 1955.

Dardi, Gopal Singh, *Sri Guru Granth Sahib*, Tr. World Sikh Uni. Press, Delhi.

Das, Kankan, *Gur Katha*, Khalsa College, Amritsar, 1967.

Das, Ganesh, *Char Bagh-i-Punjab,* ed. Kirpal Singh.

Dhadi, Nath Mal, *Amal Nama*, 1708, Tr. by Dr. Ganda Singh.

Dharampal, Ashta, *The Poetry of Dasam Granth*, 1959.

Dhillon, Balbir Singh and Bhullar, *Battles of Guru Gobind Singh*, Deep & Deep Publications, Delhi, 1990.

Dhillon, Balwant, *Early Sikh Scriptural Tradition*, Singh Brothers, Amritsar, 1999.

District and State Gazetteers of the Undivided Punjab, 4 bound in two, Low Price Publications, Delhi.

Elliot and Dawson, *History of India* as told by its own Historian, 1866-67, Vols. II and VII.

Fani, Mohsin, *Dabistan-i-Mazahib*, Eng. Tr. by Umrao Singh Shergil.

Foster, George, *A Journey from Bengal to England*, 2 Vols., R. Faulder, London, 1978.

Gandhi, Surjit Singh, *Sikhs in the 18th Century,* Singh Brothers, 1999.

Grewal, J.S. and Ball, S.S., *Guru Gobind Singh*, Punjab University, Chandigarh, 1967.

Guru Gobind Singh: Fateh Nama, English tr. by Devinder Singh Duggal.

——, *Guru Gobind Singh*, National Book Trust India, 1966.

Habib, Irfan, *Agrarian System of the Mughals*, Asia Publications, Delhi.

——, *Evidence for the Sixteenth Century Agrarian Condition in the Guru Granth Sahib in the Indian Economic and Social History Review*, Vol. II, No. 3, January-March, 1964.

——, *An Atlas of the Mughal Empire*, Oxford University Press, 1982.

Hussain, Yusaf, *Glimpses of Medieval Indian Culture*, Bombay.

Hutchinson and Vogel, J.P., *History of Hill States*, 2 Vols. Govt. Printing Press, Lahore, Reprint, 1982.

Iaayat Ulla Mirzaj Ahkam-i-Alamgiri, 1703-1707.

Janam Sakhi Gyan Rattnavli (Mani Singh Bhai).

Kapur, Prithipal and Singh, Dharam, *The Khalsa*, Punjabi University, Patiala, 1999.

Khan, Gulam Hussain *Siyar-ul-Mutakhirin*, 1785, English Tr. by Briggs, London, 1832.

Khan, Khafi, *Muntakhab-il-Lubab*, completed in 1731, printed in 1860-74.

Lal, Kanahya *Twarikh-i-Punjab*, Tr. by Jit Singh Sital, Punjabi University, Patiala.

Lal, Sarup, *Twarikh-i-Sikhan Va Dastur-ul-Amal*, M.S., 1855.

Latif, S.M. *History of Lahore*.

——, *History of the Punjab*, 1889 C.E.

Macauliffe, M.A., *The Sikh Religion*, Vol. I to Vol. VI, Reprint S. Chand & Co., Delhi, 1963.

McLeod, W.H., *Guru Nanak and the Sikh Religion*, Oxford, 1968.

——, W.H., *Sikhism*, Penguine Books, 1997.

——, *The Evolution of the Sikh Community*, Oxford University Press, 1975.

Muhammad Akbar, *Lahore—Past and Present*, Punjab Uni. Press, 1952.

Muhammad Akbar, *The Punjab Under the Mughals*, Idarah-i-Adabyar-i-Delhi, Reprint 1934.

Nand Lal, Bhai, Granthavli, ed. by Dr. Ganda Singh.

Nur-ul-Hassan, *Sayyad Sheikh Ahmed Sirhindi and Mughal Politics*. Proceedings, Indian History Congress. Rizvi Sayyad Atnar Abbas: Muslim Revivalist Movements in Northern India in the 16th and 17th Centuries.

Qasim, Muhammad, *Ibrat Nama*, written in 1723 C.E. Mutamid Khan-Iqbal Nama.

Qureshi, I.H., *A Short History of Pakistan*, Uni. of Karachi, Reprint.

Rai, Khushwat, *Twarikhe Sikhan*, M.S. dated 1869, Sikh History Research Department Khalsa College, Amritsar.

Rope, H.A., *Glossary of Punjab Tribes and Castes*.

Sachkhand Sri Hazur Sahib, Nander, 1999.

Sainapat: Shri Guru Gobind Singh, ed. by Ganda Singh, Punjabi University, Patiala, 1969.

Sakhi, Janam, Puratan edited by Bhais Vir Singh.

Sarkar, Sir J.N., *History of Auruangzeb*, Vol. III, Orient Longman, First edition.

——, *A Short History of Aurangzeb*, C. Sarkar and Sons, 1930.

Sen, Bhim, *Nuskha-i-Dilkhusha*, 1708.

Sharma, Sri Ram, *Religious Policy of the Mughal Emperors*.

Singh, Avtar, *Ethics of the Sikhs*, Punjabi University, Patiala, 1970.

Singh, Fauja, Hukam Name Shri Guru Tegh Bahadur, Punjab University, Patiala.

Singh, Ganda, *Hukam Name*, Punjabi University, Patiala, 1967.

——, *Makhzi-Twarikh-i-Sikhan*, Amritsar.

Singh, Giani Gian, *Sri Guru Panth Parkash*, Bhasha Vibhag, Punjab, 1970.

Singh, Harbans, *The Encyclopedia of Sikhism,* Vol. I to Vol. IV, Punjabi University, Patiala.

Singh, Ishar Giani, *Safar Nama Te Zafar Hama*, 1979.

Singh, Jodh and Singh, Dharain, *Sri Dasam Granth Text and Translation into English*, Vol. 1, and Vol. 2, Gurdwara Board, Takh.

Singh, Jodh, *Varan Bhai Gurdas*, Tr. Vols. 1 and 2, Vision and Venture, 1998.

Singh, Kahan, Nabha Guru Shabad Ratnakar, Mahan Kosh (Punjabi).

Singh, Kharak, *Fundamental Issues in Sikh Studies*, 1992.

Singh, Kirpal, *Janam Sakhi Parampara*, Punjabi University, Patiala, 1969.

Singh, Koir, Gurbilas Patshahi 10, Punjabi University, Patiala, 1968.

Singh, Randhir, Bhai, *Shabad Hurat*, S.G.P.C., Amritsar.

Singh, Sewa, *Shaheed Bilas,* ed. by Garja Singh, Punjab Sahitya Academy, Ludhiana.

Sohan Kavi, *Gur Bilas Padshahi Chhevin.*

Suri, Sohan La, *Umadat-ut-Twarikh*, Daftar Awall, Arya Press Lahore, 1885.

Toynbee, Arnold, *A Historian's Approach to Religion.*

Twarikh-i-Bahadur Shahi. Completed in 1747 C.E. Shahnawaz Khan, Nawab, Masirul Umara, Asiatic Society, Calcutta 1888-91.

Vasvani, T.L., *Sikh Sanctuary*, Madras, 1922.

William, Ershike, *History of India under Humayun*, Atlantic Publishers, Delhi, 1982.

Gazetteers

Dehradun Gazetteer.

Gujranwala Gazetteer.

Hoshiarpur District Gazetteer, Lahore, 1904.

Imperial Gazetteer of India, Oxford, 1908.

Mandi State Gazetteer.

Punjab State Gazetteer.

Sylhet District Gazetteer.

Journals and Periodicals

Abstracts of Sikh Studies, Institute of Sikh Studies, Chandigarh.

Sikh Review, Calcutta.

The Journal of Religious Studies, Punjabi University, Patiala.

The Journal of Sikh Studies, Guru Nanak Dev University, Amritsar.

The Punjab Journal of Politics.

The Punjab—Past and Present.

The Spokesman.